The Autobiography
MILES DAVIS
with Quincy Troupe

Miles

SIMON AND SCHUSTER

New York, London, Toronto, Sydney, Tokyo

Simon and Schuster
Simon & Schuster Building
Rockefeller Center
1230 Avenue of the Americas
New York, New York 10020

Designed by Karolina Harris
Picture section researched, edited and arranged by Vincent Virga
Manufactured in the United States of America

10 9 8 7 6 5 4 3 2 1

Library of Congress Cataloging-in-Publication data
Davis, Miles.
  Miles, the autobiography/Miles Davis with Quincy Troupe.
    p. cm.
  Includes index.
  1. Davis, Miles.   2. Jazz musicians—United States—Biography.
I. Troupe, Quincy.   II. Title.
ML419.D39A3   1989
788.9'2'092—dc20   89-19652
[B]   CIP
ISBN 0-671-63504-2

Prologue

isten. The greatest feeling I ever had in my life—with my clothes on—was when I first heard Diz and Bird together in St. Louis, Missouri, back in 1944. I was eighteen years old and had just graduated from Lincoln High School. It was just across the Mississippi River in East St. Louis, Illinois.

When I heard Diz and Bird in B's band, I said, "What? What is this!?" Man, that shit was so terrible it was scary. I mean, Dizzy Gillespie, Charlie "Yardbird" Parker, Buddy Anderson, Gene Ammons, Lucky Thompson, and Art Blakey all together in one band and not to mention B: Billy Eckstine himself. It was a motherfucker. Man, that shit was all up in my body. Music all up in my body, and that's what I wanted to hear. The way that band was playing music—that was *all* I wanted to hear. It was something. And me up there playing with them.

I had already heard about Diz and Bird, was already into their music—especially Dizzy's, with me being a trumpet player and all. But I was also into Bird. See, I had one record of Dizzy's called "Woody'n You" and a record of Jay McShann's with Bird on it called "Hootie Blues." That's where I first heard Diz and Bird, and I couldn't believe what they were playing. They were so terrible. Besides them I had one record of Coleman Hawkins, one record of Lester Young, and one of Duke Ellington with Jimmy Blanton on bass that was a motherfucker, too. That was it. Those were all the records

I had. Dizzy was my idol then. I used to try to play every solo Diz played on that one album I had by him. But I liked Clark Terry, Buck Clayton, Harold Baker, Harry James, Bobby Hackett, and Roy Eldridge a lot, too. Roy was my idol on trumpet later. But in 1944 it was Diz.

Billy Eckstine's band had come to St. Louis to play at a place called the Plantation Club, which was owned by some white gangsters. St. Louis was a big gangster town back then. When they told B that he had to go around to the back door like all the other black folks, he just ignored the motherfuckers and brought the whole band through the front door. Anyway, B didn't take no shit off nobody. He would cuss and knock a motherfucker out at the drop of a hat. That's right. Forget about the playboy look and air he had about himself. B was tough. So was Benny Carter. They both would drop anybody they thought was disrespecting them in a minute. But as tough as Benny was—and he was—B was tougher. So these gangsters right there on the spot fired B and brought in George Hudson, who had Clark Terry in his band. Then B took his band across town to Jordan Chambers' Riviera Club, an all-black club in St. Louis, located on Delmar and Taylor—in a black part of St. Louis. Jordan Chambers, who was the most powerful black politician back in them days in St. Louis, just told B to bring the band on over.

So when word got around that they were going to play the Riviera rather than the Plantation, I just picked up my trumpet and went on over to see if I could catch something, maybe sit in with the band. So me and a friend of mine named Bobby Danzig, who was also a trumpet player, got to the Riviera and went on in to try and catch the rehearsals. See, I already had a reputation around St. Louis for being able to play by that time, so the guards knew me and let me and Bobby on in. The first thing I see when I got inside was this man running up to me, asking if I was a trumpet player. I said, "Yeah, I'm a trumpet player." Then, he asked if I got a union card. I said, "Yeah, I got a union card, too." So the guy said, "Come on, we need a trumpet player. Our trumpet got sick." This guy takes me up on the bandstand and puts the music in front of me. I could read music, but I had trouble reading what he put in front of me because I was listening to what everybody else was playing.

That guy who ran up to me was Dizzy. I didn't recognize him at first. But soon as he started playing, I knew who he was. And like I said, I couldn't even *read* the music—don't even talk about *playing* —for listening to Bird and Diz.

But shit, I wasn't alone in listening to them like that, because the whole band would just like have an orgasm every time Diz or Bird played—especially Bird. I mean Bird was unbelievable. Sarah Vaughan was there also, and she's a motherfucker too. Then and now. Sarah sounding like Bird and Diz and them two playing everything! I mean they would look at Sarah like she was just another horn. You know what I mean? She'd be singing "You Are My First Love" and Bird would be soloing. Man, I wish everybody could have heard that shit!

Back then Bird would play solos for eight bars. But the things he used to do in them eight bars was something else. He would just leave everybody else in the dust with his playing. Talk about me forgetting to play, I remember sometimes the other musicians would forget to come in on time because they was listening to Bird so much. They'd be standing up there on the stage with their mouths wide open. Goddamn, Bird was playing some shit back then.

When Dizzy would play the same thing would happen. And also when Buddy Anderson would play. He had that thing, that style that was close to the style that I liked. So I heard all that shit back in 1944 all at once. Goddamn, them motherfuckers was terrible. Talk about *cooking!* And you know how they were playing for them black folks at the Riviera. Because black people in St. Louis love their music, but they want their music right. So you *know* what they were doing at the Riviera. You know they were getting *all* the way *down.*

B's band changed my life. I decided right then and there that I had to leave St. Louis and live in New York City where all these bad musicians were.

As much as I loved Bird back then, if it hadn't been for Dizzy I wouldn't be where I am today. I tell him that all the time and he just laughs. Because when I first came to New York he took me everywhere with him. Diz was funny back in those days. He's still funny now. But back then he was something else. Like, he'd be sticking his tongue out at women on the streets and shit—at white women. I mean, I'm from St. Louis and he's doing that to a white person, a white *woman.* I said to myself, "Diz must be crazy." But he wasn't, you know? Not really. Different, but not crazy.

The first time in my life I went on an elevator was with Diz. He took me up on this elevator on Broadway somewhere in midtown Manhattan. He used to love to ride elevators and make fun at everyone, act crazy, scare white people to death. Man, he was something. I'd go over to his house, and Lorraine, his wife, wouldn't let nobody stay there too long but me. She would offer me dinner all the time. Sometimes I'd eat and sometimes I wouldn't. I've always been funny about what and where I eat. Anyway, Lorraine used to put up these signs that said, "Don't Sit Here!" And then she'd be saying to Diz, "What you doing with all them motherfuckers in my house? Get them out of here and I mean right now!" So I would get up to leave, too, and she'd say, "Not you, Miles, you can stay, but all the rest of them motherfuckers got to go." I don't know what it was she liked about me, but she did.

It seems people loved Dizzy so much they used to just want to be with him, you know? But no matter who was around, Dizzy always took me every place he went. He would say, "Come on, go with me, Miles." And we'd go down to his booking office, or someplace else, or like I said, maybe ride in elevators, just for the hell of it. He'd do all kinds of funny shit.

Like his favorite thing was to go by where they first started broadcasting the "Today" show, when Dave Garroway was the host. It was in a studio on the street level, so people could watch the show from the sidewalk, looking through this big plate glass window. Dizzy would go up to the window while the show was on the air—they shot it live, you know—and stick out his tongue and make faces at the chimpanzee on the show. Man, he would fuck with that chimpanzee, J. Fred Muggs, so much, he would drive him crazy. The chimpanzee would be screaming, jumping up and down and showing his teeth, and everybody on the show would be wondering what the fuck got into him. Every time that chimpanzee laid eyes on Dizzy, he'd go crazy. But Dizzy was also very, very beautiful and I loved him and still do today.

Anyway, I've come close to matching the feeling of that night in 1944 in music, when I first heard Diz and Bird, but I've never quite got there. I've gotten close, but not all the way there. I'm always looking for it, listening and feeling for it, though, trying to always feel it in and through the music I play every day. I still remember when I was just a kid, still wet behind the ears, hanging out with all these great musicians, my idols even until this day. Sucking in everything. Man, it was something.

Chapter 1

the very first thing I remember in my early childhood is a flame, a blue flame jumping off a gas stove somebody lit. It might have been me playing around with the stove. I don't remember who it was. Anyway, I remember being shocked by the whoosh of the blue flame jumping off the burner, the suddenness of it. That's as far back as I can remember; any further back than this is just fog, you know, just mystery. But that stove flame is as clear as music is in my mind. I was three years old.

I saw that flame and felt that hotness of it close to my face. I felt fear, real fear, for the first time in my life. But I remember it also like some kind of adventure, some kind of weird joy, too. I guess that experience took me someplace in my head I hadn't been before. To some frontier, the edge, maybe, of everything possible. I don't know; I never tried to analyze it before. The fear I had was almost like an invitation, a challenge to go forward into something I knew nothing about. That's where I think my personal philosophy of life and my commitment to everything I believe in started, with that moment. I don't know, but I think it might be true. Who knows? What the fuck did I know about anything back then? In my mind I have always believed and thought since then that my motion had to be forward, away from the heat of that flame.

Looking back, I don't remember much of my first years—I never liked to look back much anyway. But one thing I do know is that the year after I was born a bad tornado hit St. Louis and tore it all up. Seems like I remember something about that—something in the bottom of my memory. Maybe that's why I have such a bad temper sometimes; that tornado left some of its violent creativity in me. Maybe it left some of its strong winds. You know, you need strong wind to play trumpet. I do believe in mystery and the supernatural and a tornado sure enough is mysterious *and* supernatural.

I was born May 26, 1926, in Alton, Illinois, a little river town up on the Mississippi River about twenty-five miles north of East St. Louis. I was named after my father; he was named after his father. That made me Miles Dewey Davis III, but everybody in my family called me Junior. I always hated that nickname.

My father was from Arkansas. He grew up there on a farm that his father, Miles Dewey Davis I, owned. My grandfather was a bookkeeper, so good at what he did he did it for white people and made a whole lot of money. He bought five hundred acres of land in Arkansas around the turn of the century. When he bought all that land, the white people in the area who had used him to straighten out their financial matters, their money books, turned against him. Ran him off his land. In their minds, a black man wasn't supposed to have all that land and all that money. He wasn't supposed to be smart, smarter than them. It hasn't changed too much; things are like that even today.

For most of my life my grandfather lived under threats from white men. He even used his son, my Uncle Frank, as a bodyguard to protect him from them. The Davises were always ahead of the game, my father and grandfather told me. And I believed them. They told me that people in our family were special people—artists, businessmen, professionals, and musicians—who played for the plantation owners back in the old days before slavery was over. These Davises played classical music, according to my grandfather. That's the reason my father couldn't play or listen to music after slavery was over, because my grandfather said, "They only let black people play in gin houses and honky-tonks." What he meant was that they—the white people—didn't want to listen to no black folks playing classical music anymore; they only wanted to hear them sing spirituals or the blues. Now, I don't know how true this is, but that's what my father told me.

My father also told me my grandfather told him that whenever he got some money, no matter where or who he got it from, to count it and see if it was all there. He said you can't trust no one when it comes to money, not even people in your family. One time my grandfather gave my father what he said was $1,000 and sent him to the bank with it. The bank was thirty miles away from where they lived. It was about 100 degrees in the shade—summertime in Arkansas. And he had to walk and ride a horse. When my father got down there to the bank, he counted the money and there was only $950. He counted it again and got the same amount: $950. So he went on back home, so scared he was just about ready to shit in his pants. When he got back he went to my grandfather and said that he lost $50. So Grandpa just stood there and looked at him and said, "Did you count the money before you left? Do you know if it was all there?" My father said, no, he didn't count the money before he left. "That's right," my grandfather told him, "because I didn't give you nothing but $950. You didn't lose anything. But didn't I tell you to count the money, anybody's money, even mine? Here's $50. Count it. And then go ahead on back and put that money in the bank like I told you." Now what you got to keep in mind about all of this is that not only was the bank thirty miles away but it was hotter than a motherfucker. It was cold of my grandfather to do that. But sometimes you've got to be cold like that. It was a lesson my father never forgot and he passed it on to his kids. So today I count *all* my money.

My father, like my mother, Cleota Henry Davis, was born in 1900 in Arkansas. He went to elementary school there. My father and his brothers and sisters didn't go to high school, just skipped right over it and went straight to college. He graduated from Arkansas Baptist College, from Lincoln University in Pennsylvania, and from Northwestern University's College of Dentistry, so my father received three degrees and I remember looking at them motherfuckers up on his office wall after I got older and saying, "Goddamn, I hope he won't ask *me* to do that." I also remember seeing a picture somewhere of his graduating class from Northwestern and counting only three black faces there. He was twenty-four when he graduated from Northwestern.

His brother, Ferdinand, went to Harvard and some college in Berlin. He was a year or two older than my father, and like my father, he skipped over high school. He went straight into college after passing the entrance exam with high scores. He was a brilliant guy also; used to talk to me all the time about Caesar and Hannibal, and black history. He traveled all over the world. He was more intellectual than my father, and a ladies' man and player, editor of a magazine called *Color*. He was so smart he made me feel almost dumb; he was the only person I knew growing up who made me feel this way. Uncle Ferdinand was something else. I loved being around him, hearing him talk and tell stories about his travels, his women. And he was stylish as a motherfucker, too. I hung around him so much that my mother would get mad.

My father got out of Northwestern and married my mother. She played the violin and the piano. Her mother had been an organ teacher in Arkansas. She never talked much about her father, so I don't know much about her side of the family, never did, never asked either. I don't know why that is. From what I have heard of them, though, and the ones I did meet, they seemed to be middle class and a little uppity in their attitudes.

My mother was a beautiful woman. She had a whole lot of style, with an East Indian, Carmen McRae look, and dark, nut-brown, smooth skin. High cheekbones and Indian-like hair. Big beautiful eyes. Me and my brother Vernon looked like her. She had mink coats, diamonds; she was a very glamorous woman who was into all kinds of hats and things, and all my mother's friends seemed just as glamorous to me as she was. She always dressed to kill. I got my looks from my mother and also my love of clothes and sense of style. I guess you could say I got whatever artistic talent I have from her also.

But I didn't get along with her too well. Maybe it was because we both had strong, independent personalities. We seemed to argue all the time. I loved my mother; she was something else. She didn't even know how to cook. But, like I said, I loved her even if we weren't close. She had her mind about the way I should be doing things and I had mine. I was this way even when I was young. I guess you could say I was more like my mother than my father. Although I've got some of him in me, too.

My father settled first in Alton, Illinois, where me and my sister Dorothy were born, then moved the family to East St. Louis, on 14th and Broadway, where my father had his dental practice up over Daut's Drugstore. At first we lived upstairs behind his office, in the back.

Another thing I think about with East St. Louis is that it was there, back in 1917, that those crazy, sick white people killed all those black people in a race riot. See, St. Louis and East St. Louis were—

and still are—big packing-house towns, towns where they slaughter cows and pigs for grocery stores and supermarkets, restaurants and everything else. They ship the cows and pigs up from Texas or from wherever else it is that they come from and then they kill them and pack them up in St. Louis and East St. Louis. That's what the East St. Louis race riot in 1917 was supposed to be about: black workers replacing white workers in the packing houses. So, the white workers got mad and went on a rampage killing all them black people. That same year black men were fighting in World War I to help the United States save the world for democracy. They sent us to war to fight and die for them over there; killed us like nothing over here. And it's still like that today. Now, ain't that a bitch. Anyway, maybe some of remembering that is in my personality and comes out in the way I look at most white people. Not all, because there are some great white people. But the way they killed all them black people back then—just shot them down like they were out shooting pigs or stray dogs. Shot them in their houses, shot babies and women. Burned down houses with people in them and hung some black men from lampposts. Anyway, black people there who survived used to talk about it. When I was coming up in East St. Louis, black people I knew never forgot what sick white people had done to them back in 1917.

My brother Vernon was born the year the stock market crashed and all the rich white men started jumping out of them Wall Street windows. It was 1929. We had been living in East St. Louis for about two years. My older sister, Dorothy, was five. There was just three of us, Dorothy, Vernon, and me in the middle. We have always been close all our lives, my sister and my brother, even when we are arguing.

The neighborhood was very nice, with row houses, something like the ones they have in Philadelphia or Baltimore. It was a pretty little city. It's not like that anymore. But I remember it was that way back then. The neighborhood was also integrated, with Jews and Germans and Armenians and Greeks living all around us. Catercorner across the street from the house was Golden Rule's Grocery Store, owned by Jews. On one side was a filling station, with ambulances coming in all the time, sirens blasting, to fill up with gas. Next door was my father's best friend, Dr. John Eubanks, who was a physician. Dr. Eubanks was so light he almost looked white. His wife, Alma, or Josephine, I forget which, was almost white, too. She was a fine lady, yellow, like Lena Horne, with curly black, shiny hair. My mother would send me over to their house to get something and his wife would be sitting there with her legs crossed, looking finer than a motherfucker. She had great legs and she didn't mind showing them either. As a matter of fact she looked good everywhere! Anyway, Uncle Johnny—that's what we called her husband, Dr. Eubanks— gave me my first trumpet.

Next to the drugstore under us, and before you got to Uncle Johnny's house, was a tavern owned by John Hoskins, a black man who everybody called Uncle Johnny Hoskins. He played saxophone in the back of his tavern. All the old-timers in the neighborhood went there to drink, talk, and listen to music. When I got older, I played there once or twice. Then there was a restaurant owned by a black man named Thigpen down the block. He sold good soul food; the place was real nice. His daughter Leticia and my sister, Dorothy, were good friends. Next to the restaurant was a German lady who owned a dry goods store. This was all on Broadway going toward the Mississippi River. And there was the Deluxe Theatre, a neighborhood movie theater on 15th going toward Bond Street, away from the river. All along 15th paralleling the river toward Bond were all kinds of stores and places like that owned by blacks, or Jews, or Germans, or Greeks, or Armenians, who had most of the cleaning places.

Over on 16th and Broadway this Greek family owned a fish market and made the best jack salmon sandwiches in East St. Louis. I was friends with the son of the guy who owned it. His name was Leo. Everytime I'd see him, as we got bigger, we'd wrestle. We were about six. But he died when the house he lived in burned down. I remember them bringing him out on a stretcher with his skin all peeling off. He was burnt like a hot dog when you fry it. It was grotesque, horrible-looking shit, man. Later, when somebody asked me about that and whether Leo said anything to me when they brought him out, I remember saying, "He didn't say, 'Hello, Miles, how you doing, let's wrestle,' or nothing like that." Anyway, that was shocking to me because we were both around the same age, though I think he was a little older. He was a nice little cat. I used to have a lot of fun with him.

The first school I went to was John Robinson. It was located on 15th and Bond. Dorothy, my sister, went one year at a Catholic school, then transferred over to John Robinson, too. I met my first best friend in the first grade there. His name was Millard Curtis, and for years after we met we went almost everywhere together. We were the same age. I had other good friends in East St. Louis later, as I got more into music—musician friends—because Millard didn't play music. But I knew him the longest and we did so many things together that we were almost like brothers.

I'm pretty sure Millard came to my sixth birthday party. I remember this birthday party because my boys, guys I was hanging out with at the time, said to me, let's go hang out on the runway—the wooden scaffolding that runs across sign boards, them billboards that have them ads all pasted over them. We would go and climb up on them, sit on the scaffolds with our feet dangling down in the air and eat crackers and potted ham. Anyway, my boys told me we might as well go do this because later I was having a birthday party, so wasn't none of them going to school that day. See, it was supposed to be a surprise birthday party, but all of them knew it and told me all about what was happening. Anyway, I think I was six; I could have been seven. I remember this cute little girl named Velma Brooks being at the party. Her and a whole lot of other pretty little girls with short dresses, like miniskirts, on. I don't remember any little white girls and boys being there; there might have been some—maybe Leo before he died and his sister, I don't know—but I don't remember any being there.

The *real* reason I remember that party was because I got my first kiss from a little girl there. I kissed all the little girls, but I remember kissing Velma Brooks the longest. Man, was she cute. But then my sister, Dorothy, tried to ruin everything by running and telling my mother that I was in there kissing all over Velma Brooks. My sister did this to me all my life; she was always telling on me or my brother Vernon about something. After my mother told my father to go in there and stop me from kissing on Velma, he said, "If he was kissing on a boy like Junior Quinn, now that would be something to tell. But kissing on Velma Brooks ain't nothing to tell; that's what the boy supposed to be doing. So as long as it ain't Junior Quinn he's kissing on, then everything's cool."

My sister left in a huff with her mouth stuck out, saying over her shoulder, "Well, he's in there kissing on her and somebody ought to stop him before he give her a baby." Later, my mother told me that I had been a bad boy kissing all over Velma and that I shouldn't do that and if she had it to do all over again that she wouldn't have had no son like me who was so bad. Then she slapped the shit out of me.

I never forgot that day. At that age, I used to remember feeling that nobody liked me, because they always seemed to be whipping on me for something, but they never beat on my brother Vernon. I mean, his feet hardly ever touched the floor. He was like a little black doll for my sister and my mother and everybody else. They spoiled the shit out of him. Every time Dorothy had her friends over, they would bathe him, comb his hair, and dress him up just like he was a little baby girl doll.

Before I was into music I was really into sports—baseball, football, basketball, swimming, and boxing. I was a small, skinny kid, with the skinniest legs anybody ever had—my legs stayed skinny until today. But I loved sports so much I couldn't be intimidated or scared by people bigger than me. I ain't never been the scaredy type, never was. And if I liked someone I liked them, no matter what. But if I didn't like you, I didn't like you. I don't know why that is but that's the way I am. That's the way I've always been. For me, it's always been a vibe thing, a spiritual thing, whether I like someone or not. Like people say that I'm arrogant, but I've always been the way I am; I haven't changed that much.

Anyway, Millard and I would always be looking to find a game of football or baseball to play. We'd play a game called Indian ball, too, which was a kind of baseball game played with three or four guys to a team. If we weren't playing this, we were playing regular baseball on some vacant lot or baseball diamond. I played shortstop and could play my ass off. I could really field the ball and I was a pretty good hitter, though I didn't hit too many home runs because of my small size. But man, I loved baseball, and swimming and football and boxing.

I remember we used to play tackle football on the little plots of grass in between the sidewalk and the curb. This was on 14th Street in front of Tilford Brooks's house, who later got a Ph.D. in music and lives in St. Louis today. Then we'd go over and play in front of Millard's house. Man, we'd be getting tackled and falling on our heads and busting them wide open and bleeding like butchered hogs. Scarring up our legs and giving our mothers fits. But it was fun, man, it was a lot of fun.

I liked to swim, I loved to box. Even today those are the favorite sports I like to do. I would swim every chance I got then, and I swim every chance I get now. But boxing was and is my heart. I just love it. I can't explain why. Man, I would listen to all of Joe Louis's fights like everybody else. We'd be all crowded around the radio waiting to hear the announcer describe Joe knocking some motherfucker out. And when he did, the whole goddamn black community of East St. Louis would go crazy, celebrate in the streets, drinking and dancing and making a lot of noise. But it was joyful noise. And they did the same thing—but not as loud—when Henry Armstrong won, because he was from across the river, from St. Louis, so that made him a black local, a hometown hero. But Joe Louis was the man.

Even though I loved boxing, I didn't get into fights when I was young. We would body punch, you know, hit each other in the chest, but nothing more serious than that. We were just like every other normal bunch of kids, growing up and having fun.

But there were gangs all around East St. Louis, bad gangs like the Termites. And they had some real bad ones over in St. Louis. East St. Louis was a rough place to grow up in, because you had a lot of cats, black and white, who didn't take no shit off nobody. I wasn't into fighting until I got to be a teenager. I wasn't into no gangs when I was growing up because I was into music so much. I even stopped playing sports because of music. Now, don't get me wrong, I used to fight with motherfuckers and shit, especially when they called me Buckwheat, because I was little, skinny and dark. I didn't like that name, so if anybody called me that they had to fight. I didn't like the name Buckwheat because I didn't like what the name meant, what it represented, that stupid *Our Gang* bullshit image white people had about black people. I knew *I* wasn't like that, that I came from people who were somebodies and that whenever anybody called me by that name they were trying to make fun of me. I knew even way back then that you've got to fight to protect who you are. So, I'd fight a lot. But I never was in no gangs. And I don't think I'm arrogant, I think I'm confident of myself. Know what *I* want, always have known what I wanted for as long as I can remember. I can't be intimidated. But back then, when I was growing up, everybody seemed to like me, even though I didn't talk too much; I still don't like to talk too much now.

It was even tough in the schools as well as out in the streets. They had an all-white school up the street from where I lived, Irving School, I think it was called, that was clean as a whistle. But couldn't no black kids go there; we had to go past it to get to our school. We had good teachers, like the Turner sisters at John Robinson where I went. They were the great-granddaughters of Nat Turner and they were race-conscious just like he was. They taught us to have pride in ourselves. The teachers were good, but the black schools were all fucked up, with running toilets and things like that. They stunk like a motherfucker, man, like open cesspools in Africa where poor people live. I mean that shit made me not want to eat while I was going to elementary school, made me sick to my stomach then—and now whenever I think about it. They treated us black kids like we was just a bunch of cattle. Some people I went to school with say it wasn't this bad, but that's the way I remember it.

That's why I used to love to go to my grandfather's place in Arkansas. Down there out in the fields, man, you could walk with your shoes off and you wouldn't step into no pile of shit and get it all running and sticky and funky all over your feet, like in elementary school.

My mother was always—it seems now—putting me, my brother, and my sister on trains when we were real young to go visit my grandfather. She pinned name tags on us, gave us boxes of chicken, and put us on the train. And man, that chicken was gone soon as the train left the station. Then we'd starve all the way to wherever we were going. We always ate up the chicken too fast. Never did stop doing that. Never did learn to eat that chicken slowly. It was so good we couldn't wait. We'd be crying all the way to my grandfather's house, hungry and mad. Soon as we got to his place, I always wanted to stay. My grandfather gave me my first horse.

He had a fish farm down in Arkansas. We would catch fish all day long, buckets of them, tubs of them. Man, we ate fried fish all day long, and talk about good? Shit, that fish was a motherfucker. So, we'd run around all day. Ride horses. Go to bed early. Get up early. And do the same thing all over again. Man, it was fun being on my grandfather's farm. My grandfather was about six feet tall, brown-skinned with big eyes; looked something like my father, only taller. My grandmother's name was Ivy, and we called her Miss Ivy.

I remember getting into all kinds of things there you couldn't get into back in a town like East St. Louis. One time me and my Uncle Ed, my father's youngest brother, who was a year younger than me, went out one morning busting up nearly all of Grandpa's watermelons. We went from one watermelon patch to another and busted up every watermelon we could find. We took the heart, the center, out of them, ate some, but mostly left all the rest behind. I think I was ten and he was nine. Later, back in the house, we laid up laughing like two motherfuckers. When Grandpa found out, he told me, "You can't ride your horse for a week." *That* cured me forever of busting up watermelons. Like my father, my grandfather was something else, didn't take no shit off no one.

When I was about nine or ten I got me a paper route and started delivering papers on weekends to make some extra money. Not that I needed it, because my father by now was making a whole lot of money. I just wanted to make my own money and not have to ask my parents for anything. I've always been like that, always been independent, always wanted to make it on my own. I didn't make much, maybe sixty-five cents a week, but it was mine. I could buy me some candy. I kept a pocketful of candy and a pocketful of marbles. I would trade candy for marbles and marbles for candy, soda, and chewing gum. Somehow I learned back then that you've got to make deals—and I don't really remember who I learned it from, but it could have been from my father. In the middle of the Depression, I remember a lot of people were hungry and poor. But not my family, because my father was taking care of the money side.

I used to deliver papers to the best barbecue man in East St. Louis, old man Piggease. His place was located around 15th and Broadway, where they had all the rest of those businesses. Mr. Piggease had the best barbecue in town because he'd get the fresh meat from them packing houses in St. Louis and East St. Louis. His barbecue sauce was just outta sight. Man, that shit was so good I can taste it now. Nobody made barbecue sauce like Mr. Piggease, nobody, then or now. Nobody knew how he made his sauce, nobody knew what he put in it. He never told nobody. Then, he made this dip for the bread and that was a motherfucker, too! Plus fish sandwiches that were outta sight. His jack salmon sandwiches eventually got as good as my friend Leo's father's.

Mr. Piggease didn't have nothing but a shack that he sold his barbecue out of. Only about ten people could get in there at any one time. He had his barbecue grill laid with bricks, made it himself. He also built the chimney and you could smell that charcoal smoke all over 15th Street. So everybody got themselves a sandwich or one of those bad small ends of barbecue before the day was out. The stuff was ready about six o'clock; he had it all cooked and done. I'd be there at six on the dot, giving him his paper, the Chicago *Defender* or the Pittsburgh *Courier,* both black newspapers. I'd give him both of those papers and he'd give me two pig snouts; pig snouts cost fifteen cents apiece. But because Mr. Piggease liked me, thought I was smart, he'd let me slide for the dime and sometimes throw in an extra pig snout, or pig ear sandwich—that's where he got his nickname "Mr. Pig Ears"—or rib tip, whatever he felt like giving me that day. Sometimes he'd throw in a piece of sweet potato pie or candied yams and a drink of milk. So, he put that shit on paper plates, which would absorb all that fucking great flavor, in between slices of that funky, tasty bread he got from the bakery. Then, he'd wrap it all up in newspapers, yesterday's newspapers. Man, that was good. Ten cents for a jack salmon, fifteen cents for a snout. So I'd get my shit and sit down and talk to him for a while, with him behind the counter, dealing with everybody. I learned a lot from Mr. Piggease, but mainly he taught me—along with my father—to avoid unnecessary bullshit.

But I learned the most from my father. He was something else. He was a good-looking guy, about my height but a little bit on the plump side. As he got older, he began to lose his hair—which fucked with his head a little bit, in my opinion. He was a well-bred man, liked nice things, clothes and cars, just like my mother.

My father was pro-black, very pro-black. Back in those days someone like him was called a "race man." He was definitely not an "Uncle Tom." Some of his African classmates at Lincoln University, like Nkrumah of Ghana, became presidents of their countries, or high up in their country's governments. And so my father had these connections over in Africa. He liked Marcus Garvey more than the politics of the NAACP. He felt that Garvey was good for the black race, because he got all those black people together back in the 1920s. My father thought that was important and hated the way people like William Pickens of the NAACP thought and talked about Garvey. Pickens was a relative, an uncle, I think, of my mother's, and sometimes when he was passing through St. Louis he would call her up and come over. At the time I think he was high up in the NAACP, a secretary or something. Anyway, I remember him calling up to come by one time and when my mother told my father, he said, "Fuck William Pickens, because the son of a bitch never did like Marcus Garvey and Marcus Garvey didn't do anything other than get all those black people together to do something for themselves, and that's the most black people have ever been together in this country. And this cocksucker is opposed to him. So fuck the motherfucker, fuck him and all his stupid ideas."

My mother was different; she was all for the uplifting of the black race, but she saw it like somebody in the NAACP would see it. She thought that my father was too radical, especially later when he started getting into politics. If I got my sense of style and clothes from my mother, I think I got most of my attitude, my sense of who I was, my confidence and race pride from my father. Not that my mother wasn't a very proud person, she was. But most of it I picked up from my father, the way I looked at certain things.

My father didn't take no shit off nobody. I remember one time when this white man came by his office for something. He was the one who sold my father gold and stuff. Anyway, my father's office was real crowded when this white man comes in. Now, my father had a sign behind the reception desk that read, "Do Not Disturb," which he used when he was working on somebody's mouth. The sign was up, but the white man, after waiting about a half an hour, says to me—I was about fourteen or fifteen, working the receptionist's desk that day—"I can't wait any longer, I'm going on in." I say to him, "The sign says 'Do Not Disturb,' can't you see what the sign says?" The man just ignores me and goes on in to my father's office where he does the teeth. Now, the office is full of black people who *know* my father don't tolerate that kind of shit. So, they just kind of smile and lay back, to see what was going to happen. No sooner did the gold man get into my father's office when I hear my father say to him, "What the fuck are you doing in here? Can't you read, mother-fucker? You dumb white motherfucker! Get the fuck on out of here!" The white man came on out of there quick, looking at me like I was crazy or something. So I told the motherfucker as he was going out the door, "I told you not to go in there, stupid." That was the first time I ever cussed a white man who was older than me.

Another time my father went looking for a white man who had chased me and called me a nigger. He went looking for him with a loaded shotgun. He didn't find him, but I hate to think of what would have happened if he had. My father was something. He was a strong motherfucker, but he was weird in the way he looked at things, too. Like he wouldn't cross certain bridges going from East St. Louis to St. Louis because he said he knew who built them, said they were thieves and that they probably didn't build the bridges very strong because they were likely cheating on the money and the building materials. He actually believed that them bridges would fall into the Mississippi one day. And to the day he died he believed this was so and was always puzzled by the fact that they never did fall. He wasn't perfect. But he was a proud man and was probably way ahead of his time for a black man. Shit, he even liked to play golf way back then. I used to caddy for him over on the golf course in Forest Park in St. Louis.

He was one of the pillars of the black community in East St. Louis, because he was a doctor and got into politics. Him and Dr. Eubanks, his best friend, and a few other prominent black men. My father carried a lot of weight and influence in East St. Louis while I was growing up. So some of his importance was carried over to his kids and that's probably why a lot of people—black people—in East St. Louis treated my brother and sister and me as if we were kind of special. Now, they didn't kiss our asses or nothing like that. But they did treat us most times like we were different. They expected us to make something important of ourselves. I guess this kind of special treatment helped us have a positive attitude about ourselves. This kind of thing is important for black people, especially young black people—who mostly hear all kinds of negative things about themselves.

My father was a strict man when it came to discipline. He made us all aware that we had to keep our shit together. I think I got my bad temper from him. But he never, ever whipped me. The maddest he ever got with me was once when I was about nine or ten and he had bought me a bike, I think my first bike. So me being mischievous, I used to ride the bike off the stairs. We were still living on 15th and Broadway, and hadn't yet moved to the house at 17th and Kansas. Anyway, I rode my bike down these real high stairs and had a curtain rod in my mouth. I was going so fast that I couldn't stop and ran into the front door of the garage behind our house. The curtain rod jammed back into my mouth and busted it wide open. Well, when he found out what had happened he got so mad I thought he was going to kill me.

Another time that he got very mad with me was when I set fire to the shed, or the garage, and almost burned the house down. He didn't say nothing, but if looks could kill I would have been dead. Then later when I got older and thought I knew how to drive, I backed the car all the way across the street and ran it into a telephone pole. Some of my friends had been teaching me how to drive, but my father wouldn't let me practice, because I didn't have a license. And me being like I was—headstrong—I wanted to see if I could drive. When he found out about my crashing the car, he didn't do nothing but shake his head.

The funniest thing I can remember happening when I did something wrong was when he took me over to St. Louis and bought me all of these clothes. I think I was about eleven or twelve and I was just getting into clothes. Anyway, it's Easter time and my father wants me and my sister and brother to look good in church. So he takes me over to St. Louis and buys me a pleated, gray double-breasted suit; some Thom McAn boots; a yellow, striped shirt; a hip beanie cap; and a leather change purse that he put thirty pennies in. Now I know I'm clean, right?

When we get back home my father goes upstairs to get something from his office. I got these thirty pennies burning a hole in the new change purse he just bought me. Now, you know I've just got to spend this money—hip and clean as I am, right? So I go into Daut's Drug-store and tell Mr. Dominic, the owner, to give me twenty-five cents' worth of them juicy chocolate soldiers—my favorite candy at that time. You could get three chocolate candy soldiers for a penny, so he sells me seventy-five of them. Now I got my big bag of candy, and I'm standing out in front of my father's office, sharp as a tack, and I'm eating the candy soldiers faster than nobody's business. I ate so many of them I got sick and just started spitting them out. My sister, Dorothy, sees me and thinks I'm spitting up blood, and runs and tells my father. So he comes downstairs and says, "Dewey, what are you doing? This is my place of business. People come to see me here and they'll think that I done killed somebody, think all this chocolate is dried-up blood, so get upstairs."

Another time around Easter, the next year, I think it was, my father bought me an outfit to go to church, a blue suit with short pants and socks. Along the way while me and my sister was going there, I saw some of my boys playing in the old factory house. They asked me to join them and I told my sister that I'd catch up with her. I went on in that factory house and all of a sudden it's so dark in there I can't see. I trip, fall, and I'm crawling around. I fall into this puddle of dirty water with my good new clothes on. And it's Easter. You know how I felt. So, I didn't go to church. I just went back home and my father didn't do anything. But he did tell me that if I so much as "ever stumble again like that, and you're not supposed to stumble, I'm going to kick your motherfucking ass." So that stopped me from doing really silly shit like that again. He said, "That could have been acid or anything you fell in. You could have been dead, going in a strange dark place like that. So don't you ever do it again." And I didn't.

Because it wasn't so much the clothes he was concerned about. It didn't bother him that I ruined them. It was *me* he was worried about. I never forgot that, that he was only concerned about me. So we always got along well. He was always behind me 100 percent, whatever I wanted to do, and I believe that his confidence in me made me have confidence in myself.

But my mother would whip the shit out of me at the drop of a hat. She was into whipping so much that one time, when she couldn't do it because she was sick or something, she told my father to do it. He took me into a room, closed the door, and told me to scream like he was beating me. "Make some noise, like you're getting beat," I remember him saying. And then me screaming at the top of my lungs and him sitting there looking at me all steely-eyed. That was some funny shit, man. But now that I think about it, I would have almost preferred his whipping me to the way he used to look right through me like I was nothing. When he did that he made me *feel* like I was nothing. That feeling was worse than a whipping could ever have been.

My mother and father never did get along well. They saw most things through different eyes. They had been at each other's throats since I was a little kid. The only thing I ever saw that really connected them up was later when I got my bad heroin habit. When that happened, they seemed to forget their differences and pulled together to try to save me. Other than that time, they always seemed to me to be fighting like cats and dogs.

I remember my mother picking up things and throwing them at my father and saying all kinds of off-the-wall, nasty things to him. Sometimes he would get so mad that he'd also pick up something and throw it at her, whatever he could get his hands on—a radio, the dinner bell, anything. And she'd be screaming, "You're trying to kill me, Dewey!" I remember one time after an argument my father had gone outside to cool himself out. When he came back my mother wouldn't open the door and let him back in—he had forgotten his key. He was standing out there screaming for her to open the door, and she wouldn't. It was one of those glass doors that you could see through. He got so mad with her he punched her right in the mouth through the glass. He knocked a couple of teeth right out of her mouth. They were best apart, but they gave each other grief until they finally got divorced.

I think part of their problem was that they had different temperaments. But it wasn't only that. They developed a typical doctor-wife relationship in that he was seldom ever at home. It didn't bother us kids too much because we were always doing something. But I think it bothered her a lot. And then when he got into politics he was there even less. Plus, they always seemed to be arguing about money, even though my father was considered wealthy. At least, he was for a black man.

I remember when he ran for State Representative of Illinois. He was running because he wanted to put a fire department out where he had his farm in Millstadt. Some white people wanted to give him money not to run, but he ran anyway and lost. My mother got on him for not taking the money. She said that they could have used that money to go on a vacation or something. Plus, she was mad at him later for losing most of his fortune gambling; my father lost over a million dollars gambling like he did. And she never did like all that radical political shit my father was into. But after they broke up she told me later that if she had it to do all over again, she would have treated my father differently. But by then, it was way too late.

None of our parents' problems seemed to affect the fun that me, my sister, and my brother were having, although looking back I guess it really did. It had to affect us somehow, although I don't really know how. I just thought it was a drag to watch them fighting all the time. Like I said, my mother and I didn't get along too well and so I guess I blamed her for all the problems. I know my father's sister, Corrine, blamed her; she never did like my mother.

My Aunt Corrine had a lot of money and shit, but everybody thought she was weirder than a motherfucker. I did too. But they were close, my father and his sister. And even though she was against my father marrying my mother, people said that when they got married my aunt said, "Lord, help that poor woman. Because she don't know the trouble she's getting into."

Aunt Corrine was a doctor of metaphysics or something like that. She had her office right next to my father's. There was a sign out in front saying "Dr. Corrine, Reader, Healer," with an open palm facing the viewer. She told people's fortunes. She'd be in her office lighting all them candles and shit and smoking them cigarettes. Man, she'd be up in her office behind all those clouds of smoke, talking weird shit. People were scared of her; some thought she was a witch, or some kind of voodoo queen. She liked me. But she must have thought that *I* was weird, because as soon as I walked in her office she started lighting those candles and smoking cigarettes. Ain't that a bitch; she thought *I* was weird.

All of us kids—my brother and my sister and me—liked artistic things when we were young, especially Vernon and me, but Dorothy, too. When I was growing up—before I really got into music—me and Dorothy and Vernon used to have our own talent shows. We were still living on 15th and Broadway when we started. I think I was about nine or ten. Anyway, I was just beginning to play trumpet, just getting into it. As I said, Uncle Johnny had given it to me. So, I would play trumpet—as much as I could play back then—and Dorothy would play piano. Vernon would dance. We had a lot of fun. Dorothy could play a few church songs. But other than that, she couldn't play. Mostly we would do little skits—funny shit, you know—talent shows with me being the judge. Man, I was hard on them. Vernon could always sing, draw, and dance. So, he'd be singing and Dorothy would be dancing. By this time my mother was sending her to dancing school. Anyway, that's the kind of shit we was doing. But as I got older, I got more serious, especially about my playing music.

The first time I really paid attention to music was when I used to listen to a radio show called "Harlem Rhythms." I was about seven or eight. The show used to come on at fifteen minutes to nine every day, so I was late to school a lot because I was listening to that program. But I *had* to hear that show, man, had to. Most of the time they played black bands, but sometimes when they had a white band on I would cut it off, unless the musician was Harry James or Bobby Hackett. But that program was really great. It had all them great black bands on there and I remember being fascinated by hearing the records of Louis Armstrong, Jimmie Lunceford, Lionel Hampton, Count Basie, Bessie Smith, Duke Ellington, and a whole bunch of other bad motherfuckers on that program. Then when I was nine or ten I started taking some private music lessons.

But before the lessons, I also remember how the music used to sound down there in Arkansas, when I was visiting my grandfather, especially at the Saturday night church. Man, that shit was a motherfucker. I guess I was about six or seven. We'd be walking on these dark country roads at night and all of a sudden this music would seem to come out of nowhere, out of them spooky-looking trees that everybody said ghosts lived in. Anyway, we'd be on the side of the road—whoever I was with, one of my uncles or my cousin James— and I remember somebody would be playing a guitar the way B. B. King plays. And I remember a man and a woman singing and talking about getting *down!* Shit, that music was something, especially that woman singing. But I think that kind of stuff stayed with me, you know what I mean? That *kind* of sound in music, that blues, church, back-road funk kind of thing, that southern, midwestern, rural sound and rhythm. I think it started getting into my blood on them spook- filled Arkansas back-roads after dark when the owls came out hoot- ing. So when I started taking music lessons I might have already had some idea of what I wanted my music to sound like.

Music is a funny thing when you really come to think about it. Because it's hard to pinpoint where it all began for me. But I think some of it had to have started on that Arkansas road and some on that "Harlem Rhythms" radio show. When I got into music I went all the way into music; I didn't have no time after that for nothing else.

by the time I was twelve, music had become the most important thing in my life. I probably didn't realize how important it would become, but looking back, I can see just how important it was. I still played baseball and football, still hung out with my friends like Millard Curtis and Darnell Moore. But I was seriously taking trumpet lessons and was really into my horn. I remember going to Boy Scout camp near Waterloo, Illinois, when I was about twelve or thirteen. It was Camp Vanderventer, and Mr. Mays, the Head Scoutmaster, knew that I played trumpet. He gave me the job of playing taps and reveille. I remember how proud I was for him to ask me, picking me out from everyone. So I guess by then I was starting to play all right.

But I really started to stretch on out as a player after I left Attucks Junior High and went to Lincoln High School. My first great teacher, Elwood Buchanan, was at Lincoln. Lincoln was both a junior and senior high school; I went there for junior high and stayed all the way to graduation. When I started playing in the band I was younger than everybody else. After my father, Mr. Buchanan was the biggest influence on my life up until then. He was definitely the person who took me all the way into music at that time. I knew I wanted to become a musician. That was all I wanted to be.

Mr. Buchanan was one of my father's patients and drinking buddies. My father told him how interested I was in music and in playing trumpet, specifically. So he said he would give me trumpet lessons and that was that. I was going to Attucks when I first started taking lessons from Mr. Buchanan. Later, after I started going to Lincoln High School, he still sort of looked after me to keep me on the right track.

On my thirteenth birthday, my father bought me a new trumpet. My mother wanted me to have a violin, but my father overruled her. This caused a big argument between them, but she soon got over it. But Mr. Buchanan was the reason I got a new trumpet, because he knew how bad I wanted to play.

It was about that time that I first started having serious disagreements with my mother. Up until then, it had been over small things. But it just kind of went downhill. I don't really know what her problem was. But I think it had something to do with her not talking real straight to me. She was still trying to treat me like I was a little baby, the way she was treating my brother, Vernon. I think this had something to do with him becoming a homosexual. The women—my mother, my sister, and my grandmother—always treated Vernon like a girl. So, I wasn't having none of that shit from them. It was a matter of talking straight to me or not talking to me at all. My father told my mother to leave me alone when we started having problems. And she did most of the time, but we really got into some bad arguments. Despite all that, my mother did buy me two records by Duke Ellington and Art Tatum, though. I used to listen to them all the time and that helped me later in understanding jazz.

Because Mr. Buchanan had already given me trumpet lessons at Attucks before I came to Lincoln, I was advanced on the instrument. I was already playing pretty good. Then in high school I also started studying with a great German trumpet teacher named Gustav who lived over in St. Louis and played first trumpet with the St. Louis Symphony Orchestra. He was a bad motherfucker. He also made great trumpet mouthpieces, and I use one of his design even today.

At Lincoln High, the band under Mr. Buchanan's direction was a motherfucker. We had a hell of a cornet and trumpet section. It was me, Ralaigh McDaniels, Red Bonner, Duck McWaters, and Frank Gully—who played first trumpet and was a bad motherfucker. He was about three years older than I was. Because I was the smallest and youngest person in the band, some of the kids would pick on me. But I was mischievous, too, playing little pranks on people and shit —throwing spitballs and hitting people upside the head when they weren't looking. You know, little kid, teenage shit, wasn't none of it serious.

Everybody always seemed to like my tone, which I kind of got from the way Mr. Buchanan played at the time. This was on cornet. As a matter of fact, Red and Frank and everybody else who was playing cornet or trumpet in the band used to pass around Mr. Buchanan's instrument; I think I was the only one in the cornet section who had his own instrument. But even though they were all older than me and I had a lot to learn, they all encouraged me, liked the way I sounded, the way I approached playing. They always used to tell me I had a lot of imagination on the instrument.

Mr. Buchanan kept us playing strictly marches and shit like that. Overtures, real good background music, John Philip Sousa marches. He didn't let us play no jazz shit while he was around, but when he would leave the band room for a while we would try to get into some jazz. One of the hippest things Mr. Buchanan taught me was not to play with vibrato in my tone. At first, I used to like to play with vibrato because of the way most of the other trumpet players played the instrument. One day while I was playing in that style, with all this vibrato, Mr. Buchanan stopped the band and told me, "Look here, Miles. Don't come around here with that Harry James stuff, playing with all that vibrato. Stop shaking all those notes and trembling them, because you gonna be shaking enough when you get old. Play straight, develop your *own* style, because you can do it. You got enough talent to be your own trumpet man."

Man, I never forgot that. But at the time, he hurt and embarrassed me. I just loved the way Harry James played. But after that I started to forget James and found out that Mr. Buchanan was right. At least, he was right for me.

By the time I was in high school I started getting really serious about my clothes. I started caring about the way I looked, trying to look hip and everything, because about this time girls started paying attention to me—although at age fourteen I wasn't really into them yet. So I started dressing real hip, taking a lot of time about selecting the clothes I bought and wore to school. Me and a couple of my friends—who were also into clothes—started comparing notes on what was hip and what wasn't. I liked the dress style of Fred Astaire and Cary Grant back then, so I created a kind of hip, quasi-black English look: Brooks Brothers suits, butcher boy shoes, high top pants, shirts with high tab collars that were so stiff with starch that I could hardly move my neck.

One of the most important things that happened for me in high school—besides studying under Mr. Buchanan—was when one time the band went to play in Carbondale, Illinois, and I met Clark Terry, the trumpet player. He became my idol on the instrument. He was older than me and was a drinking buddy of Mr. Buchanan. Anyway, we went down there to Carbondale to play and I saw this dude and walked right up to him and asked him if he was a trumpet player. He turned and asked me how I knew he was a trumpet player. I told him I could tell by his embouchure. I had on my school band uniform and Clark had on this hip coat and this bad, beautiful scarf around his neck. He was wearing hip butcher boy shoes and a bad hat cocked ace-deuce. I told him I could also tell he was a trumpet player by the hip shit he was wearing. He kind of smiled at me and said something that I have forgotten. Then, when I asked him some things about playing trumpet, he sort of shined on me by telling me that he didn't want to "talk about no trumpet with all them pretty girls bouncing around out there." Clark was really into the girls at that time, and I wasn't. So what he said to me really hurt me. The next time we met it was a different story altogether. But I never forgot that first time me and Clark met, how hip he was. I decided then I was going to be that hip, even hipper, when I got my shit together.

I started hanging out with my friend Bobby Danzig. Bobby was about the same age as me and was a hell of a trumpet player. We used to go around listening to music and sitting in wherever we could. We went everywhere together, we were both into clothes, even thought a lot alike. But he was more outspoken than me. He would tell a motherfucker off in a minute. Man, we'd go to a club and listen to a band and if the horn player was standing wrong, or the drummer had his drums set up wrong, Bobby would say, "Let's get out of here, man, because this motherfucker can't play. Look at how the drummer done set up his drums, man; they're wrong. And look at how that trumpet player's standing. His posture's all fucked up. Now you *know* that motherfucker can't play standing up there on the bandstand like that! So let's get out of here!"

Man, Bobby Danzig was something else. He was a great trumpet player and he was even a greater pickpocket. He'd get on one of them trolleys that was running in St. Louis and by the time it had reached the end of the line, Bobby would have himself $300, or more on a great day. I met Bobby when I was sixteen and I think he was the same age. We joined the union together and we'd go everywhere together. Bobby was my first musical best friend, my running partner. Like I said, it was him who went with me to the Riviera when I went to audition for the Billy Eckstine band, and he could play trumpet like a motherfucker. I later became good friends with Clark Terry, but Clark was about six years older than I was and so we were into different head sets. But Bobby was right there in the things we liked to do together. Except I was never into picking pockets like he was. He was the best at it I have ever seen.

After I studied trumpet with Mr. Buchanan I began studying with a great teacher named Gustav. He played trumpet with the St. Louis Symphony Orchestra. He also made some great trumpet mouthpieces, and I use a mouthpiece of his design even today. Anyway, Gustav also taught a trumpet player named Levi Maddison. Levi was his star pupil, and man, he was a motherfucker. Back in those days, around 1940, St. Louis was a great city for trumpet players and Levi was one of the baddest, if not *the* baddest. But Levi was a crazy motherfucker who went around laughing to himself all the time. Once he started laughing at something he couldn't stop. A lot of people said he was laughing all the time because he was despondent. I don't know *what* Levi was despondent over, but I know he could sure play the trumpet. I used to love to watch him. His trumpet was an extension of him. But all of the trumpet players from St. Louis played like that—Harold "Shorty" Baker, Clark Terry, and myself. We all played like that, had what I called "that St. Louis thing."

Levi would always be smiling with that crazy look in his eyes. That distant thing. He was out and he was always being confined in the nuthouse for a few days. He didn't never hurt nobody, wasn't violent or anything like that. But I guess people back in those days didn't want to take no chances. Later, after I left St. Louis to live in New York, every time I would come back home for a visit I would go and see Levi. Finding him was sometimes difficult. When I found him, though, I would ask him to put the trumpet to his mouth just because I loved the way he held it. And he would, with a big smile on his face. Then once when I came back I couldn't find him. They said he started laughing one day and couldn't stop. So they took him to the sanatorium and he never came out again. Or, at least, nobody ever saw him again. But the thing Levi used to do on trumpet was just too bad, man, he was a hell of a musician. When he picked up the horn you would hear all this tone and brilliance, you know? Nobody else had it and I have yet to hear a tone like that. It's almost like mine, but it was rounder—sort of in between Freddie Webster's and mine. And

Levi had that air about him when he picked up his horn that you were going to hear something you'd never heard before in your life. Only a few people had that attitude. Dizzy had it and I think I have it. But Levi was the man. He was a motherfucker. If he hadn't gone crazy and went to the nuthouse, people would have been talking about him today.

Gustav would tell *me* I was the worst trumpet player in the world. But later, when Dizzy had a hole in his lip that wouldn't heal and so he went to see Gustav about changing mouthpieces, he said Gus told him that I was his best pupil. All I know is that Gus never told me that to my face.

Maybe Gus thought that by telling me I was his worst student that I would play harder. Maybe he thought that was the way to get the best out of me. I don't know. But it didn't bother me. As long as he taught me that half an hour for the $2.50 I paid him, he could say anything he wanted. Gus was a technician. He could run chromatic scales about twelve times in one breath. He was something. But by the time I was going to him for lessons I already had some confidence in my playing. I knew I wanted to be a musician and so everything I did was leaning toward that.

While I was in high school I started hanging out with a piano player named Emmanual St. Claire "Duke" Brooks. (His nephew, Richard Brooks, an all-American football player, is now the principal of Miles Davis Elementary School.) He got his nickname "Duke" because he knew and could play all of Duke Ellington's music. He used to play with the bassist Jimmy Blanton at a place across the street from where I lived called the Red Inn. Duke Brooks was two or three years older than me, but he had a big influence on me because he was into the new music that was happening at the time.

Duke Brooks was a hell of a piano player. Man, the motherfucker played like Art Tatum. He used to teach me chords and shit. He lived in East St. Louis and had a room by himself in his parents' house, off the porch. I'd go over to his house and listen to him at lunchtime when I was going to Lincoln High School. He lived about two or three blocks from school. He smoked a lot of reefer and I think he was the first person I knew who did that. I never did it with him, though. I never did like reefer too much. But then, at that time, I wasn't doing nothing, not even drinking.

Duke eventually got killed when he was hoboing a ride on a train somewhere in Pennsylvania. He was in one of those cars filled with gravel and sand. I heard the shit fell on him and he suffocated. I think this was in 1945. I still miss him and think about him even up until today. He was a hell of a musician and if he hadn't gotten killed, he would have been a motherfucker on the music scene.

I was starting to play the running trumpet style that I was hearing around St. Louis. Me and Duke and a drummer named Nick Haywood—who had a hump in his back—had a little group together. We used to try to play like the black guys who played in Benny Goodman's band. Benny had a black piano player named Teddy Wilson. But Duke played hipper than Teddy Wilson. Duke played piano then like Nat "King" Cole. He was just that slick, Duke was.

The only new records we had during this time were mostly the records they took out of jukeboxes and sold you for a nickel. And if you didn't have money to buy it then you'd just have to go and cop it by listening to the jukebox. I was playing by ear back then. Anyway, our little group would play tunes like "Airmail Special." We'd play it with those hip accents. Duke was such a motherfucker on the piano that it made me play in the running style he had.

About this time I was starting to have a little reputation around East St. Louis as an up-and-coming trumpet player. People—musicians—thought I could play, but I wasn't vain enough to admit it out loud. But the way I was beginning to think to myself was that I could play as good as any motherfucker walking. I probably thought I could play better. Because when it came to reading music and remembering the parts, I had a photographic memory. I didn't forget anything. I was also improving as a soloist from working with Mr. Buchanan and being around guys like Duke Brooks and Levi Maddison. So, a lot of things were starting to fall into place. Some of the best musicians around East St. Louis wanted me to play with them. I was beginning to think I was the hippest thing around.

Maybe one of the reasons I didn't say it out loud was because Mr. Buchanan was still on my back to get better at Lincoln High. Although he leaned toward me in the band after Frank Gully graduated —I was playing most of the first parts—he still came down on me hard sometimes. He'd say my sound was too small or he'd tell me he couldn't hear me sometimes. But he was always like that—hard on you, especially if he thought you could play. Once when I was younger and everybody was thinking I was going to be a dentist, he had told my father, "Doc, Miles ain't gonna be no dentist. He's gonna be a musician." So he'd already seen something in me even back then. He told me later that it was my curiosity, wanting to know so much about music, that was my edge. That was carrying me forward all the time.

Duke Brooks and Nick Haywood, some other guys, and me used to play at a place called Huff's Beer Garden. Frank Gully used to play there with us sometimes. We'd make some pocket change on Saturdays. But it wasn't nothing to call home about. We'd just make the gigs for the fun of it. We played all kinds of little gigs in East St. Louis: social clubs, church affairs, any place we could play. Sometimes we'd make as much as six dollars a night. We used to practice in my basement too. Man, did we play loud. I remember one time my father came by Huff's to hear us play. When he told me about it the next day, he said all he could hear was the drums. Anyway, we were trying to play all of Harry James's tunes. But after a while, I quit the band, because outside of Duke's playing there wasn't nothing happening for me in it.

Thinking about nothing but music cut me out of the gang wars and shit, and limited the time for playing sports. I was practicing every chance I got—fucking around trying to learn how to play piano, too. I was learning how to improvise and really getting deep into jazz. I wanted to be able to play the things I heard Harry James playing. So I quickly got tired of listening to motherfuckers who couldn't play hip shit. Some of the guys who weren't advanced in music started to laugh at me for trying to play the newer music. But I didn't give a fuck about what they were talking about. I *knew* that I was on the right track.

About the time I was sixteen I had a chance to play some gigs on the road—Belleville, Illinois, places like that. My mother said I could play on weekends. This was with a guy named Pickett. We used to play shit like "Intermezzo," "Honeysuckle Rose," and "Body and Soul." I would just play the melodies because nothing else hip was happening. We were making a little pocket change. But I was learning all the time. Pickett played that roadhouse music, or what some call honky-tonk. You know. That shit that they play in black "bucket of blood" clubs. "Bucket of blood" refers to the fights that were likely to jump off in those clubs. But after a while I got tired of asking when I was going to be able to get off—play the hip shit I was getting into. It wasn't long before I quit Pickett's band.

By the time I was fifteen or sixteen, I had learned how to play chromatic scales, too. When I started playing that shit everybody around Lincoln stopped and asked me what I was doing. They started looking at me differently after that. Also, me and Duke were beginning to catch jam sessions in Brooklyn, Illinois—just up the road from East St. Louis. One of my father's best friends was the mayor of Brooklyn, so he let me play even though I was too young to be going into clubs. A lot of really fine musicians played those riverboats on the Mississippi from New Orleans to St. Louis. They were always sitting in up in those all-night Brooklyn nightspots. Man, them places was always jumping, especially on weekends.

East St. Louis and St. Louis were country towns full of country people. Both towns are real square, especially the white people from around there—*really* country, and racist to the bone. Black people from around East St. Louis and St. Louis were country, too, but kind of hip in their countryness. It was a hip place. A lot of people from that area had a whole lot of style back in those days—still probably do. Black people from that area of the country are kind of different from black people in other places. And I think when I was growing up it was because of the people—especially black musicians—moving back and forth from New Orleans. St. Louis is close to Chicago and Kansas City, as well. So people would bring the different kinds of styles of those places back to East St. Louis.

There was a hipness in the black people then. After St. Louis closed down at night, everybody over there came to Brooklyn to listen to the music and party all night long. People in East St. Louis and St. Louis worked their asses off in them packing and slaughterhouses. So you know they was mad when they took off work. They didn't want to hear no dumb shit off nobody, and would kill a motherfucker quick who brought them some stupid shit. That's why they were serious about their partying and listening to music. That's why I loved playing up in Brooklyn. People were really into listening to what you were playing. If you weren't playing anything, the people in Brooklyn would let you know it quick. I've always liked honesty and can't stand people being any other way.

About this time I was starting to make a little money, not much. My teachers at Lincoln knew that I was serious about being a musician. Some of them heard me up in Brooklyn on weekends or at other jam sessions. But I made it a point to do real good in my studies, because if I didn't, I knew my mother and father weren't going to let me play. So I studied harder.

When I was sixteen, I met Irene Birth, who was going to Lincoln with me. She had real pretty feet. I was always a sucker for pretty little feet. She was about five feet six inches tall and weighed about 103 pounds. A slender woman, but a real nice figure—reminded me of a dancer's body. She was half yellow-looking in color. You know, kind of light-skinned, but half-assed light skin. Outside of her being pretty and hip, with a good body, her feet is what really attracted me. She was a little older than I was—I think she was born May 12, 1923—and a couple of grades ahead of me. But she liked me and I liked her and she was the first real girlfriend that I had.

She lived up on Goose Hill, which is a part of East St. Louis that is over by the packing houses and the pens where they used to keep the cows and pigs after they unloaded them from the trains. The neighborhood was poor and black. There was always a real bad smell in the air, of burnt meat and hair. The smell of manure and cow shit mingled with this smell of death. What a weird, funky smell. Anyway, it was a long distance from where I lived, but I used to walk over there to see her. Sometimes alone and sometimes with my friend Millard Curtis, who was by then a star football and basketball player; I think he was captain of the football team.

I was really into Irene. I got my first orgasm with her. I remember the first time I bust my nuts I thought I had to pee and jumped up and ran to the bathroom. I had had a wet dream before, when I thought I had rolled over on an egg and burst it. But, man, I had never experienced nothing like that first nut.

Irene and I used to take the trolley car across the bridge over the Mississippi River to St. Louis on weekends. We'd go all the way out to Sarah and Finney—which was the richest black neighborhood in St. Louis back then—to the Comet Theatre, the best black movie house in town. The whole trip cost about forty cents for both of us. I used to carry my horn every place we went, because I figured I might get a chance to play. Always wanted to be ready if the opportunity presented itself, and sometimes it did.

Irene used to dance in one of those groups they had around East St. Louis. She could really dance. I never was a good dancer. But I could dance with Irene for some reason; she seemed to be able to pull the shit out of me and not make me stumble all over the place and look like a fool. She actually made me look like I knew what I was doing. But Irene was one of the only girls—besides my sister, Dorothy—I could dance with. I didn't like to dance because I was too shy back then.

Irene grew up with her mother, who was a good woman, strong and fine like Irene. Her father, Fred Birth, was a numbers writer. He was a gambler, a real tall dude. She had a younger half-brother named Freddie Birth who I used to give trumpet lessons to. He was a pretty good player, but I was hard on him, like Mr. Buchanan was hard on me. After I left Lincoln, Freddie played first trumpet in the school band. He is a school principal back in East St. Louis today. Freddie Jr. grew up to be a very nice and hip dude.

Irene also had a little brother named William, about five or six years old, I think, who I liked very much. William was a real cute little boy, with curly hair, but thin and always coughing. He had gotten real sick with pneumonia, or something like that. So anyway, this doctor came over to see William. Because Irene knew that I had thought of being a doctor—following in my father's footsteps, but on the medical, not dental side (something few people knew about me) —she called me to watch what he did. The doctor came and took one look at William and flat out said, without any emotion, that there was nothing he could do. He said that William was going to be dead before morning. Man, that shit made me so fucking mad. You know, for a long time I couldn't understand how he could say something like that and be so cold about it. It just turned my stomach, man. William did die early the next day in his mother's arms at home without the doctor ever taking him to the hospital, and that shit hurt me so bad.

After this happened, I went to my father and asked him how a doctor could come to see William and tell his family that he was going to be dead before morning and not do nothing about it. He's a doctor, ain't he? Is it that they don't have no money, or what? So my father, knowing that I was asking these questions because of my interest in medicine, said, "If you go to some doctors with a broken arm, they will just cut it off instead of setting it because it might be real hard for them to set it. It might take too much effort. So it's easier for them to cut it off. He's one of them kind of doctors, Miles. There are plenty of them in the world. Those kinds of people, Miles, are only in medicine for the prestige and money that it brings them. They don't love it like I do, or like some of my friends do. You don't go see him if you're really sick. The only people that go to see him are poor black people. Those doctors and he don't care nothing about them. That's why he was so cold to William and his family. He don't care nothing about them, do you understand?"

I nodded that I understood. But, man, that shit shocked me, disturbed the fuck out of me. Then, I found out later that this doctor had this real big house, that he was rich and had his own airplane. He had all this shit that he made off people—poor black people that he didn't give a fuck about. That shit made me sick. So I thought about William's death and what my father told me about how some doctors were. I just couldn't understand how someone could look at somebody whose heart is still beating and just say that that person's going to die tomorrow morning and not try to do something about it —at least try to ease the pain. It just seemed to me, at that time, that if someone's heart is still beating then that person's still got a chance to live. I decided that I wanted to be a doctor so that I could try and save the lives of people like William.

But you know how it is. You say you want to be this, you want to be that. And then, finally, something else just comes along and moves it out of your head, especially when you're young. Music just moved medicine out of my head. That is, if it ever really was there in the first place. I had in my head that if I didn't make it as a musician by the time I was twenty-four, I was going to do something else. That something else, in my mind, was medicine.

Anyway, going back to Irene. I think William's dying like he did brought Irene and me closer. We got real tight after that. She used to go everywhere with me. My father never liked Irene, though. My mother did. I really don't know why he didn't like her, but he didn't. Maybe he thought she wasn't good enough for me. Maybe he thought that she was too old and would misuse me. I don't know what it was, but it didn't change the way I felt about her. I was really into her.

Irene was the person who, when I was seventeen, dared me to call up Eddie Randle and ask him for a job in his band. Eddie Randle's Blue Devils band was hot, man; them motherfuckers could play their asses off. I was over to her house when she dared me, so I told her to give me the phone, and I called him up. When he answered the phone, I said, "Mr. Randle, I hear you need a trumpet player; my name is Miles Davis."

He said, "Yeah, I need a trumpet player. Come on over and let me hear you."

So I went over to the Elks Club in downtown St. Louis where the Rhumboogie Club was located. It was on the second floor, up a long, narrow flight of stairs, in a building sitting off by itself. It was in the black community, so the place would be packed with black people who really were into music. This was where Eddie Randle played. His band was also billed as the Rhumboogie Orchestra. I auditioned with another trumpet player and got the job.

The Blue Devils played hot dance music so good and there were so many good musicians in that band that everybody used to come hear us play, no matter what kind of music they themselves played. Duke Ellington came through and heard Jimmy Blanton, the great bass player, sitting in with us one night and hired him on the spot.

There was an alto saxophone player in the Blue Devils named Clyde Higgins, who was one of the baddest motherfuckers I ever heard. His wife, Mabel, played piano with the Blue Devils. She was a great musician and a great woman. She was fatter than a mother-fucker, though, and Clyde was skinnier than a motherfucker. But she was something else, a beautiful person. I spent a lot of time learning from her. She showed me a lot of shit on piano, which helped me to develop even faster as a musician.

Another dude who played a great alto was Eugene Porter. He was almost as bad. He was younger than Clyde and wasn't in the band, but he sat in a lot. Eddie Randle played a mean trumpet himself. But Clyde Higgins was so bad that when him and Eugene Porter went down to audition for a gig with Jimmie Lunceford's band, Clyde blew them all away. See, Clyde was a tiny, real black man, and he looked like a monkey. Back during those days a lot of bands that played for white people liked to hire light-skinned musicians, and so Clyde was too dark for them. Eugene said when Clyde went for the audition and told Lunceford he was a saxophone player, everybody laughed at him and started calling him "the little monkey." They gave him the toughest music they had in their book to play. Clyde, being the great musician that he was, ran right through it like it wasn't nothing. At least, that's what Eugene said. When Clyde got through playing, all them cats in Lunceford's band had their mouths hanging open. So Lunceford said to them, "Well, how y'all like that?" Nobody said nothing. Clyde didn't get the job, though. Eugene did, because he was better-looking and light-skinned, and a real good alto player. But he wasn't even close to Clyde Higgins. And he told everybody that Clyde should have gotten the job. But that's the way things were back then in those days.

Playing with Eddie Randle had to be one of the most important steps in my career. It was with Eddie Randle's band that I really started opening up with my playing, really got into writing and arranging music. I became the musical director of the band, because most of the other guys in the band were working regular gigs in the daytime, so they didn't have the time to get the music together. I was in charge of setting up rehearsals and rehearsing the band. They had other acts at the Rhumboogie, like dancers and comedians, singers, shit like that. So sometimes the band accompanied another act and I had to get the band ready for that. We traveled some and played all over the St. Louis and East St. Louis areas. I met many other great musicians when they came through. I learned a lot being in Eddie Randle's band, and I made more money than I had ever made, about $75 or $80 a week.

I stayed with Eddie Randle's band for about a year, from 1943 to 1944, I think. I used to call him "Bossman," because that's what he was to me—the boss—and he ran a tight band. I learned a lot from him about how to run a band. We used to do the musical charts and arrangements of Benny Goodman, Lionel Hampton, Duke Ellington, and all them bad cats that were playing back then. There were a lot of great bands around St. Louis, like the Jeter-Pillars Band and George Hudson's band. Man, both of *them* bands was motherfuckers, too. But Ernie Wilkins, who was the arranger for the Blue Devils when I was in that band, and Jimmy Forrest came out of Eddie Randle's band, so I guess I would have to say that he—Eddie Randle —was a leader of great musicians. But George Hudson was a mean trumpet player, too. St. Louis, like New Orleans, is a big trumpet player's town, maybe because of all those marching bands in St. Louis. All I know is that some bad motherfuckers on trumpet came out of there and when I was growing up trumpet players from all over the country used to come through to play in those jam sessions. But I hear it's a lot different today.

I remember when I ran into Clark Terry again at the Rhumboogie; it was a different story from when I had first met him. Now, here he comes into the Rhumboogie to hear *me* play. I said to him when he ran up to me telling me how bad I was, "Yeah, motherfucker, you come up to me now saying that shit, when you wouldn't even talk to me when I first met you over in Carbondale; I'm the little dude you shined on over there." So man, we just laughed, and have been great friends ever since. But him telling me I was bad and could really play at that time did a lot of good. I already had confidence, but Clark telling me this just gave me more. After Clark and I became friends, we hung out all over the St. Louis area, sitting in and going to jam sessions, and when people heard that Clark and I were going to be sitting in on a particular night, the place would fill up quick, be jammed-packed with people. Clark Terry was the one who really opened up the St. Louis jazz scene for me, taking me with him when he would go sit in. I learned a lot from listening to him play the trumpet. He introduced me to the fluegelhorn, too, which I played for a while, calling the one I had "my fat girl," because of the way it was shaped.

But I had an impact on Clark also, because he used to borrow my fluegelhorn and keep it for a couple of days because I preferred playing the trumpet. That's how he started playing fluegelhorn, and he's still playing it today and is one of the best in the world at playing it, if not *the* best. All through this period I loved Clark Terry—still do to this day—and I think he felt the same way about me. Every time I got a new horn back in those days, I would go looking for Clark to fix up my horn, get the valves to working, and he would fix it up like nobody else could. Man, Clark had a way of twisting and lightening the spring action of the pumps of a trumpet, just by adjusting the springs around, that would make your horn sound altogether different. It made your horn sound like magic, man. Clark was a magician with that shit. I used to love for Clark to fix my valves. And he used to always use those Heim mouthpieces of Gustav's design with his instrument, because they were very thin but very deep, and gave a big, round, warm sound. All the St. Louis trumpet players used them. One time I lost mine and Clark got me a new one. After that, every time he would find an extra one he'd get it for me in St. Louis.

While I was with Eddie Randle's band, like I said, a lot of other great musicians used to come and listen to the band—people like Benny Carter and Roy Eldridge, and the trumpet player Kenny Dorham, who came all the way from Austin, Texas, to hear me play. He had heard about me all the way down there. Then there was Alonzo Pettiford, who also played trumpet, and who was the bass player Oscar Pettiford's brother. He was from Oklahoma and was one of the baddest trumpet players around back in those days. Man, could that motherfucker play fast—his fingers were a blur. He played that real fast, hip, slick Oklahoma style. Then there was Charlie Young, who played both saxophone *and* trumpet, and played both of them *real* good. And then I met "the President," Lester Young, when he would come down from Kansas City to play in St. Louis. He'd have

Shorty McConnell on trumpet in his band, and sometimes I'd come over with my horn to where they were playing and sit in. Man, playing with Prez was something. I learned a lot from the way he played the saxophone. As a matter of fact, I tried to transpose some of his saxophone licks over to my trumpet.

Then there was "Fats" Navarro, who came through from Florida or New Orleans. Nobody knew who he was, but that motherfucker could play like I had never heard nobody play before. He was young, like me, but he was already advanced in his concept of how to play the instrument. Fats was in a band of Andy Kirk's and Howard McGhee's, who was also a fantastic trumpet player. One night him and me got into a jam session on trumpet that was a motherfucker, turned the whole place out. I think this was sometime in 1944. After I heard that band, Howard became my idol, replacing Clark Terry for a while, until I heard Dizzy.

I also met Sonny Stitt around this time. He was playing in Tiny Bradshaw's band and so in between sets at the club he was playing at he would come over to the Rhumboogie to catch our set. After Sonny Stitt heard the band and my playing, he approached me about going on the road with Tiny Bradshaw's band. Man, talk about excited, I couldn't wait to get home to ask my parents if I could go. Plus, Sonny had told me I looked like Charlie Parker. All the cats in the band had their hair slicked back, was wearing hip shit—tuxedos and white shirts—and acting and talking like they was the baddest motherfuckers in the world. You know what I mean? They impressed the fuck out of me. But when I got home and asked my parents, they said no, because I hadn't finished high school yet. I would have been making only $60, $25 less than I was making with Eddie Randle's Blue Devils. I think it was the idea of traveling on the road with a big time band that impressed me the most. Plus, they seemed so hip and were wearing such hip shit. At least, it seemed that way to me back then. I got other offers from Illinois Jacquet, McKinney's Cotton Pickers, and A. J. Sullivan to travel on the road playing in their bands. I also had to turn them down until I graduated from high school. Man, I wanted to hurry up and graduate so that I could get on with playing music and living my life. I was still quiet. Still didn't talk much. But I was changing on the inside. And I really was into clothes—I was clean as a motherfucker, or like they used to say back in St. Louis, cleaner than a broke-dick dog.

Things were going great for me musically, but things at home were not going so good. My parents were getting along worse than ever and were just about to separate. They did separate around 1944, I forget which year it was. My sister, Dorothy, was starting college at Fisk, and by this time people in East St. Louis felt that Vernon was on his way to being a homosexual. Back in them days that was some other kind of shit.

My father had bought a three-hundred-acre farm in Millstadt, Illinois, before he and my mother separated. But she didn't like being out there with all the horses, cows, and prize-winning pigs my father was raising. My mother wasn't into the country living like my father was. But he started spending a lot of time out on his farm and this probably caused them to break up quicker than they would have. My mother didn't cook or do housework. So we had a cook and a maid. But that still didn't seem to make her happy. I liked it out in Millstadt —riding horses and all. It was peaceful and beautiful. I've always been into shit like that. In fact, it reminded me of my grandfather's place, only it was bigger. The house was white, with colonial-style columns, and had about twelve or thirteen rooms. It was two stories high and had a guesthouse. It was really a beautiful place, with a lot of grounds and trees and flowers. I used to love to go out there.

After my mother and father separated, things got real bad between my mother and me. I stayed with her after they separated, but we didn't seem to agree on anything, and with my father not there to keep her off me, there were a lot of screaming arguments. I was getting independent, but I think that the real cause of the problem with my mother was my relationship with my girlfriend Irene Birth.

My mother liked Irene, but she was pissed off when Irene got pregnant. She had plans for me going to college and this was going to cause a problem. My father, like I said, didn't like Irene, although he warmed up to her later. So when I first heard about Irene being pregnant, I went and told my father and he said, "So? So what? I'll take care of it for you."

So I said, "No, Dad, it don't go like that. I'll take care of it myself. I helped do it and I got to be man enough to take care of it." So he kind of paused for a minute and then he said, "Listen, Miles, the baby might not even be yours, because I know all them other niggers she's been fucking. So don't be walking around thinking you are the only one. There's others, plenty of others." I knew Irene was messing around with another dude named Wesley, I forgot his last name, who was older than me. And I knew she was going with a drummer named James—a little bitty guy—who used to play around East St. Louis; I would see her with him from time to time. But then again, Irene was fine and popular with the men. So my father wasn't telling me nothing I didn't already know. But I was convinced that the baby was mine and that I was doing the right thing by owning up to it. My father was really pissed off with Irene for getting pregnant. I think it was one of the things that stood between them ever really getting tight as they could have been. Anyway, I graduated from Lincoln in January 1944, although I didn't get my degree until that June. We had our first child, a daughter, Cheryl, that year.

Meanwhile, I was making about $85 a week playing in Eddie Randle's band and with other people, and I was buying myself some hip Brooks Brothers suits. I had myself a new horn, so I wasn't doing too bad. But the problems with my mother were getting out of hand, and I knew I had to do something about that and also do something about taking care of my family. I never married Irene legally, but we were still like man and wife. But I started to see some other things about how women were with men. I was also starting to think seriously about leaving the St. Louis area to live in New York.

Marghuerite Wendell (later Willie Mays's first wife) used to work the door at the Rhumboogie. Me and her got to be good friends. She was from St. Louis and was one of the hippest women I ever met. Anyway, she used to come up to me and tell me how handsome all the women, her friends, thought I was. But I didn't pay much attention to that kind of shit. That just seemed to make them bitches more serious about getting me in bed with them. You know what I mean? I remember this one woman named Ann Young, who turned out to be Billie Holiday's niece, coming up to me one night telling me she wanted to take me to New York and buy me a new trumpet. I said I got a new trumpet and I don't need nobody to take me to New York because I'm going to get there anyway. Well, the bitch got madder than a motherfucker and told Marghuerite that I was silly. Marghuerite just laughed, because she knew how I was.

Another time when I was in Eddie Randle's band, there was this dancer named Dorothy Cherry, who was finer than ten motherfuckers. Man, she was so fine guys used to send her roses every night. Everybody wanted to fuck her. She was an exotic dancer and we used to play behind her act at the Rhumboogie. Anyway, one night I was passing by her dressing room and she said for me to come in. Now, this bitch had a fine, low ass, long legs, hair down her back;

just a pretty, Indian-looking woman. Dark, with a great body and beautiful face. I guess I was about seventeen at the time and she was about twenty-three or twenty-four. Anyway, she tells me she wants me to hold a mirror under her pussy while she shaved her pubic hairs. So I did. I held the mirror while she did it and didn't think nothing of it. The bell rang announcing that intermission was over and it was time for the band to play again. I told the drummer in the band what had happened and he looked at me really funny and said, "So, what did you do?" I told him I just held the mirror for her. And he said, "That's all? That's all you did?"

I said, "Yeah, that's all I did; what else was I supposed to do?" The drummer, who was about twenty-six or twenty-seven, just shook his head and started laughing and then he said, "You mean with all these sex-fiend motherfuckers in this band she lets *you* hold that goddamn mirror? Aw, man, ain't *that* a bitch!" Then he started looking for somebody to tell. For a while after that, the guys in the band looked at me kind of funny. I just figured that it was just show business, right, everybody helping each other out.

But after I got to thinking about it later, that fine bitch having me hold that mirror for her and me looking at that sweet pussy—what was on her mind? I never found out. But she would look at me in that sly way women look at men who are sort of innocent. It's like they're wondering how it would be to teach you all they know. But I was stupid about women then—except for Irene—and I didn't know when I was being hit on.

Once I had graduated from high school I was finally free to do what I wanted to do for at least a year or so. I had decided to try to go to the Juilliard School of Music in New York City. But I couldn't get in until September, and I still would have to pass an audition to be accepted. So I decided to get in as much playing and traveling as I could before I went to Juilliard.

In June 1944, I decided to leave Eddie Randle's band to play with a group out of New Orleans called Adam Lambert's Six Brown Cats. They had a kind of modern swing style, and Joe Williams, the great jazz singer—who was unknown at the time—was singing with them. Their trumpet player, Tom Jefferson, had gotten homesick for New Orleans while the band was playing in Springfield, Illinois, and decided to go home. I was recommended to take his place and they paid me good money. So I went with them to Chicago—the first time I had been to that city.

After a few weeks with the band, I came back home because I didn't like what they were playing. That's when Billy Eckstine's band came to St. Louis and I got that chance to play with them for two weeks. This really made up my mind for me to go to New York and attend Juilliard. My mother wanted me to go to Fisk, where my sister, Dorothy, was. She was telling me about how good Fisk's music department was and about the Fisk Jubilee Singers. But after I had heard and played with Charlie Parker, Dizzy Gillespie, Buddy Anderson (the trumpet player I replaced in the band in St. Louis; he got sick with tuberculosis and went back to Oklahoma and never played again), Art Blakey, Sarah Vaughan, and Mr. B himself, I *knew* I had to be in New York, where the action was. But my father had to settle the argument between my mother and me over my choice of school, and even though Juilliard was a world-famous music school, it still didn't make no difference to my mother. She wanted me to go to Fisk, where my sister could keep an eye on me. But I wasn't having none of that.

East St. Louis and St. Louis were getting so depressing to me around this time that I had to go someplace, even if it was wrong. I especially felt like this after Clark Terry left and joined the Navy. For a while, I was so down, I thought of joining the Navy myself so I could play with the great Navy band they had up there in the Great Lakes. Man, they had Clark, Willie Smith, Robert Russell, Ernie Royal and the Marshall brothers, and a whole lot of other dudes who used to play with Lionel Hampton's band, and Jimmie Lunceford's band. They didn't have to do no drills or duty or nothing; all they had to do was play music. They went to boot camp, but that was it. But finally, you know, I said, fuck it, because Bird and Dizzy weren't there and that's where I wanted to be, around them; that was where it ultimately was at and they were in New York, so that's where I took my ass. But I came real close to joining the Navy in 1944 after I got out of high school. Sometimes I wonder what would have happened if I had done that instead of moving to New York.

I left East St. Louis for New York in early fall 1944. I had to pass my audition to get into Juilliard, and I passed with flying colors. The two weeks I had spent with B's band in St. Louis had been good for me, but I had been a little hurt when B didn't take me with them to play in Chicago's Regal Theatre. B had gotten Marion Hazel to replace me, since Buddy Anderson wasn't coming back. That had hurt my confidence a little. But playing around East St. Louis and St. Louis again before I went up to New York helped me regain my confidence in myself. Plus Dizzy and Bird had told me to look them up if I ever came to the Big Apple. I knew I had learned all I could from playing around St. Louis, knew it was time to move on. So I packed up my stuff in the early fall of 1944 and took a train up to New York City, confident in my heart that I was going to have some shit for them motherfuckers playing up there. I ain't never been scared of doing new things, and I wasn't scared when I got to New York City. But I knew I had to get my shit together if I was going to hang with the big boys. I also knew I *was* going to do just that. I thought I could play the trumpet with anybody.

i arrived in New York City in September 1944, not in 1945 like a lot of jive writers who write about me say. It was almost the end of World War II when I got there. A lot of young guys had gone off to fight the Germans and the Japanese and some of them didn't come back. I was lucky; the war was ending. There were a lot of soldiers in their uniforms all around New York. I do remember that.

I was eighteen years old, wet behind the ears about some things, like women and drugs. But I was confident in my ability to play music, to play the trumpet, and I wasn't scared about living in New York. Nonetheless, the city was an eye-opener for me, especially all the tall buildings, the noise, the cars, and all those motherfucking people, who seemed to be everywhere. The pace of New York was faster than anything I had ever seen in my life; I thought St. Louis and Chicago were fast, but they weren't anything like New York City. So that was the first thing I had to get used to, all the people. But getting around by subway was a gas, it was so fast.

The first place I stayed was at the Claremont Hotel, which was on Riverside Drive right across from Grant's Tomb. The Juilliard School got me a room there. Then I found me a room up on 147th Street and Broadway, in a rooming house run by these people named Bell, who were from East St. Louis and knew my parents. They were nice people and the room was big and clean and cost me a dollar a week. My father had paid for my tuition and had given me some pocket money beyond my rent, enough to last me for about a month or two.

I spent my first week in New York looking for Bird and Dizzy. Man, I want everywhere looking for them two cats, spent all my money and didn't find them. I had to call back home and ask my father for some more money, which he sent me. I still was living clean, not smoking or drinking or using dope. I was just into my music and that was a total high for me. When school started at Juilliard, I would take the subway to 66th Street where the school was located. Right off the bat, I didn't like what was happening at Juilliard. The shit they was talking about was too white for me. Plus, I was more interested in what was happening in the jazz scene; that's the *real* reason I wanted to come to New York in the first place, to get into the jazz music scene that was happening around Minton's Playhouse in Harlem, and what was going on down on 52nd Street, which everybody in music called "The Street." That's what I was really in New York for, to suck up all I could from those scenes; Juilliard was only a smokescreen, a stopover, a pretense I used to put me close to being around Bird and Diz.

After I got to 52nd Street, I found Freddie Webster, who I had met back in St. Louis when he passed through playing in Jimmie Lunceford's band. Then I went and heard the Savoy Sultans at the Savoy Ballroom in Harlem; me and Freddie went to see them. They was badder than a motherfucker. But I was trying to find Bird and Dizzy and, although I was liking what I was seeing, still, it wasn't what I really came to New York to see.

The second thing I looked for was the horse stables. Since my father and grandfather had horses and since I had been riding them most of my life, I loved them as spirits and loved to ride them. I thought they would be in Central Park, so I used to walk up and down the Park, from 110th Street to 59th Street, looking for the horse stables. I never found them. Finally, one day I asked a policeman where I could find them, and he told me they were somewhere on 81st or 82nd Street. I went there and rode me a couple of horses. The attendants looked at me strange, I guess because they weren't used to seeing a black person coming to ride horses. But I just figured that that was their problem.

I went up to Harlem to check out Minton's, on 118th Street between St. Nicholas and Seventh Avenue. Next to Minton's was the Cecil Hotel, where a lot of musicians stayed. It was a hip scene. The first dumb motherfucker I saw on the corner of St. Nicholas and 117th Street was a cat named "Collar." It was in the little park they called Dewey Square, where all the musicians used to sit and get high. I never knew Collar's real name. He was from St. Louis. He used to be the Dexedrine king there and would supply Bird with Dexedrine and nutmeg and shit when he came through St. Louis. So, anyway, here's Collar up in Harlem, clean as a broke-dick dog, white-on-white shirt, black silk suit, his hair all slicked back and down to his shoulders. He said that he was in New York trying to play saxophone at Minton's. But he couldn't play too tough when he was back in St. Louis. He just wanted to be in the life of a musician. He was a *real* funny motherfucker on top of all of this. So here he was, trying to sit in at Minton's, the black jazz capital of the world. He never made it. Nobody never paid no attention to Collar up at Minton's.

Minton's and the Cecil Hotel were both first-class places with a lot of style. The people that went there were the cream of the crop of Harlem's black society. That great, middle-class building across the street from Dewey Square was called Graham Court. A lot of society black people lived in those huge, fabulous apartments; you know, doctors and lawyers and head-nigger-in-charge-type blacks. A lot of people from around the neighborhood, from Sugar Hill, came to Minton's and the neighborhood was first-class back in those days before the drugs really came in and destroyed it during the 1960s.

People who came to Minton's wore suits and ties because they were copying the way people like Duke Ellington or Jimmie Lunceford dressed. Man, they was cleaner than a motherfucker. But to get into Minton's didn't cost anything. It cost something like two dollars if you sat at one of the tables, which had white linen tablecloths on them and flowers in little glass vases. It was a nice place—much nicer than the clubs on 52nd Street—and it held about 100 or 125 people. It was mainly a supper club and the food was prepared by a great black woman cook named Adelle.

The Cecil Hotel was also a nice place, where a lot of the black musicians visting from out of town would stay. The rates were reasonable and the rooms were big and clean. Plus, they had a few high-class hustlers and prostitutes who hung around there and so if a cat wanted to get his balls up out of sand he could pay for a fine woman and get himself a room.

Minton's was *the* ass-kicker back in those days for aspiring jazz musicians, not The Street like they're trying to make out today. It was Minton's where a musician *really* cut his teeth and *then* went downtown to The Street. Fifty-second Street was easy compared to what was happening up at Minton's. You went to 52nd to make money and be seen by the white music critics and white people. But you came uptown to Minton's if you wanted to make a reputation among the musicians. Minton's kicked a lot of motherfuckers' asses, did them in, and they just disappeared—not to be heard from again. But it also taught a whole lot of musicians, made them what they eventually became.

I ran into Fats Navarro again up at Minton's and we used to jam up there all the time. Milt Jackson was there. And Eddie "Lockjaw" Davis, the tenor saxophonist, led the house band. He was a motherfucker. See, the great musicians like Lockjaw and Bird and Dizzy and Monk, who were the kings of Minton, never played no ordinary shit. They did this to eliminate a whole lot of people who couldn't play.

If you got up on the bandstand at Minton's and couldn't play, you were not only going to get embarrassed by people ignoring you or booing you, you might get your ass kicked. One night this guy who couldn't play worth shit got up to try and do his thing—bullshit—and style himself off to get some bitches, playing anything. A regular street guy who just loved to listen to all the music was in the audience when this dumb motherfucker got up on the stage to play, so the man just got up quietly from his table and snatched this no-playing cat off the stage, dragged him outside and into the alcove between the Cecil Hotel and Minton's, and just kicked this motherfucker's ass. I mean *real* good. Then he told the dude not to never take his ass up on the bandstand at Minton's again until he could play something worth listening to. That was Minton's. You had to put up or shut up, there was no in between.

A black man named Teddy Hill owned Minton's Playhouse. Bebop started at his club. It was the music laboratory for bebop. After it polished up at Minton's, *then* it went downtown to 52nd Street—the Three Deuces, the Onyx, and Kelly's Stable—where white people heard it. But what has to be understood in all of this is no matter how good the music sounded down on 52nd Street, it wasn't as hot or as innovative as it was uptown at Minton's. The idea was that you had to calm the innovation down for the white folks downtown because they couldn't handle the *real* thing. Now, don't get me wrong, there were *some* good white people who were brave enough to come up to Minton's. But they were few and far between.

I hate how white people always try to take credit for something after *they* discover it. Like it wasn't happening before they found out about it—which most times is always late, and they didn't have nothing to do with it happening. Then, they try to take *all* the credit, try to cut everybody black out. That's what they tried to do with Minton's Playhouse and Teddy Hill. After bebop became the rage, white music critics tried to act like they discovered it—and us—down on 52nd Street. That kind of dishonest shit makes me sick to my stomach. And when you speak out on it or don't go along with this racist bullshit, then you become a radical, a black troublemaker. Then they try to cut you out of everything. But the musicians and the people who really loved and respected bebop and the truth know that the *real* thing happened up in Harlem, at Minton's.

Every night after I finished my classes, I would either go down to The Street or up to Minton's. For a couple of weeks I didn't find Bird or Dizzy nowhere. Man, I was going to the 52nd Street clubs like the Spotlite, the Three Deuces, Kelly's Stable, and the Onyx looking for them. I remember when I went down to the Three Deuces for the first time and saw how little that place was; I thought it was going to be bigger. It had such a big reputation in the jazz scene that I thought it would be all plush and shit. The bandstand wasn't nothing but a little tiny space that could hardly hold a piano and didn't seem like it could ever hold a whole group of musicians. The tables for the customers were all jammed together and I remember thinking that it wasn't nothing but a hole in the wall, and that East St. Louis and St. Louis had hipper-looking clubs. I was disappointed in the way the place looked, but not in the music I heard. The first person I heard there was Don Byas, who was a hell of a tenor saxophone player. I remember listening with awe to him playing all that shit on that little bitty stage.

Then I was finally able to get in touch with Dizzy. I got his number and called him up. He remembered me and invited me over to his apartment on Seventh Avenue in Harlem. It was great to see him. But Dizzy hadn't seen Bird, either, and didn't know how or where to get in touch with him.

I kept looking for Bird. One night I found myself just sort of standing around in the doorway at the Three Deuces when the owner came up and asked me what I was doing there. I guess I looked young and innocent; I couldn't even grow a moustache back then. Anyway, I told him I was looking for Bird and he told me he wasn't there and that I had to be eighteen to come in the club. I told him I *was* eighteen and all I wanted to do was to find Bird. Then the dude start telling me what a fucked-up motherfucker Bird was, about him being a dope addict and all that kind of shit. He asked me where I was from and when I told him, he come telling me that I ought to go on back home. Then he called me "son," a name I never liked, especially from some white motherfucker who I didn't know. So I told him to go fuck himself and turned around and left. I already *knew* Bird had a bad heroin habit; he wasn't telling me nothing new.

After I left the Three Deuces, I walked up the street to the Onyx Club and caught Coleman Hawkins. Man, the Onyx was jam-packed with people there to see Hawk, who played there regularly. So, because I still didn't know anybody I just hung around the doorway like I had done at the Three Deuces, looking for a face I might recognize, you know, maybe somebody from B's band. But I didn't see anyone.

When Bean—that's what we called Coleman Hawkins—took a break, he came over to where I was, and until this day I don't know why he did this. I guess it was a lucky break. Anyway, I knew who he was and so I spoke to him and introduced myself and told him that I had played with B's band back in St. Louis and that I was in New York going to Juilliard but really trying to find Bird. I told him that I wanted to play with Bird and that he had told me when I got to New York to look him up. Bean kind of laughed and told me that I was too young to get mixed up with somebody like Bird. Man, he was making me mad with all this shit. This was the second time I had heard this that night. I didn't want to hear it no more, even if it came from somebody that I loved and respected as much as Coleman Hawkins. I got a real bad temper, so the next thing I know I'm saying to *Coleman Hawkins* something like, "Well, you know where he is or not?"

Man, I think Hawk was shocked by a young little black motherfucker like me talking to him like that. He just looked at me and shook his head and told me the best place to find Bird was up in Harlem, at Minton's or Small's Paradise. Bean said, "Bird loves to jam in those places." He turned to walk away, then added, "My best advice to you is just finish your studies at Juilliard and forget Bird."

Man, those first weeks in New York were a motherfucker—looking for Bird, and trying to keep up with my studies. Then somebody told me that Bird had friends in Greenwich Village. I went down there to see if I could find him. I went to coffeehouses on Bleecker Street. Met artists, writers, and all these long-haired, bearded beatnik poets. I had never met no people like them in all my life. Going to the Village was an education for me.

I began to meet people like Jimmy Cobb and Dexter Gordon as I moved around Harlem, the Village, and 52nd Street. Dexter called me "Sweetcakes" because I was drinking malted milks and eating cakes, pies, and jelly beans all the time. I was even getting friendly with Coleman Hawkins. He took a liking to me, watched out for me, and helped me all he could to find Bird. By now Bean thought I was really serious about the music and he respected that. But, still no Bird. And not even Diz knew where he was at.

One day I saw in the paper where Bird was scheduled to play in a jam session at a club called the Heatwave, on 145th Street in Harlem. I remember asking Bean if he thought Bird would show up there, and Bean just kind of smiled that slick, sly smile of his and said, "I'll bet *Bird* doesn't even know if he'll really be there or not."

That night I went up to the Heatwave, a funky little club in a funky neighborhood. I had brought my horn just in case I did run into Bird —if he remembered me, he might let me sit in with him. Bird wasn't there, but I met some other musicians, like Allen Eager, a white tenor player; Joe Guy, who played a great trumpet; and Tommy Potter, a bass player. I wasn't looking for them so I didn't pay them hardly no attention. I just found a seat and kept my eye fixed on the door, watching out for Bird. Man, I had been there almost all night waiting for Bird and he hadn't shown up. So I decided to go outside and catch a breath of fresh air. I was standing outside the club on the corner when I heard this voice from behind me say, "Hey, Miles! I heard you been looking for me!"

I turned around and there was Bird, looking badder than a moth-erfucker. He was dressed in these baggy clothes that looked like he had been sleeping in them for days. His face was all puffed up and his eyes were swollen and red. But he was cool, with that hipness he could have about him even when he was drunk or fucked up. Plus, he had that confidence that all people have when they *know* their shit is bad. But no matter *how* he looked, bad or near death, he still looked good to me that night after spending all that time trying to find him; I was just glad to see him standing there. And when he remembered where he had met me, I was the happiest motherfucker on earth.

I told him how hard it had been to find him and he just smiled and said that he moved around a lot. He took me into the Heatwave, where everybody greeted him like he was the king, which he was. And since I was with him and he had his arm around my shoulder, they treated me with a lot of respect, too. I didn't play that first night. I just listened. And, man, I was amazed at how Bird changed the minute he put his horn in his mouth. Shit, he went from looking real down and out to having all this power and beauty just bursting out of him. It was amazing the transformation that took place once he started playing. He was twenty-four at the time, but when he wasn't playing he looked older, especially off stage. But his whole appearance changed as soon as he put that horn in his mouth. He could play like a motherfucker even when he was almost falling-down drunk and nodding off behind heroin. Bird was something else.

Anyway, after I hooked up with him that night, I was around Bird all the time for the next several years. He and Dizzy became my main influences and teachers. Bird even moved in with me for a while, until Irene came. She came to New York in December 1944. All of a sudden, there she was, knocking on my motherfucking door; my mother had told her to come. So I found Bird a room in the same rooming house, up on 147th and Broadway.

But I couldn't handle Bird's lifestyle then—all the drinking and eating and using dope. I had to go to school in the daytime and he'd be laying up there fucked up. But he was teaching me a lot about music—chords and shit—that I would go and play on the piano when I got to school.

Almost every night I was going somewhere with Diz or Bird, sitting in, soaking up everything I could. And like I said, I had met Freddie Webster, who was a great trumpet player about the same age as me. We would go down to 52nd Street and listen in amazement at how fast Dizzy could play tempos on the trumpet. Man, I hadn't never heard no shit like they was playing on 52nd Street and up at Minton's. That was so good it was scary. Dizzy started showing me shit on the piano so I could expand my sense of harmony.

And Bird introduced me to Thelonious Monk. His use of space in his solos and his manipulation of funny-sounding chord progressions just knocked me out, fucked me up. I said, "Damn, what is this motherfucker doing?" Monk's use of space had a big influence on the way I played solos after I heard him.

Meanwhile I started really getting pissed off with what they was talking about at Juilliard. It just wasn't happening for me there. Like I said, going to Juilliard was a smokescreen for being around Dizzy and Bird, but I did want to see what I could learn there. I played in the school symphony orchestra. We played about two notes every ninety bars, and that was that. I wanted and needed more. Plus, I knew that no white symphony orchestra was going to hire a little black motherfucker like me, no matter how good I was or how much music I knew.

I was learning more from hanging out, so I just got bored with school after a while. Plus, they were so fucking white-oriented and so racist. Shit, I could learn more in one session at Minton's than it would take me two years to learn at Juilliard. At Juilliard, after it was all over, all I was going to know was a bunch of white styles; nothing new. And I was just getting mad and embarrassed with their prejudice and shit.

I remember one day being in a music history class and a white woman was the teacher. She was up in front of the class saying that the reason black people played the blues was because they were poor and had to pick cotton. So they were sad and that's where the blues came from, their sadness. My hand went up in a flash and I stood up and said, "I'm from East St. Louis and my father is rich, he's a dentist, and I play the blues. My father didn't never pick no cotton and I didn't wake up this morning sad and start playing the blues. There's more to it than that." Well, the bitch turned green and didn't say nothing after that. Man, she was teaching that shit from out of a book written by someone who didn't know what the fuck he was talking about. That's the kind of shit that was happening at Juilliard and after a while I got tired of it.

The way I was thinking about music was that people like Fletcher Henderson and Duke Ellington were the real geniuses at arranging music in America. This woman didn't even know who these people were, and I didn't have the time to teach her. She was supposed to be teaching me! So, instead of listening to what she and the other teachers said, I was looking up at the clock and thinking about what I would be doing later that night, wondering when Bird and Diz would be going downtown. I was thinking about going home to pick up some clothes to wear over to Bickford's at 145th Street and Broadway, to pick up fifty cents worth of soup so I could have the strength to play later on that night.

On Monday nights at Minton's, Bird and Dizzy would come in to jam, so you'd have a thousand motherfuckers up there trying to get in so they could listen to and play with Bird and Dizzy. But most of the musicians in the know didn't even think about playing when Bird and Dizzy came to jam. We would just sit out in the audience, to listen and learn. The rhythm section for them might be Kenny Clarke on drums and sometimes Max Roach, who I met up there. Curly Russell would be playing bass and Monk was on the piano sometimes. Man, people would be fighting over seats and shit. If you moved you'd lose your seat and have to argue and fight again. It was something. The air was just electric.

The way the shit went down up at Minton's was you brought your horn and hoped that Bird and Dizzy would invite you to play with them up on stage. And when this happened, you'd better not blow it. I didn't. The first time I played there I wasn't great but I was playing my ass off in the style I played, which was different from Dizzy's, although I was influenced by his playing at this time. But people would watch for clues from Bird and Dizzy, and if they smiled when you finished playing, then that meant that your playing was good. They smiled when I finished playing that first time and from then on I was on the inside of what was happening in New York's music scene. So after that I was like an up-and-coming star. I could sit in with the big boys all the time.

That's what I was thinking about in my classes at Juilliard, instead of having my mind on what they was teaching me. That's why I eventually quit Juilliard. They weren't teaching me nothing and didn't *know* nothing to teach me because they were so prejudiced against all black music. And that's what I wanted to learn.

Anyway, after a while I was sitting in up there at Minton's whenever I wanted to and people were coming to hear *me* play. I was getting a reputation. One of the things that surprised me about being in New York was that when I first got there, I thought all the musicians would know more about music than they did. So I was shocked to find out that among the older guys, Dizzy, Roy Eldridge, and long-haired Joe Guy were the only ones I could listen to and learn something from. I expected everybody was going to be a motherfucker and was surprised when I knew a lot more about music than most of them.

Another thing I found strange after living and playing in New York for a little while was that a lot of black musicians didn't know anything about music theory. Bud Powell was one of the few musicians I knew who could play, write, and read all kinds of music. A lot of the old guys thought that if you went to school it would make you play like you were white. Or, if you learned something from theory, then you would lose the feeling in your playing. I couldn't believe that all them guys like Bird, Prez, Bean, all them cats wouldn't go to museums or libraries and borrow those musical scores so they could check out what was happening. I would go to the library and borrow scores by all those great composers, like Stravinsky, Alban Berg, Prokofiev. I wanted to see what was going on in all of music. Knowledge is freedom and ignorance is slavery, and I just couldn't believe someone could be that close to freedom and not take advantage of it. I have never understood why black people didn't take advantage of all the shit that they can. It's like a ghetto mentality telling people that they aren't supposed to do certain things, that those things are only reserved for white people. When I would tell other musicians about all this, they would just kind of shine me on. You know what I mean? So I just went my own way and stopped telling them about it.

I had a good friend named Eugene Hays, who was from St. Louis and studied classical piano at Juilliard with me. He was a genius. If he had been white, he would have been one of the most highly regarded classical pianists in the world today. But he was black and he was ahead of his time. So they didn't give him anything. He and I took advantage of these music libraries. We would take advantage of everything we could.

Anyway, at the time I was hanging out with musicians like Fats Navarro—who everybody called "Fat Girl"—and Freddie Webster, and I had gotten kind of close with Max Roach and J. J. Johnson, the great trombone player from Indianapolis. We was all trying to get our master's degrees and Ph.D.'s from Minton's University of Bebop under the tutelage of Professors Bird and Diz. Man, they was playing so much incredible shit.

One time after the jam session was over and I had gone home to sleep, there was this knock on my door. I got up and went to the door with sleep in my eyes, madder than a motherfucker. I opened the door and there was J. J. Johnson and Benny Carter standing there with pencils and paper in their hands. I asked them, "What do you motherfuckers want this early in the morning?"

J. J. said, " 'Confirmation.' Miles, do 'Confirmation' for me, hum it."

The motherfucker ain't even said hello, right? That's the first thing out of his mouth. Bird had just written "Confirmation" and all the musicians just loved that tune. So, here's this motherfucker at six in the morning. We had just finished jamming "Confirmation" earlier, me and J. J., at the jam session. Now he's talking about humming the tune.

So I started humming it through my sleep, in the key of F. That's what it's written in. Then J. J. says to me, "But Miles, you left out a note. Where's the other note, what's that other note in the tune?" So I remember it and tell him.

He said, "Thanks, Miles," wrote something down, and then left. J. J. was a funny motherfucker, man. He used to do that shit to me all the time. He figured I knew what Bird was doing technically because I was going to Juilliard. I'll never forget that first time he did it, and we laugh about it even today. But that's how much everybody was into Bird's and Dizzy's music. We lived and slept it every day.

Me and Fat Girl used to sit in a lot together up at Minton's. He was so big and fat until he lost all that weight right before he died. If he didn't like what some motherfucker was playing up at Minton's, Fat Girl would just block the cat from getting the microphone. He'd just turn sideways and block whoever it was and motion for me to play. Cats used to get mad with Fat Girl, but he didn't care, and whoever he did it to knew they couldn't play. So they'd stay mad for only so long.

But my real main man during those first days in New York was Freddie Webster. I really liked what Freddie was doing on the horn then. He had a style like the players from St. Louis, a big, singing sound, and he didn't play too many notes or play those real fast tempos. He liked medium-tempo pieces and ballads a lot, like I did. I loved the way he played, that he didn't waste notes and had a big, warm, mellow sound. I used to try to play like him, but without the vibrato and "shaking about the notes." He was about nine years older than me, but I used to show him everything they taught me at Juilliard about technique and composition, technical things, which Juilliard *was* good for. Freddie was from Cleveland and grew up playing with Tadd Dameron. We were as close as real brothers and a lot alike. We were about the same size and used to wear each other's clothes.

Freddie had a lot of bitches. Women were his thing, besides music and heroin. Man, people would be coming by telling me about Freddie being a violent cat who carried a .45 gun and shit like that. But everybody who knew him well knew this wasn't true. I mean he didn't take no shit, but he didn't go around fucking with nobody. He even stayed with me for a while after Bird moved out. Freddie spoke his mind and didn't take shit off nobody. He was a complex guy, but we got along real well. We were so close that I paid his rent a lot. Whatever I had was his. My old man was sending me about forty dollars a week, which was a nice amount of money in those days. Whatever I didn't spend on my family I shared with Freddie.

The year 1945 was a turning point in my life. So many things started happening for me and to me. First off, from hanging around with so many musicians and being in so many clubs, I started to drink a little during that year and I started to smoke. And I was playing with more people. Me and Freddie, Fat Girl, J. J., and Max Roach were jamming all over New York and Brooklyn, wherever we could. We'd play downtown on 52nd Street until about twelve or one in the morning. Then, after we finished playing there, we'd go uptown to Minton's, Small's Paradise, or the Heatwave and play until they closed—around four, five, or six in the morning. After we'd be up all night at jam sessions, me and Freddie would sit up even longer talking about music and music theory, about approaches to the trumpet. At Juilliard I'd sleepwalk through them sorry-ass classes, bored to tears, especially in my chorus classes. I'd be sitting there yawning and nodding. Then, after classes, me and Freddie would sit around and talk more music. I hardly slept. And with Irene home, well, I had to be taking care of my husband duties with her sometimes, you know, being with her, shit like that. Then Cheryl would be crying. It was a motherfucker.

During 1945, me and Freddie Webster used to go down almost every night to catch Diz and Bird wherever they were playing. We felt that if we missed hearing them play we were missing something important. Man, the shit they were playing and doing was going down so fast you just had to be there in person to catch it. We really studied what they were doing from a technical point of view. We were like scientists of sound. If a door squeaked we could call out the exact pitch.

There was a white teacher named William Vachiano that I was studying with who helped me. But he was into shit like "Tea for Two" so he'd ask me to play stuff like that for him. We'd have arguments that became legendary among musicians in New York, because he was supposed to be this great teacher of advanced students, like I was. But me and that motherfucker went around on each other's back a lot of times. I would say, "Hey, man, you're supposed to be teaching me something, so do it and cut out the bullshit." Well, when I would say something like that, Vachiano would get madder than a motherfucker and turn all red in the face. But I got my point across to him.

It was playing with Bird that really got my shit to going. I could sit and talk, eat and hang out with Dizzy, because he's such a nice guy. But Bird was a greedy motherfucker. We didn't never have too much to say to each other. We liked playing with each other and that was it. Bird didn't never *tell* you what to play. You learned from him by just watching him, picking up shit that he did. He never did talk about music much when you were alone with him. But we talked a few times about it when he was living with me, and I picked up some things, but mostly I just learned by listening to him play.

Dizzy *liked* to talk a lot about music, though, and I picked up a lot from him in that way. Bird might have been the spirit of the bebop movement, but Dizzy was its "head and its hands," the one who kept it all together. I mean, he looked out for the younger players, got us jobs and shit, talked to us, and it didn't matter that he was nine or ten years older than I was. He never talked down to me. People used to put Dizzy down because he acted so crazy and shit. But he wasn't really crazy, just funnier than a motherfucker and really into the history of black people. He was playing music from Africa and Cuba a long time before it got popular anywhere else. Dizzy's apartment —at 2040 Seventh Avenue, in Harlem—was the gathering place for many of the musicians in the daytime. There got to be so many of us that his wife, Lorraine, started putting motherfuckers out. I'd be there a lot. Kenny Dorham would be over there, Max Roach, Monk.

It was Dizzy who made me really learn how to play piano. I'd be over there watching Monk doing his weird shit with space and progressive chords. And when Dizzy would practice, man, I would be soaking up all that good shit. But then again, I showed Diz something that I'd learned at Juilliard, the Egyptian minor scales. With the Egyptian scale you just change the flats and sharps where you want the note flatted and where you want it sharp, so you have two flats and one sharp, right? That means you will play E flat and A flat and then the F will be sharp. You put in the note that you want, like in the C scale's minor Egyptian scale. The shit looks funny because you have two flats and a sharp. But it gives you the freedom to work with melodic ideas without changing the basic tonality. So I turned Dizzy on to that; it worked both ways. But I learned way more from him than he did from me.

Bird could be a lot of fun to be around, because he was a real genius about his music, and he could be funnier than a motherfucker, talking in that British accent that he used to use. But he still was hard to be around because he was always trying to con or beat you out of something to support his drug habit. He was always borrowing money from me and using it to buy heroin or whiskey or anything he wanted at the time. Like I said, Bird was a greedy motherfucker, like most geniuses are. He wanted everything. And when he was desperate for a fix of heroin, man, Bird would do anything to get it. He would con me and as soon as he left me, he would run around the corner to somebody else with the same sad story about how he needed some money to get his horn out of the pawnshop, and hit them up for some more. He never paid nobody back, so in that way Bird was a motherfucking drag to be around.

One time I left him in my apartment when I went to school and when I got back home the motherfucker had pawned my suitcase and was sitting on the floor nodding after shooting up. Another time, he pawned his suit to get some heroin and borrowed one of mine to wear down to the Three Deuces. But I was smaller than he was so Bird was up there on the bandstand with suit sleeves ending about four inches above his wrist and suit pants ending about four inches above his ankles. That was the only suit I had at the time, so I had to stay in my apartment until he got his suit out of the pawnshop and brought mine back. But man, the motherfucker walked around for a day looking like that, just for some heroin. But they said Bird played that night like he had on a tuxedo. That's why everybody loved Bird and would put up with his bullshit. He was the greatest alto saxophone player who ever lived. Anyway, that's the way Bird was; he was a great and a genius musician, man, but he was also one of the slimiest and greediest motherfuckers who ever lived in this world, at least that I ever met. He was something.

I remember one time we was coming down to The Street to play from uptown and Bird had this white bitch in the back of the taxi with us. He done already shot up a lot of heroin and now the motherfucker's eating chicken—his favorite food—and drinking whiskey and telling the bitch to get down and suck his dick. Now, I wasn't used to that kind of shit back then—I was hardly even drinking, I think I had just started smoking—and I definitely wasn't into drugs yet because I was only nineteen years old and hadn't seen no shit like that before. Anyway, Bird noticed that I was getting kind of uptight with the woman sucking all over his dick and everything, and him sucking on her pussy. So he asked if something was wrong with me, and if his doing this was bothering me. When I told him that I felt uncomfortable with them doing what they was doing in front of me, with her licking and slapping her tongue like a dog all over his dick and him making all that moaning noise in between taking bites of chicken, I told him, "Yeah, it's bothering me." So you know what that motherfucker said? He told me that if it was bothering me, then I should turn my head and not pay attention. I couldn't believe that shit, that he actually said that to me. The cab was real small and we all three were in the backseat, so where was I supposed to turn my head? What I did was to stick my head outside the taxi window, but I could still hear them motherfuckers getting down and in between, Bird smacking his lips all over that fried chicken. Like I said, he was something, all right.

So I looked up to Bird for being a great musician more than I liked him as a person. But he treated me like his son, and he and Dizzy were like father figures to me. Bird used to always tell me that I could play with anybody. So he would almost push me up on stage sometimes to play with somebody who I didn't think I was ready for, someone like Coleman Hawkins or Benny Carter or Lockjaw Davis. I might have been confident in my playing with most people, but I was still only nineteen and felt that I was too young to play with certain other people—though there weren't many that I felt that way about. But Bird used to build up my confidence by saying he had gone through the same bullshit when he was younger back in Kansas City.

I did my first recording date, in May 1945, with Herbie Fields. Man, I was so nervous about making that date that I couldn't even hardly play. Even in the ensemble playing—I didn't get to play no solos. I remember Leonard Gaskin on bass on that date, and a singer named Rubberlegs Williams. But I tried to put that record out of my mind and I forgot who else was on that date.

I also got my first important nightclub gig at that time. I played with Lockjaw Davis's group for a month at the Spotlite on 52nd Street. I had been sitting in with him a lot up at Minton's, so he knew how I played. Around that time—maybe a little bit before this, I don't exactly remember—I started sitting in with Coleman Hawkins's band at the Downbeat Club on 52nd Street. Billie Holiday was the star singer with the group. The reason that I got to sit in a lot was because Joe Guy, Bean's regular trumpet player, had just gotten married to Billie Holiday. Sometimes, they'd be so high off heroin and be fucking so good that Joe would miss his gig. So would Billie. So, Hawk would use me when Joe didn't show up. I used to check with Hawk down at the Downbeat every night to see if Joe had shown up. If he didn't, then I would play the set.

I loved playing with Coleman Hawkins and behind Billie when I got the chance. They were both great musicians, really creative and shit. But nobody played like Bean. He had such a big, huge sound. Lester Young—Prez—had a light sound and Ben Webster used to be running all kinds of funny-ass chords, you know, like a piano, because he also played piano. And then there was Bird who also had his own thing, his sound. But Hawk started liking me so much that Joe got his act together and stopped missing sets. Then the gig with Lockjaw came around.

After the gig with Lockjaw was over, people started using me a lot on The Street. What was happening was that white people, white critics, were now beginning to understand that bebop was some important shit. They began talking and writing a lot about Bird and Dizzy, but only when they played on The Street. I mean, they wrote and talked about Minton's, but only after they had made The Street the place for white people to come to and spend a lot of money to hear this new music. Around 1945 a lot of the black musicians were playing down on 52nd Street, for the money and the media exposure. It was around this time that the clubs on 52nd—like the Three Deuces, the Onyx, the Downbeat Club, Kelly's Stable, and others—started being more important for musicians than the clubs uptown in Harlem.

A lot of white people, though, didn't like what was going on on 52nd Street. They didn't understand what was happening with the music. They thought that they were being invaded by niggers from Harlem, so there was a lot of racial tension around bebop. Black men were going with fine, rich white bitches. They were all over these niggers out in public and the niggers were clean as a motherfucker and talking all kind of hip shit. So you know a lot of white people, especially white men, didn't like this new shit.

There were a couple of white music critics, like Leonard Feather and Barry Ulanov, who were co-editors of *Metronome* music magazine and who understood what was going on with bebop, who liked it and wrote good things. But the rest of them white motherfucking critics hated what we were doing. They didn't understand the music.

They didn't understand, and hated, the musicians. Still, the people were packing into the clubs to hear the music, and Dizzy's and Bird's group at the Three Deuces was the hottest thing in New York.

Bird himself was almost a god. People followed him around everywhere. He had an entourage. All kinds of women were around Bird, and big-time dope dealers, and people giving him all kinds of gifts. Bird thought this was the way it was supposed to be. So he just took and took. He began missing sets and whole gigs. This was fucking with Dizzy's head, because though he might have acted a little crazy, he was always organized and took care of business. Dizzy didn't believe in missing gigs. So he would sit down with Bird, beg him to pull his act together, threaten to quit if he didn't. Bird didn't, so finally Dizzy quit, and that was the end of the first great group in bebop.

Dizzy's quitting the group shocked everybody in the music world, and upset a lot of musicians who loved to hear them play together. Now, everybody realized that it was over and we weren't going to hear all that great shit they did together no more, unless we heard it on record or they got back together. That is what a lot of people hoped would happen, including me, who took Dizzy's place.

When Dizzy left their band at the Three Deuces, I thought Bird was going to take a band uptown, but he didn't, at least not right away. A lot of club owners on 52nd began asking Bird who his trumpet player was going to be since Dizzy quit. I remember being with Bird one time in a club when the owner asked that, and Bird turned to me and said, "Here's my trumpet player right here, Miles Davis." I used to kid Bird by saying, "If I hadn't joined your band, *you* wouldn't even have a job, man." He would just smile, because Bird enjoyed a good joke and one-upmanship. Sometimes it didn't work —me being in the band—because the owners liked Bird and Dizzy together. But the owner of the Three Deuces hired us in October of 1945. The group had Bird, Al Haig on piano, Curly Russell on bass, Max Roach and Stan Levey on drums, and me. It was the same rhythm section that Bird and Dizzy had right before Dizzy quit. I remember the gig at the Three Deuces being for about two weeks. Baby Laurence, the tap dancer, was the floor show. He took four and eights with the band and was a motherfucker. Baby was the greatest tap dancer that I have ever seen, or heard, because his tap dancing sounded just like a jazz drummer. He was something else.

I was so nervous on that first real gig with Bird that I used to ask if

I could quit every night. I had sat in with him, but this was my first real paying gig with him. I would ask, "What do you need me for?" because that motherfucker was playing so much shit. When Bird played a melody I would just play under him and let him lead the fucking note, let him sing the melody and take the lead on every-thing. Because what would it look like, me trying to lead the leader of all the music? Me playing lead for Bird—are you kidding? Man, I was scared to death I was going to fuck up. Sometimes I would act like I was quitting, because I thought he might fire me. So I was going to quit before he did, but he would always encourage me to stay by saying that he needed me and that he loved the way I played. I hung in there and learned. I knew everything Dizzy was playing. I think that's why Bird hired me—also because he wanted a different kind of trumpet sound. Some things Dizzy played I could play, and other things he played, I couldn't. So, I just didn't play those licks that I knew I couldn't play, because I realized early on that I had to have my own voice—whatever that voice was—on the instrument.

That first two weeks with Bird was a motherfucker, but it helped me grow up real fast. I was nineteen years old and playing with the baddest alto saxophone player in the history of music. This made me feel real good inside. I might have been scared as a motherfucker, but I was getting more confident too, even though I didn't know it at the time.

But Bird didn't teach me much as far as music goes. I loved playing with him, but you couldn't copy the shit he did because it was so original. Everything I learned about jazz back then I learned from Dizzy and Monk, maybe a little from Bean, but not from Bird. See, Bird was a soloist. He had his own thing. He was, like, isolated. And there was nothing you could learn from him unless you copied him. Only saxophone players could copy him, but even they didn't. All they could do was try to get Bird's approach, his concept. But you couldn't play that shit he played on saxophone with the same feeling on trumpet. You could learn the notes but it won't sound the same. Even great saxophonists couldn't copy him. Sonny Stitt tried, and Lou Donaldson a little later, and Jackie McLean a little later than both of them. But Sonny had more of Lester Young's style. And Bud Freeman used to play a lot like Sonny Stitt played. I guess Jackie and Lou came the closest to Bird, but only in their sound, not in *what* they played. Nobody could play like Bird, then or now.

As for my concept of music, back then my main influences besides

Dizzy and Freddie Webster were Clark Terry with his approach to the horn, and Thelonious Monk with his harmonic sense—the way he played chords was something else. But I guess Dizzy was my main influence. One day after I first came to New York, I asked Dizzy about a chord and he said, "Why don't you sit down and play it on piano?" So I did. You know, I was asking him for the chords, but I already knew them in my head, I just wasn't playing them. Because when I first went with Bird's band I knew everything Dizzy was playing on trumpet with Bird. I had studied that shit up and down, backwards and forward. I couldn't play it high, but I knew *what* he was playing. I just couldn't play it high like Dizzy could because my chops weren't that developed and I didn't *hear* the music up in that high register. I always heard the music better and clearer coming from me in the middle registers.

I asked Dizzy one day, "Man, why can't I play like you?" He said, "You *do* play like me, but you play it down an octave lower. You play the chords." Dizzy is self-taught, but he knows everything about music. So when he told me that I heard everything down lower, in the middle register, it just made sense to me, because I didn't hear anything up, you know? Now I can, but not then. And one time a little after this conversation with Dizzy, he came up to me after I had played a solo and said, "Miles, you're stronger now; your chops are better than they were when I first heard you." What he meant was that I was playing higher and stronger than I was before.

In order for me to play a note it has to sound good to me. I've always been that way. And a note has to be in the same register that the chord was in when I played it back, at least then it did. Back in bebop, everybody used to play real fast. But I didn't ever like playing a bunch of scales and shit. I always tried to play the most important notes in the chord, to break it up. I used to hear all them musicians playing all them scales and notes and never nothing you could remember.

See, music is about style. Like if I were to play with Frank Sinatra, I would play the way he sings, or do something complementary to the way he sings. But I wouldn't go and play with Frank Sinatra at breakneck speed. I learned a lot about phrasing back then listening to the way Frank, Nat "King" Cole, and even Orson Welles phrased. I mean all those people are motherfuckers in the way they shape a musical line or sentence or phrase with their voice. Eddie Randle used to tell me to play a phrase and then breathe, or play the way you breathed. So, the way you play behind a singer is like the way Harry "Sweets" Edison did with Frank. When Frank stopped singing, then Harry played. A little before and a little afterwards, but not ever over him; you never play *over* a singer. You play between. And if you play the blues you just have to play a feeling; you have to feel it.

I learned all that back in St. Louis, so I always wanted to play something different than the way most trumpet players played. Still, I wanted to play high and fast like Dizzy just to prove to myself that I could do it. A lot of cats used to be putting me down back in the bebop days because their ears could only pick up what Dizzy was doing. That's what they thought playing the trumpet was all about. And when somebody like me came along, trying something different, he ran the risk of being put down.

But Bird wanted something different after Dizzy quit the band. He wanted a different trumpet approach, another concept and sound. He wanted just the opposite of what Dizzy had done, somebody to complement his sound, to set it off. That's why he chose me. He and Dizzy were a lot alike in their playing, fast as a motherfucker, up and down the scales so fast sometimes you almost couldn't tell one from the other. But when Bird started playing with me there was all this space for him to do his shit in without worrying about Dizzy being all up in there with him. Dizzy didn't give him no space. They were brilliant together, maybe the best ever at what they did together. But I gave Bird space and after Dizzy, that's what he wanted. A little while after we opened up at the Three Deuces, some people still wanted to hear Diz instead of me. I could understand that.

After a while, the group moved down the street to play the Spotlite Club. Bird replaced Al Haig on piano with Sir Charles Thompson and hired Leonard Gaskin on bass instead of Curly Russell. We didn't play there long because the police shut down the Spotlite and some of the other clubs on 52nd for some bullshit about drugs and phony liquor licenses. But the real reason I think they shut it down for a couple of weeks was because they didn't like all them niggers coming downtown. They didn't like all them black men being with all them rich, fine white women.

That part of 52nd Street was nothing but a row of three- or four-storied brownstones in the first place. Wasn't nothing fancy about the motherfucking place. Earlier, rich white people used to live on the block, between Fifth and Sixth avenues. Somebody told me that ended around Prohibition when the rich people moved out and the buildings were turned into small businesses and clubs that were on the ground floor. The clubs got real popular during the 1940s when the small bands took over from the large bands. Those clubs were too small to hold big bands. The bandstand couldn't hardly hold a five-piece combo, let alone one with ten or twelve people. So this kind of club created a new kind of musician, who was comfortable in a small-band setting. That's the kind of musical atmosphere I came into when I started playing on The Street.

But the small clubs like the Three Deuces, the Famous Door, the Spotlite, the Yacht Club, Kelly's Stable, and the Onyx also attracted hustlers and fast-living pimps with plenty of whores, hipsters, and drug dealers. I mean, these kinds of people—both black and white —were a dime a dozen on The Street. Them motherfuckers were everywhere doing whatever they wanted to do. Everyone knew that they had paid off the police, and this was all right as long as most of the hustlers were white. But when the music came downtown from uptown, the black hustlers around that scene came downtown with it, at least a whole lot of them did. And this didn't set too well with the white cops. The drug and liquor license thing was only a cover, as far as a lot of black musicians were concerned, for the real reason, which was racism. But they wouldn't admit that back then.

But anyway, after they closed down the Spotlite Club, Bird moved the group up to Minton's in Harlem. I started to play a whole lot better up there. I don't know why, maybe it was all those black people who I had played in front of who were in my corner. I can't put my finger on it. All I know is that I had more confidence in myself and in my playing, and although Bird got standing ovations all the time and wild cheers and shit like that, the people seemed to love my playing, too. I even got a few standing ovations. And Bird was smiling when I played and so were the rest of the musicians in the band. I was still struggling with tunes like "Cherokee" or "A Night in Tunisia," which Diz had just burned through because these tunes were made to order for the way he played. But I was good enough to get through them most of the time without most of the audience knowing that. But when Freddie Webster or Diz would show up out in the audience, they knew I was having trouble with these tunes, but they never came down hard on me about it, although they did let me know that they knew.

A lot of people—white people included—followed the band up-town. I think that's one of the reasons 52nd Street didn't stay closed, because them white owners began to complain about how they was losing all the money to them niggers up in Harlem. Anyway, The Street reopened a short time after Bird went uptown and began drawing all those white people up there. If it's one thing white people are united on it is that they all hate to see black people making the money they *think* belongs to *them*. They were beginning to think that they *owned* these black musicians because they was making money for them. So, the word must have gone out that these new rules was hurting these white club owners' pocketbooks, that they were about to lose the business back to Harlem. But when the clubs reopened, it seemed like the shit had changed; in the space of time that we were gone some magic, some energy, had been lost. I might be wrong, but it seemed to me that when they closed The Street, that that was the beginning of the end for everything down there. It was just a matter of time.

So that's the kind of world I was juggling when I first got to New York, both uptown and downtown. I mean I was juggling it with Juilliard, which was a whole other world from the one bebop played in. And Bird was the king of this whole scene, because he did so much of everything that world was about—like shooting heroin, fucking around with whores, borrowing money to support his heroin habit, all that shit. Bird did more weird shit than anybody I ever met.

When I decided to quit Juilliard in the fall of 1945, Freddie Webster was the first person I told. Freddie was a strong, nice dude. He told me that I ought to call up my father and tell him first before I quit. Now, I was just going to quit and tell my father later. But when Freddie said that to me I got to thinking about the whole thing. Then I told Freddie, "I can't call up my old man and say, 'Listen, Dad, I'm working with some cats named Bird and Dizzy, so I'm gonna quit school.' I can't do no shit like that. I got to go back home and tell him in person." Freddie agreed, and that's the way I did it.

I caught a train and went back to East St. Louis, walked in his office, which had out the "Do Not Disturb" sign. Of course, he was shocked to see me, but my father was cool about things like that. He just said, "Miles, what the fuck you doing back here?"

I said, "Listen, Dad. There is something happening in New York. The music is changing, the styles, and I want to be in it, with Bird and Diz. So I came back to tell you that I'm quitting Juilliard because what they're teaching me is white and I'm not interested in that."

"Okay," he said, "as long as you know what you're doing, everything is okay. Just whatever you do, do it good."

Then he told me something I will never forget: "Miles, you hear that bird outside the window? He's a mockingbird. He don't have a sound of his own. He copies everybody's sound, and you don't want to do that. You want to be your own man, have your own sound. That's what it's really about. So, don't be nobody else but yourself. *You* know what *you* got to do and I trust your judgment. And don't worry, I'll keep sending you money until you get on your feet."

That was all he said and then he went back to working on his patient. It was something else, man. But I was forever grateful to my father for understanding so well. My mother didn't like it, but she had learned by now not to say anything about something I had already decided to do. As a matter of fact, it seemed like we were getting closer. I mean, one time in a trip home I had found out that my mother could play a mean blues on the piano. Up until then I hadn't even known that she was that kind of musician. So, when I came in on this Christmas trip home from Juilliard and she was playing the blues, I told her I liked what she was playing and that I didn't even know she could play the piano like that. She kind of smiled at me and said, "Well, Miles, there's a lot of things that you don't know about me." We both just laughed and realized for the first time that it was true.

My mother was a beautiful woman, physically, and as she got older, spiritually. She had a beautiful attitude. Her face was an attitude. I picked this up from her and the older she got the more beautiful the attitude became and the closer we got to each other. But as much as I'm into music, my parents hardly ever went to nightclubs, not even to see me play.

Before I quit Juilliard, I did take Dizzy's advice to take some piano lessons. I also took some lessons in symphonic trumpet playing that helped me out with my playing. Trumpet players from the New York Philharmonic Orchestra gave the lessons, so I learned some things from them.

When I say that Juilliard didn't help me, what I mean is it didn't help me as far as helping me understand what I really wanted to play. I figured there wasn't nothing left for me to do at that school. I have hardly ever felt regret over anything I've done. I have sometimes, not often. But I didn't feel anything when I left Juilliard in the fall of 1945. Anyway, I was playing with the greatest jazz musicians in the world, so what did I have to feel bad about? Nothing. And I didn't. Never looked back.

about this time, in the fall of 1945, Teddy Reig, who was a producer for Savoy Records, approached Bird about doing a recording date for his Savoy label. Bird agreed to do the record and asked me to be on trumpet; Dizzy was on some tracks playing piano. Thelonious Monk and Bud Powell couldn't or wouldn't make it; Bud never did get along too tough with Bird anyhow. So it was Sadik Hakim on piano on some tracks Dizzy didn't play piano on, Curly Russell on bass, Max Roach on drums, and Bird on alto sax. The name of the record was *Charlie Parker's Reboppers*. It was a great record, at least a lot of people thought it was, and it definitely made my name in the bebop movement.

But getting that record finished was something else, man. I remember Bird wanting me to play "Ko-Ko," a tune that was based on the changes of "Cherokee." Now Bird *knew* I was having trouble playing "Cherokee" back then. So when he said that that was the tune he wanted me to play, I just said no, I wasn't going to do it. That's why Dizzy's playing trumpet on "Ko-Ko," "Warmin' up a Riff," and "Meandering" on *Charlie Parker's Reboppers,* because I wasn't going to get out there and embarrass myself. I didn't really think I was ready to play tunes at the tempo of "Cherokee" and I didn't make no bones about it.

One thing was funny about that recording session. When Dizzy played all them beautiful solos, I was fast asleep on the goddamn floor and missed all that bad shit he played. Later, after I heard it on record, man, all I could do was shake my head and laugh. That shit Dizzy played on that day was too bad.

But the gig itself was weird, because all these hustlers and dope dealers looking for Bird were coming by. The whole recording session was done in one day, I think. It was in late November, on a day off from playing, so it probably was on a Monday. Anyway, all these people kept coming by and Bird would disappear into the bathroom with a dope dealer and come out an hour or two later. In the meantime, everybody was sitting around, waiting on Bird to finish his nap. Then, he would come back all fucked up and shit. But after Bird got high, he just played his ass off.

When the record was released, I remember some of the reviewers put me down, especially the one in *Down Beat*. I forget his name, but I remember him saying something about how I had copied all the wrong shit from Dizzy, and that in the end it was going to be bad for me. I don't pay any attention to critics, but back then what that cat said kind of hurt me, because I was so young and all, and playing on this record and doing good was very important to me. But Bird and Dizzy told me not to pay that shit critics said no mind, and I didn't; I respected what *they*—Bird and Dizzy—had to say about how good I played. The dude who wrote that shit in *Down Beat* probably never played any instrument in his entire life. Maybe that's where my bad feelings for music critics first started, back then when they put me down so cold, when I was so young and had so much to learn. They were cold-blooded on me then, didn't show no mercy. I guess I thought that was wrong to be so hard on someone so young and inexperienced without giving no kind of encouragement.

But as good as my relationship with Bird was getting in music, our private relationship was getting worse. Like I said, Bird lived with me for a minute, but it wasn't as long as a lot of writers say it was. I mean, I got him a room in the same apartment building where me and my family lived. But he would be down to our apartment all the time, borrowing money and shit, eating Irene's cooking, passing out drunk on the couch or the floor. Plus, when he would come by, he was constantly bringing all kinds of women and hustlers, dope dealers and all kinds of dope-fiend musicians.

One of the things I never understood about Bird was why he did all the destructive shit he used to do. Man, Bird knew better. He was an intellectual. He used to read novels, poetry, history, stuff like that.

And he could hold a conversation with almost anybody on all kinds of things. So the motherfucker wasn't dumb or ignorant or illiterate or anything like that. He was real sensitive. But he had this destructive streak in him that was something else. He was a genius and most geniuses are greedy. But he used to talk a lot about political shit and he loved to put a motherfucker on, play dumb to what was happening and then zap the sucker. He used to especially like to do this to white people. And then he would laugh at them when they found out they had been had. He was something—a very complex person.

But the worst thing that Bird did back then was to take advantage of my love and respect for him as a great musician. He would tell dope dealers that I was going to be paying the money *he* owed them. So them dudes would be coming by looking like they wanted to kill me sometimes. That shit was dangerous. Finally I just told him and all the rest of them motherfuckers not to come by my house no more. That shit got so bad that Irene went back to East St. Louis, but she came back to New York as soon as Bird stopped coming around so much. Bird met Doris Sydnor about this time and he moved into her apartment, somewhere on Manhattan Avenue. But when Bird moved out of my place and before Irene came back from East St. Louis, Freddie Webster moved in and we would talk all night. He was a whole lot better to get along with than Bird was.

In between gigs with Bird, I played some with Coleman Hawkins and Sir Charles Thompson up at Minton's in the fall of 1945. Like I said, I loved playing with Bean, man, because he could play so good and he was just a beautiful person. He always treated me good, almost like his son. Man, Bean could play the hell out of a ballad, especially one like "Body and Soul." He was from Saint Joseph, Missouri, a little town near Kansas City, which is where Bird came from. We—Bird, me, and Bean—were all from the Midwest. I think that had a lot to do with us hitting it off musically, and sometimes— at least with Bird—socially; we kind of thought and saw things alike. Bean was a sweet guy, one of the most beautiful people I've ever met and he taught me a lot about music.

Plus he used to give me clothes. I'd ask him how much he wanted for a coat or a shirt, and he'd give me one for fifty cents or something like that. He bought the clothes from this hip store on Broadway near 52nd Street, then gave them to me for almost nothing. Like Bean would give me one of them hip overcoats he had for about ten dollars. One time down in Philly, I met these guys through Bean named Nelson Boyd and Charlie Shaw (who I think was a drummer, I don't remember). Anyway, Charlie used to make his own suits and he would make some for Bean. Man, them suits was motherfuckers. I said to him, "Goddamn, Charlie, why don't you make me one of them suits?" He said for me just to get the material and he would, free of charge. So I did. And he made me a bad double-breasted suit that I used to wear to death. I think a lot of them pictures that they took of me around 1945 to 1947 I was wearing Charlie Shaw's suits. After that, I have always got my suits made when I had the money.

I also got to know Thelonious Monk better when I was working with Bean; he was in the band, too. Denzil Best was playing drums. I really liked Monk's tune, " 'Round Midnight," and I wanted to learn how to play it. So I used to ask him every night after I got through playing it, "Monk, how did I play it tonight?" And he'd say, looking all serious, "You didn't play it right." The next night, the same thing and the next and the next and the next. This went on for a while.

"That ain't the way to play it," he would say, sometimes with an evil, exasperated look on his face. Then, one night, I asked him and he said, "Yeah, that's the way you play it."

Man, that made me happier than a motherfucker, happier than a pig in shit. I'd gotten the sound down. It was one of the hardest. " 'Round Midnight" was very difficult because it had a complex melody and you had to hang it together. You had to play it so you could hear the chords and changes and also hear the tops; it was just one of those tunes that you had to hear. It wasn't like a regular eight-bar melody or motif and it stopped, like in a minor key. It's a hard tune to learn and remember. I can still play it, but I don't like to do it too much now, except maybe when I'm practicing, alone. And what made it so hard for me to play was that I had to get all those harmonies. I had to hear the song, play it, and improvise so that Monk could hear the melody.

I learned about improvising from Bean, Monk, Don Byas, Lucky Thompson, and Bird. But Bird was such a great and inventive improviser that he would turn songs inside out. If you didn't know music, you didn't know where the fuck Bird was at when he was improvising. See, Bean, Don Byas, Lucky Thompson all had the same style: They would run their solos and then they would improvise. You could still hear the melody when they improvised. But when Bird played, it was totally another ball game, totally something else, something different every time. Among the masters he was *the* master.

Let's put it another way: There are painters and then there are painters among great painters. In this century, in my opinion, you had Picasso, Dali. Bird for me was like Dali, my favorite painter. I liked Dali because of his imagination when he painted death. See, I was into that kind of imagery and I liked the surrealism in his paintings. The way Dali used surrealism always had a wrinkle in it—at least for me—it was so different; you know, like a man's head in a breast. And Dali's paintings had a slick finish about them. But Picasso, besides his cubist work, had that African influence in his paintings, and I already *knew* what that was all about. So Dali was just more interesting for me, taught me a new way of looking at things. Bird was like that with music.

Bird had about five or six styles, all different. He had one like Lester Young; one like Ben Webster; one Sonny Rollins used to call "pecking," when a horn player uses real short phrases (today, Prince uses that style); and at least two others I can't describe right now. Monk was like that as a composer and as a piano player; not all the way like Bird, but similar.

I think a lot about Monk these days because all the music that he wrote can be put into these new rhythms that are being played today by a lot of young musicians—Prince, my new music, a lot of stuff. He was a great musician, an innovator, especially in his composition and writing.

Monk was also a funny cat, man, because he used to play the beats with his legs and feet moving. I used to love to watch him play piano, because if you watched his feet, you could know whether or not he was up into the music. If his feet moved all the time, then he was in it; if they didn't, then he wasn't. It was like watching and listening to sanctified church music: the beats, you know, the rhythms. A lot of his music reminds me of the West Indian music being played today, that is his accents and rhythms and the way he approached melody. You know, a lot of guys used to say that Monk didn't play piano as well as Bud Powell, because they all thought Bud was better technically because of his speed. That was some wrong shit to say, the wrong way to approach them, because they had different styles. Monk played some real hip shit and so did Bud Powell. But they were different. Bud played more like Art Tatum, and all the bebop piano players were crazy about Art. Monk was more into Duke Ellington, that stride piano thing Duke was into. But you could hear Monk's style up in Bud's playing. They were both bad motherfuckers. They just had two different styles. Like Bird and Bean are different;

like Picasso and Dali. But Monk's shit was very hip, especially his approach to composition. It was very innovative.

Now this might sound strange, but Monk and I were very close, musically speaking. He used to show me all his songs, then he would explain them to me if I didn't understand something. I used to see them all and laugh about them because they were so funny, so quirky. Monk had a great sense of humor, musically speaking. He was a real innovative musician whose music was ahead of his time. You could adapt some of his music to what's going on now in fusion and in some of the more popular veins; maybe not all of them, but the ones that got the pop in the motherfucking head, you could. You know, that black rhythmic thing that James Brown could do so good. Monk had that thing and it's all up in his compositions.

Monk was a serious musician. When I first met him, he used to stay fucked up a lot, high off Dexedrines. At least, that's what I heard. But when I was learning music from him—and I learned a lot from him—he wasn't getting high so much. He was a big, strong motherfucker, about six feet two, and over two hundred pounds. He didn't take no shit off nobody. When I heard stories later saying that me and him was almost about to fight after I had him lay out while I was playing on "Bags' Groove," I was shocked, because Monk and I were, first, very close, and second, he was too big and strong for me to even be thinking about fighting. Shit, man, he could have just squashed me if he wanted to. All I did was tell him to lay out when I was playing. My asking him to lay out had something to do with music, not friendship. He used to tell cats to lay out himself.

But as great a musician as he was, I just didn't like what he played behind *me,* that is, the way he used to play chords in the rhythm. See, you had to play like Coltrane to play with Monk—all that space and disjointed shit he used to play. But that shit was bad, now. It was some top of the shit music. But it was just different.

Monk was a quiet dude. Sometimes he and Bean used to get into these deep conversations. Bean liked to tease Monk about a lot of shit. And Monk would take it, because he loved Bean and because— as big and strong and menacing as he could look—he was a real soft, calm and gentle person, a beautiful person, almost serene. But if it had been reversed and it was Monk teasing the shit out of Bean, then Bean wouldn't have liked that.

I thought nothing of it before but now that I'm looking back, hardly any of the critics understood Monk's music. Man, Monk taught me more about music composition than anyone else on 52nd Street. He showed me everything; play this chord like that, do this, use that, do that. He wouldn't tell me quite like that; he'd just sit down at the piano and show me. But you had to be quick with Monk and be able to read between the lines, because he never did talk too much. He'd be doing what he'd be doing in that funny sort of way that he had. If you weren't serious about what *you* were doing and what *he* was *showing* you—not telling you—then, you'd be saying, "What? What was that? What's he doing?" It was over for your ass if you found yourself in that place. The shit done passed you by. And that was that. It wasn't no coming back. By that time Monk was somewhere else. Because Monk was a man who couldn't and wouldn't stand for no bullshit. And so he saw in me somebody who was serious and he gave me all he could, which was a lot. And although I really didn't hang out with Monk in a social type of way—he never did do that kind of thing no way—he also was a musical elder and teacher for me, and I really felt very close to him and him to me. I really don't think he would have done for someone else all that he did for me. I might be wrong, but I don't think so. But despite Monk being a beautiful cat, he could also be strange to people that didn't know him, like I became later for people who didn't know me.

Sir Charles Thompson was also a strange cat, but a strange that was different from Monk's, whose strangeness came mainly from him being quiet. Sir Charles would use me on trumpet with Connie Kay on drums and himself on piano. Up until that time, I had never heard that combination of instruments played together before, but that didn't bother Sir Charles—who had "knighted" himself. He was strange in that way, and he wasn't quiet.

A lot of cats used to come up and sit in with us at Minton's during the short time I played in Sir Charles's band. People like Bird, Milt Jackson, Dizzy, and a white trumpet player named Red Rodney, who was a bad motherfucker. Freddie Webster used to sit in a lot and I remember when Ray Brown first came to Minton's and blew everybody away with his playing. Sir Charles had a lot of good musicians sitting in with his band. He came out of the swing era, out of that kind of music—Buck Clayton, Illinois Jacquet, and Roy Eldridge—those kinds of musicians. He played a Count Basie-type piano. But he could copy some of Bud Powell's licks, too, when he wanted. He liked playing with the boppers. I know Gil Evans used to like him. I did, too, for a while, but I was moving in another musical direction, more into the kind of music Bird and Dizzy were playing, at least at that time.

After I started playing with Bird's band, me and Max Roach got real tight. He, J. J. Johnson, and I used to run the streets all night until we crashed in the early morning hours, either at Max's pad in Brooklyn or in Bird's place. Other cats like Milt Jackson, Bud Powell, Fats Navarro, Tadd Dameron, and Monk, sometimes Dizzy, all thought somewhat alike. We had a lot of give and take among us. And if anybody needed anything, like musical encouragement, or money, we shared what we had. If Max thought I missed something when we started out in Bird's band, he'd pull my coattails to what it was I missed. And I would do the same for him.

But it was the jam sessions, all over Harlem and Brooklyn, where we had a lot of fun just sitting in with other musicians our own age. I had mostly been around guys who had been older than me and who had something to teach me. Now, in New York, I had found a group of guys who were about my age and who I could both learn from and share my shit with. Before, I hadn't run with too many young guys. I was too advanced musically for them and they didn't have anything they could teach me; most of the time it was the other way around. But I'm the kind of person who always likes to learn different, new, innovative things. So with Max and all the other cats I mentioned before, I could sit up all night and play and talk music. That's what I have always been into.

New York was different back in those days, because you could run the streets looking for all kinds of jam sessions to play in. Plus all the great musicians would be there just like everybody else. Unlike today, in those days you didn't get too big to be sitting in at the jam sessions. Also, all the clubs were close to each other; like either on 52nd Street, or up in Harlem—at Lorraine's, or Minton's, or Small's Paradise, all around Seventh Avenue. The clubs were not so spread out like they are today. Our main interest was to be a part of the music scene. I don't think it's the same today.

I have always liked to take chances, musically speaking, and I guess with my own life as I got older. But back in 1945 all my risk taking was in music. Max Roach was like that back then too. He and I were supposed to be the next bad motherfuckers. Everybody was talking about Max being the next Kenny Clarke, who was considered bebop's top drummer during that time; everybody called Kenny Clarke "Klook." And I was supposed to be the next Dizzy Gillespie. Now, whether that was true or not, I didn't know. That's what the musicians and a lot of the people who came to listen to bebop were saying.

The critics were still putting me down, and I think some of it had to do with my attitude, because I ain't never been no grinner, or someone who went out of his way to kiss somebody's ass, especially a critic. Because *who* most critics like a lot of times depends on whether the person is nice to them. Plus most of them were white and were used to black musicians being nice to them so that the critics would write good things about them. So a lot of the guys kissed their asses, grinned up on stage and entertained, rather than just played their instruments—which is what they were there for.

As much as I love Dizzy and loved Louis "Satchmo" Armstrong, I always hated the way they used to laugh and grin for the audiences. I know *why* they did it—to make money and because they were entertainers as well as trumpet players. They had families to feed. Plus they both liked acting the clown; it's just the way Dizzy and Satch were. I don't have nothing against them doing it if they want to. But *I* didn't like it and didn't *have* to like it. I come from a different social and class background than both of them, and I'm from the Midwest, while both of them are from the South. So we look at white people a little differently. Also I was younger than them and didn't have to go through the shit they had to go through to get accepted in the music industry. They had already opened up a whole lot of doors for people like me to go through, and I felt that I could be about just playing my horn—the only thing I wanted to do. I didn't look at myself as an entertainer like they both did. I wasn't going to do it just so that some non-playing, racist, white motherfucker could write some nice things about me. Naw, I wasn't going to sell out my principles for them. I wanted to be accepted as a good musician and that didn't call for no grinning, but just being able to play the horn good. And that's what I did then and now. Critics can take that or leave it.

So a lot of critics didn't like me back then—still don't today—because they saw me as an arrogant little nigger. Maybe I was, I don't know, but I do know that I wasn't going to have to write about what I played and if they couldn't or wouldn't do that, then fuck them. Anyway, Max and Monk felt like that, and J. J. and Bud Powell, too. So that's what brought us close together, this attitude about ourselves and our music.

We were getting reputations about this time. People were following us around wherever we played—you know, Harlem, downtown on The Street, and sometimes over to Brooklyn. And a lot of women were coming around to see Max and me. But I was with Irene, and I believed at the time that a man should only have one woman. I believed that shit for a long time until I changed, when I got my heroin habit and had to use women to help support me. But back then I believed one man-one woman. But I did have a thing for a few women back then, like Annie Ross and Billie Holiday.

When The Street stayed closed throughout the last part of 1945, Dizzy and Bird decided to leave New York and go to Los Angeles. Dizzy's agent, Billy Shaw, had convinced a nightclub owner there that bebop would be sensational out on the coast. I think the club owner's name was Billy Berg. Dizzy liked the idea of spreading bebop to California, but he didn't like the idea of having to put up with Bird's shit again. He balked at first, but when they said Bird had to be a part of the deal, Dizzy finally gave in. So the group was Dizzy, Bird, Milt Jackson on vibes and Al Haig on piano, Stan Levey on drums and Ray Brown on bass. They all went to California by train, I think in December of 1945.

Since it was slow in New York, I decided to go back to East St. Louis for a rest. I closed down my apartment up on 147th and Broadway. Irene and Cheryl were with me, and we really needed a bigger place. I decided to take care of that when I got back to New York. In the meantime, we all arrived back in East St. Louis in time for Christmas.

I was still there in January when Benny Carter came to play at the Riviera over in St. Louis with his big band, so I went over to catch the band, and since I knew Benny, I went backstage. He was glad to see me and asked me to join his band. Benny's band was based in Los Angeles. Since Bird and Dizzy were out there, I called Ross Russell, who was living in New York and handling all of Bird's bookings, and told him I was going out to L.A. and wanted to look up Bird and Dizzy. He gave me Bird's number, and I called Bird up and told him I was coming to L.A.

What you've got to understand is that I was thinking only about just seeing Bird and listening to what they were playing. I had no other reason for calling Bird than that. But he started talking about me joining the band out there, about me, him, and Dizzy playing together. He said that he was lining up a record deal with Dial Records and that Ross Russell was setting it up, and wanted me to play on the date. I was flattered listening to him, praising me like that. Who wouldn't be happy if the baddest motherfucker on the scene was telling you how bad you are and that he wanted you to play with him? But when you talked to Bird there was always a chance of him trying to put something over on you for reasons other than music. And I wasn't thinking no thoughts about taking Dizzy's place. I loved him. I knew that Bird and Dizzy had had problems in the past, but I hoped they were getting along like they used to.

What I didn't know was that Bird and Ross Russell had already talked about using me. Bird wanted a different kind of trumpet player from Dizzy. He wanted someone with a more relaxed style who played in the middle register, like me. I found out after I got to Los Angeles.

When we arrived, Benny Carter had a job at the Orpheum Theatre. After we played that job the band broke up temporarily until the next job. Benny formed a small group from the larger band that had me and Al Grey, the trombonist, and some other people who I've forgotten. I think he had a guy named Bumps Meyers in the group. We started doing small clubs around L.A. and did a radio broadcast. But I didn't like the music Benny's group was playing, though I didn't tell him that right then. Benny was a nice guy and I liked how *he* played, but I couldn't use the music them other guys were playing. Plus, when I first got to L.A. I was living with Benny. I felt it would have been wrong to just up and walk out on him. So I didn't know what to do for a little while. I didn't like playing in Benny's band because they were playing a lot of old-fashioned numbers and arrangements. Benny is a hell of a musician, you know. But he wasn't confident in his playing and sometimes he'd ask if he sounded like Bird. I'd say, "No, you sound like Benny Carter." Man, when I would tell him this, he would laugh his ass off.

I was playing with Bird at an after-hours club called the Finale when I was still with Benny Carter's band. The Finale was upstairs, on the second floor, I think. It wasn't a large place, but it was a nice place and I thought it was funky because the music was funky and the musicians were getting down. They used to broadcast live from there over the radio. Bird had persuaded a guy named Foster Johnson, a retired vaudevillian hoofer who ran the club, to let him bring in the band. The Finale Club was located in a section of Los Angles called Little Tokyo. There was a black neighborhood right next to this Japanese neighborhood. I think the Finale Club was located on South San Pedro. Anyway, in Bird's band at the Finale, we had myself on trumpet, Bird on alto, Addison Farmer—the twin brother of trumpet player Art Farmer—on bass, Joe Albany on piano, and Chuck Thompson on drums. A lot of other good musicians used to sit in at the Finale. Howard McGhee would come around a lot. He ran the club after Foster Johnson managed it. Sonny Criss, an alto player, used to sit in, and Art Farmer, Red Callender, the bassist, and Red's protegé, that crazy, beautiful motherfucker, Charlie Mingus.

Charlie Mingus loved Bird, man, almost like I have never seen nobody love. Maybe Max Roach loved Bird that much. But Mingus, shit, he used to come to see and hear Bird almost every night. He couldn't get enough of Bird. He also liked me a lot. But Mingus could play the bass and everybody knew when they heard him that he would become as bad as he became. We also knew he would have to come to New York, which he did.

I got tired of the music Benny's band was playing. It wasn't music. I told my friend Lucky Thompson how sick I was of playing in the band. He told me to quit and come stay with him. Lucky was a hell of a saxophone player that I had met at Minton's. He was from Los Angeles and had come back home. I had let Lucky stay with me a couple of times when he was in New York. He had a house in Los Angeles and I went and stayed with him.

By now it was early 1946 and my girl, Irene, was back in East St. Louis, pregnant with our second child, Gregory. Now I had to think about making money to support my family. Before I quit, Benny asked me if I needed some money. He had heard that I was unhappy. I just told him, "Naw, man, I just want to quit." He was hurt, and I felt bad because he had brought me out to California and was counting on me. That was the first time I had quit a band abruptly like that. I was making about $145 a week. But I was in pain playing with Benny's band. No amount of money was going to make me happy playing those bullshit Neil Hefti arrangements Benny's band was playing.

After leaving Benny's band I didn't have no money in my pocket. So I moved in with Lucky for a while, then I started living with Howard McGhee. We got to be big buddies and he wanted to learn what I knew about the trumpet and music theory. Howard lived with this white girl, Dorothy. She was beautiful—looked just like a movie star. I think they were married; I don't know. Anyway, she kept Howard in a new car and with a pocketful of money and brand-new clothes. Howard was something else, man. Anyway, Dorothy had a friend, a blonde, beautiful woman who looked just like Kim Novak, only finer. Her name was Carol. She was one of George Raft's girls.

She'd be over to Howard's house and Howard wanted me to go with her. At this time I had probably made love to only two or three women. I had started smoking a little bit by this time, but I still didn't even know how to curse. So, here was Carol coming by to see me and I ain't paying no attention to her. She was sitting around watching me practice trumpet, which was all I was doing.

When Howard would get home after Carol had left, I would tell him, "Howard, you know Carol came by."

"And what?" Howard would say.

"And what?" I'd say, "What do you mean, 'And what?'"

"And what did you do, Miles?"

"Nothing," I said, "I didn't do nothing."

"Listen, Miles," Howard would say, "that girl is rich. I mean if she comes by, that means she likes you, so do something. You think she coming by here and by Lucky's house blowing the horn of her Cadillac for her health, man? So the next time she come by, do something. You hear what I'm telling you, Miles?"

She came by a little after that and blew the horn of that new Cadillac she had. I let her in and she asked me if I needed something. Cadillac sitting outside with the top down, she finer than a motherfucker. I hadn't messed with no white girls at that time, so I was probably a little scared of her. Maybe I had kissed one in New York. But I hadn't been to bed with one yet. So I told her I didn't need anything. So she left. When Howard got home I told him Carol had come by and asked me if I needed anything.

"And what?" Howard said.

"I told her I didn't need anything. I don't want any money or nothing."

"Are you crazy, motherfucker," Howard said, madder than a motherfucker. "When she comes by again and you tell me that shit and you don't have no money, man, I'm cutting your motherfucking nose off. Here we can't play nowhere. The black union don't want us to play because we're too modern. The white union don't like us because we're black. And here's a white woman, a whore who wants to give you money, and you ain't got none, and you say no? If you do that shit again I'm going to stab you, you jive motherfucker, you hear what I'm saying, you understand? You'd better, because I ain't bullshitting."

I knew Howard was nice and everything, but he didn't like no stupid bullshit. The next time Carol came by and asked me if I needed money, I said, "Yeah." When she offered it to me, I took it.

When I told Howard that, he said, "Good." After that I used to think about what Howard told me, I mean that shit embarrassed me, her giving me money. I hadn't been around no shit like that. But it was the first time I didn't have money, really. After that Carol used to give me sweaters and shit because it got cold in Los Angeles at night. But I never forgot that conversation with Howard. I remember it almost word for word. And that's unusual for me.

After I quit Benny's band, then I finally hooked up with Bird and played with him for a while. Howard McGhee was also taking care of Bird while he was out in Los Angeles. Bird lived with Howard for a while after he got through playing his engagement with Dizzy at Billy Berg's club. The music Diz and Bird had done at Berg's club had gone over big in Los Angeles, but Dizzy wanted to go back to New York. He bought tickets for all of the band—including Bird—to fly back to New York. Everybody went, was glad to go. Except at the last minute, Bird decided to cash in his ticket in order to buy heroin.

Early in the spring of 1946, I think it might have been March, Ross Russell set up a recording session with Dial Records for Bird. Ross made sure that Bird was sober, and hired me and Lucky Thompson on tenor, a guy named Arv Garrison on guitar, Vic McMillan on bass, Roy Porter on drums, and Dodo Marmarosa on piano.

At this time, Bird was drinking cheap wine and shooting heroin. People on the West Coast weren't into bebop like people in New York were and they thought some of the shit we were playing and doing was weird. Especially with Bird. He didn't have no money, was looking bad and raggedy, and everybody who *knew* who he was, *knew* he was a bad motherfucker who didn't care. But the rest of the people who were being told that Bird was a star could only see this broke, drunken dude playing this weird shit up on stage. A lot of them didn't buy all that shit about Bird being this genius, they just ignored him, and I think this hurt his confidence in himself and what he was doing. When Bird left New York he was a king, but out in Los Angeles he was just another broke, weird, drunken nigger playing some strange music. Los Angeles is a city built on celebrating stars and Bird didn't look like no star.

But at this recording session that Ross set up for Dial, Bird pulled himself together and played his ass off. I remember we rehearsed at the Finale Club the night before we recorded. We argued half the night about what we were going to play and who was going to play what. There had been no rehearsal for the recording date, and the musicians were pissed because they were going to be playing tunes they were unfamiliar with. Bird was never organized about telling people what he wanted them to do. He just got who he thought could play the shit he wanted and left it at that. Nothing was written down, maybe a sketch of a melody. All he wanted to do was play, get paid, and go out and buy himself some heroin.

Bird would play the melody he wanted. The other musicians had to remember what he had played. He was real spontaneous, went on his instinct. He didn't conform to Western ways of musical group interplay by organizing everything. Bird was a great improviser and that's where he thought great music came from and what great musicians were about. His concept was "fuck what's written down." Play what you know and play that well and everything will come together—just the opposite of the Western concept of notated music.

I loved the way Bird did that. I learned a lot from him that way. It would later help me with my own music concepts. When that shit works, man, it's a motherfucker. But if you get a group of guys who don't understand what's happening, or they can't handle all that freedom you're laying on them, and they play what *they* want, then it's no good. Bird would get guys in who couldn't handle the concept. He did it in the recording studio and when they were playing a live performance. That's what a lot of that argument was about at the Finale the night before we recorded.

The recording session took place in Hollywood at a studio called Radio Recorders. Bird was a motherfucker on that date. We recorded "A Night in Tunisia," "Yardbird Suite," and "Ornithology." Dial released "Ornithology" and "A Night in Tunisia" on a 78 rpm record in April of that year. I remember Bird recording a tune on that date called "Moose the Mooch" that was named after the cat who used to get Bird's heroin. I think he got something like half of Bird's royalties from that record date for supplying Bird with heroin. (It was probably written into Bird's contract in some kind of way.)

I think everyone played well on this date but me. This was my second recording date with Bird but I don't know why I didn't play as well as I could have. Maybe I was nervous. It's not that I played terrible. It's just that I could have played better. Ross Russell—a jive motherfucker who I never did get along with because he was nothing but a leech, who didn't never do nothing but suck off Bird like he was a vampire—said something about my playing was flawed. Fuck that jive white boy. He wasn't no musician, so what did he know what Bird liked! I told Ross Russell he could kiss my ass.

I remember playing with a mute on that date so I would sound less like Dizzy. But even with the mute I still sounded like him. I was mad with myself, because I wanted to sound like myself. I still felt that I was close to getting to the place where I would have my own voice on trumpet. I was anxious to be myself even then, and I was only nineteen. I was impatient with myself and most everything else. But I kept it to myself and kept my eyes and ears wide open so that I could keep on learning.

After the recording session, I think it was around that time, maybe in early April, the police closed the Finale, which was then run by Howard and Dorothy McGhee. Howard was constantly being fucked over by the white police because he was married to a white woman. When Bird started living in their garage and drinking, with all them pimps, dope dealers, and hustlers around, the police began to notice and turned up the heat. They really started messing with them even more. They were a tough couple though, so it didn't make them change what they were doing. The police had closed the Finale because they said dope was being dealt from there—and it was. But they didn't never bust nobody. So they closed it down because of suspicion.

There weren't many places for jazz musicians—especially black jazz musicians—to play in the first place. So there was hardly any money to make. After a while I started getting some money from my father, so I wasn't doing too bad. But I wasn't doing real good, either. About this time heroin got hard to get in Los Angeles. This didn't bother me because I wasn't using it, but Bird was all the way into it. He was a real bad junkie by then, so he started going through severe withdrawal. He just disappeared. Nobody knew he was living with Howard, and Howard didn't tell nobody that he was there going cold turkey. But when Bird gave up heroin, he only switched to drinking more heavily. I remember him telling me once that he was trying to kick heroin and that he hadn't had any for a week. But he had two gallons of wine on the table, empty quart whiskey bottles in the trash can, bennies spilled all over the table, and a crowded tray overflowing with cigarette butts.

Bird drank a lot before, but nowhere near as much as he did after he kicked heroin. Then he started drinking a fifth of anything he could get his hands on. He liked whiskey, so if he had that it would be gone in no time. Wine he drank even more of. That's what Howard later told me Bird survived on when he was going cold turkey, port wine. Then he started taking pills, Benzedrine, really messing his body up.

The Finale was opened up again in May of 1946. Bird used Howard on trumpet instead of me and for some reason the month stayed in my mind. I think Bird had Howard, Red Callender, Dodo Marmarosa, and Roy Porter in that group. Bird was breaking down physically right in front of everyone, but he was playing good, too.

I started hanging out with some of the younger musicians of Los Angeles, like Mingus, Art Farmer, and, of course, Lucky Thompson —my main man during the time I stayed out on the West Coast. I think I played another gig with Bird in April, but I'm not sure. Seems like I played at a place called the Carver Club, on UCLA's campus. I think Mingus, Lucky Thompson, Britt Woodman, and maybe Arv Garrison were on that job. Work was getting hard to find in Los Angeles and by May or June I was tired of living out there. The scene was too slow. I wasn't learning nothing.

I had first met Art Farmer at the black union office, which was located in downtown Los Angeles, in the black community. I think it was Local 767. I was talking to a trumpet player named Sammy Yates, who played in Tiny Bradshaw's band. Some other guys were standing around asking me about what was happening with the new music, bebop, and what was New York like. Questions like that. I was telling them what I could. I remember this real quiet cat standing off to the side who couldn't have been more than seventeen or eighteen, watching everything I was saying, soaking it all up. I remembered him when I would see him at some of the jam sessions. That was Art Farmer. And then I played with his twin brother and found out that he played trumpet and fluegelhorn too. So we'd have these short conversations about music. I liked him, because he was a real nice cat and he could really play, for someone as young as he was.

I think I ran into him the most over at the Finale. I knew him better after he moved to New York later on. But I met Art Farmer the first time I went to Los Angeles. A lot of the young musicians in Los Angeles who were serious about playing would come up and ask me questions about what was happening in New York. They knew I had played with a lot of the bad cats and so they wanted to pick my brains.

By the summer of 1946 I was working with Lucky Thompson's band at a place called the Elks Ballroom, farther south on Central

Avenue, where we got the black crowd from Watts. They were some country motherfuckers but they used to like the music we played because they could dance to it. Mingus played bass in that band. Lucky used to rent the place three nights a week and advertise by saying something like, "Lucky Thompson's All Stars, featuring the brilliant young trumpet player Miles Davis, last heard here with Benny Carter." Man, that shit was funny. Lucky Thompson was something else. That gig lasted for about three or four weeks and then Lucky left with Boyd Raeburn's band.

Around this time I was on an album with Mingus, *Baron Mingus and His Symphonic Airs.* Mingus was a crazy, brilliant person and I never knew what he meant by that title. He tried to explain it to me once, but I don't think even *he* knew what he meant by it. But Mingus didn't do nothing halfway. If he was going to make a fool out of himself, he was going to do it better than anybody else ever did it. A lot of people didn't like Mingus calling himself Baron, but it didn't bother me. Mingus might have been crazy, but he was also ahead of his time. He was one of the greatest bass players who ever lived.

Charlie Mingus was a motherfucking man who didn't take no shit off nobody. And I admired that in him. A lot of people couldn't take him, but they were scared to tell him to his face. I used to. It didn't scare me that he was so big. He was a gentle, nice cat who wouldn't hurt nobody unless they fucked with him. Then, watch out! We used to argue and scream at each other all the time. But Mingus never threatened to hit me. In 1946, after Lucky Thompson left town, Mingus became my best friend in Los Angeles. We would rehearse together all the time, talk about music all the time.

Bird was worrying me because he was drinking like a fish and getting fat. He was in such bad physical shape that for the first time since I had known him, his playing was really bad. He was now drinking about a quart of whiskey a day, up from a fifth. See, junkies have routines. First thing they do is satisfy the habit. Then they can operate, play music, sing, whatever. But Bird was out of his routine in California. When you're in a new place and you can't consistently find what you need, you find something else—for Bird it was drinking. Bird was a junkie. His body was used to heroin. But his body wasn't used to all the drinking he was doing. He just went crazy. It happened to him in Los Angeles, and later on in Chicago and Detroit.

It really started to show when Ross Russell organized another Dial Records session in July of 1946, but Bird couldn't hardly play. Howard McGhee, who played trumpet on that date, organized the band. Bird was pitiful; he couldn't play anything. Being in Los Angeles, and being neglected, and not having any drugs, and drinking all them quarts of whiskey and downing bennies finally had wasted him. He seemed drained and I really thought it was over. I mean I thought he was going to die. Later that night after the set, he went back to the hotel room and got so drunk he fell asleep smoking and he set fire to the bed. When he put the fire out and then wandered into the street naked, the police arrested him. They thought he was crazy and took him to Camarillo State Hospital. He stayed there for seven months. It probably saved his life, though they did some fucked-up shit to him.

When they took Bird away it really shocked everybody on the scene, especially in New York. But what horrified everybody was that they gave Bird shock treatment while he was in Camarillo. One time they gave him so much that he almost bit off his tongue. I couldn't understand why they gave him shock treatments. They said it helped him. But for an artist like Bird the shock treatments just helped to fuck him up more. They did the same thing to Bud Powell when he got sick, and it didn't help him. Bird got in such bad shape, the doctors told him that if he got even a bad cold—or pneumonia, again—he would die.

After Bird went off the scene, I would rehearse with Charlie Mingus a lot. He wrote tunes that Lucky and him and me would rehearse. Mingus didn't give a fuck what kind of musical ensemble it was; he just wanted to hear his shit played all the time. I used to argue with him about using all those abrupt changes in the chords in his tunes.

"Mingus, you so fucking lazy, man, that you won't modulate. You just, bam! hit the chord, which is nice sometimes, you know, but not all the fucking time."

He would just smile and say, "Miles, just play the shit like I wrote it." And I would. It was some strange-sounding shit back then. But Mingus was like Duke Ellington, ahead of his time.

Mingus was playing really different shit. All of a sudden he started doing this strange-sounding music, almost overnight. Now, nothing in music and sounds is "wrong." You can hit anything, any kind of chord. Like John Cage playing the shit he's playing, making all them strange sounds and noises. Music is wide open for anything. I used to tease him, "Mingus, why you playing like that?" Like, he'd be playing "My Funny Valentine" in a major key and it's supposed to be played in D minor. But he would just smile that sweet smile of his and keep doing what he was doing. Mingus was something else, man, a pure genius. I loved him.

Anyway, during the summer of 1946—late August I think—Billy Eckstine's band came to Los Angeles. Fats Navarro had been their regular trumpet player, but he had quit the band to stay in New York. So B got in touch with me because Dizzy had told him I was out in L.A., and he asked me if I wanted to play in his band. "Hey, Dick"— B called me Dick—"well, you ready now, motherfucker?"

"Yeah," I said.

"Dick, I'm gonna give you $200 a week, whether we play or not. But don't tell nobody else," he said. "If you do I'll kick your ass."

"Okay," I said, with a big smile on my face.

See, B had asked me to join his band before I left New York. He had wanted me real bad. That's the reason he paid me so much now. But back then I was enjoying myself playing in the little groups, and Freddie Webster had told me, "Miles, you know playing with B is nothing but death for you. If you go with him you're going to die as a creative musician. Because you can't do what *you* want to. You can't play what *you* want to. They're going to South Carolina and you ain't like that. You can't grin. You ain't no Uncle Tom and you're going to do something and them white folks down there are going to shoot you. So don't do it. Tell him you don't want to go with him."

And I did, because Freddie was my main man and he was very wise. When I tried to say that B didn't take shit off nobody, so why wouldn't they shoot him in the South, too, Freddie said, "Miles, B is a star and a big money-maker. You ain't. So don't put yourself in the same league with him, yet." That's the reason B said to me, "Well, Dick. You ready now, motherfucker?" when he asked me to join his band in Los Angeles. He was pulling my leg for not having joined the band back in New York. But he respected me for having turned him down.

B had Sonny Stitt, Gene Ammons, and Cecil Payne in the saxophone section; Linton Garner—Erroll Garner's brother—on piano; Tommy Potter on bass and Art Blakey on drums. Hobart Dotson, Leonard Hawkins, King Kolax, and me were the trumpet section.

By this time B had become one of the most famous singers in the United States, ranking up there with Frank Sinatra, Nat "King" Cole, Bing Crosby, and others. He was a sex object among black women, a star. He was that for white women, too, but they didn't love him or buy his records the way black women did. He was a rough motherfucker who didn't take no shit off no one, woman or man. He'd just knock the shit out of the first person to get out of line.

But B thought of himself more as an artist than as a star. He could have made a lot of money for himself if he had dropped the band and gone out on the road as just a singer. That band, like all the others before it, was very tight, very disciplined. They played the shit out of anything B wanted. The band would get down especially after B had done his numbers. He would just stand there with this big grin on his face, loving what everybody was doing. B's band was never recorded correctly. The record label was more interested in B as a singer, so they put the emphasis on him and on popular music. He had to do the pop stuff to keep the band going.

B had, I think, a nineteen-piece orchestra, and around that time all them big bands were breaking up because of money. One day when the band had been off for a week, B brought me all this money. I said, "B, I can't take this money, man, because the rest of the guys ain't getting paid."

B just smiled and put the money back in his pocket and never did that to me again. It wasn't that I couldn't have used the money. I could have used it on my family; Irene was in East St. Louis with the two kids, Cheryl and Gregory. But I just couldn't take it knowing the rest of the guys weren't getting paid.

When we weren't working dances and shit all over Los Angeles, we broke down into small groups and played little clubs, like the Finale. We stayed out in Los Angeles about two or three months before working our way back to New York in late fall 1946, with stops in Chicago.

I had played all over California with B's band, so my reputation there was growing. When I got ready to leave Los Angeles with B's band, Mingus got real mad at me. He thought I was abandoning Bird, who was still up in Camarillo. He asked me how I could go back to New York without Bird. He was madder than a motherfucker. I couldn't say nothing, so I didn't. Then, he said that Bird was like my "papa." I told him that there wasn't anything I could do for Bird. I remember saying, "Listen, Mingus, Bird's in a mental hospital and no one knows *when* he'll get out. Do you, man? Bird's all fucked up, can't you see that?"

Mingus went on: "Like I said, Miles, Bird is your musical papa. You're an asshole, Miles Davis. That man *made* you."

Then I said, "Fuck you, Mingus. Ain't no motherfucker made me, nigger, but my *real* daddy. Bird might have helped me, and he did.

But the motherfucker didn't *make* me, man. So fuck that shit. I'm tired of this jive-ass Los Angeles. I've got to go back to New York where the shit is really happening. And don't worry about Bird, Mingus. Because Bird *will* understand even if *you* don't."

Talking to Mingus like that really hurt me, because I loved him, and I could see that my leaving hurt him real bad. He gave up trying to convince me to stay. But I think that argument really hurt our friendship. We played together after that, but we weren't as close as we had been. We were still friends, though, no matter what some of the people said who wrote about us in their books. Those writers never talked to me. How would they know how *I* felt about Charlie Mingus? Later on in our lives, Mingus and me just went our separate ways, like a whole lot of other people do. But he was my friend, man, and *he* knew it. We might have had disagreements, but we always did, even before that Bird argument.

I started snorting cocaine while I was in B's band. Hobart Dotson, the trumpet player who sat right next to me, turned me on. He gave me a pure rock one day. We were in Detroit on our way back to New York. The person who first turned me on to heroin—which I also did while I was in B's band—was Gene Ammons, in the reed section. I remember when I snorted cocaine for the first time. I didn't know what it was, man. All I know is that all of a sudden everything seemed to brighten up and I felt this sudden burst of energy. The first time I used heroin, I just nodded out and didn't know what was happening. Man, that was a weird feeling. But I felt so relaxed. Then the idea was going around that to use heroin might make you play as great as Bird. A lot of musicians did it for that. I guess I might have been just waiting for his genius to hit me. Getting into all that shit, though, was a very bad mistake.

Sarah Vaughan had left the band by this time and a singer named Ann Baker had taken her place. She was a good singer. She was also the first woman to tell me "a hard dick has no conscience." She used to just open up my hotel door and come right in and fuck me. She was something.

We used to travel around by bus and if B caught somebody asleep on the bus with his mouth open, he would drop salt in his mouth and wake him up. Man, everybody would be dying laughing at the poor sucker, coughing and shit, eyes all bugged out. Yeah, man, B was funnier than a motherfucker.

B was so clean and fine back in them days that women were all over his ass. He was so handsome that I used to think he looked like a girl sometimes. A lot of people thought that because B was so handsome that he was soft. But B was one of the toughest mother-fuckers I ever met. One time we were in Cleveland or Pittsburgh and everybody was waiting on B outside his hotel in the bus, ready to go. We were about an hour late in leaving. Now here comes B out of the hotel with this fine woman. He said to me, "Hey, Dick, this is my woman."

She said something like, "I got a name, Billy, tell him my name."

B turned around and said, "Bitch, shut up!" He slapped the shit out of her right there.

She says to B, "Listen, you motherfucker, if you wasn't so pretty I'd break your motherfucking neck, you jive bastard."

B was just standing there laughing and shit, saying "Aw, shut up, bitch. Wait 'til I get some rest. I'm gonna knock your fucking ass out!" The woman was madder than a motherfucker.

Later on in New York, after the band broke up, me and B used to meet and hang out on The Street. By this time I was snorting coke, so B would be buying all the coke a motherfucker could snort. They used to sell it to you in these little packages. B would be counting the packages, saying "How many packages you got, Dick?"

When I was younger I used to have B's problem of looking almost too pretty in the face. I was so young-looking in 1946, people used to say I had eyes like a girl. If I went into a liquor store to buy myself or someone else some whiskey, they would always ask how old I was. I'd tell them that I had two kids and they'd still ask for I.D. I was small and had this young girl's face. But B was debonair and a ladies' man. I also learned a lot from him about dealing with people you didn't want around. You just tell them to get the fuck out of your face. That's it. Anything else is a waste of time.

On the way back to New York we went through Chicago, Cleve-land, Pittsburgh, and some other places, I forget now. When we got to Chicago, I went home to see my family and my new son for the first time. This was around Christmas, so I spent the holidays with my family. After that, the band stayed together through the first two months of 1947 before we broke up. I had gotten some good news: *Esquire* magazine had voted me its New Star award for trumpet, I think because of my playing with Bird and B's band. Dodo Marma-rosa won it for piano and Lucky Thompson for tenor saxophone, and we all three had played with Bird. So it was a rough year but it was a good year, too.

back in New York, The Street was open again. To have experienced 52nd Street between 1945 and 1949 was like reading a textbook to the future of music. You had Coleman Hawkins and Hank Jones at one club. You had Art Tatum, Tiny Grimes, Red Allen, Dizzy, Bird, Bud Powell, Monk, all down there on that one street sometimes on the same night. You could go where you wanted and hear all this great shit. It was unbelievable. I was doing some writing for Sarah Vaughan and Budd Johnson. I mean everybody was there. Nowadays you can't hear people like that all at once. You don't have the opportunity.

But 52nd Street was something else when it was happening. It would be crowded with people, and the clubs were no bigger than apartment living rooms. They were so small and jam-packed. The clubs were right next to each other and across the street from one another. The Three Deuces was across from the Onyx and then across from there was a Dixieland club. Man, going in there was like going to Tupelo, Mississippi. It was full of white racists. The Onyx, Jimmy Ryan's club, could be real racist, too. But on the other side of the street, next to the Three Deuces, was the Downbeat Club and next to that was Clark Monroe's Uptown House. So you had all these clubs right next to each other featuring people like Erroll Garner, Sidney Bechet, Oran "Hot Lips" Page, Earl Bostic every night. Then there would be other jazz going on at other clubs. That scene was

My father, Miles Dewey Davis, in his graduation photo from Northwestern University Dental School.

My mother, Cleota Henry Davis, was a beautiful woman and a good blues piano player.

THAT'S me on the left, with my sister, Dorothy, my brother, Vernon, and my mother.

Me around the time I began playing the trumpet.

Some of the images of black people that I would fight against throughout my career. I loved Satchmo (5), but I couldn't stand all that grinning he did. Beulah (6), Buckwheat (7), and Rochester (8) influenced too many white people's attitudes towards blacks.

My father admired Marcus Garvey for the way he got black people to stand together for themselves.

Billy Eckstine, "Mr. B." Playing in B's band in St. Louis was the greatest musical thrill in my life.

Dizzy Gillespie. Dizzy was B's trumpet player and my idol. We became great friends and still are to this day.

12 MY first professional job, with Eddie Randle's Blue Devils—the Rhumboogie Orchestra—in St. Louis, 1944. I'm at the far right in the back row.

CLARK Terry was the best-known trumpet player in St. Louis. He helped me out when I was just getting started.

14

13

CHARLIE Christian played the electric guitar like a horn and influenced the way I played trumpet.

Some other influences on me: Nat "King" Cole (15), Frank Sinatra (16), and Orson Welles (17). All of them were inventive in the way they phrased what they played and sang and spoke.

The greatest jazz club in New York, Minton's Playhouse in Harlem. Bebop was born in Minton's before it moved downtown to 52nd Street. Thelonious Monk, on the left, was one of the great pioneers of bebop. I remember how happy I was when he told me I had finally learned how to play "'Round Midnight."

18

19

20

21

5₂ND Street in the bebop days. We will never see anything like that again. Bird's groups played frequently at the Three Deuces. Onstage that's Tommy Potter on bass, Bird, me, and Duke Jordan on piano. You can't see Max Roach on drums, but he was always there, protecting the beat.

THREE DEUCES Presents

CHARLIE PARKER
AND HIS BAND
featuring
...S DAVIS
TRUMPET
MAX ROACH
DRUMS
DUKE JORDAN
PIANO
TOMMY POTTER
BASS

22

In between gigs with Bird I played with some other great musicians, like Coleman Hawkins. Like me and Bird, Bean was from the Midwest; maybe that's why we hit it off so good.

23

"Billie's Bounce," an old Savoy recording I made with Bird as part of Charlie Parker's Reboppers.

Max Roach and I were like brothers when we played with Bird.

24

25   Bud Powell played with me in some of Bird's groups. He was a beautiful person and a motherfucker on the piano.

26

After playing with Bird my reputation grew, and I put together a group called the Miles Davis All Stars. Bird and I were still playing together, but sometimes now I was the leader because Bird was too unreliable.

27

WITH Fats Navarro (left) and Kai Winding. I replaced "Fat Girl" in Tadd Dameron's group when Fats had become a junkie and couldn't play any more.

28

DEXTER Gordon. Dexter hipped me to the importance of looking sharp. I thought he was the cleanest cat around.

29

SONNY Stitt was my first choice for alto saxophone in the "Birth of the Cool" sessions. He played a lot like Bird, and like Bird he had a bad heroin habit.

31

30

"THE Birth of the Cool." We recorded "Budo" for Capitol (31) at the session photographed below, in January 1949 (32). This recording date brought together guys like Gerry Mulligan, Lee Konitz, and Kai Winding. Al Haig played the piano (33). I was moving away from the hard sound of bebop, and Gil Evans, who arranged these sessions, had been heavily influenced by Duke Ellington (34).

32

33

34

THE first time I ever left the country was with the group that Tadd Dameron (shown here with Sarah Vaughan, 35) and I took to Paris in 1949. There, I met Juliette Greco (36), who came to listen to me all the time, and we fell in love. Kenny Dorham (below, 37) is the trumpet player who took my place when I finally quit Bird's band. Kenny Clarke, "Klook," as we called him (right, 38), was the drummer in our band in France, where all these pictures were taken.

35

36

38

37

A jam session at Bop City in San Francisco, 1951. I'm in the back, toward the right, leaning over. Maybe I'm studying Dizzy's piano technique. That's my buddy Jimmy Heath up front in the striped tie.

A club date at the Hi Hat in Boston. I'm playing trumpet, of course, and the guy at the microphone is Symphony Sid, one motherfucker I never did like.

41

Fɪʀsт ladies of jazz. Billie Holiday (41) was near the end of her career by the time I met her, but I loved listening to her. Ella Fitzgerald (42) was incomparable. Sarah Vaughan (43) sang with B's band, but not when I was in it. She was great, too.

42

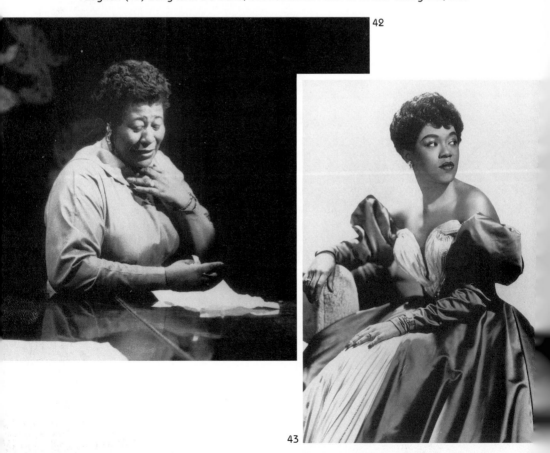

43

45

Sᴏɴɴʏ Rollins. A great saxophone player. We hung out together a lot in Harlem when I was a junkie.

AʜᴍᴀD Jamal. It was my sister, Dorothy, who first turned me on to Ahmad. I loved his lightness and understatement. He had a tremendous influence on my playing.

44

I loved boxers, and Sugar Ray Robinson was the greatest that I ever saw. I used to stop in at his club in Harlem. I told him I kicked my habit because I was inspired by his discipline.

46

47

Jᴀᴄᴋɪᴇ McLean. He was my main running buddy in my worst junkie years in the early fifties. Jackie, Sonny, and I all played together in the Miles Davis All Stars group I had then.

I liked to box, but when the trainer who was working with me, Bobby McQuillen, told me I was pitiful because of my habit, I decided to kick it.

48

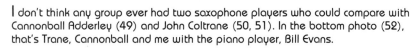

49

50

I don't think any group ever had two saxophone players who could compare with Cannonball Adderley (49) and John Coltrane (50, 51). In the bottom photo (52), that's Trane, Cannonball and me with the piano player, Bill Evans.

52

powerful. I'm telling you, I don't think we will ever see any shit like that ever again.

Lester Young used to be there, too. I had met Prez when he came through St. Louis and played the Riviera before I moved to New York. He called me Midget. Lester had a sound and an approach like Louis Armstrong, only he had it on tenor sax. Billie Holiday had that same sound and style; so did Budd Johnson and that white dude, Bud Freeman. They all had that running style of playing and singing. That's the style I like, when it's running. It floods the tone. It has a softness in the approach and concept, and places emphasis on one note. I learned to play like that from Clark Terry. I used to play like he plays before I was influenced by Dizzy and Freddie, before I got my own style. But I learned about that running style from Lester Young.

Anyway, after laying around for a while, I did a record with Illinois Jacquet in March 1947. We had a hell of a trumpet section, with me, Joe Newman, Fats Navarro, and two others—I think Illinois's brother Russell Jacquet and Marion Hazel. Dickie Wells and Bill Doggett played trombone and Leonard Feather, the critic, played piano. I liked playing with Fats again.

Dizzy was packing them in with his big band, playing bebop. He had Walter Gil Fuller, who used to write for B's band, as his musical director. Gil was a motherfucker and so there was a lot of excitement with what Dizzy's band was doing. Then, in April, Dizzy's manager, Billy Shaw, booked his big band into the McKinley Theatre up in the Bronx. What made this gig so special in my memory is that Gil Fuller hired the best trumpet section that I think has ever been in any one band. He had me, Freddie Webster, Kenny Dorham, Fats Navarro, and Dizzy himself. Max Roach was on drums. Just as we were about to do the gig, Bird came back to New York and joined the band. He had got out of Camarillo in February and hung around Los Angeles long enough to record two albums for Dial and pick up his drug habit again. But those were terrible records that Ross Russell made Bird record. Now, why did Ross do Bird like that? Man, that's the reason I didn't like Ross Russell. He was a slimy motherfucker who used the fuck out of Bird. Anyway, when Bird came back to New York he wasn't as bad off as he had been in Los Angeles, because he wasn't doing too much drinking and he wasn't shooting up as much then as he would later. But he was still using shit.

But, man, the trumpet section—the whole band on the first night

—was a motherfucker, you hear me? That music was all over the place, up in everyone's body, all up in the air. And it was so good to play with everybody like that. I loved it and was so excited about playing with everybody I didn't know what to do. It was one of the most exciting, spiritual times I have ever had, next to that first time I played with B's band in St. Louis. I remember the crowd on the first night listening and dancing their asses off. There was an excitement in the air, a kind of expectation of the music that was going to be played. It's hard to describe. It was electric, magical. I felt so good being in that band. I felt that I had arrived, that I was in a band of musical gods, and that I was one of them. I felt honored and humble. We were all there to do it for the music. And that's a beautiful feeling.

Dizzy wanted to keep the band clean and felt that Bird would be a negative influence. On the night we opened at the McKinley, Bird was up on stage nodding out and playing nothing but his own solos. He wouldn't play behind nobody else. Even the people in the audience were making fun of Bird while he was nodding up there on stage. So Dizzy, who was fed up with Bird anyway, fired him after that first gig. Then Bird talked to Gil Fuller and promised him that he would stay clean, and he wanted Gil to tell this to Diz. Gil went to Dizzy to try to talk him into letting Bird stay. And I went to Diz and told him that it would be good to keep Bird around to write some tunes for a little money; I think it was a hundred dollars a week. But Dizzy refused, saying he didn't have no money to pay him and that we would just have to get along without him.

I think we played the McKinley Theatre for a couple of weeks. Meanwhile, Bird was forming a new band and asked me to come with him, and I did. The two records Bird had recorded for Dial out in Los Angeles had been released. I was on one and Howard McGhee was on the other, I think. They had been released in late 1946 and were now big jazz hits. So, with 52nd Street open again and Bird back in town, the club owners wanted Bird. Everybody was after him. They wanted small bands again and they felt that Bird would pack them in. They offered him $800 a week for four weeks at the Three Deuces. He hired me, Max Roach, Tommy Potter, and Duke Jordan on piano. He paid me and Max $135 a week and Tommy and Duke $125. Bird made the most he had ever made in his life, $280 a week. It didn't matter to me that I was making $65 a week less than what I had made in B's band; all I wanted to do was play with Bird and Max and make some good music.

I felt good about it, and Bird was clear-eyed, not like the crazed look he had in California. He was slimmer and seemed happy with Doris. She had gone out to California to get him when he got out of Camarillo, and accompanied him east on the train. Man, Doris loved her Charlie Parker. She would do anything for him. Bird seemed happy and ready to go. We opened in April 1947, opposite Lennie Tristano's trio.

I was really happy to be playing with Bird again, because playing with him brought out the best in me at the time. He could play so many different styles and never repeat the same musical idea. His creativity and musical ideas were endless. He used to turn the rhythm section around every night. Say we would be playing a blues. Bird would start on the eleventh bar. As the rhythm section stayed where they were, then Bird would play in such a way that it made the rhythm section sound like it was on 1 and 3 instead of 2 and 4. Nobody could keep up with Bird back in those days except maybe Dizzy. Every time he would do this, Max would scream at Duke not to try to follow Bird. He wanted Duke to stay where he was, because he wouldn't have been able to keep up with Bird and he would have fucked up the rhythm. Duke did this a lot when he didn't listen. See, when Bird went off like that on one of his incredible solos all the rhythm section had to do was to stay where they were and play some straight shit. Eventually Bird would come back to where the rhythm was, right on time. It was like he had planned it in his mind. The only thing about this is that he couldn't explain it to nobody. You just had to ride the music out. Because anything might happen musically when you were playing with Bird. So I learned to play what I knew and extend it upwards—a little *above* what I knew. You had to be ready for anything.

A week or so before opening night, Bird called for rehearsals at a studio called Nola. A lot of musicians rehearsed there during those days. When he called the rehearsals, nobody believed him. He never had done this in the past. On the first day of rehearsal, everybody showed up but Bird. We waited around for a couple of hours and I ended up rehearsing the band.

Now, opening night, the Three Deuces is packed. We ain't seen Bird in a week, but we'd been rehearsing our asses off. So here this nigger comes in smiling and shit, asking is everybody ready to play, in that fake British accent of his. When it's time for the band to hit, he asks, "What are we playing?" I tell him. He nods, counts off the beat and plays every motherfucking tune in the exact key we had rehearsed it in. He played like a motherfucker. Didn't miss one beat, one note, didn't play out of key all night. It was something. We were fucking amazed. And every time he'd look at us looking at him all shocked and shit, he'd just smile that "Did you ever doubt this?" kind of smile.

After we got through with that first set, Bird came up and said—again in that fake British accent—"You boys played pretty good tonight, except in a couple of places where you fell off the rhythm and missed a couple of notes." We just looked at the motherfucker and laughed. That's the kind of amazing shit that Bird did on the bandstand. You came to expect it. And if he didn't do something incredible, *that's* when you were surprised.

Bird often used to play in short, hard bursts of breath. Hard as a mad man. Later on Coltrane would play like that. Anyway, so then, sometimes Max Roach would find himself in between the beat. And I wouldn't know what the fuck Bird was doing because I wouldn't have never heard it before. Poor Duke Jordan and Tommy Potter, they'd just be there lost as motherfuckers—like everybody else, only more lost. When Bird played like that, it was like hearing music for the first time. I'd never heard anybody play like that. Later, Sonny Rollins and I would try to do things like that, and me and Trane, playing those short, hard bursts of musical phrases. But when Bird played like that, he was outrageous. I hate to use a word like "outrageous," but that's what he was. He was notorious in the way he played combinations of notes and musical phrases. The average musician would try to develop something more logically, but not Bird. Everything he played—when he was on and *really* playing—was terrifying, and I was there every night! And so we couldn't just keep saying, "What? Did you hear *that!*" all night long. Because then *we* couldn't play nothing. So we got to the point where, when he played something that was just so outrageous, we blinked our eyes. They would just get wider than they were, and they already were *real* wide. But after a while it was just another day at the office playing with this bad motherfucker. It was unreal.

I was the one who rehearsed the band and kept it tight. Running that band made me understand what you had to do to have a great band. People said it was the best bebop band around. So I was proud of being the band's musical director. I wasn't twenty-one years old yet in 1947, and I was learning real quick about what music was all about.

Bird never talked about music, except one time I heard him arguing with a classical musician friend of mine. He told the cat that you
can do anything with chords. I disagreed, told him that you couldn't
play D natural in the fifth bar of a B flat blues. He said you could.
One night later on at Birdland, I heard Lester Young do it, but he
bent the note. Bird was there when it happened and he just looked
over at me with that "I told you so" look that he would lay on you
when he had proved you wrong. But that's all he ever said about it.
He knew you could do it because he had done it before. But he didn't
get up and show nobody *how* to do it or nothing. He just let you pick
it up for yourself, and if you didn't, then you just didn't.

I learned a lot from Bird in this way, picking up from the way he
played or didn't play a musical phrase or idea. But like I said, I never
did talk to Bird much, never talked to him over fifteen minutes at a
time, unless we were arguing about money. I'd tell him right up front,
"Bird, don't fuck with me about money." But he always did.

I never liked the way Duke Jordan played piano and neither did
Max, but Bird kept him in the band anyway. Me and Max wanted
Bud Powell on piano. Bird couldn't get him though, because Bud and
Bird didn't get along. Bird used to go by Monk's house and try to talk
to Bud, but Bud would just sit there and not say anything to him. Bud
would come to a gig wearing a black hat, white shirt, black suit, black
tie, black umbrella, cleaner than a motherfucker and wouldn't speak
to nobody but me or Monk, if he was there. Bird would beg him to
join the group and Bud would just look at him and drink. He wouldn't
even smile at Bird. He'd just sit out in the audience drunk as a
motherfucker, high off heroin. Bud got too high and stayed that way,
like Bird. But he was a genius piano player—the best there was of
all the bebop piano players.

Max used to always want to fight Duke Jordan for fucking up the
tempo in the group. Max would get so mad that he wanted to physically beat Duke up. Duke wouldn't listen. He'd just be playing and
Bird would do something and Duke would lose time. This would fuck
Max up if I wasn't counting the time for him. Then Max would
scream at Duke, "Clear the fuck out of the way, motherfucker, you
fucking up the time again."

We did replace Duke Jordan with Bud Powell on a record for
Savoy around May of 1947. I think the record was called the *Charlie
Parker All Stars*. It had everyone in Bird's regular group on it except
Duke. I wrote a tune for the album called "Donna Lee," which was

the first tune of mine that was ever recorded. But when the record came out it listed Bird as the composer. It wasn't Bird's fault, though. The record company just made a mistake and I didn't lose no money or nothing.

Bird was still under contract to Dial Records when he made this record for Savoy, but that kind of shit didn't ever stop Bird from doing what he wanted to do. Whoever had the money right then was who he went with. Bird recorded four albums that I played on in 1947, I think three on Dial and one on Savoy. He was real active musically that year. Some people think that 1947 was Bird's greatest year. I don't know about that and I don't like to make statements like that. All I know is he played great music then. And he played great music after that, too.

It was through "Donna Lee" that I met Gil Evans. He had heard the tune and went to see Bird about doing something with it. Bird told him that it wasn't his tune but that it was mine. Gil wanted the lead sheet for the tune in order to write an arrangement of it for the Claude Thornhill orchestra. I met Gil Evans for the first time when he approached me about arranging "Donna Lee." I told him he could do it if he got me a copy of Claude Thornhill's arrangement of "Robbin's Nest." He got it for me and after talking for a while and testing each other out, we found out that I liked the way Gil wrote music and he liked the way I played. We heard sound in the same way. I didn't really like what Thornhill did with Gil's arrangement of "Donna Lee," though. It was too slow and mannered for my taste. But I could hear the possibilities in Gil's arranging and writing on other things, so what they did on "Donna Lee" bothered me less, but it did bother me.

Anyway, I think that Savoy record with Bird was my best recording up until that time. I was getting more confident in my playing and was developing a style of my own. I was getting away from Dizzy's and Freddie Webster's influences. But it was at the Three Deuces, playing every night there with Bird and Max, that really helped me find my own voice. Musicians were constantly sitting in with the band and so we were always adjusting to different styles. Bird liked this shit a lot and I liked it too, sometimes. But I was more interested in developing the band's sound than I was in sitting in with a bunch of different motherfuckers every night. But Bird had come from that tradition in Kansas City and kept it going up at Minton's and the Heatwave in Harlem, so it was something he always liked to do and felt comfortable with. But when somebody who couldn't play the tunes sat in, then that was a drag.

Playing with Bird and being seen and heard every night on 52nd Street helped lead to my first record date as a leader. The record was called *Miles Davis All Stars*. I cut the record for the Savoy label. Charlie Parker played tenor sax, John Lewis piano, Nelson Boyd bass, and Max Roach drums. We went in the studio in August of 1947. I wrote and arranged four tunes for the album: "Milestones," "Little Willie Leaps," "Half Nelson," and "Sippin' at Bell's," a tune about a bar in Harlem. I also recorded on an album with Coleman Hawkins. So I was busy in 1947.

Irene had come back to New York with our two kids and we found a place out in Queens that was a lot bigger than the place we used to have. I was snorting coke, drinking, and smoking some by now. I didn't smoke pot because I never liked it. But I still wasn't using heroin. As a matter of fact, Bird once told me that if he ever caught me shooting heroin he would kill my ass. What was starting to get me into trouble though was all the women hanging around the band and me. But I still wasn't really into them yet. I was still so much into the music that I was even ignoring Irene.

There was a concert that a lot of cats played in at Lincoln Square, which was a ballroom that was located where Lincoln Center is now. Man, that was a great concert of All Stars. Art Blakey, Kenny Clarke, Max Roach, Ben Webster, Dexter Gordon, Sonny Stitt, Charlie Parker, Red Rodney, Fats Navarro, Freddie Webster, and myself. I think it cost something like $1.50 to get in and hear all those great musicians. Some people danced and some just listened.

I remember that concert because it was one of the last times Freddie Webster played in New York. When Freddie died, in 1947, it made me sick. Everybody else, too, especially Diz and Bird. Webs—that's what we called him—died in Chicago of an overdose of heroin that was meant for Sonny Stitt. Sonny had been beating everybody out of their money to support his habit. So he did it in Chicago when he and Freddie were playing there. Whoever he beat arranged to give him some bad shit, probably battery acid or strychnine. I don't know what it was. Anyway, Sonny gave it to Freddie, who shot it and died. I was sick over that for a long time. We were almost brothers, me and Freddie. I think about him, even today.

We went on the road to Detroit in November of 1947. We were supposed to play a club called the El Sino there, but they canceled on us after Bird showed up at the club and walked out. When Bird left New York he always had trouble buying heroin. Then he would drink a lot, which is what he did this night, and he couldn't play. After he got into the argument with the manager and walked out, he went back to the hotel and got so mad he threw his saxophone out of the window and smashed it up on the street. Billy Shaw bought him another one, though, a brand-new Selmer.

After coming back to New York and recording another record (which had J. J. Johnson on it), the group came back to Detroit to fulfill the broken contract we had with the El Sino club. This time everything was all right and Bird played his ass off. Betty Carter sat in with the group on this trip. She left right after this, though, to go with Lionel Hampton's band. I think it was in Detroit that Teddy Reig approached Bird to do another album for him on Savoy. Billy Shaw, who had a lot of influence over Bird and was, I think, a co-manager, told Bird that he had to stop recording for small labels like Dial and stick with a big label, like Savoy. See, everybody knew that the American Federation of Musicians was calling for a ban against recording because of a contract dispute. So Bird—who was always needing cash—signed with Reig and Savoy and went immediately into the studio. I think it was the Sunday before Christmas.

After finishing this album—I think it was called *Charlie Parker Quintet*—and the one we made in Detroit, Bird went out to California to join Norman Granz's Jazz at the Philharmonic for a concert tour of the Southwest. I went to Chicago to see my sister and her husband, Vincent Wilburn, for Christmas. Then I went back to New York and joined up with Bird again. He had gone off to Mexico and married Doris, missing a concert to do it and fucking up Norman Granz. Bird got star billing on the tour. He was the *main* attraction, so when he missed that concert people got mad and took it out on Norman. But Bird didn't care about that kind of shit. He could always talk his way back into a person's good graces.

Bird was full of confidence after the Philharmonic tour. He had just been named best alto saxophonist of the year by *Metronome* magazine. He seemed happier than I had ever seen him. We played the Three Deuces again and the lines got longer each night. But it seemed to me that every time Bird was just about to get himself together, he always fucked up. It was as if he were afraid of living a normal life; people might think he was square or something. It was tragic, because he was such a genius and a nice person, when he wanted to be. But the constant heroin use really started to fuck with him. Drug dealers went everywhere we went. This shit started to get out of hand in 1948.

I remember this time in '48 when we were out in Chicago to play the Argyle Show Bar. The band was there to start the show but Bird hadn't shown up yet. When he did, he was so fucked up on heroin and alcohol he couldn't play. He was half asleep up on stage. Me and Max played four bars apiece trying to wake him up. The tune would be in F, and Bird would start playing a different tune. So Duke Jordan, who couldn't play anyway, would start to follow Bird's fucked-up lead. It was so bad, they fired us. Bird left the club and peed in a telephone booth, thinking it was a toilet. The white guy who owned the club told us that we had to pick up our money from the black union office. Now, they got this tough black union local in Chicago, right? And we ain't got no money. But I ain't worried about that because my sister lives in Chicago and I could stay there. They would give me some money. But I was worried about the rest of the band. Anyway, Bird said for us to meet him at the black musicians' local the next day to pick up our money.

Bird walks into Union President Gray's office and tells him that he wants his money. Now, keep in mind none of these guys like the way Bird plays anyway. They see him as an overrated junkie, all fucked up and everything, right? So when Bird says this to President Gray, Gray just reaches into his drawer and pulls out a gun. He tells us to get the fuck out of his office or he's going to shoot us. So we get the fuck out of there *real* quick. On the way out, Max Roach says to me, "Don't worry. Bird will get the money." Max believed Bird could do anything. Bird wanted to go back and fight the guy, but Duke Jordan stopped him. That black motherfucker Gray would have shot Bird, because he was a mean guy and didn't give a fuck about who Bird was.

But Bird got his revenge on the club owner of the Argyle when we came back there later in the year. While everybody was playing, Bird laid down his saxophone after finishing his solo, walked off the stage, and out into the Argyle lobby. He walked into a telephone booth in the lobby and peed all over the booth, man. I mean a whole lot of pee. It ran all out of the booth and out on the motherfucking carpet. Then, he came out of the booth smiling, zipped up his pants, and walked back up on the bandstand. All these white people were watching. Then he started playing again and played his ass off. He wasn't high or nothing that night; he was just telling the owner in so many words—without even saying them—not to fuck with him. And you know what? The owner didn't say shit, acted like he didn't see what Bird did. He paid him. But we never did get that money from Bird.

Around this time 52nd Street started to decline. People kept coming to the clubs to hear the music but the police were everywhere. There were a lot of hustlers on the street, so the police put pressure on the owners to clean up their club acts. The police started to arrest some of the musicians and a lot of the hustlers. People were coming to hear Bird's group, but other groups weren't doing so good. Some of the clubs on The Street had stopped featuring jazz and had turned into strip joints. Also, in the past, a lot of the crowd had been good-time-loving-servicemen, but now that the war was over, people were stiffer and not as lenient.

The music scene was hurt by the decline of The Street and the continuing recording ban. The music wasn't being documented. If you didn't hear bebop in the clubs then you forgot it. We were playing regularly at a few places, the Onyx and the Three Deuces. But Bird was fucking with everybody's money and that was messing with our heads. I used to look at Bird as if he were a god, but I wasn't looking at him that way no more. I was twenty-two years old, had a family, had just won the 1947 *Esquire* New Star Award for trumpet, and had tied Dizzy for first place in the critics' *Down Beat* poll. It wasn't that I had gotten a big head, but I was beginning to know who *I* was musically. Bird's not paying us was not right. He showed us no respect at all and I wasn't going to take it.

I remember one time the band went from Chicago to Indianapolis to play a gig. Max and I were roommates and went everywhere together. On the way we stopped in some little diner somewhere in Indiana, an integrated place, to get something to eat. We're sitting there eating, minding our own business, when four white guys walk in and sit down across from us. They were drinking beer and getting drunk, laughing and talking louder than anybody else, like drunken hillbillies can do. Being from East St. Louis, I knew what kind of white people they were, but Max, being from Brooklyn, didn't. I knew they were ignorant motherfuckers. And them drinking beer just made it worse, right? Anyway, so one of them leans over and says, "What do you boys do?"

Now, Max, who is intelligent but who don't know what he's in for, turns to the guy and says with a smile, "We're musicians." See, Max don't understand, this is redneck-cracker shit. Being from Brooklyn, he ain't never been around it. So then the white guy says, "Why don't you play something for us if y'all so good?" When he said that, I *knew* what was coming next, so I just picked up the whole table-cloth with everything on it and threw it all over the motherfuckers before they could say or do anything. Max was throwing shit and screaming. Those white boys was so shocked they just sat there with their mouths open, not saying nothing. When we left I told Max, "Next time just ignore them; this ain't Brooklyn."

By the time I got to Indianapolis to play that night, I'm madder than a motherfucker. And here comes Bird, after we get through playing, telling us that he ain't got no money and that we'd have to wait until the next time we played to get paid because the owner didn't pay him. Everybody else goes for it, but me and Max go up to Bird's room. His wife, Doris, is there, and when we walk in I see Bird putting a lot of money under his pillow. So then he blurts out, "I ain't got no money. I need this for something else. I'll pay you when I get back to New York."

Max says, "Okay, Bird, anything you say."

I said, "Come on Max, he's taking our money, again. He's bull-shitting."

Max just shrugged his shoulders and didn't say anything. He was always on Bird's side no matter what Bird did, you know. So I said, "I want my fucking money, Bird."

Bird, who used to call me Junior, says, "You will not get one penny, Junior, nothing, no money at all."

Max says, "Yeah, I can dig that Bird, I can wait, yeah I can dig it. I can dig that, Miles, because Bird has been teaching us."

I picked up a beer bottle and broke it and with it poised in my hand said to Bird, "Motherfucker, give me my money or I'm gonna kill you." And I had him by his collar.

He reached under the pillow real fast then and handed me the money and said with a shit-eating grin on his motherfucking face, "See, you got mad, didn't you. Did you see that, Max? Miles got mad at me after all I've done for him."

Max comes down on his side, saying, "Miles, Bird was just testing you to see where you were at. Yeah, he didn't mean nothing."

That's when I seriously started to think about quitting the group.

Bird high all the time, not paying us, and me working like a dog to keep the band and music together. He was fucking up. Plus, I thought too much of myself to be treated like that. And Doris, his wife, looked just like Olive Oyl to me. I can't stand nobody talking to me if they ain't together. Especially if they hand out shit like white people do when they think they're the boss. That's the way Doris was. She was nice and all and in Bird's corner, but she liked acting like the boss, especially over black people. When we would be going somewhere to play, Bird would send Doris down to the train station with the tickets. Here'd be this bitch looking just like Olive Oyl, standing in the middle of Penn Station lording it over a group of great musicians like she was our mother or something. I didn't like no ugly women acting like they owned me. But Doris loved it, being surrounded by all these fine black men. She was in heaven. And Bird was someplace high, or trying to get high. He was just insensitive.

Since 52nd Street was going down fast, the jazz scene was moving to 47th and Broadway. One place was the Royal Roost, owned by a guy named Ralph Watkins. It was originally a chicken joint. But in 1948 Monte Kay talked Ralph into letting Symphony Sid produce a concert on an off-night there. Monte Kay was a young white guy who was hanging around the jazz scene. Back then he used to pass himself off as a light-skinned black guy. But when he got some money, he went back to being white. He's made millions producing black musicians. Today he's a millionaire living in Beverly Hills. Anyway, Sid picked Tuesday night and did a concert with me and Bird, Tadd Dameron, Fats Navarro, and Dexter Gordon. They had a non-drinking section in the club where young people could come and sit and listen to the music for ninety cents. Birdland did that too, later on.

This was the time when I got to know Dexter Gordon. Dexter had come east in 1948 (or somewhere around that time), and he and I and Stan Levey started hanging out. I had first met him in Los Angeles. Dexter was real hip and could play his ass off, so we used to go around and go to jams. Stan and I had lived together for a while in 1945, so we were good friends. Stan and Dexter were using heroin together but I was still clean. We would go down to 52nd Street to hang out. Dexter used to be super hip and dapper, with those big-shouldered suits everybody was wearing in those days. I was wearing my three-piece Brooks Brothers suits that I thought were super hip, too. You know, that St. Louis style shit. Niggers from St. Louis had the reputation for being sharp as a tack when it came to clothes. So couldn't nobody tell me nothing.

But Dexter didn't think my dress style was all that hip. So he used to always tell me, "Jim" ("Jim" was an expression a lot of musicians used back then), "you can't hang with us looking and dressing like that. Why don't you wear some other shit, Jim? You gotta get some vines. You gotta go to F & M's," which was a clothing store on Broadway in midtown.

"Why, Dexter, these some bad suits I'm wearing. I paid a lot of money for this shit."

"Miles, that ain't it, 'cause the shit ain't hip. See, it ain't got nothing to do with money; it's got something to do with hipness, Jim, and that shit you got on ain't nowhere near hip. You gotta get some of them big-shouldered suits and Mr. B shirts if you want to be hip, Miles."

So I'd say, all hurt and shit, "But Dex, man, these are nice clothes."

"I know you think they hip, Miles, but they ain't. I can't be seen with nobody wearing no square shit like you be wearing. And you playing in Bird's band? The hippest band in the world? Man, you oughta know better."

I was hurt. I always respected Dexter because I thought he was super hip—one of the hippest and cleanest young cats on the whole music scene back then. Then one day he said, "Man, why don't you grow a moustache? Or a beard?"

"How, Dexter? I ain't even got no hair growing nowhere much except on my head and a little bit under by arms and around my dick! My family got a lot of Indian blood, and niggers and Indians don't grow beards and be hairy on their faces. My chest is smooth as a tomato, Dexter."

"Well, Jim, you gotta do something. You can't be hanging with us looking like you looking, 'cause you'll embarrass me. Why don't you get you some hip vines since you can't grow no hair?"

So I saved up forty-seven dollars and went down to F & M's and bought me a gray, big-shouldered suit that looked like it was too big for me. That's the suit I had on in all them pictures while I was in Bird's band in 1948 and even in my own publicity shot when I had that process in my hair. After I got that suit from F & M's, Dexter came up to me grinning that big grin of his and towering over me, patting me on my back, saying, "Yeah, Jim, now you looking like something, now you hip. You can hang with us." He was something else.

More and more now I was really leading Bird's band because he was never around except to play and pick up his money. I was showing Duke chords every day, hoping he would pick up shit, but he never did listen. We never got along. Bird wouldn't fire him, and I couldn't because it wasn't my band. I'd ask Bird to fire him all the time. Me and Max wanted Bud Powell in the band instead of Duke Jordan. But Bird stuck with Duke.

But there was a problem with Bud. What happened was that one night a few years earlier he had gone up to the Savoy Ballroom in Harlem dressed in his all-black outfit that he used to like to wear. He had his boys from the Bronx with him, who, he used to brag, "would kick anybody's ass." So he goes up to the Savoy without any money in his pocket, and the bouncer, who knew him, told him he couldn't go in without any money. But he's saying this to Bud Powell, the greatest young piano player in the world, and Bud knew this. So Bud just walked right past the motherfucker. The bouncer did what he was being paid to do. He broke Bud's head all the way open, cracked him upside his head with a pistol.

After that, Bud started shooting heroin like it was going out of style, and he was the last person who should have been shooting heroin, because it made him crazy. And he never could drink but now he started drinking like it was going out of style, too. Then Bud started acting crazy, throwing fits and going for weeks not speaking to anyone, including his mother and his oldest friends. Finally his mother sent him over to the Bellevue psychiatric ward in New York City; this was in 1946. They started giving him shock treatments. They really thought he was crazy, too.

So that was that. After them shock treatments, Bud wasn't never the same, as a musician and as a person. Before Bud went to Belle-vue, everything he played had a wrinkle in it; there was always something different about the way the music came off. Man, after they bashed his head in and gave him shock treatments, they would have done better cutting off his hands, instead of cutting off his creativity. Sometimes I used to wonder if them white doctors gave him shock treatments on purpose, to cut him off from himself, like they did to Bird. But Bird and Bud were different. Where Bird was ornery, Bud was passive. Bird survived his shock treatments; Bud didn't.

Before all this happened, Bud Powell was a bad motherfucker. He was the missing link that kept our band from really being maybe the greatest bebop group of all time. With Max pushing Bird and Bird pushing Bud, and me floating over all that bad music—man, it's too painful to think about. Al Haig, the piano player Bird had in the group in 1948, played good enough. He was all right. And John Lewis, who also played with us, played nice enough, too. But Duke Jordan was just there taking up space. And Tommy Potter used to choke the bass like he was strangling somebody he hated. We'd always be saying to him, "Tommy, let that woman loose!" Although Tommy's time wasn't bad. But if Bud had been there, well, what can you say; it didn't happen, but it could have happened.

For some reason, Bud's mother trusted and liked me. But then, people used to like me a lot, I mean all kinds of people. Sometimes I think it might have had something to do with the fact that I used to be a paper boy back in East St. Louis. Having a paper route, you had to learn to talk to all kinds of people. So Bud's mother liked me because whenever I saw her, I talked to her. After Bud went crazy like he did, she would let him go places with me. She knew I hardly drank or used drugs like a lot of the other people always hanging around Bud.

I would come by and sneak him a bottle of beer—he couldn't take more than that without going off in his head. He would sip on that, sit there, and say nothing. He would sit there in front of the piano in their apartment up on St. Nicholas in Harlem. I would ask him to play "Cherokee," and he would, brilliantly. He was like a thorough-bred horse on the piano, even after he was ill. And he would try to play after he was sick because he never thought he couldn't. But no matter how great he might play "Cherokee" or anything else after he got sick he could never play the way he could before. But not to know how to play, man, Bud didn't know what that was, at least not inside his own head. Bird was the same way. In fact, Bird and Bud are the only two musicians that I've known like that.

Sometimes, when I was living in Harlem, Bud would come over to my apartment up on 147th Street and not say anything. He did this every day for two weeks one time. Didn't say a word to nobody, me or Irene or our two kids. He would just sit there and stare off into space with this sweet smile on his face.

Years later, in 1959, we went on tour, me and Lester Young—it was the same year that Lester died—and Bud. Bud wouldn't say nothing to nobody; he'd just sit there and smile. He used to look at this musician named Charlie Carpenter. One day Bud was sitting there as usual, not saying nothing to nobody, just smiling at Charlie. So Charlie said, "Bud, what are you always smiling about?" Bud, without changing expression, said, "You." Lester Young just fell out laughing, because Charlie *was* a sad motherfucker and that's what Bud was smiling about all the time.

Before that, when Bud got out of the crazy house where they had put him, he came downtown one night to listen to Bird's band, wearing his usual black suit, black umbrella, white shirt, black tie, black shoes, black socks, and his black hat. We came outside on break and there he was standing there, real clean and sober. Now, you see, the reason Bird didn't want Bud in the band was not because he didn't like the way he played. He told Max and me that he didn't want Bud in the band because he "got too high." Now can you imagine Bird saying that somebody got "too high"? As high as he got?

So this time Max and me said, "Bud, stay right here, we'll be right back. Don't go nowhere." He just grinned at us and didn't say anything. We ran into the club, did our set, and told Bird, "Bud's outside and he's clean."

Bird said, "Oh, yeah? I don't believe it."

We said, "Come on, Bird, we'll show you." So me and Max took Bird outside and there was Bud standing by the car where we had left him, like a zombie. He looked at Bird and his eyes rolled up in his head. Then he just started sliding right down the side of the motherfucking car, to the ground. "Bud, where you been?" I said. He just mumbled something about how he had been around the corner to the White Rose tavern. He had gotten drunk that quick.

Later, after he got so far gone, he wouldn't even hardly talk to nobody. It was a shame. He was one of the greatest piano players in this century.

Things in the band were bad by now. Bird was hocking his horn all the time. He didn't have one most of the time, so he was borrowing other people's saxophones. It got so bad that the Three Deuces had a guy, I think he was a janitor or something, who would go to the pawnshop every day just to get Bird's horn out of hock and then return it to the pawnshop after Bird got through playing.

By this time, Max and I were confident we could make it by ourselves and we were fed up with Bird's childish, stupid bullshit. All we wanted to do was play great music, and Bird was acting like a fool, some kind of motherfucking clown. He was treating us like we were nothing, like we were one foot high, and we knew different.

One time at the Three Deuces Bird came in late and went in the dressing room, where he opened up sardines and crackers. The owner was trying to get him to hurry up to the bandstand and Bird was just casually eating, grinning like a motherfucking fool, you know what I mean? The owner was begging him to play and Bird was offering him crackers. Man, that was a funny scene. I laughed until I almost died. Finally he came on out of the dressing room and played. But by that time he had made fools out of the owners, who never forgot it. After that, Bird moved the group to the Royal Roost and we never played the Three Deuces again.

From, I think, September of 1948 until December of that year, we played the Royal Roost. It was good at the Roost because Symphony Sid was broadcasting from there and so we were heard by a wider audience. I also started playing with other groups besides Bird's and with my own band. The music I played during this time was what I played with Bird and other groups, but also what I was playing of my own music, which was a lot different from the other stuff. I was finding my own voice and that's what I was mainly interested in.

It was right around this time that Bird's group got to record the first time in 1948, I think it was in September. I got Bird to replace Duke Jordan with John Lewis on that record. Duke got real mad with me, but I didn't care *what* he thought because I was only interested in the music. Curly Russell was on this record, too.

Later, Al Haig came into the group as Duke's permanent replacement. This was around December of 1948. I wasn't crazy about Bird bringing in Al. I didn't have nothing against him personally but thought that John Lewis and Tadd Dameron were better piano players. I think Bird's decision had something to do with showing everybody that he, not me, was in control. Everybody knew who I wanted in the group, so for Bird it might have been about saving face. I don't know really. Bird and I never talked too much, probably fifteen minutes at the most through all the time I knew him. And in 1948 we were talking less than we had before. After Al Haig was brought in, Bird replaced Tommy Potter with Curly Russell. Then he switched back up and replaced Curly with Tommy.

Right after this I brought a group, a nonet, into the Roost. I had Max Roach, John Lewis, Lee Konitz, Gerry Mulligan, Al McKibbon on bass and Kenny Hagood on vocals. I also had Michael Zwerin on trombone, Junior Collins on French horn, and Bill Barber on tuba. I had started working with Gil Evans some time before this and he had done the arrangements.

Gil had stopped arranging for Claude Thornhill's band in the summer of 1948. He had hoped that he could write and arrange for Bird.

But Bird never had time to listen to what Gil did, because for Bird, Gil only provided him with a convenient place to eat, drink, shit, and be close to 52nd Street, since Gil had an apartment over on 55th Street. When Bird did finally listen to Gil's music, he liked it. But by that time Gil didn't want to work with Bird.

Gil and I had already started doing things together and everything was going real well for us. I was looking for a vehicle where I could solo more in the style that I was hearing. My music was a little slower and not so intense as Bird's. My conversations with Gil about experimenting with more subtle voicing and shit were exciting to me. Gerry Mulligan, Gil, and I started talking about forming this group. We thought nine pieces would be the right amount of musicians to be in the band. Gil and Gerry had decided what the instruments in the band would be before I really came into the discussions. But the theory, the musical interpretation and what the band would play, was my idea.

I hired the rehearsal halls, called the rehearsals, and got things done. I was doing this shit with Gil and Gerry on the side from the summer of 1948 until we recorded in January and April of 1949 and then again in March 1950. I got us some jobs and made the contact at Capitol Records to do the recording. But working with Gil really got me into writing compositions. I would play them for Gil on the piano at his apartment.

I remember when we started to get the nonet together that I wanted Sonny Stitt on alto saxophone. Sonny sounded a lot like Bird, so I thought of him right away. But Gerry Mulligan wanted Lee Konitz because he had a light sound rather than a hard bebop sound. He felt that this kind of sound was what was going to make the album and the band different. Gerry felt that with me, Al McKibbon, Max Roach, and John Lewis all in the group and all coming from bebop, it might just be the same old thing all over again, so I took his advice and hired Lee Konitz.

Max was hanging out with Gil and Gerry and me over at Gil's and so was John Lewis, so they knew what we wanted to do. Al McKibbon too. We also wanted J. J. Johnson, but he was traveling with Illinois Jacquet's band, so I thought about Ted Kelly, who was playing trombone with Dizzy's band. But he was busy and couldn't make it. So we settled on a white guy, Michael Zwerin, who was younger than me. I had met him up at Minton's one night when he was sitting in and asked him if he could rehearse the next day with us at Nola's Studio. He made it and was in the band.

See, this whole idea started out just as an experiment, a collaborative experiment. Then a lot of black musicians came down on my case about their not having work, and here I was hiring white guys in my band. So I just told them that if a guy could play as good as Lee Konitz played—that's who they were mad about most, because there were a lot of black alto players around—I would hire him every time, and I wouldn't give a damn if he was green with red breath. I'm hiring a motherfucker to play, not for what color he is. When I told them that, a lot of them got off my case. But a few of them stayed mad with me.

Anyway, Monte Kay booked us into the Royal Roost for two weeks. When we opened up at the Roost, I had the club put up a sign outside that said, "Miles Davis's Nonet; Arrangements by Gerry Mulligan, Gil Evans, and John Lewis." I had to fight like hell with Ralph Watkins, the owner of the Roost, to get him to do this. He didn't want to do the shit in the first place, because he felt it was too much for him to be paying nine motherfuckers when he could have paid five. But Monte Kay talked him into it. I didn't like Watkins too much, but I respected him for taking the chance that he did. We played the Royal Roost for two weeks in late August and September of 1948, taking second billing to Count Basie's orchestra.

A lot of people thought the shit we were playing was strange. I remember Barry Ulanov of *Metronome* magazine being a little confused about the music we played. Count Basie used to listen every night that we were there opposite him, and he liked it. He told me that it was "slow and strange, but good, real good." A lot of the other musicians who used to come hear the band liked it also, including Bird. But Pete Rugolo of Capitol Records really liked what he heard and he asked me if he could record us for Capitol when the recording ban was over.

Later in September I took another group into the Roost, with Lee Konitz, Al McKibbon, John Lewis, Kenny Hagood, and Max Roach. Symphony Sid broadcast this gig and recorded it, so there was a record of what we played. That group was happening, man. We got down on that one time we played together, you know. Max was playing his ass off.

But around this time, Gil went into a musical writing slump. It would take him a week to write eight bars. He finally got it together, though, and wrote a tune called "Moon Dreams" and some things for "Boplicity" for *Birth of the Cool*. The *Birth of the Cool* album came from some of the sessions we did trying to sound like Claude

Thornhill's band. We wanted that sound, but the difference was that we wanted it as small as possible. I said it had to be the voicing of a quartet, with soprano, alto, baritone, and bass voices. We had to have tenor, half-alto, and half-bass. I was the soprano voice, Lee Konitz was the alto. We had another voice in a French horn and a baritone voice, which was a bass tuba. We had alto and soprano up top—me and Lee Konitz. We also used the French horn for the alto voicing and the baritone sax for baritone voicing and bass tuba for bass voicing. I looked at the group like it was a choir, a choir that was a quartet. A lot of people put the baritone sax on the bottom, but it's not a bottom instrument, like a tuba is. The tuba is a bass instrument. I wanted the instruments to sound like human voices, and they did.

Gerry Mulligan would double with Lee sometimes and then double with me, and with Bill Barber, who was always on the bottom playing bass tuba. Sometimes he would come up in the register and sometimes we'd have him bring the sound up. And it worked.

We had one day in the studio with the nonet—I think it was in January 1949. Kai Winding had replaced Michael Zwerin, who had to go back to college, and Al Haig replaced John Lewis on piano, and Joe Shulman took Al McKibbon's place. At this first session I think we recorded "Jeru," "Move," "Godchild," and "Budo." We didn't use any of Gil's arrangements at that session because Pete Rugolo wanted to record the faster and medium-tempo tunes first. That first session went off almost without a hitch. Everybody played well, and Max was pushing everybody. I liked the way everybody played that day. Capitol Records liked the music so much that they released "Move" and "Budo" as 78s about a month after we recorded them, and they brought out "Jeru" and "Godchild" in April. Later we did two more recording sessions, one in March or April 1949, and another one in 1950. By then we had made more changes in the band: J. J. Johnson replaced Kai Winding on trombone; Sandy Siegelstein replaced Junior Collins on French horn and then he was replaced by Gunther Schuller; Al Haig was replaced by John Lewis on piano; Joe Shulman was replaced by Nelson Boyd on bass, who was then replaced by Al McKibbon; Max Roach was replaced by Kenny Clarke on drums, who was then replaced again by Max; and on the last date, Kenny Hagood sang the vocals. The only ones who were constants throughout the three recordings were myself, Gerry Mulligan, Lee Konitz, and Bill Barber.

Me and Gil wrote "Boplicity" but credited it to my mother, Cleo Henry, because I wanted it in a different music publishing house than the one I was signed with. So I just put her name on it.

Birth of the Cool became a collector's item, I think, out of a reaction to Bird and Dizzy's music. Bird and Diz played this hip, real fast thing, and if you weren't a fast listener, you couldn't catch the humor or the feeling in their music. Their musical sound wasn't sweet, and it didn't have harmonic lines that you could easily hum out on the street with your girlfriend trying to get over with a kiss. Bebop didn't have the humanity of Duke Ellington. It didn't even have that recognizable thing. Bird and Diz were great, fantastic, challenging—but they weren't sweet. But *Birth of the Cool* was different because you could hear everything and hum it also.

Birth of the Cool came from black musical roots. It came from Duke Ellington. We were trying to sound like Claude Thornhill, but he had gotten his shit from Duke Ellington and Fletcher Henderson. Gil Evans himself was a big fan of Duke's and Billy Strayhorn's, and Gil was the arranger for *Birth of the Cool*. Duke and Billy used to use that doubling thing up in the chords like we did on *Birth*. You always hear Duke doing that and he would always get guys with a sound that you could recognize. If they played alone in Duke's band, you could always tell who they were by their sound. If they played in a section thing, then you could still tell who they were in the section by the voicing. They put their own personality on certain chords.

So that's what we did in *Birth*. And that's why I think it got over like it did. White people back then liked music they could understand, that they could *hear* without straining. Bebop didn't come out of them and so it was hard for many of them to hear what was going on in the music. It was an all-black thing. But *Birth* was not only hummable but it had white people playing the music and serving in prominent roles. The white critics liked that. They liked the fact that *they* seemed to have something to do with what was going on. It was just like somebody shaking your hand just a little extra. We shook people's ears a little softer than Bird or Diz did, took the music more mainstream. That's all it was.

By late 1948 I was at the end of my rope with Bird, but I was just hanging in there hoping he would change and get better because I loved playing with him so much when he *did* play. But as he got more famous, he would work more as a solo act, leaving the band behind. I know he made more money for himself this way, but we were supposed to be a group and had sacrificed so much for him. He hardly introduced us at jobs, and when he finished his solos, he just left the bandstand without even looking at us. He wouldn't count off the tempo of a tune, so we didn't know *what* he was going to play.

All Bird had to do was show up on stage and play. But he was always putting shit in the game. I remember one time at the Three Deuces Bird looked at me with this annoyed, exasperated look he could give you when he wasn't pleased about something—it could be you, it could be the fact that the dope man hadn't come, it could be that his woman hadn't sucked his dick properly, it could be the owner, someone in the audience, it could be anything, but you never, never knew. Because Bird always wore a mask over his feelings, one of the best masks that I have ever seen. Anyway, he looked at me and bent over to tell me that *I'm* playing too loud. *Me,* as soft as I was playing then? I thought to myself that Bird *must* be crazy, telling me *I* was playing too loud. I never did say anything about it, because what the fuck was I supposed to say. It was, after all, *his* band.

Bird always said he hated the idea of being thought of as just an entertainer, but like I said, he was becoming a spectacle. I didn't like whites walking into the club where we were playing just to see Bird act a fool, thinking that he might do something stupid, anything for a laugh. When I first met Bird he might have been a little foolish, but he wasn't acting stupid like he was now. I remember him announcing a tune once by saying it was called, "Suck You Mama's Pussy." But people weren't sure if he said that, if they heard him right. It was embarrassing. I didn't come to New York to work with no clown.

But when he started cutting off the band just for the hell of it, after I had spent all that time rehearsing everybody in his absence—just to hear white people laugh because they thought it was funny—that was too much for me to take. It made me mad, made me lose respect for him. I *loved* Charlie Parker as a musician—maybe not as a person—but I loved him as a creative, innovative musician and artist. But here he was turning into a motherfucking comedian right before my eyes.

Other things were beginning to happen for me. Even the master himself, Duke Ellington, liked what I was doing, what I was playing in 1948, because he sent a guy to get me once. I didn't even know Duke; I had only seen him on stage and had listened to all of his records. But I really loved him, for his music, his attitude, and his style. So I was flattered when he sent this guy to bring me up to his office to talk to me. The guy's name, I think, was Joe, and he tells me that Duke likes me, likes the way I dress, likes the way I handle myself. Well, this was pretty heady shit for a twenty-two-year-old person, coming from one of his idols. Man, that shit almost took my head off my shoulders, sent my ego climbing up to the sky. Joe gave me the address to his office, which was in the old Brill Building on Broadway and 49th Street.

I go down to see Duke, cleaner than a motherfucker, go upstairs to his office, knock on the door, and there's Duke, dressed in shorts, with some woman in there sitting on his lap. I was shocked. Now here was the person that I thought was the coolest, hippest, cleanest person in the music business, sitting in his office dressed in shorts with a woman on his lap, a big grin on his face. Man, that shit fucked me all the way up. But he tells me that I'm in his plans for the fall, musically speaking, and he wants me in his band. Man, that knocked me right out. I was awfully glad, really flattered. I mean it knocked me out that one of my idols would ask me to be in his band, which was the best big band in the business. That he would even think of me, that he had even heard about me and liked the way I played just knocked me out.

But I had to tell him that I couldn't make it, because I was finishing up *Birth of the Cool.* That's what I told him and it was true, but the real reason I didn't—couldn't—go with Duke was because I didn't want to put myself in a musical box, playing the same music, night after night after night. My head was somewhere else. I wanted to go in another direction from the one he was going, although I loved and totally respected Duke. But I couldn't tell him that. So I just told him that I had to finish *Birth of the Cool,* and he understood that. I also told him that he was one of my idols and that I was flattered that he thought of me. I hoped he wouldn't hold it against me that it didn't work out. He said for me not to worry, that I had to go the way that was best for me.

When I came out of Duke's office, Joe asked me what had happened, and I told him that after I had worked with Billy Eckstine's big band I couldn't do that kind of thing anymore. I told him that I admired Duke so much that I didn't want to work with him. I never was alone with Duke again after that, never did speak to him again, and sometimes I used to find myself wondering what would have happened if I had joined his band. One thing is for certain, I'll never know.

During this time I was going over to Gil Evans's a lot, listening to what he was saying about the music. Gil and I had hit it off right away. I could relate to his musical ideas and he could relate to mine. With Gil, the question of race never entered; it was always about music. He didn't care what color you were. He was one of the first white people I had met that was like this. He was Canadian and maybe that had something to do with how he thought.

Out of *Birth of the Cool* me and Gil got to be real great friends. Gil was just the kind of guy you love being around, because he would see things nobody else saw. He loved paintings and he would show me things that I wouldn't have ever seen. Or, he would listen to an orchestration and say, "Miles, listen to the cello right here. How else do you think that he could have played that passage?" He'd make you think about shit all the time. He used to just go inside of music and pull things out another person wouldn't normally have heard. Later he would call me up at three A.M. and tell me, "If you're ever depressed, Miles, just listen to 'Springsville'" (which was a great tune we put on the *Miles Ahead* album). And then he'd hang up the phone. Gil was a thinker and I loved that about him right away.

When I first met him, he used to come to listen to Bird when I was in the band. He'd come in with a whole bag of "horseradishes"— that's what we used to call radishes—that he'd be eating with salt. Here was this tall, thin, white guy from Canada who was hipper than hip. I mean, I didn't know *any* white people like him. I was used to black folks back in East St. Louis walking into places with a bag full of barbecued pig snout sandwiches and taking them out and eating them right there, right in a movie or club or anywhere. But bringing "horseradishes" to nightclubs and eating them out of a bag with salt, and a white boy? Here was Gil on fast 52nd Street with all these super hip black musicians wearing peg legs and zoot suits, and here he was dressed in a cap. Man, he was something else.

Gil's basement apartment over on 55th Street was where a lot of musicians hung out. Gil's place was so dark you didn't know whether it was night or day. Max, Diz, Bird, Gerry Mulligan, George Russell, Blossom Dearie, John Lewis, Lee Konitz, and Johnny Carisi used to be at Gil's all the time. Gil had this big bed that took up a lot of space and this weird motherfucking cat who was always getting into everything. We would always be sitting around talking about music, or arguing about something. I remember Gerry Mulligan being very angry at that time, about a lot of shit. But so was I, and we would get into arguments sometimes. Nothing serious, just testing each other's shit. But Gil was like a mother hen to all of us. He cooled everything out because he was so cool. He was a beautiful person who just loved to be around musicians. And we loved being around him because he taught us so much, about caring for people and about music, especially arranging music. I think Bird even stayed there for a while. Gil could put up with Bird when nobody else could.

Anyway, I was moving in another direction, away from Bird. So when the shit hit the fan in December of 1948, I was already cool in my head about what I wanted to do and what I was going to do. The band's spirit was very low about the time I decided to quit. Bird and I were hardly speaking to each other and there was a lot of tension happening within the group. The final motherfucking straw happened right before Christmas. Bird and I had an argument in the Three Deuces about my money. Here he was sitting up in the club, eating a ton of fried chicken, drinking and higher than a motherfucker off some heroin, and I ain't been paid in several weeks. And here Bird is, grinning like some full-ass Cheshire cat, looking like Buddha. I ask him for my money and he just kept on eating chicken like I wasn't there. Like I'm some kind of flunky. So I grabbed the motherfucker by his collar and said something like, "Pay me, now, motherfucker, or I'm gonna kill you and I ain't bullshitting, nigger." He goes and gets me some money real quick, not all of it, but about half of it.

About a week later, right before Christmas, we were playing at the Royal Roost. Bird and I had an argument about the rest of the money he owed me before we went on stage to play. So now Bird is up on stage acting a fool, shooting a cap gun at Al Haig, letting air out of a balloon into the microphone. People were laughing and he was, too, because he thinks it's funny. I just walked off the bandstand. Max quit too, that night, but he went back until Joe Harris came and took his place. I went back, too, for a while, but finally, not too long after that, Kenny Dorham, my old friend, took my place in Bird's band.

When I quit the band, a lot of people have written that I just walked off the bandstand and never came back. That didn't happen. I didn't just quit while he was working. I wouldn't do it like that; it just isn't professional to do things like that and I have always believed in being professional. But I had hinted to Bird that I was sick and tired of what was going on, had told him that I wanted to leave and finally I *did* leave.

Soon after, when Norman Granz came and offered me and Max fifty dollars a night to go with Jazz at the Philharmonic with Bird, I said no. When he asked Max, Max wanted to hit Norman in the mouth. But I told him, "Max, all you gotta say is no, you don't have to threaten to beat up the motherfucker." So he did. Max was mad because Norman didn't like or take the kind of music we normally played seriously, and the money wasn't right. But Norman wanted Bird on the programs, and he wanted him to feel comfortable with the people around him. They had to have a drummer, a piano, and a bass, and Bird wanted me on trumpet. Norman already had Erroll Garner on piano, but Bird could play with anybody, so it didn't matter *who* the piano player was, just as long as he could hit the keys. But Erroll could play so that was something positive. But I couldn't do what Norman or Bird wanted me to do, so I just said no. It was painful to say no to Bird, but I did. I think saying it then helped me as an individual later on, helped me to know that I knew myself.

After I quit playing with Bird, I just went across the street and got a job at the Onyx Club. I got Sonny Rollins on tenor saxophone, Roy Haynes on drums, Percy Heath on bass, and Walter Bishop on piano. I tried not to look back.

After this, me and Bird played together two or three times and made some records with each other. I didn't hold anything against Bird; I'm not that kind of person. I just didn't want to be up in Bird's shit myself. I think around 1950 Red Rodney took Kenny Dorham's place in Bird's band, and Bird used to tell him how sorry he was about the way he treated us. Kenny told me the same thing and even Bird said it to us a couple of times. But that still didn't stop him from doing the same shit to every band he had after us.

But in January 1949, *Metronome* picked a group of All Stars to make a record as soon as the recording ban was lifted, which was on the first working day of 1949. So they had me on trumpet, along with Dizzy and Fats Navarro, J. J. Johnson and Kai Winding on trombone, Buddy De Franco on clarinet, Bird on alto, Lennie Tristano on piano, Shelly Manne on drums, and some other people. Pete Rugolo was the conductor. RCA did the record, the *Metronome All Stars*.

Bird was funny at that session. He kept having to do extra takes because he said he didn't understand the arrangements. But he did understand the shit. He was just doing this so he could make some more money. The new recording contract had a three-hour limit set by the union, all over that was overtime. So Bird with his extra takes and shit stretched the session about three hours over the limit, and everybody made more money. They later named a tune "Overtime" because of what Bird did.

It was a bullshit record except for what me and Fats and Dizzy played. They were limiting everybody because there were so many soloists and these were 78 rpm recordings. But the shit that the trumpet section played I think was a motherfucker. Me and Fats decided to follow Dizzy's lead and play the shit he was playing instead of playing our own styles. It was so close to what Dizzy played, *he* didn't even hardly know when he left off and when we started. Man, them trumpet licks was flying all over the place. It was something else. After that, a lot of musicians knew that I could play Dizzy's shit, too, as well as play my own style. They—the Dizzy diehards—gave me a lot of respect after they heard this record.

After I played the Onyx, I started playing the Royal Roost with Tadd Dameron's band. Tadd was a great arranger and composer, and he was a very fine piano player also. It was a steady job, and after leaving Bird I needed this to support my family. Fats Navarro had been Tadd's regular trumpet player, but he was a total junkie by now, losing a lot of weight. He was sick all the time and missed a lot of jobs. Tadd wrote a lot of shit for Fat Girl's trumpet, but in January of 1949, Fat Girl was too sick to play, so I took over for him. He still came in and played sometimes, but he wasn't the player he used to be.

Right after Tadd and I played the Royal Roost, I joined Oscar Pettiford's band, and we went into the Three Deuces with Kai Winding on trombone. The owners of the Three Deuces, Sammy Kaye and Irving Alexander, opened up a new club on Broadway called the Clique in January of 1949. They were hoping to pick up the jazz crowd that had moved from 52nd Street to Broadway, but they had to close down six months after they opened. Then new owners leased the spot, and that's where they opened up Birdland in the summer of 1949.

Anyway, Oscar Pettiford's band had some great musicians in it: Lucky Thompson, Fats Navarro, Bud Powell, and myself. But that band wasn't into playing as a group. Everybody was playing these long solos and shit, trying to outdo the next guy. It was all fucked up and it was a shame, because it could have been something else.

Early in 1949, Tadd and I took a group to Paris, France, and played opposite Bird, just like we had done at the Royal Roost. This was my first trip out of the country and it changed the way I looked at things forever. I loved being in Paris and loved the way I was treated. I had bought me some new suits that I had made, so I know I was together, man.

The band was me, Tadd, Kenny Clarke, James Moody, and a French bass player named Pierre Michelot. Our band was the hit of the Paris Jazz Festival, along with Sidney Bechet. That's where I met Jean-Paul Sartre and Pablo Picasso and Juliette Greco. I have never felt like that in my life since. The only other times that I felt that good was when I first heard Bird and Diz in B's band and that time in Dizzy's big band up in the Bronx. But that was about just music. This was different. This was about living. Juliette Greco and I fell in love. I cared a lot for Irene, but I had never felt like this before in my life.

I met Juliette at one of my rehearsals. She would come in and sit and listen to the music. I didn't know she was a famous singer or nothing like that. She was just so fine sitting there—long black hair, beautiful face, small, stylish, so different from any other woman that I had ever met. She looked different and had a different way of carrying herself. So I asked this guy who she was.

He said, "What do you want with her?"

I said, "What do you mean, what do I want with her? I want to see her."

Then he says, "Well, you know she's one of those existentialists."

So I told him, right then and there, "Man, fuck all that kind of shit. I don't care what she is. That girl is beautiful and I want to meet her."

I got tired of waiting for someone to introduce me to her, so one time when she came to the rehearsal I just took my index finger and beckoned for her to come over to me, and she did. When I finally got to talk to her she told me that she didn't like men but that she liked me. After that we were together all the time.

I had never felt that way in my life. It was the freedom of being in France and being treated like a human being, like someone impor-tant. Even the band and the music we played sounded better over there. Even the smells were different. I got used to the smell of cologne in Paris and the smell of Paris to me was a kind of coffee smell. I found out later you could smell that same kind of smell on the French Riviera, in the morning. I have never smelled smells like that since. It's kind of like coconut and lime in rum all mixed together. Almost tropical. Anyway, everything seemed to change for me while I was in Paris. I even found myself announcing the songs in French.

Juliette and I used to walk down by the Seine River together, holding hands and kissing, looking into each other's eyes, and kissing some more, and squeezing each other's hands. It was like magic, almost like I had been hypnotized, was in some kind of trance. I had never done this before. I was always so into the music I never had time for any kind of romance. Music had been my total life until I met Juliette Greco and she taught me what it was to love someone other than music.

Juliette was probably the first woman that I loved as an equal human being. She was a beautiful person. We had to communicate with each other through expressions and body language. She didn't speak English, and I didn't speak French. We talked through our eyes, fingers, stuff like that. When you communicate like that, you know the person is not bullshitting. You have to go on feelings. It was April in Paris. Yeah, and I was in love.

Kenny Clarke decided right then and there he was staying, told me I was a fool to go back to the United States. I was sad, too, because every night I would go out to the clubs with Sartre and Juliette and we would just sit in the outside cafes and drink wine and eat and talk. Juliette asked me to stay. Even Sartre said, "Why don't you and Juliette get married?" But I didn't. I stayed a week or two, fell in love with Juliette and with Paris and then left.

When I got ready to leave, there were a lot of sad faces at the airport, including mine. Kenny was there waving goodbye. Man, I was so depressed coming back to this country on the airplane that I couldn't say nothing all the way back. I didn't know that shit was going to hit me like that. I was so depressed when I got back that before I knew it, I had a heroin habit that took me four years to kick and I found myself for the first time out of control and sinking faster than a motherfucker toward death.

Chapter 6

When I got back to this country in the summer of 1949 it was just like Kenny Clarke had told me—nothing had changed. I don't know *why* I thought it would be any different than it was; I think I thought it would be different because of the way things had happened for me in Paris. I was still up into the illusion of what had happened to me there. But I knew deep down things hadn't changed in the United States. It had only been a couple of weeks. But I was living in an illusion of possibility, maybe a miracle had happened.

Paris was where I understood that all white people weren't the same, that some weren't prejudiced and others were. I had kind of known this after I met Gil Evans and some other people, but I really came to know it in Paris. It was an important thing for me to know and it made me conscious of what was happening around me politically. I started noticing things that I hadn't noticed before, political stuff—what was really happening to black people. I knew about that stuff before on account of growing up around my father. But I was so much into music that I didn't really pay any attention to it. Only when it hit me right in my face did I do something about it.

Around this time Adam Clayton Powell from Harlem and William Dawson from Chicago were the two most powerful black politicians —I used to see Adam in Harlem because he really liked music. Ralph Bunche had just won the Nobel prize. Joe Louis had been heavyweight champion of the world for a long time by then, and he was every black person's hero—and a lot of white people's, too. Sugar Ray Robinson wasn't far behind him in popularity. Both of them used to hang out up in Harlem. Ray had a club up on Seventh Avenue. Jackie Robinson and Larry Doby were playing baseball in the major leagues. Things were beginning to happen for black people in this country.

I had never been too political, but I knew how white people treated black people and it was hard for me to come back to the bullshit white people put a black person through in this country. To realize you don't have any power to make things different is a bitch.

In Paris—shit, whatever we played over there, right or wrong, was cheered, was accepted. That ain't good either, but that's the way it was and we came back over here and couldn't even find no work. International stars and couldn't get jobs. White musicians who were copying my *Birth of the Cool* thing were getting the jobs. Man, that shit hurt me to the quick. We got a few gigs here and there and I think we rehearsed an eighteen-piece band that summer, but that was it. I was only twenty-three years old in 1949 and I guess I expected more. I lost my sense of discipline, lost my sense of control over my life, and started to drift. It wasn't like I didn't know what was happening to me. I did, but I didn't care anymore. I had such confidence in myself that even when I was losing control I really felt I had everything under control. But your mind can play tricks on you. I guess when I started to hang like I did, it surprised a lot of people who thought I had it all together. It also surprised me how fast I eventually lost control.

I remember starting to fuck around a lot uptown in Harlem after I got back from Paris. There was a lot of dope around the music scene and a lot of musicians were deep into drugs, especially heroin. People—musicians—were considered hip in some circles if they shot smack. Some of the younger guys like Dexter Gordon, Tadd Dameron, Art Blakey, J. J. Johnson, Sonny Rollins, Jackie McLean, and myself—all of us—started to get heavily into heroin around the same time. *Despite* the fact that Freddie Webster had died from some bad stuff. Besides Bird, Sonny Stitt, Bud Powell, Fats Navarro, Gene Ammons were all using heroin, not to mention Joe Guy and Billie Holiday, too. They were shooting up all the time. There were a lot of white musicians—Stan Getz, Gerry Mulligan, Red Rodney, and Chet Baker—who were also heavy into shooting drugs. But the press back then used to try and make out like it was only black musicians who were doing it.

I wasn't never into that trip that if you shot heroin you might be able to play like Bird. I knew a lot of musicians who were into that, and Gene Ammons was one of them. That ain't what got me into heroin. What got me strung out was the depression I felt when I got back to America. That and missing Juliette.

And then there was cocaine, which was a real big Latin thing. Guys like Chano Pozo were heavy into cocaine. Chano was a percussionist in Dizzy's band. He was a black Cuban and the baddest conga player on the scene then. But he was a bully. He used to take drugs from people and wouldn't pay them. People were scared of him because he was a hell of a street fighter and would kick a motherfucker's ass in a minute. He was a big man and mean and used to carry this big knife. He would terrorize people uptown. He got killed in 1948 after he slapped some Latin coke dealer upside his head up in Harlem in the Rio Cafe, on Lenox Avenue around 112th or 113th. The guy asked Chano for some money that he owed him and Chano just slapped the guy's face. The dealer got his gun and shot Chano to death. Man, him dying like that shook everybody up. This happened before I went to Paris, but it was a big part of what the whole drug scene was about.

Searching for dope uptown kept me away from my family even more. I had moved them into an apartment in Jamaica, Queens, then to St. Albans. So I was driving back and forth in my 1948 Dodge convertible—Sonny Rollins used to call it the "Blue Demon."

Irene and I didn't have any kind of family life anyway. We didn't have a whole lot of money to do things with, with the two kids and ourselves to feed and all. We didn't never go anywhere. Sometimes I used to stare into space for two hours just thinking about music. Irene would imagine that I was thinking about another woman. She'd find hair on my suit coat or my overcoat and she would swear that I had been out fucking with somebody. One reason Irene accused me of having other women was that I bought clothes off Coleman Hawkins, who was a notorious ladies' man with all kinds of hair on his clothes. But I wasn't into women at that time. So we would just get into these arguments over nothing. It used to piss me off. I really liked Irene and everything. She was a very nice person, a good woman, but for someone else. She was a real classy lady and fine. It was me who wanted something different. It was me, not her, who started fucking up royally. After I met Juliette Greco, I kind of knew what I wanted in a woman. If it wasn't going to be Juliette, then it was going to be someone with her way of looking at life and her style, both in and out of bed. She was independent, her own thinker, and I liked that.

I basically left Irene sitting at home with the kids because I didn't want to be there. One of the reasons why I stopped coming home was that I felt so bad that I couldn't hardly face my family. Irene had had such confidence and faith in me. Gregory and Cheryl, the kids, were still young and didn't know exactly what was going on. But Irene knew. It was all there in her eyes.

I left her in the care of Betty Carter, the singer. If it hadn't been for Betty Carter I don't know what Irene would have done. Because of the way I treated Irene back in those days, I think Betty Carter, even today, don't like me much. I can't blame her, because I was a no-count motherfucker in those days as far as providing for my family went. I didn't mean to leave Irene stranded the way I did, but I was sick with a heroin habit and my dreams of the woman I wanted, and that's all I could think about.

When you're doing heroin all the time, you really lose your desire to have sex with a woman, at least I did. But people like Bird seemed to want to have sex whether they were off heroin or shooting every day. It didn't seem to make a difference to them. I enjoyed having sex with Irene—like I enjoyed having Juliette. But after I got my habit, I didn't even think about having sex, and I didn't enjoy it when I did. The only thing I could think about was how I was going to cop me some more heroin.

I wasn't shooting it in my veins yet, but I was snorting as much as I could get my hands on. One day I was standing on this corner in Queens with my nose running and shit. I felt like I had a fever or a cold. This hustler friend of mine who called himself "Matinee" came up and asked what I had been doing. I told him I had been snorting heroin and coke and that I had been doing it every day and on this particular day I hadn't gone into Manhattan where I used to cop the shit. Matinee looked at me like I was a fool and told me that I had a habit.

"What do you mean, a habit?" I said.

Matinee told me, "Your nose is running, you got chills, you weak. You got a motherfucking habit, nigger." Then he bought me some heroin in Queens. I had never bought heroin in Queens. I snorted the stuff Matinee copped for me and I felt just fine. My chills went away, my nose stopped running, and I didn't feel weak no more. I continued my snorting but when I saw Matinee again he said. "Miles, don't waste that little money on getting some to snort, because you still gonna be sick. Go on and shoot it, then you'll feel much better." That was the beginning of a four-year horror show.

After a while, I was driven to getting dope, because I knew if I didn't get it I was going to be sick. And when you got sick it was like having the flu. Your nose would run, your joints would ache real bad, and if you didn't shoot some heroin into your veins, pretty soon you would start to vomit. That shit was terrible. So I avoided being in that situation at all costs.

When I first started shooting heroin, I shot up by myself. Then I started hanging out. Me, a tap dancer named Leroy, and a guy we called Laffy was copping up on 110th, 111th, and 116th streets up in Harlem. We were hanging in bars like the Rio, the Diamond, Sterling's, LaVant's pool hall, places like that. We were snorting coke along with heroin, all day long. When I wasn't with Leroy, I was with either Sonny Rollins or Walter Bishop—and a little later on, with Jackie McLean or maybe Philly Joe Jones, who was around then, too.

We'd buy $3 caps of heroin and shoot it up. We'd do four or five caps a day, according to how much money we had. We'd go over to Fat Girl's apartment in the Cambridge Hotel, on 110th Street between Seventh and Lenox; or sometimes to Walter Bishop's house to shoot up. We'd have to go to Bishop's house to get our "works"— our needles and whatever we was using to tie our arms up with so we could "pop" or "hit," make the veins we were going to be shooting the dope into stand up so we could see them. Sometimes we'd get so high that we'd leave our works at Bishop's house. Then we'd go hang around Minton's and watch the tap dancers dueling each other.

I loved to look at and listen to tap dancers. They are so close to music in the way they make their taps sound. They are almost like drummers and you can learn a lot from just listening to the rhythms they get from their taps. In the daytime, outside Minton's next to the Cecil Hotel, tap dancers used to come up there and challenge each other on the sidewalk. I especially remember duels between the dancers Baby Laurence and a real tall, skinny dude named Ground Hog. Baby and Ground Hog were junkies, and so they used to dance a lot in front of Minton's for their drugs, because the dealers liked to watch them. They gave them shit for free if they got down. There'd be a crowd all around and they would be dancing like motherfuckers. Baby Laurence was so bad, man, it's hard to describe how great he was. But Ground Hog didn't take no backseat to Baby, now. He was real hip and cleaner than a broke-dick dog, you know, his clothes and everything. Barney Biggs was another great tap dancer, and so was a guy named L. D., and Fred and Sledge, and the Step Brothers. Most of these guys were dope addicts, though I don't know about the Step Brothers. Anyway, if you weren't in the "in" crowd you didn't know nothing about the dancing in front of Minton's. Those tap dancers used to talk about Fred Astaire and all of them other white dancers like they were nothing, and they weren't nothing compared to how these guys could dance. But they were black and couldn't ever hope to get no break dancing for real money and fame.

By this time I was getting really famous and a whole lot of musicians were starting to kiss my ass like I was somebody important. I was into whether I should stand like this or that, should I hold my trumpet this way or that way when I played. Should I do this or that, speak to the audience, tap my right foot or left foot. Should I tap my foot inside of my shoe so nobody would see me doing it? I was into that kind of shit when I got to be twenty-four. Plus, while in Paris, I had found out that I wasn't as bad a player as a lot of them old-time motherfuckers had said I was. My ego was bigger than it had been before I left. I changed from a real shy person into someone confident.

By 1950 I had moved back to Manhattan and was staying in the Hotel America down on 48th Street. A lot of musicians were living there, like Clark Terry, who had finally come up to New York. Clark was playing in Count Basie's band then, I think, and so he'd be out on the road a lot. Baby Laurence used to hang out there at the hotel, too. A lot of junkies were living there also.

I was really heavy into heroin and also began to hang out with Sonny Rollins and his Sugar Hill Harlem crowd. This group included, besides Sonny, the pianist Gil Coggins, Jackie McLean, Walter Bishop, Art Blakey (who was actually from Pittsburgh, but who hung out a lot up in Harlem), Art Taylor, and Max Roach, who was from Brooklyn. I also think I met John Coltrane for the first time during this period while he was playing in one of Dizzy's bands. I think I first heard him play at a club up in Harlem.

Anyway, Sonny had a big reputation among a lot of the younger musicians in Harlem. People loved Sonny Rollins up in Harlem and everywhere else. He was a legend, almost a god to a lot of the younger musicians. Some thought he was playing the saxophone on the level of Bird. I know one thing—he *was* close. He was an aggressive, innovative player who always had fresh musical ideas. I loved him back then as a player and he could also write his ass off. (But I think later Coltrane's playing affected him and made him change his style. If he had kept doing what he was doing when I first heard him, I think he would have been an even greater player than what he is now, today—and he's still a *very* great player.)

Sonny had just got back from playing a gig out in Chicago. He knew Bird, and Bird really liked Sonny, or "Newk" as we called him, because he looked like the Brooklyn Dodgers' pitcher, Don Newcombe. One day, me and Sonny was in a cab coming from buying some dope, when the white cabdriver turned around and looked at Sonny and said, "Damn, you're Don Newcombe!" Man, the guy was totally excited. I was amazed, because I hadn't thought about it before. We just put that cabdriver on something terrible. Sonny started talking about what kind of pitches he was going to throw Stan Musial, the great hitter for the St. Louis Cardinals, that evening. So Sonny was feeling mischievous on this day and tells the cabdriver that he would leave tickets in his name at the gate. After that, the cabdriver treated us like gods.

I had a job at the Audubon Ballroom and so I asked Sonny to join the band, and he did. Coltrane was in that band, as was Art Blakey on drums. All of them—Sonny, Art, and Coltrane—were using a lot of heroin at the time, so being around them a lot like I was just got me into it deeper.

By this time, Fats Navarro was a real bad junkie, pitiful. Fat Girl's wife, Lena, was worried about him all the time. She was white. They had a little girl named Linda. He was a jolly kind of person, short and fat before the drugs got to him. But by now, he was skin and bones, walking around with this terrible cough wracking through his body all the time. He would literally shake all over every time he coughed. It was sad to see him like that. He was such a beautiful cat, man, and a great trumpet player. I really loved him. I would hang with him sometimes and shoot up with him, too. Me and Fat Girl and Ben Harris, another trumpet player. Fat Girl hated him. I knew it, but I thought Benny was all right. After we'd get off, we'd sit around and talk about music, about the old days up at Minton's when Fat

Girl would be blowing away everybody that came through the door. I would tell him shit—technical shit—about the trumpet, because, see, Fat Girl was a natural musician, a natural genius player and so I would be showing him stuff to play. Like, he couldn't play ballads for shit. I'd tell him to play softer, or to invert some of the chords he played. He used to call me "Millie." He always used to talk about changing, getting off heroin, but he didn't. He never did make it.

Fat Girl made his last record with me in May of 1950. He died a few months after making that gig. He was just twenty-seven. It was sad to listen to him that last time, trying to hit notes he used to hit like they was nothing. I think that record was called the *Birdland All Stars,* because that's where the gig was. J. J. Johnson, Tadd Dameron, Curly Russell, Art Blakey, Fat Girl, a saxophone player named Brew Moore, and myself were on that gig. Later I made a record with Sarah Vaughan, playing trumpet in Jimmy Jones's band. Some time in here, I think I played in another All Star band with Fat Girl, and that might have been the last time we played together. I'm not sure, but I think that was a Birdland All Star band, too, with Dizzy, Red Rodney, Fat Girl, and Kenny Dorham on trumpet; J. J., Kai Winding, and Bennie Green on trombone; Gerry Mulligan, Lee Konitz on sax; Art Blakey on drums; Al McKibbon on bass; and Billy Taylor on piano.

I remember everybody playing all these great fucking solos and then fucking up everything when we all tried to play together. If I remember correctly, nobody knew the arrangements, which were out of Dizzy's big band musical book. I seem to remember the owners of Birdland wanting to call the band Dizzy Gillespie's Dream Band, but Diz wouldn't go for that because he didn't want to step on nobody else's toes. Then they wanted to call the band Symphony Sid's Dream Band. Now ain't that some white people's racist shit? But even Sid was too hip and cool to go for that. So they ended up calling it the Birdland Dream Band. I think they recorded the band.

After this, I think I played the Black Orchid Club, which used to be called the Onyx Club. I had Bud Powell, Sonny Stitt, and Wardell Gray in that band, and I think Art Blakey on drums, but I'm not positive who the drummer was. This was around June 1950. I know Fat Girl died in July.

Later that summer 52nd Street closed down, then Dizzy broke up his big band, and the music scene just seemed to be falling apart. I started to believe that all this shit was happening for a specific reason, although I didn't know what the reason was. See, I'm a very intuitive person. I've always been able to predict things. But I fucked up when it came to predicting what was going to happen to me with the drugs. I'm a number six in numerology, a perfect six, and six is the number of the Devil. I think I have a lot of the devil in me. After I found this out I also came to the realization that it was hard for me to like most people—even women—beyond six years. I don't know what it is, call it superstition if you like. But in my own head, I believe that all this shit is true.

In 1950 I was coming up on living in New York for six years, so in my head maybe I thought that all of this fucked-up shit was supposed to happen to me and I couldn't seem to do nothing about it. I wanted to stop shooting drugs almost from the first time I realized I had a bad habit. I didn't want to end up like Freddie Webster or Fat Girl. But I couldn't seem to stop.

Shooting heroin changed my whole personality from being a nice, quiet, honest, caring person into someone who was the complete opposite. It was the drive to get the heroin that made me that way. I'd do anything not to be sick, which meant getting and shooting heroin all the time, all day and all night.

I started to get money from whores to feed and support my habit. I started to pimp them, even before I realized that this was what I was doing. I was what I used to call a "professional junkie." That's all I lived for. I even chose my jobs according to whether it would be easy for me to cop drugs. I turned into one of the best hustlers because I had to get heroin every day, no matter what I had to do.

I even beat Clark Terry out of some money once in order to buy some drugs. I was down around the Hotel America, where Clark lived, too, sitting on the curb thinking about how and where I was going to get some money to get off when Clark walked up. My nose was runny and my eyes were all red. He bought me some breakfast and afterward he took me to his room at the hotel and told me to get some sleep. He was going out on the road with Count Basie and about to leave. He told me when I felt well enough to leave to just lock the door behind me, but I could stay as long as I wanted to. That's how tight we were. He knew what I was doing but he just figured I would never do nothing fucked up to him, right? Wrong.

As soon as Clark left to catch his bus, I opened up his drawers and closets and took everything I could get my hands on to carry. Took a horn and a lot of clothes straight to the pawnshop and what I couldn't pawn, I sold for whatever little money I could get for the stuff. I even sold Philly Joe Jones a shirt that Clark later saw him in. Later I found out that Clark didn't catch the bus. He had waited but the bus had taken longer than he thought. He came back to his hotel room to check on how I was doing and found his door wide open. Clark called home to St. Louis and told his wife, Pauline, who was still living there, to call my father and tell him what bad shape I was in. When she called him, my father got on her case.

"The only thing that's wrong with Miles now is those damn musicians like your husband that he's hanging around with," he said to her. My father believed in me and it was hard for him to accept that I was in real deep trouble, and so he blamed Clark. My father felt that Clark had been the reason that I had gone into music in the first place.

Since Clark knew my father, he knew where he was coming from, and on top of everything, Clark forgave me for what I had done to him. He knew that if I hadn't been sick that I would never have done it to him. But for a little while after that, I avoided being anyplace I thought Clark was going to be. When we did finally run into each other, I apologized and we went on like nothing had ever happened. Now, that's a good friend. A long time after that every time he caught me in a bar drinking with my change on the counter, he'd take it for payment on what I had stolen. Man, that was some funny shit.

Irene and I were behind in our rent payments at the Hotel America. I had pawned a lot of my shit, including my own horn, and was renting a trumpet from Art Farmer for ten dollars a night. One time when he had to play, I wanted to rent it and he said I couldn't, so I got real upset. And when he did lend the horn, he would come around where I was playing so that he could pick it up. He didn't trust me to keep it overnight. I was also behind in my car payments. The people who sold me the Blue Demon were constantly on my case about repossessing it, so I always had to be figuring out secret places where I could park it. Everything was falling apart.

In 1950 me and Irene and the kids drove back to East St. Louis in the Blue Demon. We told ourselves it would be a break from New York and maybe we could pull it together. In the back of my mind I knew that it was over between us. I don't know how Irene felt at the time, but I *do* know that she was sick and tired of my silly shit.

As soon as we got into East St. Louis and I parked the Blue Demon in front of my father's house, the finance company took the car off the street. Everybody kind of wondered what that was all about, but nobody said anything. There were rumors back home that I was hooked on drugs, but it wasn't all the way into the open yet. Anyway, people in East St. Louis weren't around a lot of drug addicts, so they didn't know how drug addicts looked or acted. To them I was just Miles, the weird musician son of Dr. Davis who was living up in New York with all of those other weird musicians. At least that's what I thought they thought.

A friend of mine had told me that Irene was pregnant with another guy's child. This time I knew it couldn't have been mine, because I wasn't having sex with her. This friend told me he had seen her coming out of a hotel in New York with this guy. We never did get legally married, so we didn't have to get no divorce. At the end, we didn't have no argument or nothing like that; it was just over.

See, Irene had followed me to New York and she used to follow me around town, like to my Uncle Ferdinand's (my father's brother) in Greenwich Village. Uncle Ferd was a drunk. I used to hang with him and a couple of his black journalist friends. These guys were drinking together a lot and I didn't particularly like her seeing all these guys falling down drunk, especially my uncle. One time my mother asked me what I had been doing. When I told her that I had been hanging out with Uncle Ferd, she said, "Oh, y'all two together, huh; the blind leading the blind." Well, my mother was trying to tell me that he and I had the same kind of personality—addictive. But at the time she told me, my "jones" was music. Later, it was heroin, and then I knew what she was trying to tell me.

Anyway, Irene stayed in East St. Louis, and that's where Miles IV was born, in 1950. I came back to New York for a while and then I got a job back in Billy Eckstine's band, they were going out to Los Angeles to play and so I went with them. I needed some steady money and I didn't have anything better to do. I didn't like the music B was playing, but Art Blakey was in the band and some other musicians that I respected, so I thought that I would do it until I got myself together.

Los Angeles was the last stop on the tour, and it had been one of those long bus-ride things where we went from city to city. We didn't know where to cop on the road, and because I wasn't getting good dope on a regular basis, I began to think I had broken my habit. Dexter Gordon, Blakey, and I think Bird was with us, were on our way to the Burbank airport. Art wanted to stop somewhere and buy some drugs from a guy he knew. We did and the police busted us at the airport. They had followed us from the dealer's house. They put us in their car and said, "All right, we know who you all are and what you're doing." They were all white guys and straight as arrows. They asked us for our names. I gave them mine, Bird gave them his, Dexter gave them his, but when it came to Blakey, he tells them his name is Abdullah Ibn Buhaina, his Moslem name. So the policeman taking everything down says, "Cut that shit out and give me your fucking American name, your right name!" So Blakey tells him that he already gave him his right name. The cop got mad, took us and booked us and put us in jail. I really think he would have let us go if Blakey had given the guy his right name. So now we're in jail and I had to call my father to help get me out. He called a friend living in L.A., a dentist he went to school with named Dr. Cooper, who got in touch with a lawyer, Leo Branton. The lawyer came down and got me out.

I had all these old needle tracks on my arm, which the police noticed, but I wasn't using nothing at the time. I told Leo Branton this and he told me something which shocked the fuck out of me. He said that Art told the police that *I* was using so that they might go light on him. I didn't believe it, but one of the cops said it was true. I never said nothing to Art about it and this is the first time that I ever said anything about it publicly.

This was the first time that I had been busted for anything, the first time that I had gone to jail, and I didn't like that shit at all. They dehumanize you, and you feel so goddamn helpless behind all them steel bars with your life in the hands of someone who don't give a fuck about you. Some of them white guards are totally racist and would just as soon kick you as anything else, or kill you just like they was killing a fly or a roach. So my time in jail was an eye-opener, a real revelation.

After I got out of jail I stayed with Dexter for a while in Los Angeles. We worked some but mostly we didn't. Dexter was shooting a lot of heroin and liked being at home where he could get really good stuff. So I started shooting all over again.

I had met Art Farmer when I first went out there, and when I returned in 1950 I got to know him better. After staying with Dexter for a while, I got a place at the Watkins Hotel, which was located on West Adams around Western Avenue. I'd get together with Art and we'd talk about music. I think I was the first one to tell him about Clifford Brown, who I had heard somewhere. I thought he was good and that Art would like hearing him. Clifford wasn't famous yet, but a lot of musicians from around Philly were already talking about him. Art was and is a real nice dude, real quiet, but a hell of a trumpet player.

Toward the end of the year *Down Beat* magazine wrote this story about how heroin and drugs were ruining the music scene and they talked about how Art Blakey and myself had been busted in Los Angeles. Well, after that, everything was out in the open and I could hardly buy a music job. The club owners just froze me out.

I soon got tired of L.A., so I came on back east. I stopped at home for a hot minute, then went on to New York. But wasn't nothing happening for me there either but shooting dope with Sonny Rollins and all them guys from Sugar Hill. Wasn't no gigs happening for me.

Waiting for the trial in L.A. was hard, because hardly anybody believed that I was innocent. Around Christmas, I finally got a job playing with Billie Holiday at the Hi-Note in Chicago. This lasted about two to three weeks and I had a great time.

It was a great experience. While I was doing that gig, I got to know her and Anita O'Day, the white jazz singer, real well. I found Billie to be a very sweet, beautiful, extremely creative person. She had such a sensuous mouth and always wore a white gardenia in her hair. I thought she was not only beautiful but sexy. But she was sick because of all the drugs she did, and I understood that because I was sick, too. Still, she was a warm person, nice to be around. Years later when she was real sick, I used to visit her at her house out on Long Island and do whatever I could. I would take my son Gregory, who she loved, with me and we'd sit and talk for hours, drinking gin after gin.

This young white guy named Bob Weinstock had started a new jazz label called Prestige, and he was looking for me to make a record for him. He hadn't been able to find me and was out in St. Louis on business. Since he knew I was from around there, he called up all the Davises in the East St. Louis and St. Louis telephone books until he reached my father, who told him I was working up in Chicago. It was right after Christmas in 1950 when he ran me down at the Hi-Note, where I was playing with Billie. We signed a one-year contract beginning in January when I would be back in New York. It wasn't much money—I think something like $750—but it gave me a chance to lead a group of my own choosing, lay down some music that I wanted to record, and put a little money in my pocket. I spent the rest of the time in Chicago thinking about who I was going to record with.

I was acquitted in January 1951, and a real heavy load was lifted off my mind. But the damage had been done. My acquittal didn't make the headlines of *Down Beat* like my getting busted did; as far as all the club owners were concerned, I was just another junkie.

I thought that the nonet recordings would be good for my career, and they were, to a certain extent. Capitol Records, who had recorded the nonet sessions, didn't make the money they thought they were going to make and so they weren't interested in recording any more of the material. And because I didn't have an exclusive recording deal with Capitol I was free to go with Prestige and I did. I still hadn't gotten the recognition I thought I deserved. Toward the end of 1950 I was voted into *Metronome* magazine's All Star Band by its readers. But everybody was white in that band except for me and Max. Bird didn't even make it—they picked Lee Konitz over him, Kai Winding over J. J. Johnson, and Stan Getz over all them great black tenor players. I felt funny being picked over Dizzy. Plus a lot of white musicians like Stan Getz, Chet Baker, and Dave Brubeck—who had been influenced by my records—were recording all over the place. Now they were calling the kind of music they were playing "cool jazz." I guess it was supposed to be some kind of alternative to bebop, or black music, or "hot jazz," which in white people's minds, meant black. But it was the same old story, black shit was being ripped off all over again.

Bird broke up with Doris Sydnor—"Olive Oyl"—in 1950 and started living with Chan Richardson. Chan was an improvement over Doris; at least she was good to look at and understood the music and musicians. Doris didn't. Bird wasn't looking so good—but neither was I. He had gained a lot of weight and was looking a whole lot older than he was. The hard living was starting to get to him. But Bird had moved downtown to East 11th Street and things looked good for him. He had a new record contract with a big label, Verve, and he asked me to record with him in January of 1951. I agreed and was looking forward to it. I was looking forward to the new year, to moving ahead with my life and my music, and the contract with Prestige also helped my spirits. Nineteen fifty had been the worst year of my life. I figured there wasn't nowhere for me to go but up. I was already on the bottom.

Chapter 7

i came back to New York in high spirits. I didn't have my own place so I stayed with Stan Levey, the drummer, until I could get back on my feet. Then, in the middle of January 1951, around the seventeenth, I played on three recording sessions: one with Bird for Verve Records early in the day, then on my own date for Prestige, and then on a date for Sonny Rollins. On Bird's date, I think we had Bird, myself, Walter Bishop on piano, a guy named Teddy Kotick on bass, and Max Roach on drums. Bird was in good form that day and played great. So did everyone else. The music had a Latin base and was interesting. It was one of the most organized sessions I'd ever seen Bird put together. Everything went smoothly, although, as usual, there wasn't a lot of rehearsing. I remember thinking that things seemed like they were going well for Bird. He seemed happy, and that was a good sign.

After I finished Bird's session, I went over to record my first date as a leader for Prestige. I hired Sonny Rollins, Bennie Green, John Lewis, Percy Heath, and Roy Haynes for the date. Bob Weinstock, the producer, didn't like the idea of my using Sonny because he didn't think he was ready, but I talked him into it and even convinced him that he should give Sonny his own record date, and he did on that same day.

I didn't play well on this date because I was tired from playing the sessions with Bird. I remember that day being a cold and mushy day, a day when snow can't seem to decide if it wants to be snow; a fucked-up, raw day. I had started to shoot heroin again and so my body and chops weren't in the best shape. But I think everyone else played well—especially Sonny on a couple of tracks. Bob Weinstock knew I was a junkie, but he was willing to take a chance that I would eventually come around.

At Sonny's session John Lewis had to leave so I ended up playing piano. Everybody else on that date was the same as on my session. After it was all over, everybody teased me about playing the piano better than I had played the trumpet on my own date. I think Sonny recorded one tune that time and I think I did four and that was it. I remember feeling good when everything was over. I was back in New York and playing again and had a contract to do two more records. And I remember thinking, as Sonny and I were on our way uptown through the slush to buy some heroin, "If only I could kick this habit, then things might be all right." But I was a long way from kicking the habit and deep down, I knew it.

To make ends meet and support my habit I started transcribing music from records for lead sheets, the first eight bars of a melody, for twenty-five or thirty dollars. It was easy work and I could do a job in a couple of hours. I'd get the money and go uptown and get off. But soon even this wasn't enough to keep my habit satisfied. My health was poor and there weren't that many gigs coming where I could play regularly; my embouchure was in bad shape. A trumpet is a very demanding instrument to play. You have to keep in pretty good physical shape to play it well. Also, where I used to be a fashion-plate dresser, now I was wearing anything that would cover my body. I was beginning to think I was real cool before all this heroin shit came down on me, wearing my marcel processed hair down to my shoulders. Shit, couldn't nobody tell me I wasn't slick. But when my heroin habit started to get the best of me, all that fell apart— including my attitude—and I couldn't even support my hair being fried, done up, because I didn't have no extra money to do it. After a while I started looking bad about the head, hair all frazzled and shit, sticking out from my head like needles. I looked like a porcupine who somebody had made mad. That five dollars it used to cost me to get my hair done I just put in my arm to feed the monster. I was shooting heroin in my veins so that the monster inside wouldn't get hungry and make me sick. In 1951, I wasn't ready to admit to myself that I was sick, so I kept on sliding down that long, dark, ice-slicked road into deeper addiction.

A few days after I recorded for Prestige, I went back in the studio to record with the 1951 *Metronome All Stars* for Capitol Records. The session was nothing to write home about. It was professional-sounding and that was it; didn't no earth-breaking shit happen. I remember that they were pushing Lennie Tristano and that we recorded some tunes by George Shearing. Altogether, it was only a few minutes of music that was tightly structured and arranged. Nothing could come out of an atmosphere like that. It was just publicity bullshit, trying to push white musicians with me and Max—the only blacks among eleven musicians—being used as tokens. It didn't really matter, except that white musicians were making most of the money. Everybody knew where the action was really at, and that was with black musicians. I picked up my money and went uptown to cop.

About a month or so later I took my band into Birdland. I had Sonny Rollins, Kenny Drew, Art Blakey, Percy Heath, and Jackie McLean. Bud Powell had told me that I ought to use Jackie because he knew Jackie and was high on him. I had seen Jackie around because he came from Sugar Hill up in Harlem. He knew Sonny Rollins well because they came from the same neighborhood, around Edgecombe Avenue. Jackie wasn't even twenty when he made that Birdland gig. But he could already play his ass off. That first night, he was so scared and high that after playing about seven or eight bars of his solo, he suddenly ran off the stage and out the back door. Now, the rhythm section is still playing, and the crowd's out there with their mouths open, wondering what the fuck was going on. I left the bandstand to go back and see what happened to Jackie, although in the back of my head I'm thinking that he might have become sick from heroin, because I already knew that Jackie was using. Oscar Goodstein, the owner of Birdland, follows me outside. There's Jackie puking his brains out into a garbage can, vomit all over his mouth. I asked him if he was all right and he nodded his head that he was. I told him to wipe off his horn and come on back and play. We could hear the rhythm section still walking. Oscar's standing there with this disgusted look all over his face and says to Jackie as he's passing him, "Here kid, wipe your face," and he threw him this towel and turned and walked back into the club ahead of us. Jackie went back in there and played his ass off. I mean he was something that night.

After the gig that night, I went out to Long Island where I was now staying with Stan Levey and thought about Jackie. The next day I called and asked him to come out and go over some tunes with me, so he did. After that, I asked him to join a band I was putting together —Art Blakey, Sonny Rollins, Percy Heath, and Walter Bishop—and then we became roommates off and on for about two or three years.

Me and Jackie started hanging out a lot together, shooting dope and going to the movies on 42nd Street. Mostly, now after I moved out of Stan Levey's, I was staying in and out of hotels with bitches who were giving me what I needed to support my habit. I was staying at the University Hotel down on 20th Street and in and out of the Hotel America on 48th Street. Jackie and I used to ride the subway higher than a motherfucker, laughing at the corny shoes and clothes people was wearing. We'd just look at somebody and if we thought they looked funny, we'd just crack up. Jackie was a funny guy, man, and he used to like to play pranks on people. I would stay with him and his girlfriend sometimes, down on 21st Street, when I was too high to leave. We'd go up to Stillman's Gym and watch the boxers train, but mostly we were running partners, buying and shooting up dope. I was twenty-four going on twenty-five when Jackie and I hooked up and had already done a lot of things. He was only nineteen and hadn't been nowhere. I already had a reputation, so Jackie looked up to me, treated me with great respect, like an elder.

I was hanging with Sonny Rollins too. I remember we used to hang out at a place uptown called Bell's ("Sippin' at Bell's" is a tune I wrote about that bar). It was a classy bar, on Broadway in the 140s, and everyone that came there was clean. Or we would hang out at Sonny's apartment over on Edgecombe. We would get high and look at that beautiful view he had of that park across from where he lived. You could see Yankee Stadium from there.

If we didn't hang out over Sonny's house, or Walter Bishop's, we'd go to Jackie's parents' (I liked Jackie's mother and father) or we'd sit out in the little square down on St. Nicholas and 149th or 150th Street—especially in the summertime. It would be me, Jackie, Sonny, Kenny Drew, Walter Bishop, and Art Taylor.

I loved it in Harlem—hanging out in the clubs, in the park on 155th and St. Nicholas, going swimming in the Colonial Pool on Bradhurst around 145th Street with Max. We were all getting high and there were so many places to do it, even at Art Taylor's house. His mother, a very nice lady that I liked a lot, worked all day and so we could just have the run of the house.

After we got down, we might go by Bud Powell's and sit and listen to him play. There he'd be, not saying a word, but with that big sweet smile all over his face. We might go to Sugar Ray Robinson's night-club. That place was jumping too, not to mention Small's Paradise, Lucky's, and all the rest of them hip clubs. So I was spending a lot of time in Harlem, chasing down that heroin. Heroin was my girlfriend.

After I did the Birdland gig, I think I recorded with Lee Konitz, as a sideman, for Prestige. Max Roach was on that date and George Russell and some other guys I have forgotten. We did some of George's compositions and arrangements; he was always a very interesting composer. The playing as I remember it was good, but not startling. For me it was just another job to get some money. The club owners blacklisted me; the only person who would hire me more than once was Oscar Goodstein, at Birdland.

I played Birdland in June with J. J. Johnson, Sonny Rollins, Kenny Drew, Tommy Potter, and Art Blakey. I think they recorded a Sat-urday session on their regular Saturday-night broadcast. Everyone played well on this date, though I know my chops were still in bad shape. Then, in September, me and Eddie "Lockjaw" Davis took a band into Birdland that had Charlie Mingus, Art Blakey, Billy Taylor, and a tenor saxophonist named George "Big Nick" Nicholas. The music was good. I played better than I had been playing.

I always loved the way Lockjaw played, ever since I first heard him up at Minton's. He had such an energetic style. If you were going to play again with Lockjaw, then you'd better not be bullshitting be-cause he would embarrass you, just like Big Nick would. Nick never got a big reputation, but everybody back on the scene then knew he could play his ass off; I never knew why Nick didn't get any wider recognition. With all this energy around me, I probably played harder on these sets than I had in a long time. See, Lockjaw was one of the elders of the music scene. Same thing with Big Nick, who used to play with Dizzy and lead a great house band in Harlem at Small's Paradise Club. He used to play regularly with Monk and Bird there. So I couldn't be fucking around with these guys, because they would just blow your ass up out of the club if you was half-stepping. As high as I was, I still knew that when I played with guys like that I had a reputation to protect. So on this gig I practiced and came out playing as hard as I could.

It was good to play with Mingus again. He had been hanging around New York doing nothing ever since he quit Red Norvo's trio because he wasn't getting no billing. He was getting a few jobs here and there, and I thought that playing Birdland might help him get his thing together. He was a great bass player. But he was hard to get along with, especially about music, because he had his own definite ideas about what was good and what was bad, and he didn't mind telling anybody what he had on his mind. In that way, we were a lot alike. Our musical ideas were different sometimes. But I was glad to play with him again because he was always an inventive, hard driving, imaginative musician.

My second date with Prestige in 1951 was coming up in October, and I wanted to make a better record than I did the first time around. Plus Prestige was going to record me using a new technology they were calling "microgroove." Bob Weinstock told me that it would allow me to grow outside the three-minute time limit we were allowed on 78 rpm records. We could stretch out our solos like we played them live in clubs. I was going to be one of the first jazz artists to make 33⅓ rpm recordings, which until then had been used exclusively for live performances, and I was excited about the freedom this new technology would give me. I had gotten tired of that three-minute lockstep that the 78s had put musicians in. There wasn't any room for really free improvisation; you had to get in your solo real quick and then get out. Bob told me that Ira Gitler was going to be the producer on the album. I got Sonny Rollins, Art Blakey, Tommy Potter, Walter Bishop, and Jackie McLean for the date; it was Jackie's recording debut.

This was the set where I recorded my best work in a long time. I had been practicing and I rehearsed the band, so everybody was familiar with the material and arrangements. Sonny played his ass off on this album and so did Jackie McLean. That album was called the *Miles Davis All Stars;* sometimes it was just called *Dig.* We did "My Old Flame," "It's Only a Paper Moon," "Out of the Blue," and "Conception" on this album. Mingus had come with me to the studio with his bass; he played a few things in the background on "Conception." He didn't get listed on the album because of his exclusive contract with Verve. Charlie Parker came by and sat in the engineer's booth. Since this was Jackie McLean's first recording, he was already nervous about that, but when he saw Bird it just flipped him out. Bird was his idol, so he kept going over to Bird and asking him what he was doing there, and Bird kept telling him that he was just hanging out and listening. Man, Jackie must have asked Bird that a thousand times. But Bird understood and so he was cool. Jackie wanted Bird to leave so that he could relax. But Bird kept telling him how good he sounded and encouraging him like that. After a while Jackie relaxed and played his ass off.

I liked what I played on *Dig,* because my sound was really becoming my own thing. I wasn't sounding like nobody else, and I was getting my tone back—especially on "My Old Flame," which calls for a very melodic approach. I also remembered liking what I did on "It's Only a Paper Moon" and "Blueing." The new long-playing format was made to order for the way I played. But then when we left the recording studio, the same old bullshit was out there waiting for me.

I was in a deep fog, high all the time and pimping women for money to support my habit through the rest of 1951 and the early part of 1952. At one time, I had a whole stable of bitches out on the street for me. I was still living in and out of hotels. But it wasn't like people thought it was; these women wanted someone to be with and they liked being with me. I took them to dinner and shit like that. We'd get down on the sex thing, too, but that wasn't much, because heroin takes away your sex drive. I just treated the prostitutes like they were like anybody else. I respected them and they would give me money to get off in return. The women thought I was handsome and for the first time in my life, I began to think I was, too. We were more like a family than anything. But even the money they were giving me wasn't enough. I still found myself coming up short.

By 1952 I knew I had to try to do something to get off drugs. I had always loved boxing, so I thought that maybe I could get into that. If I trained every day, then maybe I could do something about seriously kicking my habit. I had already met Bobby McQuillen, who was a trainer at Gleason's Gym in midtown Manhattan. When I'd go there, he and I would sit around and talk about boxing. He'd been a top welterweight fighter until he killed a guy in the ring and then he quit and started coaching and training fighters. One day—I think this was early in 1952—I asked him if he would train me. He said he would think about it. I went to a fight in Madison Square Garden and afterwards I went back to Bobby's fighter's dressing room to see if Bobby was going to train me or not. Bobby looked at me with this real disgusted look and told me that he wasn't going to be training nobody that had a drug habit. So I told him that I didn't have a drug habit— and me standing there higher than a motherfucker, almost nodding I was so high. He told me that I couldn't fool him and that I should go back to St. Louis and try to kick my habit. Then he told me to get out of the dressing room and go and get myself together.

Nobody had ever talked to me like that before, and especially not about my using drugs. Man, Bobby made me feel like I was about one foot tall. I was always around musicians who either used drugs or ones who didn't but who didn't say nothing about those who did. So to hear that shit like that was something else, man.

After Bobby told me that, in a moment of clarity, I called my father and told him to come and get me. Then I hung up the phone and went back to shooting drugs.

One night I was playing the Downbeat Club. I had Jackie McLean on alto sax, Jimmy Heath on tenor sax, his brother Percy Heath on bass, Gil Coggins on piano, and Art Blakey on drums. I looked out at the audience and there was my father—standing there, in a raincoat—looking at me. I knew I was looking bad, because I owed people money, and I was playing with borrowed trumpets. I think I had borrowed Art Farmer's that night. The club owner had a lot of pawn tickets that I had given him as collateral when I borrowed money. I was in bad shape and knew it. So did my father. He was looking at me with this disgusted look that made me feel like I was a piece of shit. I walked over to Jackie and said, "That's my father down there, man. So finish out the set while I go have a little talk with him." Jackie said, "Okay," looking at me funny as hell. I must have been looking a little weird.

I left the stage and my father followed me to the coat room. The owner came in, too. My father looked me straight in the eye and told me how terrible I looked and that I was going back to East St. Louis with him that night. The owner told my father that I had to finish out the week, but my father said I wasn't finishing out anything, that he would have to get someone else to take my place. Me and the owner agreed on J. J. Johnson, who I called right then and who agreed to substitute for me on trombone.

Then the owner brought up the matter of the pawn tickets, and my father wrote him out a check and turned to me and told me to get my things. I said, "Okay," but that I had to go back out and tell the band what was happening. He said he would wait for me.

After the set was over, I pulled Jackie McLean to one side and told him J. J. was taking my place and was going to finish out the week. "I'll call you when I'm coming back, but my old man came to get me and I can't do nothing but go with him." Jackie wished me good luck and me and my father caught a train to East St. Louis. I felt like a little boy again going with his daddy. I had never felt like that before and probably haven't felt like that since.

On the way home I told him that I was going to give up dope and that all I needed was a little rest and that it would be good to be at home where there wasn't much dope around. My father was living in Millstadt, Illinois, where he had his farm and he had bought a place over in St. Louis. I stayed on the farm for a little while, riding horses and shit, just trying to relax. But that shit got boring quick, plus I started to get sick because my jones started to come down on me. So I hooked up with some people who knew where to buy heroin. Before I knew it, I was shooting up again and borrowing money from my father to support my habit, twenty, thirty dollars at a time.

About this time, I hooked up with Jimmy Forrest, who was a hell of a tenor saxophonist from St. Louis. He was also a junkie and knew where the best shit was. Me and Jimmy started playing a lot at a club out on Delmar, in St. Louis, called the Barrelhouse. Mostly white people came out to this club and that was where I met this young, fine, rich white girl whose parents owned a shoe company. She liked me a lot and she had a lot of money.

One day I felt myself getting sick, so I went to my father's office to ask him for some more money. He told me he wasn't going to give it to me, that my sister, Dorothy, had told him that I wasn't doing nothing with it but shooting it all up. At first my father didn't want to believe that I was still shooting drugs, because I had told him that I had stopped, but after Dorothy told him that I was lying, he told me he wasn't giving me no more money.

When my father told me that, I just lost it, man, and started cursing him out, calling him all kinds of names and shit. That was the first time in my life that I had done something like that. And although something deep inside me was telling me not to do it, that need to get heroin was stronger than the fear of cursing my father out. He just let me curse him out without doing or saying nothing. The people in his office were all sitting there shocked with their mouths hanging open. I was cursing so hard and so loud that I didn't even notice that he had made a phone call. Before I knew it, these two big black motherfuckers had done come in and grabbed me and took me off to a jail in Belleville, Illinois, where I stayed for a week, madder and sicker than a motherfucker, throwing up all the time. I felt like I was dying. But I didn't die and I think this was the first time that I thought to myself that I could kick this habit cold turkey; all I had to do was make up my mind to do it.

Because my father was a sheriff in East St. Louis, he had arranged for my arrest not to be official so it didn't show up on my arrest record. I learned a lot about stealing and picking pockets from all them criminals that they had in there. I even had a fight with this guy who kept fucking with me. So I just knocked him right out and then I got some respect after that. But then, man, when they found out that I was Miles Davis, because a lot of them had listened to my music, they respected me a *lot*. After that, they didn't bother me with no kind of stupid bullshit. Then, I got out. The first thing I did when I got out was run and get high. But my father had decided he was going to do something else about my problem; he was going to take me down to the federal prison for drug addiction and have me check myself in for rehabilitation. When I had cursed him out, he thought that I had lost my mind and that I really needed help. And at that moment, I agreed with him.

We drove down to Lexington, Kentucky, in my father's new Cadillac with his second wife, Josephine (Hanes was her maiden name). I had told my father that I would go into the rehabilitation program because I was doing real bad and also because I didn't want to disappoint him; I thought that I had already disappointed him enough. I figured that this might be a way to kick the habit, which I was getting tired of, and to please my father, too. But I was really getting sick of heroin by this time. I hadn't used it but one time since I had gotten out of jail, so maybe I felt that now was the time to try and beat it.

When we got to Lexington, I saw that I had to volunteer myself in order to get in, since I hadn't been busted for no criminal offense. But I couldn't do it, *couldn't* and *wouldn't* sign myself into no prison, rehabilitation or not; shit, I wasn't going to *volunteer* myself into no joint. I was never in love with being in jail and because I hadn't shot dope for almost two weeks now, maybe I thought that I had already kicked my habit. (Some musicians who were in Lexington then later told me that they heard through the prison grapevine that I was there to sign myself in and so some of them had come down to greet me before they found out that I hadn't checked myself in.) I told myself now that I was doing this mainly to satisfy my father, not myself. I convinced him that I was all right, so he gave me some money. He didn't even hold it against me that I had cursed him out like that—at least he never said anything else about it to me—because he knew I was sick. But I knew he was concerned when I didn't check myself into Lexington that time—though he didn't say nothing

—because I could see the worry in his face when we said goodbye. He wished me luck, and he and his wife drove on over to Louisville to see her father. I came on back to New York.

On the way back to New York, I called Jackie McLean and told him that I was coming. I had already talked to Oscar Goodstein at Birdland, and he gave me a date to play, so I needed to put together a group. I wanted Jackie and Sonny Rollins in the band, but Jackie told me that Sonny was in jail, busted for drugs or something. Anyway, I told Jackie that I had Connie Kay on drums, but that I needed a piano player and a bass player to open with me at Birdland. Jackie brought Gil Coggins and Connie Henry into the band for that gig. Jackie said I could stay with him, and as soon as I got back to New York, I went back to shooting drugs again; not all at once, but kind of gradually, and before I knew it I was back into the shit again. I had fooled myself into thinking I had kicked my habit by doing just a little bit at first. Then I got mad at myself for not checking into Lexington. Still, I was happy to be in New York, because in the back of my head I knew that I had to either kick my habit or die, and since I wasn't ready to die, I figured that sooner or later I would kick my habit, though I didn't know when. Going cold turkey in jail back home had given me the confidence that I could do it when I set my mind to it. But setting my mind to doing it was a bigger thing than I could have ever imagined.

Back in New York, Symphony Sid was putting together a concert tour and asked me if I would join it. I said yes, because I definitely needed the money. Also I was opening at Birdland in May with the group Jackie McLean helped me put together: me, Jackie, Connie Kay on drums, Connie Henry on bass, Gil Coggins on piano, and a cat named Don Elliott on mellophone.

We didn't have no time to rehearse, since I had just got back, and I think the playing showed that. But I remember Bird was in the audience one night and he kept applauding everything that Jackie played, even if it was wrong, which wasn't often because Jackie was playing his ass off during this engagement. One time, Bird ran over and kissed Jackie on the neck or on the cheek after we had finished a set. But all through this, Bird didn't say nothing to me, so I guess I might have gotten upset, but I don't think I did. It just struck me as kind of strange because I hadn't seen Bird act like that before. I was wondering if he was fucked up or something, because when he was doing all this applauding for Jackie, he was one of the only ones doing it. Jackie was playing good, but he wasn't playing *that* moth-erfucking good. I kept wondering why Bird was doing it and whether he was trying to psych me out or trying to make me look bad by cheering for Jackie and ignoring me. But Bird applauding Jackie like that made a whole lot of critics start paying more attention to what Jackie was playing. That particular night really put Jackie on the musical map.

Although Jackie could play his ass off, he still had a problem with his discipline and learning to play certain tunes. A little while after the Birdland gig, we had a real big argument in the recording studio over the way he *wasn't* playing "Yesterdays," or "Wouldn't You." Jackie had a lot of natural ability, but he was lazy as a motherfucker back then. I would tell him to play a certain tune, and he would tell me he "didn't know it."

"What do you mean you don't know it? Learn it," I would say.

So he would tell me some shit about the tunes being from another time period, and that he was a "young guy" and he didn't see why he had to learn "all that old shit."

"Man," I said, "music has no periods; music is music. I like this tune, this is *my* band, you're in my band, I'm playing this tune, so you learn it and learn *all* the tunes, whether you like them or not. Learn them."

One particular day in 1952 I was doing my first recording for Alfred Lion's Blue Note label (my deal with Prestige wasn't exclu-sive). Gil Coggins played piano that session; J. J. Johnson, trombone; Oscar Pettiford, bass; Kenny Clarke—who had come over from Paris —was on drums; and Jackie was on alto. I really thought people played good on that album; I thought I played well also. I think we recorded "Woody 'n' You," Jackie's "Donna" (which was called "Dig" on the other album and was credited as my tune), "Dear Old Stockholm," "Chance It," "Yesterdays," and "How Deep Is the Ocean." Jackie pulled his same shit on me while we were recording "Yesterdays." I just blew the fuck up and cursed Jackie out so cold I thought he was going to cry. He never played it right so I just told him to lay out on that tune; that's the reason he wasn't on that tune on that album. I think this was the only album I made in 1952.

One time we were down in Philadelphia playing a club, me and Jackie, Art Blakey, Percy Heath, and, I think, Hank Jones on piano. Anyway, in walks Duke Ellington, Paul Quinechette, Johnny Hodges, and some other members of Duke's band. I said to myself, "Man, we gotta hit it now." So I called out "Yesterdays." I start the melody with Jackie, and then I played a solo and motioned for him to play a solo. Now, usually on "Yesterdays" I didn't let Jackie play, but he had promised me again that he was going to learn it. I wanted to see if he had kept his word.

He started playing around with the melody and fucked it up again, right? After the set was over and I'm introducing everybody in the band over the microphone—I used to do that shit back in the real old days—when I get to Jackie I said, "Ladies and gentlemen, Jackie McLean, and I don't know *how* he got his union card, since he never does know how to play 'Yesterdays.' " Well, the audience didn't know whether I was joking or not, whether to applaud for Jackie or to boo the motherfucker. After the set, Jackie runs up to me in the alley behind the club where Art and I were getting high and says, "Miles, that wasn't right, man, embarrassing me like that in front of Duke, man, who is my fucking musical daddy, you motherfucker!" He was crying!

So I said to him, "Fuck you, Jackie, you ain't nothing but a big, fucking baby! Always talking about some shit that you're a young cat and so you can't learn that old music. Fuck that and you too! I told you, music is music. So you'd better learn your music or you ain't gonna be in my fucking band for much longer, you hear me? Learn the music that's required of you in order to play. You talking about Duke being out in the audience and that I embarrassed you when I introduced you like that. Well, motherfucker, you embarrassed *yourself* when you didn't play 'Yesterdays' right. Man, you don't think Duke Ellington knows how that tune goes? Are you crazy? I didn't embarrass you, you embarrassed your motherfucking self! Now, fuck all that crying and let's go back to the hotel."

Jackie just got quiet, then I told him a true story about how, when I was in B's band that first time, I had to run errands for B while he'd be sitting with some beautiful woman. Told Jackie how B would call out, "Where's Miles!" and make me go get his suits, or make sure his shoes were shined or send me out to get him some cigarettes; how B used to make me sit on a Coke box when I first joined the trumpet section. And all because he was the bandleader and I was the youngest guy in the band, a kid, and how this was making me pay some dues because he was the leader and could do this kind of shit to me. I told Jackie, "So don't be telling me nothing about what I say *to* you or *about* you, man, because you ain't even started paying no dues yet. You're just a spoiled brat and you're gonna learn how to play this music or you're gonna get the fuck out of my band."

He was stunned, but he didn't say nothing. I think if Jackie *had* said something right then I would have kicked his motherfucking ass, because I was telling him some shit that was going to help not hurt him.

Later, when Jackie was out of the band, every time that I would go to see him play he would play a couple of them older tunes, especially "Yesterdays." After the set he would come up to me and ask me how he did on them. By then he had become a master and could play the fuck out of anything! So I'd tell him, "You did all right for a young man," and he'd laugh his ass off. After a while, when they asked him where he studied music, he'd tell them, "I studied at the University of Miles Davis." I thought that said it.

Sometime that year, I used John Coltrane as a replacement for Jackie. I wanted to use two tenors and an alto, but I couldn't pay three horns. So I used Sonny Rollins and Coltrane on tenors at a gig I had at the Audubon Ballroom (where Malcolm X was later killed). I remember Jackie getting nervous when I told him I was using Trane instead of him: he thought I was firing him. But I just couldn't pay three horns and after I explained to him it was only for one night, he was cool. But Sonny was awesome that night, scared the shit out of Trane, just like Trane would do to him a few years later.

After those incidents, though, me and Jackie's relationship wasn't what it had been. Me talking to him like I had when I cursed him out put a strain on our friendship, so we kind of drifted apart and he left the band, although we played together some after these incidents.

Jackie introduced me to a lot of good players, like Gil Coggins. He was a hell of a piano player. But he decided to go into real estate because he didn't really like the musician's lifestyle and the money wasn't coming in regular enough back in those days. Gil was a real nice, middle-class dude and he was thinking about security. But I liked the way he played and if he had stayed at it I think he would have been one of the best piano players around. When Jackie first introduced me to him I didn't dig him. Then he played behind me on "Yesterdays" and just knocked me out. I think I met Gil when I had just come back from home that time my father took me to Lexington. Later, Jackie introduced me to the bassist Paul Chambers and the drummer Tony Williams. I think I also met the drummer Art Taylor through either Jackie or Sonny Rollins, but I think it was Jackie. I met a lot of the uptown Harlem Sugar Hill connection through both Jackie and Sonny. And all them Sugar Hill musicians could really play back in those days. They were super hip.

Except for a few gigs here and there, I spent the rest of my time running down drugs. Nineteen fifty-two was another terrible year, and the years seemed like they was getting worse after that high point of 1949. I also began for the first time to doubt myself, my own ability and discipline; for the first time I began to wonder if I could really make it in music, if I had the inner strength to keep it all together.

A lot of white critics kept talking about all these white jazz musicians, imitators of us, like they was some great motherfuckers and everything. Talking about Stan Getz, Dave Brubeck, Kai Winding, Lee Konitz, Lennie Tristano, and Gerry Mulligan like they was gods or something. And some of them white guys were junkies like we were, but wasn't nobody writing about that like they was writing about us. They didn't start paying attention to white guys being junkies until Stan Getz got busted trying to break into a drugstore to cop some drugs. That shit made the headlines until people forgot and went back to just talking about black musicians being junkies.

Now, I'm not saying here that these guys weren't good musicians, because they were; Gerry, Lee, Stan, Dave, Kai, Lennie, all of them were good musicians. But they didn't start nothing, and they knew it, and they weren't the best at what was being done. What bothered me more than anything was that all the critics were starting to talk about Chet Baker in Gerry Mulligan's band like he was the second coming of Jesus Christ. And him sounding just like me—worse than me even while I was a terrible junkie. Sometimes I found myself wondering if he could really play better than me and Dizzy and Clifford Brown, who was just really coming on to the scene. Now, I knew that among all the younger players, Clifford was head and shoulders above the rest, at least in my opinion he was. But Chet Baker? Man, I just couldn't see it. The critics were beginning to treat me like I was one of the old guys, you know, like I was just a memory —and a bad memory at that—and I was only twenty-six years old in 1952. And sometimes I was even thinking of myself as a has-been.

Chapter 8

We had signed on to do Symphony Sid's tour in the early summer—I think—of 1952 and the tour would be taking us to several cities. Sid's tour band had me on trumpet, Jimmy Heath—Percy's brother—on tenor, J. J. Johnson on trombone, Milt Jackson on vibes, Percy Heath on bass, and Kenny Clarke on drums. Zoot Sims couldn't make it, and so they replaced him with Jimmy Heath. I first met Jimmy when I was in Bird's band and we went to Philly back in 1948 to play the Downbeat Club. Jimmy used to loan Bird his horn, because Bird's was in the pawnshop, then wait until the gig was over and pick it up since he couldn't trust Bird not to pawn it. Bird would catch the train back to New York, because Philly was always hard on junkies; the police would bust a junkie in a minute.

Jimmy had small feet and he used to wear some dynamite shoes. And he could dress his ass off, too. So I would see him when I went down to Philly, where he was from. His mother loved jazz musicians. Besides Percy and Jimmy, there was Albert, or "Tootie" as all the guys in music called him, who was a drummer. The Heath brothers were a family of musicians and their mother could really cook, so a lot of musicians used to hang out at their house. Jimmy had a big band that Coltrane came out of. They was some bad motherfuckers, hip and everything.

Plus Jimmy was really into heroin, so I know me and him probably started shooting up together before he joined Symphony Sid's tour. I know he used to shoot up with Bird. I think maybe I recommended Jimmy for the band because I needed somebody else in the band that got down on heroin like me. By this time, everybody else who was in this band had quit. And with Zoot—who also got off—quitting, I was by myself.

We all felt that we should have been called something else besides The Symphony Sid All Stars, but there wasn't nothing we could do about it if we wanted our money. Because of his radio broadcast from Birdland, Sid was more of a celebrity than we were, a voice in the night coming into people's homes introducing all the great music that was changing people's lives. So he was famous and everyone thought he had discovered all of us, that *he* was the reason that this music existed. Now I will admit that *white* people might have come out to see the show because a white man like him was involved in it. But *black* people came to see *us* play and the majority of shows were for black people. He was paying us maybe $250, $300 a week, which was a good sum back in those days. But he was making two or three times that much just for his name and for saying a few words. So it really pissed everyone off.

We played Atlantic City. I remember on that gig we didn't have a piano player because somehow Milt's vibes were taking up that spot, so it was an interesting musical setup. When somebody *did* want a piano, either I or one of the other guys played piano behind whoever wanted it, so it was a learning experience for everyone. If nobody wanted piano then whoever was playing could just stroll, which meant playing whatever you wanted with only drum and bass behind you and that empty spot where the piano ordinarily would be. It was like walking down the street on a bright, sunny day without nobody or anything being in your way. That's what *I* meant by strolling; also, using your own imagination. Playing without the piano freed up the music. I found out on this tour that sometimes a piano got in the way, that you didn't need it when you wanted to get a looser, freer sound.

Next we played the Apollo Theatre on 125th Street in Harlem, which was a motherfucker of a gig. Man, the place was packed with niggers who loved—I mean *loved*—what we did, what everybody played. I remember that night playing almost above myself for the first time in a long time because the crowd was so great. Man, we were up there in our processes and I had my suits out of the pawnshop, so you couldn't tell me we weren't doing it, with all those people out there cheering. I had my "do"—process—done at Rogers up on Broadway. I was clean and I was playing my ass off at the Apollo Theatre with a group of great musicians. I was high and was going to get paid some decent money, so what else could a nigger want?

Then we went out on the road for real, to places like Cleveland, the Graystone Ballroom in Detroit, and so on, and that's when things started to go bad, because it was hard for me and Jimmy to make connections for the heroin we needed. These weren't like concerts, but more like dances, with Sid introducing the whole show. That's all he did besides collect the money and pay us.

Out in the Midwest we couldn't get no dope, or we had a hard time finding it. Sometimes we were late getting to gigs and the rest of the band would have to start without us. This would happen at intermission too. Me and Jimmy would find someone in the audience who was holding and so we'd run off back to the hotel room to get down and be late getting back. After a while, the other guys in the band started to get mad and started telling us to get our act together. Jimmy's brother, Percy, was especially giving him a hard time. But they would come down on me collectively. They were sick and tired of covering for me and Jimmy. The guys who were especially on my back were Kenny, Milt, and Percy.

Also, a lot of bullshit built up between Sid and all the musicians. In Buffalo, Sid didn't show up and so we split his $200 among ourselves. He took us to the union when we wouldn't give him the money and he lost. Then one time we found out when we were playing Chicago that Sid had sold the package for $2,000 and told us he had gotten $700. Milt Jackson overheard the conversation between Sid and the club owner. Now Sid's the booking agent for the show, so he gets the agent's fee, which was five or ten percent back then, plus he's the announcer—and, he thought, star—of the show, so he gets that money, too. Here he's taking all of that *and all* of the $1,300, the difference between $700 and $2,000. All of that is going in his pocket.

Meanwhile, *we* were making about $500 a show to split between six guys and he's making $200 a show just to do the announcing and walk around and act important and shit. So when we confront him with it, he denies it and gets mad and tells us we are ungrateful. Now ain't that just like a white man? By the time we had gotten back to New York, everybody was really fed up with Sid's conniving bullshit. Didn't nobody hate him; we just didn't want to be around him.

When the tour was ending in New York, Sid owed J. J. fifty dollars, and J. J. asked him for it. Sid fluffed him off. Sid was an arrogant motherfucker. So J. J. just up and knocked Sid's false teeth out of his mouth; They went skipping and sliding across the floor. I didn't see it happen, but Milt told me what had gone down when we came walking in high and late. Then Sid called in these gangsters who came down to the club to kick J. J.'s ass, maybe kill him. We were standing there when they all walked in like they were right out of a gangster movie. Big hats, cigars, black suits and shit and looking like they could kill a brick. They asked me if I was with J. J. and I said that if anything was going to happen to J then *I* was in it, too. All the guys joined in behind J. Sid, who was wrong in the first place, cooled everything out and gave J the money, but it was kind of scary before that.

By this time I was hanging out with a white girl named Susan Garvin, who was blond, had big, nice breasts, and looked like Kim Novak. I later wrote "Lazy Susan" for her. She was good to me because she kept me with some money and she was a good woman. She loved me. I liked her a lot, too, but because of my habit we didn't have a lot of sex, although when we did I enjoyed being with her. I had other girls, too, that gave me money, a whole stable of them. But Susan was who I was with most of the time. I was also seeing this same rich white girl who I'd met in St. Louis; she had come up to New York to check me out. Let's call her "Alice," because she's still alive and I don't want to cause her trouble; plus she's married. They were both fine and were both giving me money. But I used to like Susan a lot and she would come around to the clubs with me.

Besides this, wasn't too much happening for me in 1952. I was still trying to get my life together. But there is one story that came out around that time that Cecil Taylor says happened but I can't remember no shit like that ever happening. The story is about Joe Gordon, a real fine trumpet player who was from Boston, where Cecil Taylor's from. Now, Cecil says that Joe came to Birdland one night to sit in with me and that after he sat in, that I just walked off the bandstand—because he played so good—until Bird ran up to me and told me, "Man, you're Miles Davis; you can't let nobody do that to you." Supposedly I then went back up on the bandstand and just stood around. Somebody wrote that this guy fucked me up only because I was looking at him from my own "distorted perspective in 1952." I really can't remember nothing like that ever happening to me. Maybe it did, but I don't think so. (Joe Gordon died in a fire in 1963 and never did nothing much but once one time with Thelonious Monk on one of his albums. So he can't verify this story, and the other guy, Cecil Taylor, has always hated me since I said he couldn't play, so he might say anything to get back at me.)

Nineteen fifty-three began all right with me making a record for Prestige with Sonny Rollins (who had gotten out of jail), Bird (who appeared on the album as "Charlie Chan"), Walter Bishop, Percy Heath, and Philly Joe Jones on drums (who I was hanging with a lot at the time). Bird had an exclusive contract with Mercury (I think he had left Verve by then), so he had to use a pseudonym on record. Bird had given up shooting heroin because since Red Rodney had been busted and sent back to prison at Lexington, Bird thought the police were watching him. In place of his normal big dosages of heroin, now he was drinking an enormous amount of alcohol. I remember him drinking a quart of vodka at the rehearsal, so by the time the engineer was running the tape for the session, Bird was fucked up out of his mind.

It was like having *two* leaders at the session. Bird treated me like I was his son, or a member of *his* band. But this was *my* date and so I had to get him straight. It was difficult, because he was always on my back about one thing or another. I got so angry with him that I told him off, told him that I had never done that to him on one of his recording sessions. Told him that I had always been professional on his shit. And do you know what that motherfucker said to me? He told me some shit like, "All right, Lily Pons . . . to produce beauty, we must suffer pain—from the oyster comes the pearl." He said that to me in that fucked-up, fake British accent. Then, the motherfucker fell asleep. I got so mad all over again that I started fucking up. Ira Gitler, who was producing the record for Bob Weinstock, came out of the booth and told me *I* wasn't playing shit. At this point, I was so fed up that I started packing up my horn to leave when Bird said to me, "Miles, what are you doing?" So I told him what Ira had said, and Bird said, "Ah, come on Miles, let's play some music." And so we played some real good stuff after that.

I think we made that record in January 1953. I do know that a little while after that, I cut another record for Prestige with Al Cohn and Zoot Sims on tenors, a cat named Sonny Truitt on trombone, John Lewis on piano, Leonard Gaskin on bass, and Kenny Clarke on drums. Bob Weinstock had gotten real upset over what happened on that last album with Bird, so he put together a group of more "respectable" musicians, at least in the studio; guys who wouldn't be getting high and acting the fool. But me and Zoot were the junkies in that band and we got off before we recorded that day. The date was all right in the end, because everybody played pretty well. Nobody hardly solos on the album—I think I had one and John Lewis had one; the album was full of ensemble playing. I was playing better now than I had for a while.

A little while after this album I made another one for Blue Note with J. J., Jimmy Heath on tenor, Gil Coggins on piano, Percy Heath on bass, and Art Blakey on drums. I remember that date because besides the music that we played, me and Jimmy Heath were trying to figure out how we could buy some heroin from Elmo Hope, the piano player, who was living over on 46th Street and doing a little dealing. We were recording in the neighborhood and wanted to buy some heroin to get high before recording. Jimmy and I were getting sick because we had to feed our hungry monsters. We told Alfred Lion, the producer and owner of Blue Note, that Jimmy had to get some reeds for his horn. Then I told Alfred that I had to go with Jimmy to help him carry the box of reeds back. Now, man, you know a box of reeds ain't no bigger than a bar of soap, and you know you don't need two guys to carry something that small. I don't know whether Alfred believed us or just went along with us. So we were higher than a motherfucker when we made that record. Art Blakey was high, too, but after that shit that went down in Los Angeles with Art and me getting busted and him telling on me, I never got high with Art again.

We cut one of Jimmy Heath's tunes called "CTA," the initials of this fine half-Chinese and half-black woman he was going with named Connie Theresa Ann. I remember one time me and Jimmy and Philly Joe played a job in Philly at Reynolds Hall—I had Susan, who was white and fine, Jimmy had Connie, and Philly Joe had this fine Puerto Rican girl. They was all fine and everybody at the gig was knocked out by these girls. We used to call them the "United Nations Girls."

I did one more recording in 1953, and I did another when they made a recording of a job I had at Birdland substituting for Dizzy in his band. I did two nights at Birdland and made the record in between those nights, my chops were pretty good around this time because I was playing regularly. The record date was with a quartet —me, Max Roach, John Lewis, and Percy Heath; we cut the record for Prestige. I had a chance to stretch out my own playing for this date because I was the main soloist. Plus Charlie Mingus played piano on one tune, "Smooch," I think it was. Everyone played well on this album.

But it was the dates at Birdland that made me mad, not because of the musicians in the band, who were really fine, but because of this singer named Joe Carroll, who always played the fool. I love Dizzy, but I hated that clowning shit he used to do for all them white folks. But that was *his* business because it was *his* band. But when I had to watch Joe Carroll them two nights, man, that shit just made me sick to my stomach. But I needed the money and I would do anything for Dizzy. I decided right then and there that I wasn't never going to be part of no bullshit like that. When people came to hear me, they were going to be coming to hear my music, only.

My habit started getting real bad. By this time, policemen routinely would make me roll up my shirtsleeves, looking for fresh needle marks. That's why guys who were junkies started shooting the dope into the veins of their legs. When them police would pull you off the stage and check you out, man, that shit was embarrassing. They were especially bad on musicians in L.A. and Philly because as soon as you said you were a musician, all the white policemen would think you were a junkie.

I was getting by with the help of women; every time I really needed something during this period I had to go to women to get it. If it hadn't been for the women who supported me, I don't know how I would have made it without stealing every day like a lot of junkies were doing. But even with their support, I did some things that I was sorry for later, like what I did to Clark Terry, or like the time I beat Dexter Gordon out of some money so that I could buy some heroin. I did things like that all the time. I pawned everything I could and sometimes pawned other people's shit and lost it—horns, clothes, jewelry—because I couldn't come up with the money to get them out of hock. I didn't have to steal and run the risk of going to jail, although after that *Down Beat* story on Art Blakey and myself, and then after Cab Calloway told that shit about us junkies to Allan Marshall that was published in *Ebony* magazine where he mentioned my name along with a bunch of others, we might as well have been in jail. Because we couldn't buy a job nowhere.

It was bad enough playing the kind of music that we played, but with a habit, it was worse. People started looking at me another way, like I was dirty or something. They looked at me with pity and horror and they hadn't looked at me that way before. They put my picture and Bird's in that article. I never forgave Allan Marshall after that, or Cab Calloway, either, for saying the shit that he said in that article. Those things cost us all pain and suffering. A lot of people he talked about never recovered from what he said, because he was very popular back then and everybody listened to what he said.

I have always thought that narcotics should be legalized so that it wouldn't be that much of a street problem. I mean, why should someone like Billie Holiday have to die from trying to kick a habit, from trying to start all over again? I think the drugs should have been made available to her, maybe through a doctor, so she wouldn't have had to hustle for it. The same thing goes for Bird.

I was standing outside of Birdland one night in the late spring or summer of 1953. It was right after, or during, the time I was taking Dizzy's place there. Now, people have said that this incident happened in California, in 1953; they got the year right but they got the wrong place. It happened in New York. I was standing outside of Birdland higher than a motherfucker, nodding and shit and wearing some dirty old clothes when Max Roach walked up and looked at me and told me that I was "looking good." Then, he put a couple of new $100 bills in my pocket, right? Now he's standing there cleaner than a motherfucker, looking like a million dollars, because he was taking care of himself.

Now Max and me were just like brothers, right? Man, that shit embarrassed me so bad that instead of taking the money and going and shooting up like I normally would, I called my father and told him that I was coming home to try to get it together again. My father was behind me all the way, so he told me to come on home and I did, catching the next bus for St. Louis.

When I went back to East St. Louis, I started seeing my girlfriend Alice again. But like it always happens, pretty soon I started getting bored out of my brain and started shooting dope again. Not a lot, but enough to make me worried. In late August or early September 1953, Max Roach called from New York or Chicago and told me that he was driving to Los Angeles with Charlie Mingus to take Shelly Manne's place in Howard Rumsey's Lighthouse All Stars. He was passing through East St. Louis and he'd like to stop and see me. So I told him to come on through, that they could spend the night out at my father's place in Millstadt. They were shocked at how big my father's place was, that he had a maid and a cook and all that kind of shit, that he had cows and horses and prize-winning pigs. I had Max and Mingus decked out in silk pajamas. Anyway, it was good seeing them. Max was clean as usual and driving a brand-new Olds-mobile because he was making money by then. Plus he had a girl who had plenty of money and gave a lot of it to him.

We stayed up all night talking about music. Man, we had a ball. And by them being there like that, I saw how much I had missed the guys on the music scene in New York. By then I wasn't like any of my old friends in East St. Louis, although I really loved them like brothers. I couldn't hang around that town any longer; I didn't fit because my mind was like a New Yorker's. When Max and Mingus were getting ready to leave the next day, I decided to go with them. My father gave me some money and I left for California.

That drive to California was something else. Me and Mingus ar-gued all the way out there, and Max was like the mediator. We got into this discussion about white people, and Mingus just fucking flipped out. Back in those days, Mingus was death on white people, couldn't stand nothing white, especially a white man. In his sex thing, he might like a white girl, or an Oriental girl, but him liking a white girl didn't have nothing to do with how much he disliked the Ameri-can white male, or what people call WASPs. Then we got into this discussion, Max and Mingus and me, about animals. This was after Mingus had talked about white people like they was nothing but beasts. Then, Mingus wants to talk about real live animals, so he says, "If you were to see an animal and you're driving your new car and the animal is in the street, would you swerve to keep from hitting him and crash your car, or would you try to stop or would you just hit it? What would you do?"

Max says, "Well, I'd hit the motherfucker, because what should I do, stop and get all fucked up if a car is behind me, get my new car all smashed up?"

Mingus told him, "See there, you got the same ideas that white people have; that's just how a white man thinks. He would hit the poor animal, too, wouldn't care if he killed him or not. Me? I would smash up my car before I would kill a little defenseless animal." So this is how the conversation went all the way to California.

Somewhere out in the middle of nowhere, in Oklahoma I think, we had eaten up all the chicken that my father's cook had made for us, so we stopped to get something to eat. We told Mingus to go and get the food because he was real light-skinned and they might think he was a foreigner. We knew we couldn't eat in the place so we just told him to get some sandwiches to bring out. Mingus gets out of the car and goes into the restaurant. Then I tell Max that maybe we shouldn't have let him go in by himself on account of how crazy he was.

All of a sudden, here comes Mingus out of the restaurant madder than a motherfucker. "Them white motherfuckers won't let us eat in there; I'm gonna blow up their fucking place!"

I said, "Man, will you sit down. Mingus, just sit down and shut your fucking mouth for once. If you say another word I'm gonna break a bottle over your head, because we're going to end up going to jail over your loud mouth."

He quieted down for a while, because out in that neck of the country, they would as soon shoot a black man as look at him, back in those days. And they would get away with it because they were the law. So shit went like that all the way to California, where Mingus was from.

I didn't know Mingus as well as I thought I did. I had been on the road with Max, so we knew how each other was. But I had never traveled anywhere with Mingus and so I didn't really know how he was off the bandstand, although we had had that disagreement over Bird that time in California. I was quiet and didn't like to talk that much and so was Max. But Mingus? Man, that motherfucker would talk all the time. Now he would be talking about some heavy shit a lot of the time, but sometimes that shit was lighter than a mosquito's peter. After a while all that talking just got on my nerves and that's when I threatened to hit him with a bottle because I just couldn't take it no more. But Mingus was a big motherfucker, so I don't think he was scared of me or nothing like that. But he did shut up—for a while—and then he started talking all over again.

By the time we got to California everybody was whipped, so we dropped Mingus off and me and Max went to his hotel room. Max was playing at the Lighthouse in Hermosa Beach, which is about a block from the ocean. Now, one day Max let Mingus use his car and Mingus knocked a wheel off the car. Guess how he wrecked it. He ran into a fire hydrant trying not to hit a cat. Man, I liked to died laughing because that was the same shit we had been talking about out on the road. But Max was madder than a motherfucker, man, and so they got into it again.

Some good things happened while I was in California. I sat in with some of the musicians at the Lighthouse on a few occasions and they made a record out of that. By this time, Chet Baker was considered the hottest young trumpet on the jazz scene, and he was from California. He played in a session at the Lighthouse on the same day I sat in. That was the first time that we met, and he seemed embarrassed that he had just won the *Down Beat* poll for Best Trumpet of 1953. I think he knew he didn't deserve it over Dizzy and a lot of other trumpet players. I didn't hold it against him personally, although I was mad at the people who picked him. Chet was a nice enough guy, cool and a good player. But both him and me knew that he had copied a lot of shit from me. So that first time I met him he told me afterwards that he was nervous playing with me there in the audience.

The other good thing that happened to me on this trip was that I met Frances Taylor. She was later to become my wife—the first woman I ever legally married. I was trying to keep up my appearance better than I did when I was in New York, so I got me some nice shit on my back and my hair all done up in a marcel process. One day Buddy, this jewelry artist I used to hang out with, comes by and picks me up on his way to deliver a box of jewelry—a birthday gift from this rich white guy—to this girl who was dancing in Katherine Dunham's group. Buddy tells me that the dancer is a fox by the name of Frances and that he wants me to see her.

When we get out there on Sunset Boulevard, Frances comes down the steps and Buddy gives her the box of jewelry. As she's taking the box from Buddy, she's looking at me and smiling. I was dressed sharp as a tack. She was so fine she almost took my breath away, so I take out a piece of paper and sign my name on it with my phone number and give it to her and tell her she don't have to stare. She blushed and when we left she was walking up the stairs, looking back at me over her shoulder. I knew she liked me right then. Buddy kept raving about her all the way back, about how he could tell she liked me.

At that time Max was going with this fine black girl named Sally Blair and she was driving him crazy. She was a fine woman, from Baltimore, looked like a brown Marilyn Monroe. He was having a lot of trouble with her. I always had to keep a straight face with Max, because he was very sensitive about certain things. He didn't try to fuck up on whoever he was going with. But Sally was driving him nuts with the kind of shit she was doing, so Max was starting to look around for somebody else.

He had met Julie Robinson (who is now married to Harry Belafonte) and he liked her a lot. He told me Julie had a friend that he wanted me to meet. He started telling me about how fine this girl was. So I said okay, get us together.

My head at that time was at a place where I thought that I could get any woman that I wanted. We go out to pick them up and there's Frances. When Frances sees me, she says, "You came out with Buddy to my motel when he brought me that jewelry." So I say, "That's right." Right away Frances and I are getting tight. Max is shocked. He tells me this was the girl he was telling me about. It was a coincidence that I met her like that that first time. But after Max got us together I knew something was meant to happen between us and so did she.

On that first date, Max and Julie sat up in the front of Max's car while Frances and another dancer named Jackie Walcott and I sat in the back. We were riding around when Julie says she feels like screaming. So Max said, "Everything is everything, scream if you want." So Julie starts screaming as loud as she can.

I say to Max, "Man, are you crazy? Don't you know where we are? We're in Beverly Hills and we black and she's white. These police will beat all our asses. So stop this crazy shit." So she did. But we had a ball that night. Went out to B's house and partied with him and listened to all his bullshit. He's up there talking about, "Dick, where you get them ugly-ass bitches from? Man, they ain't nothing but mules." That's the way B would put you on. It was fun.

Before long I had made a connection to get me some heroin and so I started coming around to the Lighthouse at Hermosa Beach high and this started embarrassing the hell out of Max. Everything was going real well for Max at the time. My habit was dragging me down again, and I still wasn't admitting it. Anyway, I'm out there with Max —I think it was on his birthday—at the Lighthouse. We were standing outside. I had been taking judo lessons while I was home in East St. Louis and so I had this knife and I was going to show him how I could take it from someone about to stab me. I give it to him and tell him to act like he's going to stab me. When he does it, I take the knife from him and throw him over my shoulder, right? So he says, "Man, Miles that's something." I put the knife back in my pocket and forget about it.

Later, we were standing at the bar having drinks, and Max says, "You pay for us." I say, kidding, "You got the money and it's your birthday, so you pay." But the bartender who heard this conversation and who didn't like me says to me, as Max is going up on the stage to play, "Come on, man, I want my money." I tell him that Max is going to pay when he gets through with his set. Me and the bar-tender started arguing back and forth until finally he tells me, "I'm gonna kick your ass when I get off from work." He's white, right? Max came back and says to this dude, "Why you say that? He ain't doing nothing." So Max pays him, but by this time this dude is mad. Max starts to laugh and looks at me as if to say, "Uh-oh, you're supposed to be bad. Let's see how you handle this nut." Then he went back on stage to finish his last set. The guy says some more shit about kicking my ass, so I told him, "You don't have to wait 'til you get off from work, motherfucker, you can get off right *now* and we can settle this right here." So now here comes this fool right across the bar. I had noticed the dude was left-handed, so I just moved away from his punch and hit him upside his head and threw him all up in the seats among the customers. Max was up on stage with this shocked grin on his face. People were screaming and running for cover. A bunch of the guy's friends jumped me and then somebody called the police. The whole time Max didn't even get off the stage. All the while, he was still up there playing.

Before the guy's friends could hurt me, the bouncer breaks up the shit. The police come. Now, everybody in the club is white, except me and Max. Black people couldn't even come out to the Lighthouse back then. The police take me down to the station and I tell them that the guy had called me a "black motherfucking nigger"—which he did—and threw the first punch. Then I remember that I got this knife. I got scared as a motherfucker because if they find this, I know my ass is going to jail. But they didn't search me. Then I remember my uncle William Pickens was high up in the NAACP, so I tell the policemen this and they just let me go. About this time, Max comes walking into the police station and takes me home. I was madder than a motherfucker, and I said, "You motherfucker, you just let them take me away like that." But Max is laughing his ass off.

Things started to go bad again, and even Max got tired of my shit. I called up my father, once again, and asked him to send me bus fare home. This time I was determined to kick my habit and when I went home, that was the only thing on my mind.

When I got back to East St. Louis, I went straight out to my father's farm in Millstadt. My sister came down from Chicago and me and her and my father took a long walk around the grounds. Finally, my father said, "Miles, if it was a woman that was torturing you, then I could tell you to get another woman or leave that one alone. But this drug thing, I can't do nothing for you, son, but give you my love and support. The rest of it you got to do for yourself." When he said that, he and my sister just turned around and left me out there by myself. He had a guest house with a little two-room apartment in it and that's where I went. I locked the door and stayed until I kicked the habit cold turkey.

I was sick. I wanted to scream but couldn't scream because my father would have come from his big white house next door to see what was wrong. So I had to keep it all down inside of me. I used to hear him outside, walking past the guest house, stopping and listening to see what was going on. When he'd do that I wouldn't say nothing. I'd just lay up there in the dark, sweating like a motherfucker.

I was so sick trying to kick that habit. I got to feeling bad all over, all stiff in my neck and legs and every joint in my body. It was a feeling like arthritis, or a real bad case of the flu, only worse. The feeling is indescribable. All of your joints get sore and stiff, but you can't touch them because if you do you'll scream. So nobody can give you a massage. It's the kind of hurt I later experienced after an operation, when I had hip replacement. It's a raw kind of feeling that you can't stop. You feel like you could die and if somebody could guarantee that you would die in two seconds, then you would take it. You would take the gift of death over this torture of life. At one point I even started to jump out the window—the apartment was on the second floor—so I could knock myself unconscious and get some sleep. But I thought that with my luck I would just break my motherfucking leg and be laying out there suffering.

This went on for about seven or eight days. I couldn't eat. My girlfriend Alice came over, and we fucked, and damn if that didn't make it worse. I hadn't had an orgasm in about two or three years. It hurt the fuck out of my balls and everyplace else. It went on like this for a couple more days, then I started drinking orange juice, but I would throw it up.

Then one day it was over, just like that. Over. Finally over. I felt better, good and pure. I walked outside into the clean, sweet air over to my father's house and when he saw me he had this big smile on his face and we just hugged each other and cried. He knew that I had finally beat it. Then, I sat down and ate up everything in sight because I was hungrier than a motherfucker. I don't believe I have ever eaten like that, before or since. Then I sat down and started thinking about how I was going to get my life back together, which wasn't going to be an easy task.

s soon as I kicked my habit I went to Detroit. I didn't trust myself being in New York where everything was available. I figured that even if I did backslide a little, then the heroin that I would get in Detroit wasn't going to be as pure as what I would get in New York. I figured that this could help me and I needed all the help that I could get.

When I got to Detroit I began playing in some local clubs with Elvin Jones on drums and Tommy Flanagan on piano. I did use some heroin up there, but it wasn't so strong and there wasn't a lot of it around. I still hadn't gotten dope all the way out of my head, but I was close, and I knew it.

I stayed in Detroit for about six months. I was pimping a little then. I had me two or three girlfriends. I was even enjoying sex once again. One of the girls was a designer who tried to help me all she could. I don't want to name her; she's a very prominent person now. She took me to a sanatorium to talk with this shrink. He asked me did I ever masturbate and I told him, no. He couldn't believe that. He told me that I should do that every day instead of shooting dope. I thought that maybe he should put his own goddamn self in the nuthouse if that's all the motherfucker had to tell me. Masturbating to break a habit? Shit, I thought that motherfucker was crazy.

It was so hard to break that habit. But I finally did. But goddamn it took a long time, because I just couldn't seem to stop altogether. I would dip and dabble and tell myself I was clean and then I would start all over again.

I had this real raunchy friend named Freddie Frue, at least that's what we called him. Anyway, I was staying in a hotel, and I would never eat or anything. He was my dope contact in Detroit. Freddie would come upstairs and bring my care package for the day. It was hard to kick my habit because of guys like him and because I was weak. I had to make up my mind in my own head all over again to kick the habit. I even thought marrying somebody might help; I was thinking about asking Irene. So I took a trip to St. Louis and asked my father if he could marry us. But then I thought again. Rather than do that shit, though, I just up and left and went back to Detroit.

I had met a nice young girl while I was staying in Detroit. She was real sweet and beautiful. But I was fucking her over like I was fucking over all the women I knew at that time. If they didn't have no money I didn't want to see them, because I still hadn't gotten that monkey off my back yet. He was loosening his grip but he hadn't completely let go yet. I was still thinking like a junkie.

I knew this guy named Clarence who was in the numbers business in Detroit. He used to say, "Man, why do you do that girl like that? She's a real nice person and she cares about you. So why you treat her so bad?" I looked at him and said, "What the fuck are you talking about?"

So here's this big gangster motherfucker, got his boys all around everywhere. He's got guns and shit in his pocket and I'm getting an attitude with him, right? But see, it wasn't me talking that simple shit, it was the drugs. He looked at me real strange, like he was trying to figure out if he ought to shoot me or something. But he respected me because he loved the music and he loved the way I played. He said, "I *said,* why you treating that girl like that? You heard what I said?"

All I'm thinking about is another fix, so I tell him, "Fuck you. What I do ain't none of your business."

He looked at me like he's about one second away from killing my ass. But then this pity came into his cold eyes. He studied me for a second, looking at me like I was some scroungy dog that had crawled in out of the streets. "Man, you're fucking pathetic, a pitiful, misera- ble motherfucker who don't even deserve to live. You're a fucking junkie, you sorry motherfucker. And if I thought it would do any good, I'd kick your fucking ass all over Detroit. But I'm telling you this shit: you fuck over that lady again and I'll do more than that to your sorry, junkie ass!" Then turned and left.

Man, that shit fucked me up, because he was right about everything he had said. When you're getting high you just don't care because you're just trying to keep from hurting, from being sick. But after that, after Clarence shamed me so bad, I started really trying to clean up my act.

The dope was so bad in Detroit—it was like Philly Joe used to say about some dope, "You could have bought a Hershey bar and saved your money"—because it was cut so much. And so that gradually makes your tolerance for it go away; shooting it wasn't doing nothing for me except putting more holes in my arms. I was only doing it for that fucking feeling you get sticking a needle in your arm. And then all of a sudden I didn't want to put no more holes in my arms, so I stopped.

There were some good musicians in Detroit and I was starting to play with some of them. That helped me and a lot of them were clean. A lot of musicians in Detroit looked up to me because of all the things I had done. And so one of the things that made me stay clean was that they did look up to me and since they were clean it made me want to stay that way. There was this great trumpet player named Clair Rockamore, I think that was his name. Man, that motherfucker was bad. He was one of the best I ever heard. And then me and Elvin Jones was getting it on. People were packing in to see us when we played this little club called the Blue Bird.

One of the things that I want to clear up about when I was staying in Detroit is this story about me and Clifford Brown and Max Roach at Baker's Keyboard Lounge. I had been playing the Blue Bird for several months as a soloist—a guest soloist—in Billy Mitchell's house band. The band also had Tommy Flanagan on piano and Elvin Jones on drums. Betty Carter used to come and sit in with Yusef Lateef, Barry Harris, Thad Jones, Curtis Fuller, and Donald Byrd. It was a real hip city for music. Now, when Max came to town with Clifford and their new group—Richie Powell (Bud's little brother) on piano, Harold Land on tenor, and George Morrow on bass—Max asked me to sit in with them at Baker's.

But they got the story all wrong when they say that I just came stumbling in out of the rain with my horn in a brown paper bag and walked up on stage and started playing "My Funny Valentine." They say Brownie—that's what we called Clifford—let me play because he felt sorry for me, that he stopped the band from playing whatever it was that they were playing, and then I stumbled off the bandstand and back out into the rain. I guess that would make a nice scene in a movie, but it didn't happen. Now, in the first place, I wouldn't ever just walk up on Max and Brownie's gig like that without asking them if I could sit in. Second, I wouldn't have been carrying my trumpet around in no fucking brown paper bag in the rain because my instrument is too important to me. Also, I wouldn't have let Max see me if I was so down on my luck that I had to walk around with my shit in a paper bag. I got too much pride for that.

What really did happen at Baker's is that Max asked me to play because he used to like to hear me play like Freddie Webster. I could play like Freddie and I could buzzzzz the trumpet like Freddie down in the lower register; it's a kind of tonguing, buzzing sound. That was the only time I played with that band. But I don't know where that other story came from. That's just legend. I might have been a junkie but I wasn't as strung out as all that; I was on the road to kicking my habit.

Anyway, I really kicked my habit because of the example of Sugar Ray Robinson; I figured if he could be as disciplined as he was, then I could do it, too. I always loved boxing, but I really loved and respected Sugar Ray, because he was a great fighter with a lot of class and cleaner than a motherfucker. He was handsome and a ladies' man; he had a lot going for him. In fact, Sugar Ray was one of the few idols that I have ever had. Sugar Ray looked like a socialite when you would see him in the papers getting out of limousines with fine women on his arms, sharp as a tack. But when he was training for a fight, he didn't have no women around that anybody knew of, and when he got into the ring with someone to fight, he never smiled like he did in those pictures everybody saw of him. When he was in the ring, he was serious, all business.

I decided that that was the way I was going to be, serious about taking care of my business and disciplined. I decided that it was time for me to go back to New York to start all over again. Sugar Ray was the hero-image that I carried in my mind. It was him that made me think that I was strong enough to deal with New York City again. And it was his example that pulled me through some real tough days.

I came back to New York in February 1954, after spending about five months in Detroit. I really felt good for the first time in a long time. My chops were together because I had been playing every night and I had finally kicked heroin. I felt strong, both musically and physically. I felt ready for anything. I got me a hotel room. I remember calling up Alfred Lion at Blue Note Records and Bob Weinstock at Prestige and telling them that I was ready to record again. I told them I had kicked my habit and that I wanted to do a couple of albums using just a quartet—piano, bass, drums, and trumpet—and they were happy about that.

The scene in New York had changed since I'd been gone. The MJQ —Modern Jazz Quartet—was big on the music scene then; the kind of "cool" chamber jazz thing they were doing was getting over big. People were still talking about Chet Baker and Lennie Tristano and George Shearing, all that stuff that came out of *Birth of the Cool*. Dizzy was still playing great as ever, but Bird was all fucked up—fat, tired, playing badly when he bothered to show up for anything. The managers of Birdland even barred him from there after he got into a shouting match with one of the owners—and Birdland had been named for him.

All I could think of when I came back to New York was playing music and making records and making up for all the time I had lost. The first two albums I made that year—*Miles Davis, Vol. 2* for Blue Note and *Miles Davis Quartet* for Prestige—were very important to me. The Prestige contract had not gone into effect yet, that's why I could make the Blue Note date with Alfred Lion, which I needed to do because my money was still short. I felt I had come on strong on those records. I got Art Blakey on drums, Percy Heath from the MJQ on bass, and a young piano player named Horace Silver, who had been playing with Lester Young and Stan Getz. I think Art Blakey turned me on to Horace, because he knew him real well. Horace was staying at the same hotel I was staying in—the Arlington Hotel on 25th near Fifth—so we got to know each other well. Horace had an upright piano in his room where I would play and compose songs. He was a little younger than me, three or four years younger I think. I used to tell him a few things and show him some shit on the piano. I liked the way Horace played piano, because he had this funky shit that I liked a lot at that time. He put fire up under my playing and with Art on drums you couldn't be fucking around; you had to get on up and play. But I had Horace playing like Monk on that first album with "Well, You Needn't" and a ballad accompaniment on "It Never Entered My Mind." We also did "Lazy Susan."

I had signed a three-year deal with Bob Weinstock and Prestige

Records. I had always appreciated what Bob Weinstock did for me before, back in the early days, because he took a chance on me when nobody else in the recording industry thought I was shit—except for Alfred Lion, who was also cool with me. The money Bob gave me for them first Prestige records wasn't much—I think something like $750 a record, plus he wanted all my music publishing rights, which I didn't give him. But that little money was something I used to help support my habit back in 1951 and the records that I made helped me later in becoming a good bandleader, helped me understand how records—*good* records—are made. We got along all right, but he always wanted to tell me what to do, how to make *my* records, and so I used to tell him, "I'm the musician and you're the producer, so you just work on the technical side and leave the creative shit to me." When he didn't quite get that, I would just say, "Fuck you, Bob, get the fuck out of here and leave us alone." If I hadn't done that, we wouldn't have had Sonny Rollins, Art Blakey (and later, Trane and Monk) playing the shit they were playing because Bob wanted them to play and record differently than they did for those sessions for Prestige.

Most white record producers just wanted to always make the shit sound whiter, and so in order to keep it black, you had to fight them every step of the way. Bob wanted to do some tired shit, some pseudo-white shit. But he changed after a while—I can say that much for him. He never did pay no real decent money—even later, when we was making all them fucking masterpieces—and he wanted me to give up everything for the little money he was paying me. That's the way they treated jazz musicians—especially black jazz musicians —back in those days. And it ain't much better for most today.

Somehow I lost my horn and had to rent Art Farmer's on several occasions. I used it on "Blue Haze" on the *Miles Davis Quartet* album for Prestige. We were recording down on 31st Street. I remember this because I wanted to turn out all the lights when we were doing "Blue Haze" so that everyone could get into a certain mood that I wanted. So when I asked them to turn out the lights in the studio, somebody said, "If we turn out the lights we won't be able to see Art or Miles." That shit was funny. They said that because Art Blakey and I are so dark. I remember Art Farmer was also there at the session and there when I had that next session in April. I think that's when Bob Weinstock started to use Rudy Van Gelder as his engineer. Rudy lived over in Hackensack, New Jersey, so we recorded right there in his house, in his living room. That's where most of Prestige's records were done until later, when Rudy had another big studio built. It was a tight little room. Anyway, I was borrowing Art Farmer's horn right through that time until one time when I came to get it for a gig I was playing, and he had a gig too. So we got into an argument over *his* horn. I was paying him ten dollars to use it and so I thought I had exclusive rights, even over *him*. After that, I used Jules Colomby's horn until I got my own. Jules worked at Prestige wrapping records and stuff; he was an amateur player and the brother of Bobby Colomby, who was later with the group Blood, Sweat and Tears.

On that April session for Prestige, Kenny Clarke replaced Art Blakey on drums because I wanted that brush stroke thing. When it came to playing soft brush strokes on the drums, nobody could do it better than Klook. I was using a mute on that date and I wanted a soft thing behind me, but a swing soft thing.

Later that month I did *Walkin'* for Prestige and man, that album turned my whole life and career around. I got J. J. Johnson and Lucky Thompson for that session because I wanted that big sound that both of them could give me. You know, Lucky for that Ben Webster thing, but a bebop thing, too. J. J. had that big sound and tone, and then we had Percy Heath on bass, Art on drums, and Horace on piano. We worked out all the concepts for the music in my room and Horace's room at the Arlington Hotel. A lot of that shit came right out of Horace's old upright piano. We knew when we finished that session that we had something good—even Bob Weinstock and Rudy were excited about what went down—but we didn't really feel the impact of that album until it was released later on that year. That record was a motherfucker, man, with Horace laying down that funky piano of his and Art playing them bad rhythms behind us on the drums. It was something else. I wanted to take the music back to the fire and improvisations of bebop, that kind of thing that Diz and Bird had started. But also I wanted to take the music forward into a more funky kind of blues, the kind of thing that Horace would take us to. And with me and J. J. and Lucky on top of that shit, it had to go someplace else, and it did.

Right around then, Capitol Records released those other "Birth of the Cool" sessions that we had recorded in 1949 and 1950. Capitol put about eight out of the twelve recordings on a single long-playing album and named the album *Birth of the Cool*. That was the first time anybody had called the music that. They left off "Budo," "Move," and "Boplicity," and that made me mad. But because of the record's release, and the title of the record, *Birth of the Cool*, which was very catchy at the time, a lot of people—especially critics, white critics—started to notice me again. I started thinking about putting together a permanent band that would tour. I wanted Horace Silver on piano, Sonny Rollins on tenor, Percy Heath on bass, and Kenny Clarke on drums. But because of Sonny's drug addiction and his always being in and out of jail, it was hard for me to put it together. But that's where my head was going at the time.

In the summer of 1954, I went into the studio again for Prestige, this time with Sonny, Horace, Percy, and Klook on drums. I had decided that for the sound that I wanted at the time, Klook gave me that dimension over Art Blakey; he was more subtle than Art. I don't mean to say that he was a better drummer than Art, but that his style of playing was what I wanted at that time.

Now, around this time, there was also a piano style that I really liked. I had been turned on by the playing and musical concepts of Ahmad Jamal, who my sister, Dorothy, had turned me on to in 1953. She called me from a pay telephone booth in the Persian Lounge in Chicago, and she said, "Junior" (my family didn't call me Miles until much later, after my father had died), "there's this piano player I'm listening to right now; his name is Ahmad Jamal and I think that you will like him." I had gone to hear him once while I was out that way and he knocked me out with his concept of space, his lightness of touch, his understatement, and the way he phrased notes and chords and passages. Plus I liked the tunes he played, like "Surrey with a Fringe on Top," "Just Squeeze Me," "My Funny Valentine," "I Don't Wanna Be Kissed," "Billy Boy," "A Gal in Calico," "Will You Still Be Mine," "But Not for Me," which were standards, and I liked some of his originals, like "Ahmad's Blues" and "New Rhumba." I loved his lyricism on piano, the way he played and the spacing he used in the ensemble voicing of his groups. I have always thought Ahmad Jamal was a great piano player who never got the recognition he deserved.

In the summer of 1954 his influence wasn't as big on me as it would become later. But it was big enough for me to include "But Not for Me" in that album I did for Prestige. The other tunes we did for that date all came from Sonny Rollins. Sonny Rollins was something else. Brilliant. He was interested in Africa, so he turned Nigeria backwards and called that tune "Airegin" for that date. His other tune was "Doxy." As a matter of fact, he brought the tunes in and rewrote them right in the studio. He would be tearing off a piece of paper and writing down a bar or a note or a chord, or a chord change. We'd go into a studio and I'd ask Sonny, "Where's the tune?" And he'd say, "I didn't write it yet," or, "I haven't finished it yet." So I would play what he had and then he might go away in the corner somewhere and write shit down on scraps of paper and come back a little while after that and say, "Okay, Miles, it's finished." One tune he wrote like that was "Oleo." He got the title from oleomargarine, which was a big thing then, a cheap butter substitute. I used a mute and we left out the bass line; Horace would come in on piano when we stopped playing. That's what made that tune unique.

What we were doing is something we used to call pecking. You divided the riffs, like a chichi riff, broke them up and darted in and out of the rhythm. You could do this real well when you had a great drummer. We had Kenny Clarke and couldn't nobody play that kind of shit better than Klook.

Although I had stopped using heroin, I would still use a little cocaine from time to time because I didn't find it habit-forming; I could take it or leave it and I didn't get sick when I didn't have it. It was especially good when you were creating and going to be in the studio for a long time. And so we had some of that liquid coke at this session. It was a good session and my confidence was growing every day. But I was disappointed that I couldn't support a working band yet, and the band that was in the studio could have turned into a great band. Kenny was committed to the MJQ, and Percy and Art and Horace were talking about forming a group a year later. So, to support myself, Philly Joe Jones and I would go from city to city playing with local musicians. Philly would go ahead of me and get some guys together and then I would show and we'd play a gig. But most of the time this shit was getting on my nerves because the musicians didn't know the arrangements and sometimes didn't even know the tunes. Things still weren't where I thought they could be.

But we were playing a lot of jam sessions during this time down at Birdland. On these occasions there would be a lot of coke floating around that all the musicians were using. That's when I found as a trumpet player taking a lot of coke that I needed a lot of liquids to keep my mouth from getting dry. My mouth might get numb, but I sure didn't run out of creative ideas; they'd be jumping out of my head.

When I was a drug addict, the club owners had treated me like I was dirt and so had the critics. Now, in 1954, when I felt myself getting stronger and was clean of heroin, I felt that I didn't have to take their stupid bullshit any longer. This feeling was deep down in my mind and wasn't something that I *knew* I was feeling or thinking about. I had a lot of anger in me about things that had happened to me in the last four years; I didn't trust hardly anyone, so I think that had something to do with my attitude. When we would go places to play, I was just cold to the motherfuckers; pay me and I'll play. I wasn't about to kiss anybody's ass and do that grinning shit for nobody. I even stopped announcing tunes around this time, because I felt that it wasn't the *name* of the tune that was important, but the music we played. If they knew what the tune was, why did I have to announce it? I stopped talking to the audience because they weren't coming to hear me speak but to hear the music I was playing.

A lot of people thought I was aloof, and I was. But most of all, I didn't know who to trust. I was leery and so that's the part of my attitude that many people saw; this wariness of hanging out with people I didn't know. And because of my former drug habit, I was also trying to protect myself by not coming into close contact with a lot of people. But the people that knew me well knew that I wasn't the way they were describing me in the newspapers.

I had convinced Bobby McQuillen that I was clean enough for him to take me on as a boxing student. I was going to the gym every chance I could, and Bobby was teaching me about boxing. He trained me hard. We got to be friends, but he was mostly my trainer because I wanted to learn how to box like him.

Bobby and I would go to the fights together and train at Gleason's Gym in midtown or at Silverman's Gym, which was up in Harlem on 116th Street and Eighth Avenue (which is now called Frederick Douglass Boulevard above 110th Street) on the fourth or fifth floor in this corner building. Sugar Ray used to train there, and when he came in to train, everybody would stop what they were doing and check him out.

Bobby knew all about the swivel, which is what I call it, the swiveling of your hips and legs when you punched a guy. When you did this when you punched, you got more power into your punches. Bobby was like Joe Louis's trainer, Blackburn, who taught Joe how to swivel when he punched. That's why Joe could knock people out with only one punch. So I think Bobby must have learned it from Joe, because they knew each other and were both from Detroit. Johnny

Bratton used to do it, too. Sugar Ray also knew about the swivel. It was just one of those moves great boxers used when they were fighting.

It's a move that you have to practice over and over again until you get it, until it becomes like a reflex action, instinctive. It's like practicing a musical instrument; you have to keep practicing, over and over and over again. A lot of people tell me I have the mind of a boxer, that I think like a boxer, and I probably do. I guess that I am an aggressive person about things that are important to me, like when it comes to playing music or doing what I want to do. I'll fight, physically, at the drop of a hat if I think someone has wronged me. I have always been like that.

Boxing is a science, and I love to watch boxing matches between two guys who know what they're doing. Like when you see a fighter put his jab on the outside of his opponent. If the guy slips the jab, moves to the right or left, you got to know which way he's going to move and throw your punch at the moment he's moving his head, so that it comes right into the line of the punch you've thrown. Now that's science and precision, rather than just some kind of fucking mayhem like people say it is.

So Bobby was teaching me Johnny Bratton's style, because that was the style I wanted to know. Boxing's got style like music's got style. Joe Louis had a style, Ezzard Charles had a style, Henry Armstrong had a style, Johnny Bratton had a style, and Sugar Ray Robinson had his style—as did Muhammad Ali, Sugar Ray Leonard, Marvelous Marvin Hagler, Michael Spinks, and Mike Tyson later. Archie Moore's peek-a-boo style was something else.

But you've got to have style in whatever you do—writing, music, painting, fashion, boxing, anything. Some styles are slick and creative and imaginative and innovative and others aren't. Sugar Ray Robinson's style was all of that, and he was the most precise fighter that I ever saw. Bobby McQuillen told me that Sugar Ray Robinson would put an opponent in four or five traps during every round in the first two or three rounds, just to see how his opponent would react. Ray would be reaching, and he would stay just out of reach so he could measure you to knock you out, and you didn't even know what was happening until, BANG!, you found yourself counting stars. Then, on somebody else, he might hit him hard in his side—BANG! —after he made him miss a couple of jabs. He might do that in the first round. Then he'd tee-off on the sucker upside his head after hitting him eight or nine more times hard in the side. Maybe he'd hit him four or five times hard upside his head. Then he'd switch back to hitting him hard in the ribs, then back to the head. So by the fourth or fifth round, the sucker don't know what Ray's going to do to him next. Plus his head and ribs are hurting real bad by this time.

You don't just learn any kind of shit like that naturally. That's something somebody teaches you, like when you teach somebody how to play a musical instrument *correctly.* After you've learned how to play your instrument the *right* way, you can turn around and play it the way you want to, anyway you hear the music and sound and want to play it. But you've got to first learn how to be cool and let whatever happens—both in music and boxing—happen. Dizzy and Bird taught it to me in music; so did Monk and so did Ahmad Jamal and Bud Powell.

When I used to watch Sugar Ray train up on 116th Street, there was this old black guy in there who they used to call "Soldier." I never did know what his real name was. Soldier was the only other guy Ray listened to besides his trainer. When Ray came out in the ring, Soldier would slide up to Ray and whisper something in his ear and Ray would just nod. Nobody ever knew what Soldier told Ray, but Ray would go back in the ring and whup up on some sorry motherfucker's ass like he had done something to Ray's wife. I really used to watch Ray, idolized him. When I told him one day that summer that he was the prime reason that I broke my heroin habit, he just smiled and laughed.

I remember hanging out at Sugar Ray's bar up on Seventh Avenue (today called Adam Clayton Powell Jr. Boulevard) around 122nd or 123rd Street. Ray would be there. That's where a lot of hip people and beautiful women hung out, fighters and big-time hustlers. So they all would be standing there, fat-mouthing and high-signing and styling. And so maybe one of the other fighters might challenge Ray in some kind of way and then Ray would look at the motherfucker and say, "You don't believe I'm the champ today? Right now? Here, as I'm standing and talking to you? You want me to give you some proof, right here, right now, where we standing, while I'm talking to you?" He'd be standing there, shoulders squared, feet apart, holding one hand in the other in front of him, rocking back and forth on his heels, cleaner than a motherfucker, grinning, his hair all processed back, smiling that crooked, cocky smile he used to smile when he was daring somebody to say anything out of the way. Great fighters are testy, just like great artists; they test everybody. Sugar Ray was king of the hill, and he knew it.

He used to come up and tell everyone that I was a great musician who wanted to be a fighter, and then laugh that high-pitched laugh of his. He liked being around musicians because he liked to play drums. He'd come up to me when Johnny Bratton was fighting—because Ray *knew* I was crazy about Johnny Bratton—and ask, "What's your boy gonna do?"

So I'd say, "Do about what?"

"You know, Miles, how's he gonna do in this fight he has coming up? I think that guy's too strong for him, got a little bit too much weight for a welterweight like Johnny." Johnny was fighting a middleweight, some guy from Canada Ray had gone ten rounds with. So Ray would shuffle his feet and square up his shoulders, grip his hands in front of him down by his groin and look at me cold, right in the eyes, and smile. Then he'd say, "What do you think, Miles, you standing here telling me he can win?"

Now, he *knows* I ain't going to say nothing against Johnny, so when I'd say, "Yeah, I think he's gonna win!" Sugar would keep smiling that cold smile. Then he would say, "Well, Miles, we'll see, you know, we'll see."

So when Johnny Bratton knocked out the Canadian guy in the first round I said, "Well, Ray, I guess Johnny knew what he was doing, huh?"

"Yeah, I guess he did. *That* time. But wait until he gets in there with me; he won't be that lucky." And when Ray *did* beat Johnny Bratton he came looking for me, then he just stood there like he always stood, rocking back and forth on his heels, crooked smile on his face, and said, "So Miles, what do you think of your boy now?" And then he laughed so hard in that high-pitched laugh of his, I thought he was going to die.

The reason I'm talking so much about Sugar Ray is because in 1954 he was the most important thing in my life besides music. I found myself even acting like him, you know, everything. Even taking on his arrogant attitude.

Ray was cold and he was the best and he was everything I wanted to be in 1954. I had been disciplined when I first came to New York. All I had to do was go back to the way I had been before I got trapped in all that bullshit dope scene. So that's when I stopped listening to just anybody. I got myself a Soldier just like Sugar Ray had; and my man for talking to was Gil Evans. And I decided if somebody wasn't saying something important to me, then I would say, "Fuck them." That got me back on the right track.

Of all the people I knew, Gil Evans was one of the only ones who could pick up on what I was thinking musically. Like when he would come to hear me play, he would ease up next to me and say, "Miles, you know you got a nice, open sound and tone on your trumpet. Why don't you use it more." And then he'd be gone, just like that, and I'd be left thinking about what he had said. I would decide right then and there that he was right. Or, he would come up and whisper—always confidentially, so no one else could hear—"Miles, now don't let them play that music by themselves. You play something over them, put your sound in it, too." Or, when I was playing with some white guys, "Put *your* sound over theirs," meaning their *white* sound and feeling. He said this meaning put my shit on top so that the black thing would be on top. Now, I knew that, but what Gil was doing was just reinforcing and reminding me not to forget.

I started going to the gym regularly in 1954 to keep myself together, my body and my mind. I already *knew* that I had it there somewhere deep down inside of me, because I had had it before I came to New York—and when I first lived there—and lost it after Paris in 1949. I also realized that a person is lucky if he's got *one* Soldier or Gil Evans in his life, someone close enough to you to pull your coattail when something's going wrong. Because who knows what I would have done or become if I hadn't had someone like Gil to remind me? Deep down inside I have always been like I was when I kicked my habit. That person with a habit was never the real me. So when I kicked, I just came back to myself and kept on trying to grow, which was what I was all about when I came to New York in the first place—growing.

That summer Juliette Greco came over to New York to talk to the producers who were filming Ernest Hemingway's book *The Sun Also Rises.* They wanted Juliette to be in the film. By now she was the biggest female star in France—or close to it—so she had a suite at the Waldorf-Astoria down on Park Avenue. She got in touch with me. We hadn't seen each other since 1949, so a lot of things had happened. We had written a couple of letters, sent messages to each other through mutual friends, but that was about it. I was curious to see how she would affect me, and I'm sure she felt the same way. I didn't know if she knew about all the shit I had been in and I was curious to find out if news of my heroin problems had gotten over to Europe.

She invited me down to see her and I went. But I remember being a little wary because of what had happened to me before when I left Paris and she was all up in my head, all up in my heart and blood. She was the first woman I think that I really loved, and being separated like that almost broke my heart and sent me falling down the pit and into heroin. I knew I wanted to see her—*had* to see her—deep down in my heart. But just in case, I took a friend with me, the drummer Art Taylor. That way, I could control the situation as best I could.

We drove on down to the Waldorf in the little used MG sports car I had and gunned the engine as we pulled into the garage. Man, this fucked up all them white people; two weird-looking niggers driving up in an MG at the Waldorf. We walked up to the front desk, and the whole lobby is looking, right? Shocked out of their fucking minds to see two niggers in the front lobby of the Waldorf who weren't hired help. I walked up to the desk and asked for Juliette Greco. The man behind the counter says, "Juliette who?" Now, this motherfucker's looking like this couldn't be real, like this nigger must be crazy. I say her name again and tell him to call upstairs. So he does, and while he's dialing he's giving me an "I can't believe this" look. When she tells him to send us upstairs, I thought the motherfucker was going to die on the spot.

So we walk back across the lobby, which is silent as a mausoleum now, catch the elevator, and go on up to Juliette's room. She opened the door, threw her arms around me, and gave me this big kiss. I introduced her to Art, who's standing behind me looking shocked, and I see the joy go out of her face. I mean, like you *know* she didn't want to see that nigger right then and there. She was real disappointed. So we go in and she's looking like a motherfucker, finer than what I remember. My heart is beating fast and I'm trying to get my emotions under control, so I reacted to Juliette by being cold to her. Went into my black pimp role. Mainly because I was scared and had also picked up a pimp's attitude while I was a junkie.

I say to her, "Juliette, give me some money, I need some money right now!" She goes in her bag and pulls out some money and gives it to me. But she's wearing this shocked look on her face like she don't believe what's happening. I take the money and walk around looking at her all cold—but inside I'm wanting to grab her and make love to her, but I'm scared of what that would do to me, scared that I might not be able to handle my emotions.

After about fifteen minutes I tell her I got something to do. She asks me if I will see her later, if I maybe could go to Spain with her while she's making the movie. So I tell her that I'll think about it and call her later. I don't think she had ever been treated like that before; so many men wanted and desired her she probably had gotten her way on anything she wanted. As I'm going out the door, she asks me, "Miles, are you really coming back?"

"Aw, bitch, shut up; I told you I would call you later!" But inside I'm hoping that she will find some way to make me stay. But I dogged her so bad on that first time I saw her again, she was too shocked to do anything but let me go. Later, I called and told her I was too busy to go with her to Spain, but that I would check her out later when I came to France. She was so shocked she didn't know what to do, but she agreed to see me later, if and when I came to France. She gave me her address and phone number and hung up and that was that.

We did eventually get together and were lovers for many years. I told her what my problem was when I met her at the Waldorf, and she understood and forgave me, though she said she had really been confused and disappointed in the way I treated her. In one of Juliette's later films—I think it was a film by Jean Cocteau—she puts a picture of me on the table by her bed and you can see it in the film.

So that was one of the ways I had changed since I had my habit; I had gone inside myself to protect me from what I thought was a hostile world. And sometimes, like in the case of Juliette Greco, I didn't know who was my enemy or my friend and many times I didn't stop to find out. I was just cold to mostly everyone. That was the way I protected myself, by not letting hardly anyone inside of my feelings and emotions. And for a long time it worked for me.

On Christmas Eve, 1954, I went into the studio with Milt Jackson, Thelonious Monk, Percy Heath, and Kenny Clarke and we cut this record for Prestige called *Miles Davis and the Modern Jazz Giants*. We went out to Rudy Van Gelder's Hackensack studio to record. Now, there's a lot of misunderstanding that has gotten around about this recording date, about the tension and the anger that was supposed to have been between Thelonious Monk and me. Mostly it is bullshit and rumors that people just kept repeating until it has become fact. What *did* happen on that day was that we all played some great music. But I want to clear up once and for all what happened between me and Monk.

I just told him to lay out, not play behind me, except on "Bemsha Swing," a tune written by Monk. The reason I told Monk to lay out was because Monk never did know how to play behind a horn player. (The only horn players he ever had that sounded good playing with him were John Coltrane, Sonny Rollins, and Charlie Rouse.) But Monk couldn't play too tough with most horn players, in my opinion, and especially trumpet players. Trumpets don't have that many notes, so you really have to push that rhythm section and that wasn't Monk's thing. A trumpet player needs the rhythm section to be hot even if he is playing a ballad. You got to have that kicking thing, and most of the time that wasn't Monk's bag. So I just told him to lay out when I was playing, because I wasn't comfortable with the way he voiced his changes, and I was the only horn on that date. I wanted to hear the rhythm section stroll without a piano sound. I wanted to hear space in the music. I was just starting to use the concept of space breathing through the music—composition and arrangements —that I had picked up from Ahmad Jamal, and we even cut a tune he used to play that I loved—"The Man I Love."

On this album Monk's playing sounds good and natural, the way I wanted to hear him. I just told him what I wanted to hear, which was the way he was going to play it anyway. So I just told him first, told him to come into the music a little after I played. And that's what he did. There wasn't any argument. So I don't know how that story got started about me and Monk arguing so bad we almost came to blows.

I mean, Monk was always saying crazy stuff and walking around like he was out of it. But that's just the way that he acted, and everyone who knew him understood. He might start talking to himself in front of a bunch of people, might say anything that came to his mind. He was a great put-on artist, too, and that's the way he kept people off him, by acting crazy like he did. He might have said something to someone when they brought up that session just to fuck with their minds. I *do* know this: Monk was like a little baby. He had a lot of love in him and I *know* Monk loved me, and I loved him, too. He wouldn't ever fight me even if I stomped down hard on his feet for a week, because he just wasn't that kind of person. Monk was a gentle person, gentle and beautiful, but he was strong as an ox. And if I had ever said something about punching Monk out in front of his face—and I never did—then somebody should have just come and got me and taken me to the madhouse, because Monk could have just picked my little ass up and thrown me through a wall.

We made some great music that day, and that record went on to become a classic, just like "Walkin' " did, and "Blue 'n' Boogie." But it was on the *Modern Jazz Giants* album that I started to understand how to create space by leaving the piano out and just letting everybody stroll. I would extend and use that concept more later; in 1954, going into 1955, it wasn't as clear in my mind as it would be later.

Nineteen fifty-four was a great year for me—although I didn't realize *how* great it was at the time. I had kicked my habit and was playing better than I ever played, and a couple of the albums that were released that year, like *Birth of the Cool* and *Walkin',* made everybody—the musicians—sit up and notice me again, more than ever before. The critics' heads were still someplace else, but a few people were starting to buy my albums. I could tell this because sometime around here, Bob Weinstock gave me about $3,000 to do my next records and that was more than he ever had given me in the past. I had the feeling that I was getting there, on my own terms. I hadn't compromised my integrity to get to this place of recognition. And if I hadn't done it up to now, then I wasn't going to do it in the future.

So I went into 1955 feeling real good. Then Bird died in March and that just fucked everyone up. Everyone knew that he was in bad shape, couldn't play no more, was fat and drunk and doped up all the time, so everybody felt that he couldn't go on like that much longer. But it was still a shock when he died like he did in Baroness Pannonica de Koenigswarter's apartment on Fifth Avenue. I had met her first in 1949 when I played in Paris and she was there. She loved black music, man, and especially Bird.

What made it even worse was that Irene had me put in jail for non-support, so I was in jail on Rikers Island when I heard about Bird's death from Harold Lovett, who later would become my lawyer and my best friend. Harold, who was always around the music scene and was Max Roach's lawyer at the time, came out to Rikers Island to try to get me out. I think Max had sent him, or he came just because he heard I was there. Anyway, he told me Bird had died and I remember it was really a downer. First of all, I was in jail with all these crazy motherfuckers—just when everything seemed to be going so good for me—and I guess that was depressing me. And, like I said, I knew Bird was bad off, knew that his health was bad—the last time I saw Bird, man, he was in terrible shape—but I guess it just came as a shock to me when he really died. I was out in that jail for three days and then Bird just ups and dies.

So Harold got me out with money he had gotten from Bob Weinstock and from some gig he had gotten me down in Philly; he made
them give me an advance. I found out later that Harold drove all the
way down to Philly and back to pick up that money. He did this even
though he hadn't even really met me. When I saw him walk into my
cell at Rikers Island, I looked at him like I'd been knowing him for
years and said, "Yeah, I knew it would be you who was coming. I
knew it would be you." That fucked him up because I wasn't surprised, but like I said, I've always been able to predict shit like that.

We got into his 1950 maroon Chevrolet and went straight up to
Harlem, to Sugar Ray's club, the Sportsman's Bar. So then after we
had hung out there, Harold took me down to my girlfriend Susan's
place in the Village, on Jones Street. So I see that I'm going to like
this guy, see the way he handled Sugar Ray when we went up to his
club, see that he's sharp. So we started hanging out and then he
started doing my business.

After Bird died like that a lot of people started trying to kick their
heroin habits, and that was good. But it just made me sad that Bird
had died like he did, because, man, he was a genius and he had so
much he could have given. But that's the way life is. Bird was a
greedy motherfucker and never did know when to stop, and that's
what killed him—his greed.

Bird was supposed to have a little funeral and a quiet burial, at
least that's what Chan planned, but I wasn't going to any kind of
funeral. I don't like going to funerals; I like to remember a person
when they were alive. But I heard that Doris—"Olive Oyl"—arrived
and fucked things up, turned everything into a circus and canceled
Chan right out of the picture. Man, that was some ridiculous and sad
shit, because Bird hadn't even seen Olive Oyl for years. So here she
comes, claiming the body and shit and having a real big funeral at
Abyssinian Baptist Church up in Harlem. That was all right, because
that was Adam Clayton Powell's church. But then Doris didn't want
nobody to play jazz or blues (just like at Louis Armstrong's funeral
later; nobody could play that). Besides all that stupid music that Diz
told me they played over Bird's body, he was laying there in a pin-
striped suit and a cravat that Doris had bought him. Man, they
turned Bird's funeral into some bullshit. Maybe that's why when they
were taking the casket out, the pallbearers almost dropped the body
after somebody slipped. Man, that was Bird protesting some silly
bullshit.

Then they shipped his body to be buried in Kansas City, a place Bird hated. He had made Chan promise him she wouldn't ever bury him there. They said Bird's burial was a motherfucker, that they buried him in a bronze coffin and that his body was under a piece of glass that somebody told me was giving off light. One guy told me that it seemed "like a halo was surrounding Bird's head." Man, that shit fucked up a lot of guys who swore Bird was a god; that shit was just the icing on the cake that he was.

Bird was dead and I had to go on with my life. In June of 1955 I took a quartet into the studio for my next record for Bob Weinstock. Because I wanted to find a piano player who played like Ahmad Jamal, I decided to use Red Garland, who Philly Joe had introduced me to back in 1953 at that session when Bird had called himself "Charlie Chan." He was into boxing and he had that light touch that I wanted on piano. He was from Texas and had been playing around New York and Philly for a few years. That's where he met Philly Joe, out on the circuit, and I liked him because he was hip. Red knew I liked Ahmad Jamal, that that was the type of piano player I was looking for, and so I asked him to give me Ahmad's sound, because Red played his best when he played like that. Philly Joe was on drums at that session and Oscar Pettiford played bass. It was a nice little album, the *Miles Davis Quartet,* and it really showed Jamal's influence on me at the time. Both "A Gal in Calico" and "Will You Still Be Mine" were tunes that Jamal always played, and with Red playing with that Jamal feeling and touch, we got close on that album to what I wanted to hear. That kind of melodic understatement that Jamal had, that lightness, we put into this album. When people say Jamal influenced me a lot, they're right; but what you've got to remember is that I was into liking this kind of feeling and was playing it myself a long time before I ever heard of Ahmad Jamal. What he did for me was just to refocus my own playing on where I had been all along. He just brought me back to myself.

As much as I liked the music I was now doing, I think my name in the clubs was still shit, and a lot of critics probably still thought I was a junkie. I wasn't real popular at this time, but that began to change after I played at the Newport Jazz Festival in 1955. This was the first festival that this couple, Elaine and Louis Lorillard, got together. They picked George Wein to produce it. I think George was from Boston. For the first festival George picked Count Basie, Louis Armstrong, Woody Herman, and Dave Brubeck. And then he had an All-

Star band that had Zoot Sims, Gerry Mulligan, Monk, Percy Heath, Connie Kay; he later added me. They played a couple of tunes without me and then I joined them on "Now's the Time," which was a tribute to Bird's memory. And then we played " 'Round Midnight," Monk's tune. I played it with a mute and everybody went crazy. It was something. I got a long standing ovation. When I got off the bandstand, everybody was looking at me like I was a king or something—people were running up to me offering me record deals. All the musicians there were treating me like I was a god, and all for a solo that I had had trouble learning a long time ago. It was something else, man, looking out at all those people and then seeing them suddenly standing up and applauding for what I had done.

They had all these parties that night in this big fucking mansion. We all go there, and all these rich white people are everywhere. I was sitting over in a corner, minding my own business, when the woman who had organized the festival, Elaine Lorillard, came over with all these grinning, silly-looking white people and said something like, "Oh, this is the boy who played so beautifully. What's your name?"

Now she's standing there smiling like she's done me a fucking favor, right? So I look at her and say, "Fuck you, and I ain't no fucking boy! My name is Miles Davis, and you'd better remember that if you ever want to talk to me." And then I walked away leaving them all shocked as a motherfucker. I wasn't trying to be nasty or nothing like that, but she was calling me "boy," and I just can't take that kind of bullshit.

So I left, me and Harold Lovett, who had come up there with me. We got a ride back to New York with Monk and this was the only time that I got into an argument with him. In the car he said that I hadn't played " 'Round Midnight" right that night. I said that was okay, but that I didn't like what he had played behind me either, but I hadn't told him *that,* so why was he telling me all this shit? So then I told him that the people liked it and that's why they stood up and applauded like they did. Then I told him that he must be jealous.

Now when I told him this, I was kidding, because I was smiling. But I guess he thought I was laughing at him, making fun of him, putting him on. He told the driver to stop the car, and he got out. Because I knew how stubborn Monk was—once he made up his mind about something, that was it, couldn't nothing budge him—I told the driver something like, "Aw, fuck that motherfucker. He's crazy. Let's go." So we did. We left Monk standing there where you catch the ferry, and drove back to New York. The next time I saw Monk, it was like that shit had never happened. Monk was like that sometimes, you know, weirder than a motherfucker. And we never said anything else about that incident ever again.

After my appearance at Newport, things began to happen for me. George Avakian, the jazz producer for Columbia Records, wanted to sign me to an exclusive contract. I told him I wanted to go with Columbia because of all the shit that he offered me, but I didn't tell him that I had a long-term deal with Prestige Records. When he found that out, he started trying to negotiate a deal with Bob Weinstock, but Bob was asking for a whole lot of money and a lot of other shit. Man, I have to admit, this shit was starting to fascinate me. These motherfuckers were talking about money, *real* money, so stuff was starting to look good. It was a good position, people talking good about you all over the place instead of bad-mouthing you. They asked me to get a group together for Cafe Bohemia, a hot new jazz club down in Greenwich Village. It felt good, all this positive attention; it felt real good.

I cut a record with Charlie Mingus for his Debut label. By now, people were saying that Mingus was one of the finest bassists living and he was also a great composer. But something went wrong at this session and nothing ever really clicked, so the playing didn't have any fire. I don't know what it was—maybe the arrangements—but something definitely went wrong; Mingus had Elvin Jones on drums and you *know* that motherfucker can put fire up under anybody.

At this time I was rehearsing my own band that I was going to open up with at the Cafe Bohemia so I might have been distracted on Mingus's date. It was going to be Sonny Rollins on tenor, Red Garland on piano, Philly Joe Jones on drums, myself on trumpet, and a young bass player that Jackie McLean had told me about who was working with the George Wallington Quintet, Paul Chambers. Paul had been in New York for only a couple of months and had already worked with J. J. Johnson and Kai Winding in the new group that they had formed. Everybody was raving about Paul, who was from Detroit. When I heard him I *knew* he was a bad motherfucker.

We opened at the Bohemia, I think in July of 1955, and the place was always packed. After my engagement at the Bohemia, Oscar Pettiford brought a quartet in there that had Julian "Cannonball" Adderley on alto sax. I used to go down to the Bohemia just to hang out with my girlfriend Susan. But Cannonball just fucked me up the way he played the blues and nobody had ever heard of him. Everybody knew right away that this big motherfucker was one of the best players around. Even white critics were raving about his playing. All the record labels were running after him. Man, he was hot that quick.

Anyway, I used to sit up and talk with him, because he was a real nice guy on top of being an unbelievable alto player. When he started getting all that attention and all those record labels started running after him, I tried to tell him who was who and who to fuck with and who not to fuck with. I recommended Alfred Lion as a person he could trust and who would also leave him alone in the studio. But he didn't listen to me. I also told him about John Levy, who became his manager. But he signed with Mercury-Emarcy, who always told him what to play and record. In the end, that shit fucked Cannonball up and he hardly played the things he wanted to play or was capable of playing. They just didn't know what to do with his talent.

He was a music teacher back in Florida where he came from, so he didn't think nobody could really tell him nothing about music. I was a couple of years older than Cannonball, and had been on the New York music scene much longer. I knew a lot of shit about music from just being around a lot of bad motherfuckers, things you couldn't pick up in no college classroom—that was the reason I had quit Juilliard. But Cannonball thought he knew everything back then, so when I would talk to him about some of the silly chords he was playing—I told him he ought to change the way he approached them —he just kind of fluffed me off. By this time he had really listened to Sonny Rollins, so he *knew* that the shit I was telling him was right on the money. After I said in an interview published a short while after this that he didn't know chords but that he could play, he came up and apologized for not listening to me when I first told him.

I could almost hear him playing in my band the first time I heard him. You know, he had that blues thing and I love me some blues. I was also worried about Sonny Rollins in my band. Not because of his playing, or anything like that, but because he was talking—again— about leaving New York for good. So I was on the lookout for a replacement for Sonny if he left. But then Cannonball went back to his teaching job in Florida and fucked everyone up, and didn't come back until the next year.

In August, after the Bohemia gig, I went back into the studio to make another record for Prestige. This time I used Jackie McLean on alto, Milt Jackson on vibes, Percy Heath on bass, Art Taylor on drums, and Ray Bryant on piano because I wanted a bebop sound. I remember Jackie got so high he got terrified he couldn't play. I don't know what that shit was all about, but after this date, I never used Jackie again.

We were recording two of Jackie's compositions for this date: "Dr. Jackle" and "Minor March." Then on "Bitty Ditty," a tune by Thad Jones, Art was having a little problem with the time. But I knew he would get it. Art is a sensitive kind of guy and you try not to come down too hard on him because he might take it to heart. All of a sudden, Jackie comes up to me, all high and shit, and says, "Miles, what's happening here? You don't treat me like you do Art when I fuck up. You let me know right away what I did. How come you don't come down on Art like you come down on me?"

So I look at Jackie—who was a good friend, although we had gone our separate ways because he was still deep into drugs and I wasn't —and say, "What's the matter with you, man, you got to pee or something?" Jackie got so mad, he packed up his horn and left the studio. That's why he's only on two tunes on that album.

During the time while we were cutting that album, a horrible thing happened—a young, fourteen-year-old black boy from Chicago named Emmett Till was lynched in Mississippi by a gang of white men for talking to a white woman. They threw his body in the river. When they found him and pulled him out he was all bloated. They took pictures of him and put them in the papers. Man, that shit was horrible and shocked everyone in New York. It made me sick to my stomach. But it just let black people know once again just how most white people in this country thought of them. I won't forget them pictures of that young boy as long as I live.

I had signed for some club dates that were to start in September and when the time came Sonny Rollins disappeared like he said he would. People told me he was out in Chicago, but I couldn't track him down. (Later, I found out that he had signed himself into Lexington to kick his heroin habit for good.) I was desperate for a tenor player, so I tried John Gilmore, who was playing with Sun Ra's Arkestra. He had moved to Philadelphia and Philly Joe knew him, had played with him a few times, and recommended him. He came to a few rehearsals but he didn't work out, although he's a hell of a player. He just didn't fit in with what I wanted to do; his sound wasn't what I heard for the band.

And then Philly Joe brought up John Coltrane. I already knew Trane from the Audubon gig we had done together several years back. But that night Sonny had just blown him away. So when Philly told me who he was bringing, I wasn't excited. But after a few rehearsals—and I could hear how Trane had gotten a whole lot better than he was on that night Sonny set his ears and ass on fire—he said he had to go back home, so he left. I think the reason we didn't get along at first was because Trane liked to ask all these motherfucking questions back then about what he should or shouldn't play. Man, fuck that shit; to me he was a professional musician and I have always wanted whoever played with me to find their own place in the music. So my silence and evil looks probably turned him off.

The group almost didn't happen when Trane went back to Philly to play with Jimmy Smith. We practically had to beg him to come join the band for this gig we had in Baltimore, in late September 1955. What happened was that I had gone out and hired the Shaw Artists Corporation to do my booking for me, since all of a sudden I was in demand. The Shaws, Milt and Billy, booked dates for me. But I told them from the beginning—they were white—what *I* wanted them to do; I wasn't going to be doing what *they* wanted me to do. Because back then white men always told black guys what to do, so I wasn't having none of that and told them that right up front.

They assigned a guy named Jack Whittemore to work with me. We became good friends after a while, but I had Harold Lovett watching him like a hawk, because regardless of the fact that I grew to like Jack, I didn't want him trying to take advantage of me. It was Jack who set up my band's first tour when Coltrane was in the band, set up a tour that went to Baltimore, Detroit, Chicago, St. Louis, and back to New York to do the Cafe Bohemia.

After all this shit was set up and Sonny Rollins hadn't come back, and Trane had gone back to Philly to play with Jimmy Smith, the organist, we found ourselves without a tenor. So Philly Joe called Trane and asked him to come with us. Trane was the only one who *knew* all the tunes, and I couldn't risk having nobody who didn't know the tunes. But after we started playing together for a while, I knew that this guy was a bad motherfucker who was just the voice I needed on tenor to set off my voice.

We didn't know until later that Trane had made up his mind that if we called him he would come back with us, because he liked the music we were playing better than he did the music of Jimmy Smith; he felt there was room to stretch out in my band. But we didn't know this. So he took Philly Joe through a little thing, Trane and his girl-friend at the time, Naima Grubbs, before he decided to meet us in Baltimore. Then, when we got there and he arrived, he and Naima got married with all of us standing up there as best men, the whole band, man. As a group, on and off stage, we hit it off together.

Now we had Trane on sax, Philly Joe on drums, Red Garland on piano, Paul Chambers on bass, and myself on trumpet. And faster than I could have imagined, the music that we were playing together was just unbelievable. It was so bad that it used to send chills through me at night, and it did the same thing to the audiences, too. Man, the shit we were playing in a short time was scary, so scary that I used to pinch myself to see if I was really there. The critic Whitney Balliett said not long after Trane and I were playing to-gether that Coltrane had a "dry, unplaned tone that sets Davis off, like a rough mounting for a fine stone." But before long, Trane was much more than that. After a while he was a diamond himself, and I knew it, and everybody else who heard him knew it, too.

the group I had with Coltrane made me and him a legend. That group really put me on the map in the musical world, with all those great albums we made for Prestige and, later, Columbia Records—George Avakian finally got his way. Not only did this group make me famous, but it started me on the road to making a lot of money, too—more money, it's been said, than any other jazz musician has ever made. I don't know about that, but that's what they say. It also brought me great critical acclaim, because most of the critics really loved this band. For the most part, they loved my playing and Trane's, too—and they made everybody in that band—Philly Joe, Red, Paul—all of us, stars.

Wherever we played the clubs were packed, overflowing back into the streets, with long lines of people standing out in the rain and snow and cold and heat. It was something else, man. And a whole lot of famous people were coming every night to hear us play. People like Frank Sinatra, Dorothy Kilgallen, Tony Bennett (who got up on the stage and sang with my band one night), Ava Gardner, Dorothy Dandridge, Lena Horne, Elizabeth Taylor, Marlon Brando, James Dean, Richard Burton, Sugar Ray Robinson, just to mention a few.

When this group was getting all this critical acclaim, it seemed that there was a new mood coming into the country; a new feeling was growing among people, black and white. Martin Luther King was leading that bus boycott down in Montgomery, Alabama, and all the black people were supporting him. Marian Anderson became the first black person to sing at the Metropolitan Opera. Arthur Mitchell became the first black to dance with a major white dance company, the New York City Ballet. Marlon Brando and James Dean were the new movie stars and they had this rebellious young image of the "angry young man" going for them. *Rebel Without a Cause* was a big movie then. Black and white people were starting to get together and in the music world Uncle Tom images were on their way out. All of a sudden, everybody seemed to want anger, coolness, hipness, and real clean, mean sophistication. Now the "rebel" was in and with me being one at that time, I guess that helped make me a media star. Not to mention that I was young and good looking and dressed well, too.

Being rebellious and black, a nonconformist, being cool and hip and angry and sophisticated and ultra clean, whatever else you want to call it—I was all those things and more. But I was playing the fuck out of my horn and had a great group, so I didn't get recognition based only on a rebel image. I was playing my horn and leading the baddest band in the business, a band that was creative, imaginative, supremely tight, and artistic. And that, to me, was why we got the recognition.

On our first tour after Coltrane joined the group in late September 1955, we were having a lot of fun together, hanging out, eating together, walking around Detroit. Paul Chambers was from Detroit and I had lived there and so for us it was like a homecoming. My man Clarence, the numbers man, brought all his boys down every night to see the shows. Detroit was a gas. And then we went to Chicago to play the Sutherland Lounge on the South Side. That was a gas, too, because I knew a lot of people there including my sister, Dorothy, who was living there and teaching school. She brought a lot of people down to hear us.

The only downer for me, really, during this entire first trip was that Paul Chambers was staying with Bird's ex-wife, Doris Sydnor, in her hotel room at the Sutherland Hotel. I told Paul not to bring that bitch around me; he could do what he wanted to, but just don't involve me with her, because I couldn't even stand to look at her. So he kept her to himself while we were there. I think he was a little disappointed that I didn't like Doris, though. He probably figured she was a catch, a feather in his cap, being Bird's former old lady. But man, she was ugly and I could never understand what Bird saw in her—or what a handsome, big guy like Paul saw in her. But I guess she had something that you couldn't see on the surface. I guess she was a motherfucker in bed.

From Chicago, we went down to play Peacock Alley in St. Louis. Now you know *I* was going to have a good time there, and we all did. It seemed like everybody in East St. Louis came over to St. Louis to see me play that week in the middle of October. All my boys that I had gone to school with showed up so it was a gas.

I was happy for my family to see me doing all right, off drugs and clean, leading a band and making some money. I could see that my father and mother were proud of me, especially after I told them about all the recording deals that I had going with Columbia and all. Columbia for them was the big time, and it was the big time for me, too. Anyway, everything just went beautifully in St. Louis while I was there—and throughout the whole tour.

I think a lot of people had expected Sonny Rollins to be in the band. Nobody in St. Louis had ever heard of Trane, so a lot of them were disappointed until he played. Then he just fucked everybody up, though some people still didn't like him yet.

By the time Sonny Rollins came back from Lexington to New York, Trane was a fixture in the band and had taken over the place reserved for Sonny. And Trane's playing was so bad by then that it even made Sonny go out and change *his* style—which was a great style—and go back to woodshedding. He even went out on the Brooklyn Bridge a few times—at least that's what someone told me —to find a private place where he could practice.

By the time we got back to New York and opened at the Cafe Bohemia, a club down in the Village on Barrow Street, the band was playing great, and Trane was blowing his ass off. George Avakian from Columbia Records used to come down almost every night to hear the band. He loved the band, thought that it was a great group, but he especially loved the way Coltrane was playing now. I remember he told me one night that Trane "seemed to grow taller in height and larger in size with each note that he played," that he "seemed to be pushing each chord to its outer limits, out into space."

But as great as Trane was sounding, Philly Joe was the fire that was making a lot of shit happen. See, he *knew* everything I was going to do, everything I was going to play; he anticipated me, felt what I was thinking. Sometimes I used to tell him not to do that lick of his *with* me, but *after* me. And so that thing that he used to do after I played something—that rim shot—became known as the "Philly lick," and it made him famous, took him right up to the top of the drumming world. After he started doing it with me, guys in other bands would be telling their drummers, "Man, give me the Philly lick after I do my thing." But I left a lot of space in the music for Philly to fill up. Philly Joe was the kind of drummer that I knew my music had to have. (Even after he left I would listen for a little of Philly Joe in all the drummers I had later.)

Philly Joe and Red Garland were the same age, about three years older than I was. Coltrane and I were born in the same year, with me being a little older. Paul Chambers was the baby in the group, being only twenty, but he was playing like he had been around forever. And so was Red; he was giving me that Ahmad Jamal light touch, and a little bit of Erroll Garner, along with his own shit up in all of that. So everything was happening.

The most stunning thing that year was that Columbia gave me a $4,000 advance for my first record with them, plus $300,000 every year. But Prestige didn't want to lose me to Columbia, not after they had put up with me when didn't nobody want me, so I had about a year to go on my contract with Prestige. Columbia wanted to start recording us right then, so somehow, and I don't know what the deal was, George Avakian convinced Bob Weinstock to let him begin recording me in six months with the agreement that Columbia wouldn't release any music until after I was finished with my contractual obligations to Prestige. In the meantime, I owed Prestige four albums that I was to give them during the next year (in the end, the music I recorded for Prestige came out to be five and a half albums). We started recording for Columbia at the end of October 1955, while we were still playing down at the Cafe Bohemia, but we didn't release these tunes until later, after the May 1956 agreement. George thought that Prestige was going to release me from my contract with them, but Bob wasn't even thinking about that.

I wanted to leave Prestige because they weren't paying me no money—not what I thought I was worth. They had signed me for peanuts when I was a junkie and had hardly ever given me any extra. When the word got around that I was leaving Bob, a lot of guys thought that I was cold-blooded to leave him like that after he had done all those records with me when nobody else would. But I had to look ahead and start thinking about my future, and the way I saw it I couldn't turn down the kind of money Columbia was offering. I mean I would have been a fool to do it. Plus, it was all coming from the white man, so why should I have second thoughts about getting what I could at the time? I appreciated what Bob Weinstock and Prestige had done for me up until this time. But with all the money and opportunities Columbia was offering me, it was just time to move on.

In November, I went into the studio to fulfill my obligations to Prestige. During that session, we recorded "There Is No Greater Love," "Just Squeeze Me," "How Am I to Know?," "Stablemates," "The Theme," and "S'posin," all standards; the collection was called *Miles*. For a long time everybody thought that this was the very first recording that this band made, since we had kept that first Columbia recording session secret. This record for Prestige was nice, but nothing like what we were going to do for them in our next sessions.

By the beginning of 1956, I was really enjoying playing with this group and enjoying listening to them play as individuals. But the club owners still wanted to pay that same little money they had been paying jazz musicians in the past. So I told Jack Whittemore we wanted more money because of all the people filling up the clubs. The owners balked at first and then they came on in. I also told Jack I didn't want to play no more of those "forty-twenty" sets the club owners wanted everybody to play. They wanted you to begin your set twenty minutes after the hour and play until the end of the hour and then come back twenty minutes later and play another set. Sometimes you could end up playing four or five sets like that during a night and be tired as a motherfucker. That's one of the reasons drugs were used—especially cocaine—because playing sets like that was tiring. One time in Philadelphia I just told the club owner that I was only going to play three sets and that was it. The owner said he wasn't going to go for it, so I told him he didn't have no deal. He changed his mind after he saw all those lines outside his club.

Then there was a concert we played during this period when I was getting something like $1,000 a concert. The promoter was a guy named Robert Reisner (who I had once asked for $25 as a stand-by, because he asked me to play at this thing called the "Open Session" he used to run, and I sat around all day without playing). He later wrote a bullshit book about Bird. Anyway, Reisner wanted to add another show after the first one sold out so fast. So he offered Jack Whittemore $500 for the second show. I told Jack I wasn't doing it because the house was going to be full, so why should I have to go up there and blow my horn for half of what I made for the first concert? I told Jack to tell the guy to rope off half of Town Hall, where we were playing, if he wasn't going to give me the rest of the money. When the promoters heard this, they came on through with the rest of the bread.

But that was the kind of shit that promoters and club owners did to jazz musicians back in those days, especially if you were black. But now that we could make money whenever and wherever we played, they gave in to our demands. That's why I had a reputation for being very difficult to handle. I stood up for my rights and wouldn't let them fuck me over. I had Harold Lovett handling a lot of this for me and he was so cold, man. He had all those club owners scared of him. Harold straightened out a lot of shit for me, and that's how I learned the importance of having a good lawyer you can trust and call on at any time. And from then on out, I've always had one.

One time I knocked out this promoter named Don Friedman—this was later in 1959—because he ran up to me wanting to fine me $100 for being late even though we weren't scheduled to go on yet. I called Harold after I had knocked Don out. Harold was a real jive-talking, loud motherfucker—so he could straighten things out, and he did. Another time before that I canceled a gig in Toronto because the club owner, who didn't like Philly Joe Jones's playing, wanted me to fire him. Trane and Paul Chambers were already on their way there. So when they got there, they had no place to play. Man, they were mad at me. But I explained my reasons to them and they understood.

It was right after this incident in Toronto, in February or March 1956, that I had my first throat operation and had to disband the group while I was recovering. I had to have a non-cancerous growth on my larynx removed. It had been bothering me for a while. After I got out of the hospital, I ran into this guy in the record business who was trying to convince me to do this deal. During the course of the conversation I raised my voice to make a point and fucked up my voice. I wasn't even supposed to talk for at least ten days, and here I was not only talking, but talking loud. After that incident my voice had this whisper that has been with me ever since. I used to be self-conscious about it, but eventually I just relaxed and went with it.

I was supposed to record again in May for Prestige, but in the meantime I relaxed for the first time in a long time. I had bought myself a white Mercedes-Benz and moved to 881 Tenth Avenue up by 57th Street. It was a nice pad, especially for a bachelor. It had one huge room and a kitchen. John Lewis was living in the building then; Diahann Carroll and Monte Kay lived right across the hall from me. I was making a little money by then, but not as much as I thought I should be making. Dave Brubeck was making much more at the time. But I was dressing real good again: Brooks Brothers suits and custom-made Italian suits. I remember one night I was so clean that I was looking in the mirror admiring myself. Harold Lovett was there. I had a gig that night and he was going with me. So I say to him, "Man, I'm cleaner than a motherfucker in this blue suit." He nodded his head and I felt so good that I walked to the door and forgot my trumpet. I was on my way out, my head in the air, when Harold hollered out from behind me, "Hey, Miles, you think they want to see you clean at the Bohemia without your trumpet?" Man, I had to laugh.

I was going out with Susan and about a hundred other women, at least it seemed like that many at the time. But I still couldn't get Frances Taylor—the dancer I had met in 1953 in Los Angeles—out of my mind. I would see her from time to time, but she was always traveling somewhere to dance. I knew that I liked her a lot, but she was just never around for long. I was just biding my time until she settled down in New York, which she said she wanted to do.

I made a record in the spring of 1956 with Sonny Rollins, Tommy Flanagan (it was Tommy's birthday), Paul Chambers, and Art Taylor. This was the half session that I owed Prestige. Then in May I reorganized my regular band with Trane, Red, Philly Joe, and Paul, and we went back to record for Prestige again over at Rudy Van Gelder's place in Hackensack, New Jersey. I remember this session well because it was long, and the playing was great. We did no second takes. We just recorded like we were playing a nightclub set. That's the recording session where you can hear Trane saying on the record, "Could I have a beer opener?" and asking Bob Weinstock, "How was that, Bob?" and "Why?" after Bob pulled my leg telling us we had to do a tune over again. The next month we sneaked back into the recording studio for Columbia and cut three or four more sides for them that came out later on 'Round About Midnight, my first Columbia album.

After I reorganized the band, we went back into the Cafe Bohemia from early spring to late autumn 1956 and played to packed houses every night. With the money I was making now I was able to send support to Irene for our three kids, so that kept her off my back. And playing at the Cafe Bohemia down in the Village got me into another kind of social situation with people. Instead of being around a lot of pimps and hustlers, now I found myself around a lot of artists— poets, painters, actors, designers, filmmakers, dancers. I found myself hearing about people like Allen Ginsberg, LeRoi Jones (now Amiri Baraka), William Burroughs (who would write *Naked Lunch,* a novel about a junkie), and Jack Kerouac.

In June 1956, Clifford Brown got killed in a car accident, along with Richie Powell, the pianist who was Bud Powell's younger brother. Man, that was some sad shit, Brownie and Richie dying like that, and they were so fucking young. Brownie wasn't even twenty-six yet. Everyone had been raving about this young trumpet player who was playing in and around Philly, who could play his ass off. I think the first time I heard him was when he was in Lionel Hampton's band, and I knew then he was going to be outstanding. He had his own way of playing and if he had lived he would have been something else. I have read in places about me and Brownie not being able to get along because of competition between us. That shit's not true. We were both trumpet players and we were trying to play the best we could. Brownie was a beautiful, sweet, hip guy who you couldn't help but like to be around. He was a clean-living guy who didn't hang out much. He and I got along real good when we saw each other; he respected me a lot and I respected him. We weren't running buddies or nothing like that, but we didn't dislike each other. Brownie's death really fucked up Max Roach because him and Brownie had a great group together and with Richie and Brownie dead, Max broke up the group. It really tore up Max's head and I don't think he has played the same since. Him and Brownie were meant for each other because of the way they both played: real fast, so they could feed off each other. I have always felt that great trumpet players need great drummers in order to get their shit off. I know it has always been that way for me. Max used to tell me all the time how he loved playing with Brownie. His death really got to Max and he didn't pull out of it for a long time.

We were about to finish up our summer-long stand at the Cafe Bohemia. At the end of September, we went back into the studio for Columbia and recorded " 'Round Midnight" and "Sweet Sue" (which was arranged by Teo Macero, who would later become my producer at Columbia). Teo had gotten "Sweet Sue" from Leonard Bernstein, who had been trying to record a jazz album, *What Is Jazz?,* and so Teo picked this cut from a rendition that Bix Beiderbecke had done. I also recorded "All of You" at this session. So we had two great ballads—"All of You" and " 'Round Midnight"—in the can from that session for the album *'Round About Midnight.* "Sweet Sue" went into the album *Basic Miles.*

Then I cut a couple of tunes as a sideman with a group that called themselves The Brass Ensemble of the Jazz and Classical Music Society. I was the principal soloist on this album, and Columbia was the label that we recorded the songs for. Then, a few days after that session, I took Trane, Red, Philly Joe, and Paul back into the studio to do my last sessions for Prestige. As usual, we went out to Rudy Van Gelder's recording studio in Hackensack. This was the time when we recorded—all in one long session—"My Funny Valentine," "If I Were a Bell," and all those other tunes that appeared on those Prestige albums called *Steamin', Cookin', Workin',* and *Relaxin'.* All of those albums came out at the end of October 1956. That was some great music we made at both those sessions and I'm real proud of it today. But this ended my contract with Prestige. I was ready to move on.

After I had been around the music scene for a while, I saw what happened to other great musicians, like Bird. One of the basic things I understood was that success in this industry always depends upon how many records you sell, how much money you make for the people who control the industry. You could be a great musician, an innovative and important artist, but nobody cared if you didn't make the white people who were in control some money. The real money was in getting to the mainstream of America, and Columbia Records served the mainstream of this country. Prestige didn't; it was making great records, but outside the mainstream.

As a musician and as an artist, I have always wanted to reach as many people as I could through my music. And I have never been ashamed of that. Because I never thought that the music called "jazz" was ever meant to reach just a small group of people, or become a museum thing locked under glass like all other dead things that were once considered artistic. I always thought it should reach as many people as it could, like so-called popular music, and why not? I never was one of those people who thought less was better; the fewer who hear you, the better you are, because what you're doing is just too complex for a lot of people to understand. A lot of jazz musicians say in public that they feel this way, that they would have to compromise their art to reach a whole lot of people. But in secret they want to reach as many people as they can, too. Now, I'm not going to call their names. It's not important. But I always thought that music had no boundaries, no limits to where it could grow and go, no restrictions on its creativity. Good music is good no matter what kind of music it is. And I always hated categories. Always. Never thought it had any place in music.

So I never, ever felt bad because a lot of people were beginning to like what I was doing. I never felt that because the music I was playing was becoming popular that meant that my music was less complex than some that wasn't as popular as mine. Popularity didn't make my music any less worthy, or great. In 1955, Columbia represented for me a doorway my music could go through to reach more listeners, and I went through that door when it opened up and never looked back. All I ever wanted to do was blow my horn and create music and art, communicate what I felt through music.

And yes, going with Columbia did mean more money, but what's wrong with getting paid for what you do and getting paid well? I never saw nothing in poverty and hard times and the blues. I never wanted that for myself. I saw what it really was when I was strung out on heroin, and I didn't want to see it again. As long as I could get what I needed from the white world on my own terms, without selling myself out to all of those people who would love to exploit me, then I was going to go for what I know is real. When you're creating your own shit, man, even the sky ain't the limit.

Around this time, I met a white woman who I will call Nancy. She was Texan and a high-class call girl who lived in Manhattan in a great penthouse overlooking Central Park in the West Eighties. I met her through a black emcee named Carl Lee who worked at the Cafe Bohemia. She fell in love with me. She was fine as a motherfucker, outspoken about anything and didn't take no shit off anyone, and that included me (although most of the time she gave me what I wanted). She was a pretty little thing, dark hair, real sensuous. Nancy was a great woman, and she was one of the people who really kept me off drugs.

Nancy never worked the streets; her customers always came from the highest levels of society, from very important men—white men, mostly—whose names I won't mention. Let's just say they were some of the most important, powerful, and richest men in this country. They really liked her, though, and after I got to know her, I could understand why. She was a warm, caring, and very intelligent person, and very, very fine, very sexy, the kind of woman men lust for. She was a motherfucker in bed, so passionate and good that it would almost make you want to cry. She really loved me and I never had to give her a dime to be with her. She was a good friend, understood exactly what I was going through and what I wanted to do. She supported me 150 percent.

She pulled me out of a lot of tight jams during the time we were together. If I was out on the road doing pick-up gigs and I was stuck somewhere, I'd call Nancy and tell her, and she'd say, "Well, get the fuck out of there! How much money do you need?" And whatever I needed, she'd send it right away.

After we cut those last sides for Prestige in October 1956, I took the group back into the Cafe Bohemia and that's where a lot of shit came out between Coltrane and me. Things had been building up for a while. Man, it was a drag to see how bad Trane was treating himself; by now he was really strung out on heroin and also drinking a lot. He was coming in late and nodding on the stage. One night I got so mad with him that I slapped him upside his head and punched him in the stomach in the dressing room. Thelonious Monk was there that night; he had come back to the dressing room to say hello and saw what I did to Trane. When he saw that Trane didn't do nothing but just sit there like a big baby, Monk got hot under the collar. He told Trane, "Man, as much as you play on saxophone, you don't have to take nothing like that; you can come and play with me anytime. And you, Miles, you shouldn't be hitting on him like that."

I was so mad I didn't care what the fuck Monk was talking about, because in the first place, it wasn't none of his business. I fired Trane that night, and he went back to Philadelphia to try and kick his habit. I felt bad about letting him go, but I couldn't see what else I could have done under the circumstances.

I replaced Coltrane with Sonny Rollins and finished out the week at the Bohemia. Right after we closed, I broke up the band and caught a plane and went straight to Paris where I had been invited to headline, along with Lester Young, an all-star group of musicians that included the Modern Jazz Quartet (Percy Heath, John Lewis, Connie Kay, and Milt Jackson) and a lot of French and German musicians. We played Amsterdam, Zurich, Switzerland, Freiburg, Germany (a city in the Black Forest), and Paris.

In Paris I hooked up again with Juliette Greco, who was a real big cabaret and movie star by now. At first she was a little apprehensive about seeing me—because of the way I had acted when I saw her the last time in New York—but when I explained why I did that, she forgave me and we got along real well, just like the first time. And of course, I also got together with Jean-Paul Sartre and we had a great time just sitting around talking in their homes or at an outside cafe. We'd use a combination of broken French, broken English, and sign language.

After we had played our concert in Paris, a lot of the musicians went over to the Club St. Germain there, a hip music spot on the Left Bank. I took Juliette with me and we went to see Don Byas, the great American black saxophone player who was playing there that night. I think all the members of the MJQ were with us and Kenny Clarke was there, too. Anyway, Bud Powell and his wife, Buttercup, came on the scene to join us. We were all glad to see Bud. He had moved to Paris permanently by this time. Me and Bud were really happy to see each other and we just hugged and carried on like long-lost brothers who had finally found one another. After a few drinks and a lot of conversation, someone said that Bud was going to play. I remember feeling real happy about that because I hadn't heard Bud play in a long, long time. So he went up to the piano and started to play "Nice Work If You Can Get It."

But after a real fast and great beginning, something happened and his playing just fell apart. It was terrible. I was shocked, like everyone else there that night. Nobody said nothing, just kind of looked at each other like we couldn't believe what we were hearing. After he finished, there was silence in the club for a while. Then Bud stood up, wiped the sweat off his face with a white handkerchief and sort of bowed. When he did that, we all clapped because we didn't know what else to do. Man, it was just pitiful to hear him play like that. As Bud left the stage, Buttercup went up to greet him and she hugged him and they talked for a moment. He looked real sad, like he knew what had happened. See, by this time in his life, he was very sick with schizophrenia and he was only a shell of his former self. She brought him back over to where we were all sitting. Man, everyone was just embarrassed as hell to see him like that, too embarrassed even to say a word, so we just had these weak smiles on our faces, trying to hide what we really felt inside. There was complete silence. Complete. You could have heard a feather hit the floor.

Then I just jumped up and went and hugged Bud and told him, "Bud, now you know you shouldn't be playing when you've been drinking like you have; now you know that, don't you?" I looked at him straight in the eyes and I said this loud enough for everyone to hear. So, he just kind of nodded and smiled that secret, faraway smile that crazy people smile and sat down. Buttercup just stood, almost crying, grateful for what I had done. Then all of a sudden, everybody started talking and everything went back to the way it was before Bud played. But, you know, I couldn't have just said nothing. Man, he was my friend and one of the greatest piano players who ever lived, until he got beat up and sent to Bellevue. Now he was over there in Paris, in a foreign country, among people who might not have understood what had happened to Bud—and maybe didn't care—and thought he might have been just a drunken bum. That was a sad sight, man, seeing and hearing Bud like that. I'll never forget it as long as I live.

I came back to New York in December 1956 and got the band back together and we went on a two-month road trip. We went to Philadelphia, Chicago, St. Louis, Los Angeles, and San Francisco, where we played the Blackhawk for two weeks.

But by the fall of '56, Trane (who was back in the band) and Philly Joe had really started to get on my nerves with their junkie shit—showing up late, sometimes not at all. Here was Trane up on the bandstand sometimes nodding out, high off heroin. By this time Trane and his wife, Naima, had moved from Philly to New York, so he was getting some strong shit that he hadn't been getting in Philly. After he moved to New York his habit got worse, and real quick, too. I didn't have no moral thing about Trane and all of them shooting heroin, because I had gone through that, and I knew that it was a sickness that was hard to get rid of. So I didn't give them no grief about doing it. What I did start to get on them about was coming late and nodding up on the bandstand; I told them I couldn't tolerate that.

Here we were getting $1,250 a week when Coltrane came back into the band—and these guys are nodding out on stage. I couldn't afford that kind of shit! People would see them nodding and think *I* was a junkie again; you know, guilt by association. And I was clean as a whistle, except for sometimes when I would snort a little coke. I was going to the gym, keeping myself in good condition, not drinking much, taking care of business. I was talking to them, trying to get them to understand what they were doing to the group and to themselves. I told Trane that record producers had been coming around listening to him, thinking about giving him a contract, but when they saw him up there nodding and shit, they held off. He seemed to understand what I was talking about, but he kept right on shooting heroin and drinking like a fish.

If it had been some other player I would have fired him again after the first couple of times. But I loved Trane, I really did, although we never did hang out too much like Philly Joe and I did. Trane was a beautiful person, a real sweet kind of guy, spiritual, all of that. So you really couldn't help loving him and caring about him, too. I figured he was making more money than he had ever made in his life, and so when I talked to him I thought he would stop, but he didn't. And that hurt me. Later I found out that Philly Joe was a bad influence on Trane while they were in the band together. At first, when Trane was using that shit I didn't look at how he was acting because the music was so strong, and he and Philly would always be promising me they was going to stop. But things got worse. Sometimes, Philly Joe would be so sick up on the bandstand he would whisper to me, "Miles, play a ballad, I'm getting ready to throw up so I gotta go to the bathroom." He'd leave the stage and go throw up and come back like nothing had happened. He'd pull some stupid shit.

I remember one time when Philly Joe and I were going out on the road and doing pick-up dates back in 1954 or early '55. It would be me and him, and we'd find a local group. They'd pay us $1,000 and we'd do the gig. I was clean by this time. We were out in Cleveland, I think, and we were trying to get back to New York. Now Joe done shot up two or three hours before, so the shit is starting to wear off. When I get to the airport to buy the plane tickets, he's already getting fidgety. I'm standing up there counting out the money to this cute little white chick who is selling the tickets when I run across a counterfeit bill—we called them "purple bills" back then—which if I don't give her we won't have enough money to buy the tickets. I'm trying not to let on that this motherfucker promoter done paid us with a counterfeit bill. I look at Philly Joe and he sees the bill and knows what I'm thinking. So he starts telling the girl how fine and pretty she is and that we were musicians and would like to write a song about her because she was so nice, so could she please give us her name. That woman started smiling from ear to ear and I didn't miss a beat when I handed her that money. She didn't even count it because she was trying to write her name so fast.

We get the tickets, and when we go to catch the plane, Philly's figuring how long it will take us to get back to New York so he can get some dope and shoot it so he won't get sick. But on the way to New York the plane was routed to Washington, D.C., because New York was snowed in. By this time, Philly's throwing up in the plane's bathroom. Once we get to Washington, same thing; New York is snowed in. So I get a refund and we're going to try to catch a train to New York. But Philly knows someone in D.C., so now he's begging me to stop by this guy's house. Now, I'm getting madder than a motherfucker. But he's got his drum cases with him and he's too sick now to pick them up. So I try to carry my shit and his shit out to a cab and I fuck up my wrist. In the meantime, he's been to the bathroom to throw up again. We catch a cab, go over to this guy's house in the snow, and have to wait for him because he was out. Philly is throwing up in this dealer's bathroom; his wife, who knew Philly, had let us in. Finally the guy comes back and Philly gets off. I had to pay for the stuff. I always kept an extra stash for emergencies, but I never let Philly know about it, because he would try to beg me out of it.

Finally, we caught the train back to New York. By this time I was not only mad, but my wrist felt like it was broken. When we're getting ready to leave each other, I tell Philly, "Man, don't you ever do that shit to me again, you hear what I'm saying?" I got my fingers all up in his face, and my eyes are bulging out, standing out there in front of Penn Station, in all that snow.

So Philly said to me with this wounded look all over his face, "Miles, why you talking to me like that? Man, I'm your brother. I love you. You know how it is when somebody gets sick! Plus, on top of that, you shouldn't be angry at me, you should be angry at all this *snow*, man, 'cause that's what caused all this bullshit in the first place. So, man, get angry with God, instead of me, because I'm your brother, who loves you."

When I heard that I almost died laughing, that shit was so funny—so quick and hip. But I still went home madder than a motherfucker and swore that I was going to try to keep out of that kind of bullshit from then on.

This kind of thing happened later on, when we were on tour with the band. I used to go to the hotel to pick up Philly Joe an hour early, just to sit in the lobby and watch him check out of hotels. He would always try to talk the front desk clerk down on his bill and that used to be some funny shit to watch. He might tell the clerk that the mattress was burnt and that it was like that when he got there. So the clerk would say something like, "That might be so, but what about the woman you had up there?"

Then Joe would say, "She didn't stay and anyway, she didn't come to see me."

"But she called you," the clerk might say.

"She called me to get in touch with Mr. Chambers, who has already left your establishment."

They would go back and forth like that: "The shower didn't work for three days," or "Two out of four lights didn't work"—anything. But he would always end up saving twenty to forty dollars for a week's stay and he'd use that money to go buy dope.

One time, I think in San Francisco, that shit didn't work. I'm across the street at a coffee place and I see Philly Joe throwing his bags and shit out of the side window into the alley. Then he goes back downstairs and I see him talking to the desk clerk. I stand outside the door and hear the desk clerk telling him that he's going to have to pay because he did this same shit to him before, and that he's going to go up and lock Joe's stuff in his room until he pays. So Joe says, "fine," that he's going to get the money from a friend of his across town. He walks out of the hotel looking all indignant while the clerk goes up to lock the room. When Joe gets outside, he runs around to the side of the hotel, picks up his bags, and walks away laughing like a motherfucker.

Philly Joe was a bitch. If he'd been a lawyer and white, he would have been president of the United States, because in order to get there you gotta talk fast and carry a lot of bullshit with you; Philly had it all and a lot to spare.

But the shit with Coltrane wasn't funny like it was with Philly Joe. You could laugh at Joe's shit, but with Trane it was getting to be pathetic. He'd be playing in clothes that looked like he had slept in them for days, all wrinkled up and dirty and shit. Then, he'd be standing up there when he wasn't nodding—picking his nose and sometimes eating it. And he wasn't into women like me and Philly were. He was just into playing, was all the way into music, and if a woman was standing right in front of him naked, he wouldn't have even seen her. That's how much concentration he had when he played. Now Philly Joe was a ladies' man. He was flashy and hip, and when we were up on stage, he got almost as much attention as I did. He was a character. But Trane was just the opposite; all he lived for was to play music. That was it.

But there was more depressing me on this trip than Philly Joe and Trane getting high. I was making $1,250 a week and that just wasn't enough to support myself and the band. I was taking $400 a week for myself out of that and dividing the rest with the group. On this trip, they were running up tabs at the bar, overdrawing the money they had coming (by the time I finally took Philly out of the band I think he must have owed around $30,000).

Here I am playing and don't have *nothing* to show for it. Going into debt and yet the clubs are crowded, lines wrapped around the block! So I just said to myself, fuck it, if they don't pay me what I want, I'm not making it anymore. I called up Jack Whittemore and told him that I couldn't be playing anymore for $1,250 a week. He said, "Okay, but you got to do it this time because you signed the contract." He was right about that, but I wasn't going to be doing it no more. After this I told him I had to get $2,500 a week and he said he'd see what he could do. We got it. And $2,500 a week was high for a black band. A lot of the club owners got mad at me for that but they gave me what I wanted.

When it came to running bar tabs, Paul Chambers was the worst. I'd give him his money and then I would bring up his bar tab, and he wouldn't want to pay. One time I had to hit him in the mouth, he made me so mad. Paul was a real nice guy, but he was just immature.

One time in Rochester, New York, the club we were playing wasn't making a lot of money. I knew the woman who ran it, and she had been nice to me before so I told her she didn't have to pay me. I gave her the money back because I wasn't hurting for bread, but I told her she had to pay everyone else, and she did. I used to do shit like that sometimes if the house wasn't making no money and if the person had been good to me. Anyway, on this trip to Rochester, Paul is drinking zombies. I ask him, "Why do you drink shit like that? Why you drink so much, Paul?"

And he says, "Aw, man, I can drink all I want. I can drink ten of these and it wouldn't bother me."

"Drink 'em and I'll pay for them," I told him. And he said, "Okay."

So he drinks about five or six of them and says, "See, it didn't bother me." After this we went to a spaghetti place to eat, Paul and me and Philly Joe. We all order spaghetti and Paul puts hot sauce all over his. I say, "Man, why you do that?"

He says, "Because I love hot sauce, that's why."

So I'm talking to Philly Joe and all of a sudden I hear this crashing sound and look around and Paul's whole head had fallen face first into the spaghetti, hot sauce and everything. Those zombies had hit him in the brain. The motherfucker was out cold. He had shot up dope and drank all them zombies and he couldn't take it. (That's how he died in 1969; drugs and too much drinking and doing everything to excess, and he wasn't but in his early thirties.)

Another time we were playing in Quebec, Canada, and they had us on a variety show. Paul was drunk and goes up to these real old white women—I mean, *real* old—and says, "What are you girls doing tonight after the show?" They got mad and went to the owner. So I go to the owner and say, "My man was obviously in the wrong, and playing this kind of place, a variety show, ain't what I really want to do. Why don't we call it quits right now; you pay us what you owe us and we'll leave." He agreed. But Joe's getting sick up there anyway because there ain't no heroin around. His shit ran out and nobody else got none. We got plane tickets but we couldn't leave because Quebec was snowed in, and I didn't have enough money to buy everybody train tickets. So I called my girlfriend Nancy and she sent the money that I needed right away.

By the time we got back to New York, in March 1957, the shit had really hit the fan, and so I finally fired Trane again and also fired Philly Joe. Trane went to play with Monk at the Five Spot and Philly just played around, because by now he was a "star." I replaced Trane with Sonny Rollins again and brought in Art Taylor on drums. It was hard for me to fire Trane again, but it was even harder to let Philly Joe go, because we were best friends and had been through a lot together. But the way I saw it, I didn't have a choice.

During the final two weeks at the Cafe Bohemia, before I fired Trane and Philly Joe, something happened that I still remember clearly. Kenny Dorham, the trumpet player, came in one night and asked me if he could sit in with the band. Kenny was a hell of a trumpet player—great style, all his own. I liked his tone and voice. And he was really creative, imaginative, an artist on that horn. He never got all the credit he deserved. Now, I don't let just anybody sit in with my band. You've got to know how to play, and Kenny could play his ass off. Plus, I had known him a long time. Anyway, the place was packed that night like it always was back in those days. After I got through playing, I introduced Kenny, who came up and played just like a motherfucker. Just kicked whatever I had played right out of everyone's head. So I was mad as hell, because nobody likes for someone to come on their gig and show them up. Jackie McLean was out in the audience and so I went up to him and asked him, "Jackie, what did I sound like?"

I know Jackie loves me, and he loves the way I play, so he ain't going to pull my leg. He looked me straight in the eye and said, "Miles, tonight Kenny is playing so beautiful you sound like an imitation of yourself."

Man, was I pissed when I heard that. I just went home without saying anything to nobody; it was the last set. I thought about that shit, because I've got a lot of pride. And when I had looked at Kenny as he was leaving, he had this shit-eating grin on his face and was walking like he was ten feet tall. He *knew* what had gone down— even if people in the audience didn't. He *knew* and *I knew* what had happened.

The next night he came back, just like I figured he would, to try to do it all over again, because he knew that I was playing to the biggest and hippest audience in the city. He asked me if he could sit in again. This time I let him play first and then I went up and just kicked his motherfucking ass. See, the night before I had been trying to play shit like Kenny plays, because I wanted to make him feel comfortable. And he knew that's what I was doing. But I came back on his ass the next night and he didn't even know what hit him. (Later, in the 1960s, in San Francisco, the same thing happened again, and that one ended in a draw, too, I think.) That's the way it was back in those days, people always trying to cut you to pieces in a jam session. Sometimes you win and sometimes you lose, but after you went through it with a great player like Kenny, you had to get something out of that. You had to have picked up something or you weren't ready to learn about music, even if sometimes it might be an embarrassing situation.

In May 1957 I went back into the studio with Gil Evans and we recorded *Miles Ahead*. It was a great experience working again with Gil. Gil and I had seen each other occasionally after we made *Birth of the Cool*. After that, we talked about getting together on an album again and we came up with the concept for the music on *Miles Ahead*. As usual, I loved working with Gil because he was so meticulous and creative, and I trusted his musical arrangements completely. We had always been a great musical team and I really realized it this time when we did *Miles Ahead*: Gil and I were something special together musically. We used a big band this time; Paul Chambers and the rest were mostly studio musicians on this date. Later, after *Miles Ahead* came out, Dizzy came by one day to see me and asked me for another copy of the record because he said he had played his so much he had worn it out in three weeks! He told me "it was the greatest." Man, that was one of the greatest compliments I've ever had, for someone like Dizzy to say that about something I've done.

While I was recording *Miles Ahead*, I was working at the Cafe Bohemia with Sonny Rollins on tenor, Art Taylor on drums, Paul Chambers on bass, and Red Garland on piano. Then we played together all summer, all over the East Coast and the Midwest. But when I was back in New York, I used to go down to the Five Spot and listen to Trane and Monk's band. By this time Trane had kicked his habit cold turkey like I had, staying at his mother's house down in Philly. And man, he was playing great, sounding good with Monk (and Monk was also sounding great). Monk had a real solid group, with Wilber Ware on bass and Shadow Wilson on drums. Trane was the perfect saxophonist for Monk's music because of the space that Monk always used. Trane could fill up all that space with all them chords and sounds he was playing then. I was proud of him for having finally kicked his habit and he was showing up regularly for the gig. And as much as I always loved Sonny's playing in my band—and Art Taylor's, too—it still wasn't the same for me as when I played with Trane and Philly Joe. I found myself missing them.

In September my band changed again: Sonny quit to form his own group, and after an argument we had at Cafe Bohemia, Art Taylor left, too. Art knew I loved the way Philly played. But Art's a real sensitive guy, and I was trying to figure out how to tell him to play certain shit that would kick the music up a notch or two, without hurting his feelings. I was hinting around, talking about sock cymbals and shit, trying to let him know what I wanted, and I could see that it was getting on his nerves. But I liked Art so I was being less direct than I usually was when I wanted to tell somebody something. This time I was beating around the bush.

Anyway, this went on for a couple of days, and then by the third or fourth night I was losing my patience. The place was packed with movie stars—I think Marlon Brando and Ava Gardner were there that night (but they were always there). Plus all of Art's uptown boys had come down to hear him. The set started, and after I finished my solo I stood right next to Art's sock cymbal, with my trumpet tucked under my arm, listening, like I always did, giving him some suggestions. He wasn't paying me any attention. He's nervous, and his boys are out in the house. But I don't care about that shit because I want him to play right and not too loud on the sock cymbal like he's been doing. So I say something else to him about the sock and he gives me this "Fuck you, Miles, get off my back" look! So I say to him under my breath, "Aw, motherfucker, don't you know how Philly makes that goddamn break!"

Art got so mad, he stopped playing right in the middle of the number, got up from the drums, walked off the stage, went into the back, and later, after the set was over, went back and packed up his drums and left. Everybody was speechless, including me. But the next night I had Jimmy Cobb take his place, and Art and I have never talked about what happened there ever since. We have never even mentioned it and I have seen him a lot since then.

Later on that week or the next, I fired Red Garland and brought in Tommy Flanagan on piano. I asked Philly to come back, and he did, and then I replaced Sonny with Bobby Jaspar, a saxophonist from Belgium who was married to my old friend Blossom Dearie. I had asked Trane to rejoin the band, but he had some commitments with Monk and couldn't leave at the time. I had also been talking to Cannonball Adderley, who was back in New York, about joining the group (he had been leading a group all summer, with his cornet-playing brother, Nat), but he couldn't do it right then, although he thought he could do it in October. So I had to go with Bobby Jaspar until I could get Cannonball. Bobby was a very good musician, but he just wasn't the right guy. When Cannonball said he was ready, I hired him in October and let Bobby go.

I had this idea in my head of expanding the group from a quintet to a sextet, with Trane and Cannonball on saxophones. Man, I could just hear that music in my head and I knew that if I got it together, it would be a motherfucker. It wasn't ready to happen yet, but I had a feeling that it would happen real soon. In the meantime, I toured around with the group I had, with Cannonball on alto, in a tour called Jazz for Moderns. I think it lasted for about a month, and we closed with a lot of other groups at Carnegie Hall.

Then I went to Paris again to play as a guest soloist for a few weeks. And it was during this trip that I met the French filmmaker Louis Malle through Juliette Greco. He told me he had always loved my music and that he wanted me to write the musical score for his new film, *L'Ascenseur pour l'Échafaud* (*Elevator to the Gallows*, or *Frantic*, as it was called in America; *Lift to the Scaffold* in Britain). I agreed to do it and it was a great learning experience, because I had never written a music score for a film before. I would look at the rushes of the film and get musical ideas to write down. Since it was about a murder and was supposed to be a suspense movie, I used this old, very gloomy, dark building where I had the musicians play. I thought it would give the music atmosphere, and it did. Everyone loved what I did with the music on that film. Later the music score was released on the Columbia album that had "Green Dolphin Street" on it, called *Jazz Track*.

While I was in Paris writing the music for Malle's film, I was playing at the Club St. Germain, with Kenny Clarke on drums, Pierre Michelot on bass, Barney Wilen on saxophone, and René Urtreger on piano. I remember this gig because a lot of French critics got mad when I wouldn't talk from the bandstand and introduce tunes like everyone else did, because I thought the music spoke for itself. They thought I was arrogant and snubbing them. They were used to all those black musicians who came over there grinning and scratching up on stage. There was only one critic who understood what I was doing and didn't come down hard on me and that was André Hodeir, who I thought was one of the best music critics I had come across. Anyway, none of that shit bothered me, and I just kept on doing what I was doing. It didn't seem to disturb the people who came to listen because the club was jam-packed every night.

I saw a lot of Juliette and I think it was on this trip that we decided we were always going to be just lovers and great friends. Her career was in France, and she loved being there, while my shit was happening in the States. And while I didn't love being in America all the time, I never thought about moving over to Paris. I really loved Paris, but I loved it to visit, because I didn't think the music could or would happen for me over there. Plus, the musicians who moved over there seemed to me to lose something, an energy, an edge, that living in the States gave them. I don't know, but I think it has something to do with being surrounded by a culture that you know, that you can feel, that you come out of. If I lived in Paris, I couldn't just go and hear some great blues, or people like Monk and Trane and Duke and Satchmo every night, like I could in New York. And although there were good, classically trained musicians in Paris, they still didn't hear the music like an American musician did. I couldn't live in Paris for all those reasons, and Juliette understood.

When I got back to New York in December 1957, I was ready to move forward with my music again. I asked Red to come back, and he did. When I heard Monk's gig at the Five Spot was ending, I called Trane and told him I wanted him back, and he said, "Okay." Man, when this happened, I knew some real great musical shit was about to go down; I could feel it in my bones. And it happened. It went all the way down.

most of what had happened up until this time in small group playing had come down from Louis Armstrong through Lester Young and Coleman Hawkins to Dizzy and Bird, and bebop had basically come from that. What everybody was playing in 1958 had mostly come out of bebop. *Birth of the Cool* had gone somewhat in another direction, but it had mainly come out of what Duke Ellington and Billy Strayhorn had already done; it just made the music "whiter," so that white people could digest it better. And then the other records I made, like "Walkin'" and "Blue 'n' Boogie"—which the critics called hard bop—had only gone back to the blues and some of the things that Bird and Dizzy had done. It was great music, well played and everything, but the musical ideas and concepts had mostly been already done; it just had a little more space in it.

Of all the stuff I had done with a small group, what we did on *Modern Jazz Giants* came closest to what I wanted to do now, that kind of stretched-out sound we got there on "Bags' Groove," "The Man I Love," "Swing Spring." Now, in bebop, the music had a lot of notes in it. Diz and Bird played a lot of real fast notes and chord changes because that's the way they heard everything; that's the way their voices were: fast, up in the upper register. Their concept of music was *more* rather than *less*.

I personally wanted to cut the notes down, because I've always felt

that most musicians play way too much for too long (although I put
up with it with Trane because he played so good and I used to just
love hearing him play). But I didn't hear music like that. I heard it in
the middle and lower registers, and so did Coltrane. We had to do
something suited for what we did best, for our own voices.

I wanted the music this new group would play to be freer, more
modal, more African or Eastern, and less Western. I wanted them to
go beyond themselves. See, if you put a musician in a place where he
has to do something different from what he does all the time, then
he can do that—but he's got to think differently in order to do it. He
has to use his imagination, be more creative, more innovative; he's
got to take more risks. He's got to play above what he knows—far
above it—and what that might lead to might take him above the
place where he's been playing all along, to the new place where he
finds himself right now—and to the next place he's going and even
above that! So then he'll be freer, will expect things differently, will
anticipate and know something different is coming down. I've always
told the musicians in my band to play what they *know* and then play
above that. Because then anything can happen, and that's where
great art and music happens.

Another thing you have to remember is that this was December
1957, not December 1944, and things were different, sounds were
different, people didn't hear things the same as they heard it back
then. It's always been that way; every time has its own style, and
what Bird and Diz did was the style for that time—and it was great.
But now it was time for something different.

If any group was going to change the concept of music and take it
someplace altogether different, a new place, forward and fresh, then
I felt this group was it. I couldn't wait for us to start playing together
so we could get used to what each musician would bring to the mix,
get used to listening to each other's voices in that mix, know each
other's strengths and weaknesses. It always takes a while for everybody to get used to one another—that's why I've always taken a new
band out on the road for a while before I take them into the studio.

The idea I had for this working sextet was to keep what we already
had going with Trane, Red, Joe, Paul, and myself and add the blues
voice of Cannonball Adderley into this mixture and then to stretch
everything out. I felt that Cannonball's blues-rooted alto sax up
against Trane's harmonic, chordal way of playing, his more free-form
approach, would create a new kind of feeling, a new kind of sound,

because Coltrane's voice was already going in a new direction. And then I wanted to give that musical mixture more space, using the concepts I had picked up from what Ahmad Jamal did. I heard my trumpet voice kind of floating over and cutting through all of this mixture, and I felt that if we could do it right, the music would have all the tension up in it.

In this group, everybody had played together for over two years, except for Cannonball. But one voice can change the entire way a band hears itself, can change the whole rhythm, the whole timing of a band, even if everyone else had been playing together forever. It's a whole new thing when you add or take away a voice.

We went out on tour in late December 1957, around Christmas time, starting at the Sutherland Lounge in Chicago. I've always tried to be in Chicago around Christmas so I can get together with my family. My brother Vernon comes up from East St. Louis, and my children, who live in St. Louis, all get together at my sister Dorothy's house in Chicago, along with some guys I grew up with who live in Chicago.

We'd all get together and drink and eat for a week or so. You know, have a ball. When we first opened with the sextet at the Sutherland, my old high school friend Darnell, who used to play piano, drove his city bus all the way from Peoria, Illinois, and parked it outside our hotel for three days! Every time we would play Chicago he would come on up. My friend Boonie used to get me the best barbecue in town, because being from East St. Louis, which is a barbecue town, I've always been a freak for good barbecue and chitlings, too. I really love great black cooking, collard greens and candied yams and cornbread and black-eyed peas and southern fried chicken—all of it—and with some bad hot sauce off to the side.

Right from the beginning the tour was just a motherfucker. BANG! We hit and tore up the fucking place and that's when I knew it was going to be something else. That first night in Chicago, we started off playing the blues, and Cannonball was just standing there with his mouth open, listening to Trane playing this way-out shit on a blues. He asked me what we were playing and I told him, "the blues."

He says, "Well, I ain't never heard no blues played like that!" See, no matter how many times he played a tune, Trane would always find ways to play it different every night. I told Trane after the set to take Cannonball in the kitchen and show him what he was doing. He did, but we had substituted so many things in the twelve-bar mode that if you weren't listening when it started off, where the soloist began, then when you *did* start to pay attention, you might not know what had happened. Cannonball had told me that what Trane was playing *sounded* like the blues, but that it really wasn't, it was something else altogether. That just fucked him up because *Cannonball* was a blues player.

But Cannonball caught on quick, just like snapping your fingers, that's how fast he picked things up. He was like a sponge; he just absorbed everything. With the blues thing, I should have told him that was just the way Trane played—far out—because Cannonball was the only one in the group who hadn't played with him. But once Cannonball caught on to what was happening, he was right in there, playing his ass off. He and Trane were very different players, but both of them were great. When Cannonball first joined the band, everyone liked him right away because he was this big, jovial guy, always laughing and real nice, a gentleman, and smart as they come.

After he'd been with us a while and then after Trane came back, the sound of the band just kept getting thicker and thicker, almost like when a woman uses too much makeup. Because of the chemistry and the way people were playing off each other, everybody started playing above what they knew almost from the beginning. Trane would play some weird, great shit, and Cannonball would take it in the other direction, and I would put my sound right down the middle or float over it, or whatever. And then I might play real fast, or buzzzzz, like Freddie Webster. This would take Trane someplace else, and he would come back with other different shit and so would Cannonball. And then Paul's anchoring all this creative tension between the horns, and Red's laying down his light, hip shit, and Philly Joe pushing everything with that hip shit he was playing and then sending us all off again with them hip-de-dip, slick rim shots that were so bad, them "Philly licks." Man, that was too hip and bad. Everybody was laying all kinds of slick shit on everyone. And I was telling them things like, "Don't leave that F until the last beat. You'll be able to play the mode five beats more than you would if you would leave it in like four beats. You leave it on the last bar, you know, and you accent the bar." And they would listen. It would be slicker than slick.

Trane was the loudest, fastest saxophonist I've ever heard. He could play real fast and real loud at the same time and that's very difficult to do. Because when most players play loud, they lock themselves. I've seen many saxophonists get messed up trying to play like that. But Trane could do it and he was phenomenal. It was like he was possessed when he put that horn in his mouth. He was so passionate—fierce—and yet so quiet and gentle when he wasn't playing. A sweet guy.

He scared me one time while we were in California when he wanted to go to the dentist to get a tooth put in. Trane could play two notes all at once and I thought his missing tooth was the cause of it. I thought it gave him his sound. So when he told me he was going to the dentist to get the tooth put in, I almost panicked. I told him that I had called a rehearsal for the same time that he was going. I asked him if he could postpone his dental appointment. "Naw," he said, "naw, man, I can't make the rehearsal; I'm going to the dentist." I asked him what kind of replacement he was going to get and he says, "A permanent one." So I try to talk him into getting a removable one that he can take out every night before he plays. He looks at me like I'm crazy. He goes to the dentist and comes back looking like a piano, he was grinning so much. At the gig that night —I think it was at the Blackhawk—I play my first solo and go back by Philly Joe and wait for Trane to play, almost in tears because I know he's fucked himself up. But when he ripped off them runs like he always did, man, talk about a motherfucker being relieved!

Trane never wrote anything down when he was with my band. All he did was just start off playing. We used to talk a lot about music at rehearsals and on the way to gigs. I would show him a lot of shit, and he would always listen and do it. I'd say, "Trane, here are some chords, but don't play them like they are all the time, you know? Start in the middle sometimes and don't forget that you can play them up in thirds. So that means you got eighteen, nineteen different things to play in two bars." He would sit there, his eyes wide open, soaking up everything. Trane was an innovator, and you have to say the right thing to people like that. That's why I'd tell him to begin in the middle, because that's the way his head worked anyway. He was looking to be challenged, and if you brought the shit to him wrong he wasn't going to listen. But Trane was the only player who could play those chords I gave him without them sounding like chords.

After the gig he would go back to his hotel room and practice while everybody else was hanging out. He would practice for hours after he had just got through playing three sets. And later in 1960, after I gave him a soprano saxophone that I got from a woman I knew in

Paris, an antique dealer, it had an effect on his tenor playing. Before he got that soprano, he was still playing like Dexter Gordon, Eddie "Lockjaw" Davis, Sonny Stitt, and Bird. After he got that horn, his style changed. After that, he didn't sound like nobody but himself. He found out that he could play lighter and faster on the soprano than he could on the tenor. And this really turned him on, because he couldn't do the things on tenor that he could on alto, because a soprano is a straight horn, and since he liked the lower register, he found he could also think and hear better with the soprano than he could with the tenor. When he played the soprano, after a while it sounded almost like a human voice, wailing.

But as much as I liked Trane we didn't hang out much once we left the bandstand because we had different styles. Before, it was because he was deep into heroin, and I had just come out of that. Now, he was clean and didn't hardly ever hang out, but would go back to his hotel room to practice. He had always been serious about music and always practiced a lot. But now it was almost like he was on some kind of mission. He used to tell me that he had messed up enough, had wasted too much time and not given enough attention to his own personal life, his family, and, most of all, to his playing. So he was only really concerned about playing his music and growing as a musician. That's all he thought about. He couldn't be seduced by a woman's beauty because he had already been seduced by the beauty of music, and he was loyal to his wife. Whereas for me, after the music was through, I was out the door seeing what pretty lady I was going to be with that night. Cannonball and I would sit and talk and hang out sometimes when I wasn't with some woman. Philly and I were still friends, but he was always running down that dope, him and Paul and Red. But we were all close and everybody got along real good together.

Back in New York, Cannonball, who had signed a deal to do a record for Blue Note, asked me to play on the date, which I did as a favor. The record was called "Something Else" and was very nice. I wanted to get my group into the studio, and in April, we recorded "Billy Boy," "Straight, No Chaser," "Milestones," "Two Bass Hit," "Sid's Ahead," and "Dr. Jackle" (listed as "Dr. Jekyll") for the album *Milestones* on Columbia. I played piano on "Sid's Ahead" because Red got mad at me when I was trying to tell him something and left. But I loved the way the band sounded on this record and I knew that we had something special. Trane and Cannon were really playing their asses off and by then were really used to each other.

This was the first record where I started to really write in the modal form and on "Milestones," the title track, I really used that form. Modal music is seven notes off each scale, each note. It's a scale off each note, you know, a minor note. The composer-arranger George Russell used to say that in modal music C is where F should be. He says that the whole piano starts at F. What I had learned about the modal form is that when you play this way, go in this direction, you can go on forever. You don't have to worry about changes and shit like that. You can do more with the musical line. The challenge here, when you work in the modal way, is to see how inventive you can become melodically. It's not like when you base stuff on chords, and you know at the end of thirty-two bars that the chords have run out and there's nothing to do but repeat what you've done with variations. I was moving away from that and into more melodic ways of doing things. And in the modal way I saw all kinds of possibilities.

After Red Garland walked out on me, I found a new piano player named Bill Evans. I wasn't mad at Red, but I had moved past the point where he could contribute what I wanted in the sound of the band. I needed a piano player who was into the modal thing, and Bill Evans was. I met Bill Evans through George Russell, whom Bill had studied with. I knew George from the days back at Gil's house on 55th Street. As I was getting deeper into the modal thing, I asked George if he knew a piano player who could play the kinds of things I wanted, and he recommended Bill.

I had gotten into the modal thing from watching a performance by the Ballet Africaine from Guinea. I was seeing Frances Taylor again; she was living in New York now and dancing in a show. I had run into her on 52nd Street and was real happy to see her. She went to all the dance performances, and I would go with her. Anyway, we went to this performance by the Ballet Africaine and it just fucked me up what they was doing, the steps and all them flying leaps and shit. And when I first heard them play the finger piano that night and sing this song with this other guy dancing, man, that was some powerful stuff. It was beautiful. And their rhythm! The rhythm of the dancers was something. I was counting off while I was watching them. They were so acrobatic. They had one drummer watching them dance, doing their flips and shit, and when they jumped he would play DA DA DA DA POW! in this bad rhythm. He would hit it when they would fall. And man, he was catching everybody that did anything. The other drummers got them, too. So they would do rhythms like 5/4 and 6/8 and 4/4, and the rhythm would be changing and popping. That's the thing, that secret, inner thing that they had. It's African. I knew I couldn't do it from just watching them dance because I'm not African, but I loved what they were doing. I didn't want to copy that, but I got a concept from it.

When Bill Evans—we sometimes called him Moe—first got with the band, he was so quiet, man. One day, just to see what he could do, I told him, "Bill, you know what you have to do, don't you, to be in this band?"

He looked at me all puzzled and shit and shook his head and said, "No, Miles, what do I have to do?"

I said, "Bill, now you know we all brothers and shit and everybody's in this thing together and so what I came up with for you is that you got to make it with everybody, you know what I mean? You got to fuck the band." Now, I was kidding, but Bill was real serious, like Trane.

He thought about it for about fifteen minutes and then came back and told me, "Miles, I thought about what you said and I just can't do it, I just can't do that. I'd like to please everyone and make everyone happy here, but I just can't do that."

I looked at him and smiled and said, "My man!" And then he knew I was teasing.

Bill brought a great knowledge of classical music, people like Rachmaninoff and Ravel. He was the one who told me to listen to the Italian pianist Arturo Michelangeli, so I did and fell in love with his playing. Bill had this quiet fire that I loved on piano. The way he approached it, the sound he got was like crystal notes or sparkling water cascading down from some clear waterfall. I had to change the way the band sounded again for Bill's style by playing different tunes, softer ones at first. Bill played underneath the rhythm and I liked that, the way he played scales with the band. Red's playing had carried the rhythm but Bill underplayed it and for what I was doing now with the modal thing, I liked what Bill was doing better. I still liked Red and brought him back on a few occasions, but I mostly liked him when we were going through that Ahmad thing. Bill could play a little like that Ahmad thing, too, although when he did, he sounded a little wild.

In the spring of 1958, we moved from the Cafe Bohemia where we had played for two years, to the Village Vanguard, a club owned and run by a guy named Max Gordon. The crowds that were coming to see us over at the Bohemia just moved on over to the Vanguard and there were full houses there, too, as long as we stayed there. I moved over to the Vanguard because Max gave me more money than the Bohemia. Before I opened he had to give me $1,000 front money in cash or I wouldn't play.

But the most important thing that happened to me in the spring of 1958 was Frances Taylor coming back into my life. Man, she was a wonderful woman and I loved just being with her. I cut everyone else loose and was just with her during this time. We were so compatible —I'm a Gemini and she's a Libra. I thought she was just outta sight. She was kind of tall, honey brown, beautiful, soft smooth skin, sensitive, artistic. An elegant, gracious, graceful person. I'm making her sound perfect, right? Well, she damn near was. Everybody else loved her, too. I know Marlon Brando did, and Quincy Jones, who was on the scene back then, too. Quincy even gave her a ring, and he still don't know what I know. Frances and I started living together in my apartment up on Tenth Avenue, and everywhere we went we stopped traffic.

I turned in my Mercedes-Benz for a white Ferrari convertible that cost me something like $8,000, which was considered a whole lot of money back then. Now, here we are riding around town in this spectacular car. A real black motherfucker like me with this stunningly beautiful woman! When she got out of the bad-ass car she seemed to be all legs, because she had these long, gorgeous, dancer's legs and she carried herself with that dancer's carriage. Man, it was something, people stopping and looking with their mouths hanging open and everything.

I was sharp as a tack every time I went out in public and so was Frances. *Life* magazine even put me in their international issue as a black person who was doing something good for his people. That was all right. But I always wondered why they didn't put me in the issue that comes out over here.

Frances was from Chicago and I was also from the Midwest, so that might have had something to do with us hitting it off so quick, because we never did have to explain a lot of shit. And she was black and that helped a lot, too, although I ain't never been into a racial thing about the women I am with; if they're cool, they're cool, no matter what color they are. I'm the same way about white men, too.

Frances was great for me because she settled me down and took me out of the streets and let me concentrate more on my music. I was basically a loner and she was, too. She used to always say, "We rehearsed for this for four years, Miles, so let's make it work." I loved Frances so much that for the first time in my life I found myself jealous. I remember I hit her once when she came home and told me some shit about Quincy Jones being handsome. Before I realized what had happened, I had knocked her down and she ran out of the apartment over to Monte Kay and Diahann Carroll's place buck naked. Then she got some clothes and went over to Gil Evans's and spent the night there because she was afraid I was going to knock down Diahann and Monte's door and hit her again. Gil called to tell me that she was there and safe. I told her not to ever mention Quincy Jones's name to me again, and she never did.

We had our verbal arguments just like all couples have, but that was the first time I had hit her—though it wouldn't be the last. Every time I hit her, I felt bad because a lot of it really wasn't her fault but had to do with me being temperamental and jealous. I mean, I never thought I was jealous until I was with Frances. Before, I didn't care what a woman did; it didn't matter to me because I was so into my music. Now it did and it was something that was new for me, hard for me to understand.

She was a star and on her way to being a superstar, probably the premier black female dancer when she went with me. She was getting all these offers to dance when she won Best Dancer for what she did in *West Side Story* on Broadway. But I made her get out of that because I wanted her at home with me. Later when Jerome Robbins personally asked her to do the movie version of *West Side Story,* I wouldn't let her do that. Or *Golden Boy* with Sammy Davis, Jr., who asked her himself when we were playing in Philadelphia. He was doing the tryouts the next morning and he asked her to come down. The next day at eight A.M., we were on the turnpike in my Ferrari on our way back to New York. That was my answer.

I just wanted her with me *all* the time. But she would argue about that shit with me, tell me that she had a career, too, that she was an artist, too, but I just didn't want to hear no shit that was going to keep us apart. After a while, she stopped talking about it and started teaching a dance class for people like Diahann Carroll and Johnny Mathis. I didn't mind her doing that because she was home with me every night.

Frances had been married before and had a little boy named Jean-Pierre, who was staying with her parents, Maceo and Ellen, in Chicago while she pursued her dancing career. When we started living together, her father called one day from Chicago and wanted to speak with me. He beat around the bush for a while before he got to the point of asking when I was going to marry Frances. He said, "Well, Miles, it seems to me if you settle for something long enough and live with it and taste it, you know how the goodies are, you know whether you want to buy it or not. So what about you and Frances, what y'all gonna do, when y'all gonna get married?"

I liked her father; he was a very nice man. But I knew how he was and we talked man to man. I knew he was concerned about his daughter because that's the kind of person he was, so I said, "It's none of your fucking business, Maceo. Frances don't mind, so what you got to do with it, man? We all grown, you know!"

He didn't say nothing else about it for a while after that, but he would bring it up from time to time and I would say the same thing until we got married, later.

Frances was dancing in *Porgy and Bess* at City Center when I first saw her again, so I went to see that a lot and that's where I got the idea to do the music on the *Porgy and Bess* album that Gil and I did in the summer of 1958. Being with Frances was a big influence on me in another way outside of music; going to see her dance all the time I really got interested in that and the theater because we started going to see a lot of plays. I even wrote a song for her called "Fran Dance" that we recorded on that "Green Dolphin Street" album. After Frances finished with *Porgy and Bess* she was in *Mr. Wonderful* with Sammy Davis, Jr.

By now people were starting to talk about "the Miles Davis Mystique." I don't know *where* that shit came from, but it was around everywhere. Even the music critics had gotten off my back by this time and many of them were calling me "Charlie Parker's successor."

The first important record the sextet made with Bill Evans in the band was the one we did in May 1958, *Jazz Track,* when we recorded "Green Dolphin Street," "Stella by Starlight," "Love for Sale," and "Fran Dance." Philly Joe was gone again by the time we recorded this and had been replaced by Jimmy Cobb, who had worked with me once when he replaced Art Taylor for a minute at the Cafe Bohemia. Everyone was tired of Philly's junkie shit by now and we just couldn't handle it any longer. He finally quit and started his own band that sometimes had Red Garland in it. I would miss that "Philly thing," that "Philly lick" on the rim. But Jimmy was a good drummer who brought his own thing to the sound of the group. And since I played with the rhythm section, played off what they did, I knew Paul and Bill and Jimmy were going to be reacting to and playing off that, off their thing together. I was going to miss Philly, but I knew I was going to like Jimmy, too.

Columbia put all the "Green Dolphin Street" recordings on the other side of the music score I had done for Louis Malle's film, *Elevator to the Gallows,* and released it over here under the title of *On Green Dolphin Street.* But that was the first recording the new group made as a band. After that, in June, I did a guest appearance on an album of the Frenchman Michel Legrand's big orchestra date that he did for Columbia. Coltrane, Paul Chambers, and Bill Evans also played on that album. Then we played around New York at the Vanguard and played up at the Newport Jazz Festival.

I came back and went into the studio with Gil to make *Porgy and Bess.* We started in late July and worked over into the middle of August. I didn't use Trane and Cannon on this album because they would have been too dominant in the saxophone section. All I wanted was straight tones. Couldn't nobody match their sounds, so I just went with guys who played those plain-Jane sounds for those plain-Jane songs. I also didn't use Bill Evans because we didn't use a piano. But I did use Paul and Jimmy Cobb and I brought in Philly Joe to do a couple of things. The rest of the musicians were mostly studio musicians and one of them, the tuba-player Bill Barber, had been on *Birth of the Cool.* That was real good to do, because I had to get close to a human-voice sound in some places. That was hard, but I did it. Gil's arrangements were great. He wrote an arrangement for me to play on "I Loves You, Porgy" and he wrote a scale that I was supposed to play. No chords. He had used two chords for the other voicing, and so my passage of scales with those two chords gives you a lot of freedom and space to hear other things.

Besides Ravel and a whole lot of others, Bill Evans had turned me on to Aram Khachaturian, a Russian-Armenian composer. I had been listening to him and what intrigued me about him were all those different scales he used. Classical composers, at least some of them, have been writing like this for a long time, but not many jazz musicians have. The musicians were giving me tunes with chords all the time, and at the time I didn't want to play them. The music was too thick.

Anyway, we did *Porgy and Bess* and then we went down to play the Showboat in Philadelphia, and that's where a narcotics policeman tried to bust Jimmy Cobb and Coltrane for drugs, but everybody was clean. One time they even came fucking with me during this engagement, looking for drugs. I just pulled down my shorts and told the motherfuckers to look up my asshole since they couldn't find no shit no place else. Man, them Philadelphia police were a bitch, always fucking with you; they were some of the most corrupt motherfuckers on the planet, and racist, too.

But things were starting to go bad in the group. After about seven months, Bill wanted to leave because he hated all the traveling and he wanted to do his own thing. Cannonball was talking about the same thing, and wanted to get his old group back together again, and even Coltrane was beginning to feel the same way. In Cannon's case, he didn't like being the road manager, paying off the guys and all. But the reason he was doing that was because he had a good head for that kind of thing and I really trusted him. Also I gave him more money for doing this so he was making more than everyone else except me. When he first joined the band, he said he would stay for a year and that year was up in October 1958. I convinced him to stay on for a little while longer and he agreed, but Harold Lovett and I really had to talk to him to keep him.

Some of the things that caused Bill to leave the band hurt me, like that shit some black people put on him about being a white boy in our band. Many blacks felt that since I had the top small group in jazz and was paying the most money that I should have a black piano player. Now, I don't go for that kind of shit; I have always just wanted the best players in my group and I don't care about whether they're black, white, blue, red, or yellow. As long as they can play what I want that's it. But I know this stuff got up under Bill's skin and made him feel bad. Bill was a very sensitive person and it didn't take much to set him off. Then a lot of people were saying he didn't play fast enough and hard enough for them, that he was too delicate. So on top of all this shit was the thing about traveling and wanting to form his own group and play his own music, which was where Coltrane and Cannonball were moving.

We were playing the same program every night and a lot of it was standards, or my music. I know they wanted to play their own stuff and establish their own musical identity. I didn't blame them for feeling that way. But we had the best group in the business and it was *my* band and so I wanted to keep it together for as long as I could. That was a problem, but it happens with most bands after a while. People just outgrow each other, like I did with Bird, and they have to move on.

Bill left the band in November 1958 and went down to Louisiana to live with his brother. Then he came back after a while and formed his own group. After a while he got Scott LaFaro on bass and Paul Motian on drums and he became very popular with that group, winning a number of Grammy Awards. He was a great little piano player, but I don't think he ever sounded as good after that as he did when he played with me. It's a strange thing about a lot of white players—not all, just most—that after they make it in a black group they always go and play with all white guys no matter how good the black guys treated them. Bill did that, and I'm not saying he could have gotten any black guys any better than Scott and Paul, I'm just telling what I've seen happen over and over again.

I asked Red Garland to replace Bill until I could find a replacement, and he stayed three months until he left to form his own trio. While he was with me Red went on the road with us for a while and then we came back and played Town Hall, and even Philly Joe played that gig because I think Jimmy Cobb was sick. It was like a reunion and everybody played their asses off. But now that we were going on the road, I had to deal with Trane, who now really wanted to leave. He was getting comfortable with himself, playing better and with more confidence than he had ever played. Plus he was happy and staying home and gaining weight. I even started kidding him about his weight, but those kinds of things didn't even cross his mind, you know, things like how much he weighed or clothes and shit like that. All he cared about was music and how he sounded playing. I was concerned because he was eating a lot of sweets in place of shooting drugs, so I offered to sell him some gym equipment so he could get his weight down.

Trane used to call me "the teacher" and it was hard for him to bring up that he wanted to leave; I would find it out from other people he had told. But he did bring it up finally and we made a compromise: I turned him on to Harold Lovett as a manager to handle his financial affairs. And then Harold got him a recording contract with Nesuhi Ertegun at Atlantic Records, who had always loved his playing since Trane had first come into the group. Trane had been doing some things for Prestige as a leader, which I turned him on to, but as usual, Bob Weinstock wasn't paying no real money.

Harold set up a publishing company for Trane (he kept it until his death, in 1967, and he also kept Harold Lovett as his manager). I had thought if Trane was going out on his own then he needed to learn something about business and be involved with someone he could trust. To keep Trane in the band longer, I asked Jack Whittemore, my agent, to get bookings for Trane's group whenever we weren't playing, and he did. So by the beginning of 1959, Trane was in a good position to get his own independent career on the road and that's what he began to do. If he wasn't playing with me he was always playing somewhere as a headliner, fronting his own band.

Cannonball was doing the same thing, so in 1959 we had three bandleaders in the group, and things started getting difficult. By now Trane had found his drummer in Elvin Jones, my old friend from Detroit, and he was constantly raving about him; but I already knew Elvin was bad. And Cannon was playing with his brother, Nat, so both of them knew where they were going. I felt good for them and bad for me, because I could see the writing on the wall, and I knew soon it was going to be over. I'd be lying if I said that that didn't make me sad, because I really loved playing with this band and I think it was the best small band of all time, or at least the best I had heard up until then.

I found a new piano player in February; his name was Wynton Kelly. There was another piano player that I liked and his name was Joe Zawinul (he would play with me later). But it was Wynton who came into the band. Wynton was from the West Indies, from Jamaica, and had played with Dizzy for a minute. I loved the way Wynton played, because he was a combination of Red Garland and Bill Evans; he could play almost anything. Plus, he could play behind a soloist like a motherfucker, man. Cannonball and Trane loved him, and so did I.

Wynton joined us just before I was going into the studio to make *Kind of Blue*, but I had already planned that album around the piano playing of Bill Evans, who had agreed to play on it with us. We went into the studio to record *Kind of Blue* on the first or second day of March 1959. We had the sextet of Trane, Jimmy Cobb, Paul, Cannon, myself, and Wynton Kelly, but he played on only one tune: "Freddie Freeloader." That song was named after this black guy I knew who was always seeing what he could get from you free, and he was always around the jazz scene. Bill Evans played on the rest of the tunes.

We made *Kind of Blue* at two recording sessions—one in March and the other one in April. In between, Gil Evans and I took a big orchestra and did a television show with a lot of the music on *Miles Ahead.*

Kind of Blue also came out of the modal thing I started on *Milestones.* This time I added some other kind of sound I remembered from being back in Arkansas, when we were walking home from church and they were playing these bad gospels. So that kind of feeling came back to me and I started remembering what that music sounded like and felt like. That feeling is what I was trying to get close to. That feeling had got in my creative blood, my imagination, and I had forgotten it was there. I wrote this blues that tried to get back to that feeling I had when I was six years old, walking with my cousin along that dark Arkansas road. So I wrote about five bars of that and I recorded it and added a kind of running sound into the mix, because that was the only way I could get in the sound of the finger piano. But you write something and then guys play off it and take it someplace else through their creativity and imagination, and you just miss where you thought you wanted to go. I was trying to do one thing and ended up doing something else.

I didn't write out the music for *Kind of Blue,* but brought in sketches for what everybody was supposed to play because I wanted a lot of spontaneity in the playing, just like I thought was in the interplay between those dancers and those drummers and that finger piano player with the Ballet Africaine. Everything was a first take, which indicates the level everyone was playing on. It was beautiful. Some people went around saying that Bill was co-composer of the music on *Kind of Blue.* That isn't true; it's all mine and the concept was mine. What he did do was turn me on to some classical composers, and they influenced me. But the first time Bill saw any of that music was when I gave him a sketch to look at just like everyone else. We didn't even have rehearsals for that music—we'd only had about five or six in the last two years—because I had great musicians in that band and that's the only way that can work.

I had Bill playing on *Kind of Blue* in a minor mode. Bill was the kind of player that when you played with him, if he started something, he would end it, but he would take it a little bit farther. You subconsciously knew this, but it always put a little tension up in everyone's playing, which was good. And because we were into Ravel (especially his "Concerto for the Left Hand and Orchestra") and Rachmaninoff ("Concerto No. 4"), all of that was up in there somewhere. When I tell people that I missed what I was trying to do on *Kind of Blue*, that I missed getting the exact sound of the African finger piano up in that sound, they just look at me like I'm crazy. Everyone said that record was a masterpiece—and I loved it too—and so they just feel I'm trying to put them on. But that's what I was trying to do on most of that album, particularly on "All Blues" and "So What." I just missed.

I remember when Billie Holiday died in July 1959. I didn't know Billie all that well; we didn't hang out or nothing like that. Billie loved my son, Gregory. She used to think he was cute. I knew that she and her husband weren't getting along because she said to me once, "Miles, I told him he could leave me alone. He could have our house, everything, but just leave me alone." But that was all I remember her telling me that was personal. She did tell me she liked a man built like Roy Campanella, the old Brooklyn Dodgers catcher, because she thought that kind of man had that sexual thrust that she liked when she was making love. She loved those short, wide, big legs, low ass; built like a buffalo. From what she told me, Billie was really into sex when that dope and alcohol didn't kill her sexual drive.

I remember her being a very warm, nice woman, and she had that smooth, light-brown skinned Indian look before drugs destroyed her face. She and Carmen McRae reminded me of the way my mother looked, Carmen more so than Billie. Billie was a beautiful woman before all the alcohol and drugs wore her down.

The last time I saw her alive was when she came down to Birdland where I was playing in early 1959. She asked me to give her some money to buy some heroin and I gave her what I had. I think it was about a hundred dollars. Her husband, John (I forget his last name), kept her on the stuff so he could control her. He was an opium user himself. He used to be telling me to come and lay on the sofa with him and smoke some opium. I never did it with him, never smoked opium once in my life. He kept all the drugs and gave them to Billie whenever he felt like it; this was his way of keeping her in line. John was one of those slick hustling street cats from Harlem who'd do anything for money.

"Miles," Billie had said, "that motherfucker John done run off with all my money. So can you loan me some to get a fix? I need it real bad." So I gave her what I had because she was looking real bad by this time, worn out, worn down, and haggard around the face and all. Thin. Mouth sagging at both corners. She was scratching a lot. Before she was such a well-built woman, but now she had lost all that weight and her face was bloated from all that drinking. Man, I felt bad for her.

Whenever I'd go see her, I always asked Billie to sing "I Loves You, Porgy," because when she sang "don't let him touch me with his hot hands," you could almost feel that shit she was feeling. It was beautiful and sad the way she sang that. Everybody loved Billie.

She and Bird died the same way. They both had pneumonia. One time down in Philadelphia they had kept Billie in jail overnight for drugs. Maybe it was a couple of days, I don't remember. But I know they had her in jail. So she's in there sweating and then being cold and stuff. When you are trying to break a habit, you get hot and cold, and if you don't get the proper medical treatment, you go right into pneumonia. And that's what happened with Billie and Bird. When somebody gets backed up with that dope—using, stopping, using, stopping—and then when it gets into your system, you die. It just kills you and that's what happened to Billie and Bird; they just gave in to all the shit they was doing. Got tired of everything and just checked out.

Except for that, in 1959 I was feeling on top of the world. The new sextet with Wynton Kelly on piano opened at Birdland to packed crowds. People like Ava Gardner and Elizabeth Taylor were in the audience every night and coming back to the dressing room to say hello. Coltrane went into the studio and recorded *Giant Steps* around this time, about two weeks after the *Kind of Blue* last session, and he did the same thing that I did with the music I recorded on *Kind of Blue:* he came into the studio with sketches of the music that none of the musicians on that date had ever heard. That was a compliment to me. We also played the Apollo Theatre in Harlem, as one of the headliners, then we went to San Francisco and spent about three weeks at the Blackhawk, which was jammed every night with overflowing audiences and lines that wrapped around the corners.

It was in San Francisco that Trane gave an interview to a writer named Russ Wilson and told him that he was seriously thinking about leaving the group, which Wilson wrote in the papers the next day. Then, the guy went on to say who was going to be replacing Trane: Jimmy Heath. Jimmy Heath did replace Trane when he left, but I didn't think it was none of Trane's business to be telling the writer what I had told Trane in private. This made me real mad, and

I told Trane not to do it anymore. I mean, what had I ever done to front him off like that? I told him I had done everything for him, had treated him like my brother and here he was doing this kind of shit to me and telling a white boy all about my business. I told him, if you want to leave, leave, but tell me before you start running around telling everybody else that shit and don't be putting it out there who's going to replace you. Everyone was praising Trane now, and I know it was hard on him not to go out on his own. But he was moving farther and farther away from the group. When we played the Playboy Jazz Festival in Chicago that summer, he didn't come with us because he had other commitments. But Cannonball played his ass off, alternating his solos with mine. Everybody was playing great that day in early August and when I got back to New York everybody was talking about how great we sounded even without Trane.

In late August we opened up at Birdland again to standing-room-only crowds. Pee Wee Marquette, the famous midget emcee, who was the mascot at Birdland, was introducing Ava Gardner from the bandstand every night, and she was throwing kisses and coming backstage and kissing me back there. One time Pee Wee came back and said Ava was looking for me out front, wanted to come back and speak to me. So I asked Pee Wee, "What for, why does she want to speak to me?"

"I don't know, but she said she wants to take you to this party."

So I said, "Okay, Pee Wee, send her back."

He brought her back, all smiling and shit, and left her with me. She kidded with me and took me to this party, because she liked me a lot. The party got boring, and so I introduced her to this big black dude named Jesse, sitting there about to have a fit looking at Ava Gardner, who was a stunningly beautiful woman, dark and sensuous with a beautiful full mouth that was soft as a motherfucker. Man, she was a hot number. I said, "Ava, kiss him on the fucking cheek so he can stop looking at you; he's almost about to have a baby." So she kissed him on the cheek and he started talking to her. Then she kissed me and froze him out and then we left and I dropped her off. We didn't get down or nothing like that. She was a nice person, though, real nice, and if I would have wanted to we could have had a thing. I just don't know why it didn't happen, but it didn't, even though a lot of people swear that it did.

The only thing negative during this time was Trane still grumbling about leaving the band, but everybody had gotten used to that. Then something happened, some real jive bullshit that changed my whole life and my whole attitude again, made me bitter and cynical again when I was really starting to feel good about the things that had changed in this country.

I had just finished doing an Armed Forces Day broadcast, you know, Voice of America and all that bullshit. I had just walked this pretty white girl named Judy out to get a cab. She got in the cab, and I'm standing there in front of Birdland wringing wet because it's a hot, steaming, muggy night in August. This white policeman comes up to me and tells me to move on. At the time I was doing a lot of boxing and so I thought to myself, I ought to hit this motherfucker because I knew what he was doing. But instead I said, "Move on, for what? I'm working downstairs. That's my name up there, Miles Davis," and I pointed to my name on the marquee all up in lights.

He said, "I don't care where you work, I said move on! If you don't move on I'm going to arrest you."

I just looked at his face real straight and hard, and I didn't move. Then he said, "You're under arrest!" He reached for his handcuffs, but he was stepping back. Now, boxers had told me that if a guy's going to hit you, if you walk *toward* him you can see what's happening. I saw by the way he was handling himself that the policeman was an ex-fighter. So I kind of leaned in closer because I wasn't going to give him no distance so he could hit me on the head. He stumbled, and all his stuff fell on the sidewalk, and I thought to myself, Oh, shit, they're going to think that I fucked with him or something. I'm waiting for him to put the handcuffs on, because all his stuff is on the ground and shit. Then I move closer so he won't be able to fuck me up. A crowd had gathered all of a sudden from out of nowhere, and this white detective runs in and BAM! hits me on the head. I never saw him coming. Blood was running down the khaki suit I had on. Then I remember Dorothy Kilgallen coming outside with this horrible look on her face—I had known Dorothy for years and I used to date her good friend, Jean Bock—and saying, "Miles, what happened?" I couldn't say nothing. Illinois Jacquet was there, too.

It was almost a race riot, so the police got scared and hurried up and got my ass out of there and took me to the 54th Precinct where they took pictures of me bleeding and shit. So, I'm sitting there, madder than a motherfucker, right? And they're saying to me in the station, "So you're the wiseguy, huh?" Then they'd bump up against me, you know, try to get me mad so they could probably knock me upside my head again. I'm just sitting there, taking it all in, watching every move they make.

I look up on the wall and see they were advertising voyages for officers to take to Germany, like a tour. And this is about fourteen years after the war. And they're going there to learn police shit. It's advertised in the brochure; they'll probably teach them how to be meaner and shit, do to niggers over here what the Nazis did to the Jews over there. I couldn't believe that shit in there and they're supposed to be protecting us. I ain't done nothing but help a woman friend of mine get a cab and she happened to be white and the white boy who was the policeman didn't like seeing a nigger doing that.

I had called my lawyer, Harold Lovett, at about three A.M. The police charged me with resisting arrest, and assault and battery of a police officer. *Me!* And I ain't done nothing! It's so late that Harold can't really do nothing. They take me downtown to police headquarters and so Harold comes down to Centre Street, where they had me in the morning.

It makes the front pages of the New York newspapers, and they repeat the charges in their headlines. There was a picture, which became famous, of me leaving the jail with this bandage all over my head (they had taken me to the hospital to have my head stitched up), and Frances—who had come down to see me when they were transferring me downtown—walking in front of me like a proud stallion.

When Frances had come down to that police station and saw me all beat up like that, she was almost hysterical, screaming. I think the policemen started to think that they had made a mistake, a beautiful woman like this screaming over this nigger. And then Dorothy Kilgallen came down and then wrote about it in her column the next day. The piece was very negative against the police, and that was of some help to my cause.

Now I would have expected this kind of bullshit about resisting arrest and all back in East St. Louis (before the city went all-black), but not here in New York City, which is supposed to be the slickest, hippest city in the world. But then, again, I was surrounded by white folks and I have learned that when this happens, if you're black, there is no justice. None.

At the hearing, the district attorney said to me, "When the policeman said, 'You're under arrest,' and you looked at him, what did that look mean?"

Harold Lovett, my lawyer, said, "What does that mean, 'What did that look mean?' " What they were trying to say was that I was going to knock the policeman down or something. My lawyers didn't put me on the witness stand, because they thought that the white judge and white jury would mistake my confidence for arrogance, and because of my bad temper, which they didn't trust me to keep in check. But that incident changed me forever, made me much more bitter and cynical than I might have been. It took two months for three judges to rule that my arrest had been illegal and dismiss the charges against me.

Later I sued the police department for $500,000. Harold wasn't doing negligence suits, so he got another lawyer, who forgot to file the claim before the statute of limitations ran out. We lost the damage suit, and I was madder than a motherfucker, but there wasn't nothing I could do about it.

The police revoked my cabaret license, and that prevented me from playing New York clubs for a while. My band had played out the last set without me, but the club made an announcement about what had happened. I heard that the band had played their asses off without me, stretching out and playing everything, every tune the way they probably would have played them in their own groups. Cannonball and Coltrane both called off the tunes after I left, so I know the place was popping. But after that shit made the front pages of the New York papers for a couple of days, everything was quiet. A lot of people forgot about it in a second. But a lot of musicians and people in the know—black and white—didn't, and thought I was a hero for standing up to the police like I did.

Around this time, people—white people—started saying that I was always "angry," that I was "racist," or some silly shit like that. Now, I've been racist toward nobody, but that don't mean I'm going to take shit from a person just because he's white. I didn't grin or shuffle and didn't walk around with my finger up my ass begging for no handout and thinking I was inferior to whites. I was living in America, too, and I was going to try to get everything that was coming to me.

Around the end of September, Cannonball left the band, so now we were back to a quintet again. He never came back. Everybody else stayed. Cannon's leaving like he did changed the sound of the band and so we went back to what we had been playing, the style before we had gone into the modal thing. Because in Wynton Kelly on piano we had a combination of Red Garland and Bill Evans, so we could go any way we wanted to. But without Cannon's alto voice up in the mix, I kind of reached a dead end of ideas for what I wanted a small group to sound like.

I just felt I needed to take a rest. I had always been looking for new things to play, new challenges for my musical ideas and most of the time I had reached them. Maybe living alone had something to do with that, being out there all the time listening to all the music and being the center of things. Now I was staying home a lot with Frances, going to dinner parties, living the couple's life. But there still remained something that I was compelled to do in late 1959, and that was to begin an album with Gil Evans that we were calling *Sketches of Spain.*

How all this came about was that in 1959 I was in Los Angeles and went to see a friend of mine named Joe Montdragon, a great studio bass player, who lived in the San Fernando Valley. Joe was a Spanish Indian from Mexico, a very handsome guy. When I got to his house, he played this recording of *Concierto de Aranjuez* by this Spanish composer, Joaquin Rodrigo, and said, "Miles, listen to this; you can do this!" So I'm sitting there listening and looking at Joe and I'm saying to myself, Goddamn, these melody lines are strong. I knew right there that I had to record it, because they just stayed in my head. When I got back to New York, I called up Gil and discussed it with him and gave him a copy of the record to see what he thought could be done with it. He liked it, too, but said we had to get some more pieces to fill out an album. We got a folklore record of Peruvian Indian music, and took a vamp from that. This was "The Pan Piper" on the album. Then we took the Spanish march "Saeta," which they do in Spain on Fridays when they march and testify by singing. The trumpet players played the march on "Saeta," like it was done in Spain.

The black moors were over there in Spain, because Africans had conquered Spain a long time ago. In the Andalusian area you have a lot of African influence in the music, architecture, and in the whole culture, and a lot of African blood in the people. So you had a black African thing up in the feeling of the music, in the bag pipes and trumpets and drums.

The "Saeta" was an Andalusian song known as the arrow of song, and it was one of the oldest religious types of music in Andalusia. It is a song usually sung alone, without any kind of accompaniment, during the Holy Week religious ceremonies in Seville, and tells about the Passion of Christ. It's a street procession, and the singer, a woman, stands on a balcony grasping the iron railing overlooking the procession, which stops beneath her balcony while she sings this song. I was supposed to be her voice on trumpet. And when I'm through, a fanfare of trumpets gives the signal for the procession to move on. All the way through the song these muffled drums underscore the singer. There's a march feeling at the end of the song because that's what's happening—they march away, leaving the woman silent on her balcony after she gets through singing. My voice had to be both joyous and sad in this song, and that was very hard, too.

Now, that was the hardest thing for me to do on *Sketches of Spain:* to play the parts on the trumpet where someone was supposed to be singing, especially when it was ad-libbed, like most of the time. The difficulty came when I tried to do parts that were in between the words and stuff when the singer is singing. Because you've got all those Arabic musical scales up in there, black African scales that you can hear. And they modulate and bend and twist and snake and move around. It's like being in Morocco. What really made it so hard to do was that I could only do it once or twice. If you do a song like that three or four times you lose that feeling you want to get there.

There was a little bit of the same thing, the same kind of voice that I played on trumpet in "Solea." "Solea" is a basic form of flamenco. It's a song about loneliness, about longing and lament. It's close to the American black feeling in the blues. It comes from Andalusia, so it's African-based. But on "Saeta," I never did play until Gil had it all together.

First, he had to reorchestrate the whole song because he had the music score and musical parts for all the voices so tight and fucking close. He had it exactly how everything was, musically speaking, so if somebody would just breathe, he would have that in there, too. Gil had like micro-beats in the score. It was so tight that one of the trumpet players—a favorite white trumpet player of mine named Bernie Glow—turned all red while he was trying to play this Mexican melody. He told me later that was the hardest passage that he ever had to play. I told Gil to write another arrangement, but he didn't feel that anything was wrong with this one and couldn't understand why Bernie was finding it so hard to play this arrangement.

Now, Gil was the type of guy who would spend two weeks writing eight bars of music perfectly. He'd go over it and over it and over it. Then he'd come back to it again and again and again. A lot of times I had to be standing over him and just take the shit from him because he'd be so long in making up his mind about putting some music in or taking some out. He was a perfectionist.

So after Bernie turned purple like that, I just went to Gil and told him, "Gil, you don't have to write that music like that. It's too close for the musicians to play. You don't have to make the trumpet players sound like they're perfect, because these trumpet players are classically trained and they don't like to miss no notes no how." So he agreed with that. In the beginning, we had the wrong trumpet players because we had those who were classically trained. But that was a problem. We had to tell them *not* to play exactly like it was on the score. They started looking at us—at Gil, mostly—like we were crazy. They couldn't improvise their way out of a paper bag. So they were looking at Gil like, "What the fuck is he talking about? This is a concerto, right?" So they know we must be crazy talking about "play what isn't there." We just wanted them to feel it, and read and play it, but these first ones couldn't do that, so we had to change trumpet players, and that's why Gil had to reorchestrate the score. Next we got some trumpet players who were both classical and could feel. There were only a few parts; it was like a marching band. And so after we changed trumpets and reorchestrated for them—and Bernie still turned purple, but he and Ernie Royal and Taft Jordan and Louis Mucci played their asses off—everything went all right. I played both trumpet and fluegelhorn on this album.

Then we had to have some drummers who could get the sound that I wanted; I wanted the snare drum to sound like paper tearing, those little tight rolls. I had heard that sound way back in St. Louis at the Veiled Prophet Parades with those marching legit drummers they had back there. They sounded like Scottish bands. But they're African rhythms, because that's where the bagpipes come from, too, Africa.

That meant we had to get a chorus of legit drummers to play in the background behind Jimmy Cobb on drums and Elvin Jones on percussion. We had that kind of sound from the drummers, the legit drummers, and we had Jimmy and Elvin to play the stuff they normally play, solo and shit. Legit drummers can't solo because they have no musical imagination to improvise. Like most other classical players, they play only what you put in front of them. That's what classical music is; the musicians only play what's there and nothing else. They can remember, and have the ability of robots. In classical music, if one musician isn't like the other, isn't all the way a robot, like all the rest, then the other robots make fun of him or her, especially if they're black. That's all that is, that's all the classical music is in terms of the musicians who play it—robot shit. And people celebrate them like they're great. Now, there's some great classical music by great classical composers—and there's some great players up in there, but they have to become soloists—but it's still robot playing and most of them know it deep down, though they wouldn't admit it in public.

So you have to have a balance on something like *Sketches of Spain,* between musicians who can read music and play it with no feeling or a little feeling, and some others who could play with real feeling. I think the perfect thing is when some musicians can both read a musical score and feel it. With me, if I read it and play it, it's not going to have that much feeling in it. But if I just listen to it and play it, it's going to have a lot of feeling in it. What I found I had to do in *Sketches of Spain* was to read the score a couple of times, listen to it a couple of times more, *then* play it. For me, it was just about knowing what it is, and then I could play it. It seemed to work out all right, because everyone loved that record.

After we finished working on *Sketches of Spain,* I didn't have *nothing* inside me. I was drained of all emotion and I didn't want to hear that music after I got through playing all that hard shit. Gil said, "Let's go listen to the tapes." I said, "*You* go listen to the tapes, because I don't want to hear it." And I didn't hear it until it came out on record over a year later. I wanted to go forward to something else. When I finally did hear it, my musical head was somewhere else, so I didn't really think nothing of it. I really only listened closely to it once. I mean, it might have been on the record player around the house—because Frances really loved it—but I only sat down once and really listened and went over every tune with a fine-tooth comb. I liked the record and thought everybody had played well on it and that Gil had arranged his ass off, but it didn't have a large impact upon me.

Joaquin Rodrigo, the composer of *Concierto de Aranjuez,* said he didn't like the record, and he—his composition—was the reason I did *Sketches of Spain* in the first place. Since he was getting a royalty for the use of the song on the record, I told his person who had played it for him, "Let's see if he likes it after he starts getting those big royalty checks." I never heard anything about or from him after that.

This woman told me she went to visit this old retired bullfighter who raised bulls for the ring. She had told him about this record that had been made by a black American musician, and he didn't believe that a foreigner, an American—and especially a black American—could make such a record, since it depended upon knowledge of Spanish culture, including flamenco music. She asked him if she could play the record for him and he said she could. He sat there and listened to it. After it was finished, he rose from his chair and put on his bullfighting equipment and outfit, went out and fought one of his bulls for the first time since he had retired, and killed the bull. When she asked him why he had done it, he said that he had been so moved by the music that he just had to fight the bull. It was hard for me to believe this woman's story, but she swore that it was true.

after *Sketches of Spain,* neither Gil nor I wanted to go back into the studio for a while. It was now early 1960, and Norman Granz had booked me and my band on a European tour. This was to be a pretty long tour, starting in March and running through April.

Trane didn't want to make the European trip and was ready to move out before we left. One night I got a telephone call from this new tenor on the scene named Wayne Shorter, telling me that Trane told him that I needed a tenor saxophonist and that Trane was recommending him. I was shocked. I started to just hang up and then I said something like, "If I need a saxophone player I'll get one!" And then I hung up. BLAM!

So when I saw Trane I told him, "Don't be telling nobody to call me like that, and if you want to quit then just quit, but why don't you do it after we get back from Europe?" If he had quit right then he would have really hung me up because nobody else knew the songs, and this tour was real important. He decided to go with us, but he grumbled and complained and sat by himself all the time we were over there. He gave me notice that he would be leaving the group when we got home. But before he quit, I gave him that soprano saxophone I talked about earlier and he started playing it. I could already hear the effect it would have on his tenor playing, how it would revolutionize it. I always joked with him that if he had stayed home and not come with us on this trip, he wouldn't have gotten that

soprano saxophone, so he was in debt to me for as long as he lived.
Man, he used to laugh until he cried about that, and then I would
say, "Trane, I'm serious." And he'd hug me real hard and just keep
saying, "Miles, you're right about that." But this was later, when he
had his own group and they was killing everybody with their shit.

Right after we got back to the States in May, Trane quit the band
and opened at the Jazz Gallery. The person I got to replace Trane
when I started playing again with my group in the summer of 1960
was my old friend Jimmy Heath, who had just gotten out of prison
for drugs.

Trane had been in the big band Jimmy used to have in Philly
around 1948, and then they both went with Dizzy's band that year.
So they had known each other for a long time. From 1955 to 1959,
Jimmy was in prison, so he was off the scene altogether. When Trane
said he was leaving for good he told me Jimmy had just gotten out of
the joint and probably needed a gig and that he also knew a lot of
music we were playing.

But my music had moved a ways since when Jimmy first played it
back in 1953, on my album *Miles Davis All Stars,* and I thought it
might be hard for him to get out of that bebop thing that he was into.
But I figured we had a while and I was willing to give Jimmy a chance.
Trane was always high on Jimmy's playing and so was I. Plus, he was
a very hip dude to be with, funny and clean and very intelligent.

We were in California, so I called him up and asked him to join
the band. He said he would love to do it, so I sent him a plane ticket
to come on out.

The first place we played was the Jazz Serville Club in Hollywood.
When Jimmy arrived I started showing him what we were doing and
I could see right away that he didn't know what the fuck it was. I
mean, he knew about modal music, but I could see that he hadn't
ever played it before, that it was new to him. He had been playing
songs with a lot of chord changes that resolve, so everything ends up
in one way. But we were playing scales and into modal stuff. For
some reason I remember Cannonball was on that gig with us, and
Jimmy was fighting the songs at first, trying to adapt to the modal
playing everyone else was into. But after a while I could hear him
relaxing and getting into the music. And then we came back East and
played French Lick, Indiana (that little hick town the basketball
player Larry Bird is from), the Regal Theatre in Chicago, and a couple of other places.

When we got back East Cannonball left for good and Jimmy went down to Philly to see his family before we were to go out and play the Playboy Festival in Chicago. That's when his parole officer told him he had to stay within a sixty-mile radius of Philadelphia as a condition of his parole. That fucked up Jimmy's music career for years. He couldn't even come to New York to play, and he was clean as a whistle the whole time we were out on tour, didn't do nothing but come to the gig and play and go back to his hotel room. Here he was making more money than he had ever made in his life, and this parole officer, an Italian dude, blocks him. Man, life is a bitch sometimes, and especially if you're black.

When Jimmy told me that shit I called some friends in Philadelphia to see what they could do, but they couldn't do nothing. I hated to see Jimmy leave the band like that because he was getting into the modal thing, and I think he would have been fine. I know that it hurt him and it hurt me, too.

Now I thought about the other guy Trane had recommended, Wayne Shorter. I called him up and asked him if he could join the band. But he was playing with Art Blakey and the Jazz Messengers and couldn't come with us. So I got Sonny Stitt, who could play both tenor and alto. He joined us about the time I was going over to Europe for another tour, stopping in London first.

Around this time I got another shock when I found out my mother had cancer. She had moved back to East St. Louis in 1959 with her husband, James Robinson. Doctors had found cancer when they operated on her that year, so that was worrying everybody. But when I talked to her she sounded strong, and she looked good when I saw her.

The 1960 European tour was the first time I had come to London, I think, and the concerts there were packed every night. We were playing these halls of from three to eight thousand. Frances went with me and just killed everyone who laid eyes on her. Man, every day in the British papers they were writing about how fine she was. It was something else. They talked about her almost as much as they talked about me. They wrote about her in a positive way, but they jumped all over me. I didn't understand it at first. They were calling me arrogant, saying that I didn't like the way the English talk, that I had bodyguards to protect me, when in fact the only people who went with me besides the members of the band were Frances and Harold Lovett. They said I didn't like white people; all kinds of shit. And then somebody told me that if you're famous that's the way the

English press does you. After that, I relaxed. After England we went on to Sweden and Paris then back to the States to finish up our tour.

I especially remember playing Philly because of an incident that Jimmy Heath and I had with the police. See, Jimmy loved cars, too, and I think he had a Triumph sports car. Anyway, I drove my Ferrari down to Philly—I used to drive it everywhere back in those days, to all my gigs that weren't on the West Coast (later I would even drive one of my Ferraris out there to some gigs). So I picked up Jimmy and we were riding around talking about music and shit and I probably was complaining to him about Sonny Stitt playing the wrong kind of shit on "So What," because he would always fuck up on that tune and so I used to tell Jimmy this every time I'd see him. So anyway, we were riding in my Ferrari and I was showing him how fast the car ran on Broad Street, where the speed limit is about twenty-five miles an hour or so. I told Jimmy this car could make all the lights before they turned red or yellow. So I gear down and the car is moving at fifty-five miles an hour before he could blink, right? His eyes were bulging all out his head and we're making all the motherfucking lights. The car is moving so fast and low it's just whistling. We're going real fast and run up on a light that changes and I got to hit my brakes, right? But I know what I got, and I know the brakes are going to hold and we're going to stop on a motherfucking dime. Jimmy's eyes are almost about to fall out of his head because he knows we're going to run right through this red light. So I gear down from about sixty miles an hour and stop on a dime, like I knew it would, and Jimmy just couldn't believe it. When we stop, there are two white, undercover narcotics policemen sitting in an unmarked car. So we stop right by them. They look over and see us and say, "That's that fucking Miles Davis and Jimmy Heath in that fucking car." So they tell us to pull over and flash their badges and shit and tell us to come over to their car. We do, because I don't want to get Jimmy in no trouble because he's on parole and shit. So, we go over and they check us out, you know, search us and everything and don't find nothing and let us go. Man, it was a drag.

There was a lot of shit happening in 1960, including a new black alto saxophonist named Ornette Coleman coming to New York City and turning the jazz world all the way around. He just came and fucked up everybody. Before long you couldn't buy a seat in the Five Spot, where he was playing every night with Don Cherry—who played a plastic pocket trumpet (Ornette had a plastic alto too, I believe), Charlie Haden on bass, and Billy Higgins on drums. They were playing music in a way everyone was calling "free jazz" or "avant-garde" or "the new thing" or whatever. A lot of the "star" people who used to come and see me—like Dorothy Kilgallen and Leonard Bernstein (who, they tell me, jumped up one night and said, "This is the greatest thing that has ever happened to jazz!")—were now going to see Ornette. They played the Five Spot for about five or six months, and I used to go and check them out when I was in town, even sat in with them a couple of times.

I could play with anybody, in any style—if you're playing one way, I can play that style—because I had learned all the trumpet styles by then. What Don Cherry was doing was just a style. But Ornette could play only one way back then. I knew that after listening to them a few times, so I just sat in and played what they played. It was just a certain tempo, that particular number we played that time. I've forgotten what the name of the song was. Don asked me to play, so I did. Don liked me a lot and he was a nice guy.

But Ornette's a jealous kind of dude, man. Jealous of other musicians' success. I don't know what's wrong with him. For him—a sax player—to pick up a trumpet and violin like that and just think he can play them with no kind of training is disrespectful toward all those people who play them well. And then to sit up and pontificate about them when he doesn't know what he's talking about is not cool, man. But you know, music's all just sounds anyway. The violin is okay as an instrument and I guess you can get away with playing it as a kind of filler in places if you don't really know how to play it. I don't mean soloing or nothing like that, just hitting a few notes here and there. But if you don't know how to play the trumpet, it sounds terrible. People who know how to play it can play it even when it's all stopped up. As long as you play in rhythm, even if the horn's all fucked, as long as it fits, you can do that. You just have to play a style. If you play a ballad, you play a ballad. But Ornette couldn't do that on trumpet because he didn't know anything about the instrument. But Ornette's cool; I just wish he wasn't so jealous.

I liked Ornette and Don as people, and I thought Ornette was playing more than Don was. But I didn't see or hear anything in their playing that was all that revolutionary, and I said so. Trane was there a lot more than I was, watching and listening, but he didn't say nothing like I did. A whole lot of the younger players and critics jumped down my throat after I put down Ornette, called me "old-fashioned" and shit. But I didn't like what they were playing, especially Don Cherry on that little horn he had. It just looked to me like he was playing a lot of notes and looking real serious, and people went for that because people will go for anything they don't understand if it's got enough hype. They want to be hip, want always to be in on the new thing so they don't look unhip. White people are especially like that, particularly when a black person is doing something they don't understand. They don't want to have to admit that a black person could be doing something that they don't know about. Or that he could be maybe a little more—or a whole lot more—intelligent than them. They can't stand to admit that kind of shit to themselves, so they run around talking about how great it is until the next "new thing" comes along, and then the next and then the next and then the next. That's what I thought was happening when Ornette hit town.

Now, what Ornette did a few years later was hip, and I told him so. But what they were doing back in the beginning was just being spontaneous in their playing, playing "free form," bouncing off what each other was doing. That's cool, but it had been done before, only they were doing it with no kind of form or structure and that's the thing that was important about what they did, not their playing.

I think Cecil Taylor came on the scene around the same time that Ornette did, maybe a little later. He was doing on piano what Ornette and Don were doing with two horns. I felt the same way about him that I felt about them. He was classically trained and could play the piano technically, but I just didn't like his approach. It was just a lot of notes being played for notes' sake; somebody showing off how much technique he had. I remember one night somebody dragged me and Dizzy and Sarah Vaughan up to Birdland to hear Cecil Taylor play. I left after hearing a little bit of what he was doing. I didn't hate him or nothing, and don't hate him today; I just didn't like what he was playing, that's all. (Somebody told me that when Cecil was asked how he liked the way I played, he said, "He plays all right for a millionaire." Now, that's funny; until I heard that I didn't think he had a sense of humor.)

Sonny Stitt left the band sometime around the beginning of 1961. I replaced him with Hank Mobley, and we went into the studio to record *Someday My Prince Will Come* in March 1961. I brought Coltrane in to play on three or four of those tunes and Philly Joe to play on one. But the rest of the band was the same: Wynton Kelly,

Paul Chambers, Jimmy Cobb, and Hank Mobley on two or three tunes. Teo Macero, my producer, had started to splice tape together on *Porgy and Bess* and then on *Sketches of Spain,* and he did it on this album, too. We post-recorded solos on those albums, with Trane and me doing some extra horn work. It was an interesting process that was done frequently after that.

It was on *Someday My Prince Will Come* that I started demanding that Columbia use black women on my album covers. So I was able to put Frances on *Someday My Prince Will Come.* (After that Frances was on two more album covers, then Betty Mabry was on *Filles de Kilimanjaro,* Cicely Tyson on *Sorcerer,* and Marguerite Eskridge on *Miles Davis at the Fillmore.*) I mean, it was my album and I was Frances's prince, and "Pfrancing" on that album was written for her. Next I got rid of all them stupid liner notes, which I had been trying to do for a long time. See, I never thought there was nothing nobody could say about an album of mine. I just want everyone to listen to the music, and make up their own minds. I never did like no one writing about what I played on an album, trying to explain what I was trying to do. The music speaks for itself.

That spring of 1961—April I think it was—I decided to drive out to California, for a gig in San Francisco at the Blackhawk. I had been playing at the Village Vanguard when I was in New York, but the music was starting to bore me because I didn't like what Hank Mobley was playing in the band. Gil and I were working a little bit on an album we wanted to do for Columbia. But other than that, everything was slow.

Playing with Hank just wasn't fun for me; he didn't stimulate my imagination. This was about the time I started playing real short solos and then leaving the bandstand. People were complaining because they were coming to see me play, or do whatever it was they thought I was supposed to do. By now they had made me a "star," and people were coming just to look at me, to see what I was going to do, what I had on, whether I would say anything or cuss somebody out, like I was some kind of freak in a glass cage at the motherfucking zoo. Man, that shit was getting depressing. And by now I was in a lot of pain all the time from what I found out was sickle-cell anemia, which was causing arthritis in my joints, especially in my left hip joint. That was irritating me, and working out in the gym didn't seem to help. So I decided that I would drive to California, just to cool myself out; go through Chicago and St. Louis and then out to California before the band got there. Maybe it would be fun. I was starting to feel like I needed a change.

Columbia recorded us at the Blackhawk, but all that equipment in the club bothered the guys in my band and me, too. Everybody was checking on the sound levels and shit, and that can throw off your timing. But there was a guy out there named Ralph J. Gleason, a writer, who I liked a lot. It was always good to see him and talk with him. He, Leonard Feather, and Nat Hentoff were the only music critics who didn't write like fools. But you could keep the rest of them.

When we came back to New York after being at the Blackhawk in April 1961, we had a date at Carnegie Hall that I was looking forward to. Not only were we going to have a small group, but we were going to have Gil Evans conducting a big orchestra, too, playing a lot of the music from *Sketches of Spain*.

This was a great night of music. The only thing that fucked it up for me was when Max Roach came with some other protesters and sat up on the stage. Man, that bothered me so I couldn't even play. The concert was a benefit for the African Relief Foundation, but Max and his friends saw it as benefiting a group they thought was a CIA front or something that was perpetuating colonialism in Africa. I didn't mind that Max thought that this group was a tool for the United States, because the group was mostly white people, you know? What I minded was him fucking with the music like he did by coming up and sitting on the stage just as we were about to play, holding up these goddamn signs. I had just started playing when he did it so it just fucked me up. I didn't know why Max did it. But Max was like my brother, and he told me later that he just wanted me to be aware of what I was getting myself into. So I just told him he should have told me another way than he did and he agreed with that. After somebody got him to move off the stage, I went back and finished playing.

Me and Max had another run-in not long after this incident. As I said before, Max had taken Clifford Brown's death back in 1956 very hard and started drinking and stuff. I wasn't seeing him much at that time. He had married Abbey Lincoln, the singer. Now he thought somehow that I was messing around with her, so he was going to get even by trying to fuck Frances. He was coming around and beating on our door when I wasn't there, demanding to get in. He came by one night and tried to break the door down, which really scared

Frances, and she told me. At first I couldn't believe what I was hearing, but then I finally realized that she was telling the truth. I got in my car and went looking for Max. I found him up at Sugar Ray's club in Harlem. I tried to explain to Max that all I had ever done to Abbey Lincoln was give her a haircut. Someone had told Max that I had "trimmed" Abbey—and he thought that meant I had fucked her. When he started to scream at me and choke me, I just hit him with an uppercut and knocked him out. Dropped him right there. He was screaming, and I had tried to leave once or twice but he wouldn't let me. Now, you know a drummer is as strong as an ox, man, and Max didn't take no shit off no one. I knew this. Frances was there, and people were looking at all of us like we were out of our minds.

Man, that was some real sad shit to be up in. That wasn't the real Max Roach screaming in that club at me, just like it wasn't the real Miles Davis who had been a junkie all them years. Drugs was talking for Max and so when I hit him like I did, I didn't feel like I was hitting the real Max that I knew. But that shit hurt me real bad, real bad, and I went home and cried like a baby in Frances's arms that night, all night. That was one of the hardest and most emotionally wrenching things that I have ever gone through. But after a while, things went back to being just like they used to be. Max and I hardly ever said anything about it after that night.

Frances and I were really getting along great in 1961. I had surprised her earlier at Birdland by giving her a star sapphire ring all wrapped up in toilet tissue. She was shocked because she didn't expect it. I think Dinah Washington was singing that night in Birdland. Also, I was staying home a lot teaching Frances how to cook. I had gotten into cooking. I just loved good food and hated going out to restaurants all the time, so I taught myself how to cook by reading books and practicing, just like you do on an instrument. I could cook most of the great French dishes—because I really liked French cooking—and all the black American dishes. But my favorite was a chili dish that I called Miles's South Side Chicago Chili Mack. I served it with spaghetti, grated cheese, and oyster crackers. I taught Frances how to make that dish and after a while she was cooking everything better than me.

Sometime during this period we moved up to 312 West 77th Street, into a converted Russian Orthodox church. I had bought the five-story building in 1960, but we hadn't really moved into it yet because it was being renovated.

It was over by the Hudson River, between Riverside Drive and West End Avenue. It had a basement, where I put a gym so I could work out, and a music room where I could rehearse without disturbing anyone else in the house. The first floor had a big living room area and a large kitchen, too. There was a staircase that led up to the bedrooms. And then we had apartments that we rented out on the top two floors. We also had a little garden in back. We were very comfortable by this time. I was making about $200,000 a year. I had invested some of my money in stocks; I used to check the papers all the time to see how they were doing.

We needed the house because by then Frances and I had all the kids living with us: my daughter, Cheryl, my sons, Miles IV and Gregory, and Frances's son, Jean-Pierre. My brother Vernon was coming up and staying sometimes and so was my sister and mother. And my father came once or twice.

I hadn't seen my mother very often, but when I did, she was something else, man. She never bit her tongue. I remember once when a guy named Marc Crawford was doing a big piece on me for *Ebony* magazine and I was in Chicago playing the Sutherland Lounge. Marc was sitting at the table with me, my mother, my sister, Dorothy, and her husband, Vincent. My mother said to me, "Miles, you could at least smile for the audience when they're clapping so hard for you. They're clapping because they love you, love what you are playing because it's beautiful."

I said, "What do you want me to be, an Uncle Tom?"

She looked at me real hard for a minute and then she said, "If I ever hear about you tomming, I'll come and kill you myself." Well, everybody at the table just sat there, because they knew how she was. But Marc Crawford's eyes got bigger than oranges. He didn't know whether to write that down or not. But that's the way my mother was, totally outspoken.

In 1961 I won another *Down Beat* poll for Best Trumpet and also for having the Best Combo. Trane's new group with Elvin Jones, McCoy Tyner, and Jimmy Garrison had won Best New Combo and Trane was named Best Tenor Saxophonist and Best New Star on Soprano Saxophone. So everything was looking good, except for my having sickle-cell anemia. It couldn't kill me, but it was serious enough to be a downer. Still, everything else was looking up.

A lot of actors were coming around when I played. Marlon Brando was coming into Birdland every night to listen to the music and lay his eyes on Frances. I remember him sitting at her table all night talking to her and grinning like a schoolboy while I was up there playing. At Birdland Ava Gardner was a regular, and Richard Burton and Elizabeth Taylor came by, too. Paul Newman also came to Birdland a lot, not just to listen to the music but also to study my attitude for a film about musicians he was making, *Paris Blues*. Out in Los Angeles, when I played there, Laurence Harvey was always coming around and parking his white Rolls-Royce (with purple upholstery) right out in front of the club, which I think was the It Club. It was owned by a black guy named John T. McClain (his son, also named John T. McClain, is one of the biggest record producers in the business today, producing people like Janet Jackson for A & M Records), who we used to call, "John T." I was also enjoying my new house in New York. Coltrane came by and we played a little down in the basement. Cannonball would come by, too. I had heard Bill Evans was strung out on heroin, and that just made me sick, man, because I had talked to Bill when he first started to experiment with it, but I guess he didn't pay me no attention. But that upset me a lot, because he was such a beautiful musician and here he was getting a habit when everyone else, even Sonny Rollins and Jackie McLean, were cleaning themselves up.

It was because of Bill's influence, I think, that I always had classical music on around the house. It was so soothing to think and work by. I mean people would come by and expect to hear a lot of jazz on the box, but I wasn't into that at the time and a lot of people were shocked to hear me listening to classical music all the time, you know, Stravinsky, Arturo Michelangeli, Rachmaninoff, Isaac Stern. Frances liked classical music, too, and I think she was a little surprised when she found out I liked it a lot.

Frances and I had finally gotten married on December 21, 1960. She went out and bought herself a five-band wedding ring. I didn't believe in wearing one, so I didn't. This was the first time I had married officially. This made Frances's parents really happy, and I found myself being happy for them. My father and mother also thought it was good, because they both liked Frances a lot, like everybody else did.

But as good as my home life was, the music wasn't going too good for me during this period. Hank Mobley left the band in 1961 and I replaced him for a hot minute with a guy named Rocky Boyd, but he didn't work out either. Like I said, by this time I was a "star" to a lot of people. In January 1961, *Ebony* had done a seven-page spread with a whole lot of pictures of me and my family and friends in my new house, pictures of my mother and father, with him out on his pig farm looking all rich and everything. It was a big thing and really put me over with black people. But none of this mattered to me now because the music wasn't happening and that was fucking me up. I was starting to drink more than I had in the past and I was taking pain medication for the sickle-cell anemia. And I was starting to use more coke, I guess because of the depression.

In 1962, J. J. Johnson was available, and Sonny Rollins came back and made some gigs, so I got a real good sextet together with Wynton Kelly, Paul Chambers, Jimmy Cobb, and myself, and we went out on the road. We played Chicago—this was the middle of May—and we went through East St. Louis to see my father. He wasn't feeling too good. Frances had come out with us to see her parents in Chicago, so she was with us, too.

My father had gotten hit by a train in his car a couple of years back —I think it was in 1960—crossing one of those unguarded country crossings. It had fucked him up because the white ambulances wouldn't pick up a black person where he got hit and so he had to wait for a black ambulance to come and take him to the hospital. Nobody told me right away because they didn't think it was too serious. Also, I was on the road and they didn't want to worry me. When I happened to call him a week or so after this happened, I asked him how he was doing and he said, "Oh, I got hit by a train." Just like that he said it, like it wasn't nothing, you know?

I said, "What? What happened?"

"Nothing. I just got hit by a train. My wife took me to get examined, and they say I'm all right."

After that, he couldn't pick up anything without his hands shaking. He would reach for an object and lean forward to pick it up but couldn't do it. His wife had been telling me he was getting worse, so I brought him to New York and had a neurosurgeon look at him, but he couldn't tell what was wrong with my father. My father was like a punch-drunk fighter now; he wouldn't let no one give him nothing. One time while he was there I went to get something for him and he told me, "Can't you tell when people don't want your help?"

He couldn't walk straight anymore, he couldn't work. When I came through in 1962, he looked the same as when I last saw him, shaking and shit and didn't want nobody to do nothing for him. But he couldn't do nothing for himself, and he was still trying and complaining every time someone did do something for him, because he was a very proud man. He was constantly telling me he was going to beat whatever it was that was making him this way, and that he was going to be back to work before anybody knew it.

But just as we were about to leave to go to Kansas City, he gave me a letter. I just gave it to Frances and hugged him and left. I forgot about the letter. Then about three days later we were playing in Kansas City and J. J. comes up to me and says, "You better sit down."

I looked at him and ask, "What the fuck for, what you gotta tell me?" But I can tell something's funny by the way he's looking at me, all sad. So I sit down, feeling a little scared. "Your father just died, man. They just called the club and told the owner; your father just died." I just looked at him, shocked, and I said, "No shit! Aw, goddamn! Man!" I'll never forget it. I just said, "No shit!" I don't know what it did to me; I wasn't crying or nothing. I was just kind of numb, probably in a state of disbelief.

Then I remembered the letter. I went right back to the hotel room and asked Frances for it. It said, "A few days after you read this I'll be dead, so take care of yourself, Miles. I truly loved you, and you made me proud." Man, that just fucked me up. I cried, cried hard, man, real hard and long. I was mad at myself for forgetting to read the letter until then. I felt real bad, real guilty. I was frustrated—so fucking frustrated, you wouldn't believe—for not being able to help my father when he was sick after all those times he had helped me. And I could see how sick he was from his handwriting because it was so shaky and uneven. I just read the letter over and over and over again, and then I read it some more and I kept it. He was sixty years old when he died. I thought he was going to live forever, because he was always there for me. I knew that I had had a great father, I mean a great one, and he had to be a bad motherfucker to tell me he was going to die like that. I didn't think he had looked good when I saw him, and after I thought back over the last visit—going back over every image I could remember of him—I remember him having that certain look that people—spiritual, country people—have in their eyes when something is very wrong. He had that look when I was saying goodbye, that sad look of "I probably won't be seeing you any more" in his eyes. But I didn't get it. And knowing that made me feel even sadder, even guiltier, that I had let my father down at the one time that he had needed me most. If I had only been paying attention! I had seen that look before, many times, like in the eyes of Bird the last time I saw him, and others.

My father's funeral in May 1962 was one of the biggest, if not *the* biggest, they had ever had for a black man in East St. Louis. It was held in the new Lincoln High School gymnasium. It was packed, man, people from everywhere came, all the doctors and dentists and lawyers he knew, a lot of people from Africa that he had known from college, a lot of white, wealthy people. I saw people I hadn't seen in years. I sat in the front row with the rest of the family. I had already gone through the sadness, so it wasn't painful, wasn't sad, to sit there and look at him for the last time. It was almost like he was just sleeping in the casket. My brother Vernon, who's crazier than I could ever be, started joking about how some woman looked. Vernon said, "Miles, look at that bitch with that big ass trying to hide it." I looked and it was true, so I almost cracked up, almost died laughing. Man, that nigger's crazy. But he relaxed everybody and I only felt real sad again after they took my father and buried him in the cemetery. When they put him in the ground then I really knew that I had seen him—his physical image—for the last time on this earth. After that I would only see him in pictures or living in my mind.

I came back to New York and tried to work, so I wouldn't have time to think about my father. We played the Vanguard, places on the East Coast. I was playing clubs and going to the gym a lot and then I recorded *Quiet Nights* with Gil Evans in July of that year. (We did other sessions in August and November.) I didn't really feel nothing about the music we did on this album. I knew I wasn't into what we were doing like I had been in the past. We were trying to get some bossa nova shit on to that record.

Then Columbia got the bright idea of making an album for Christmas, and they thought it would be hip if I had this silly singer named Bob Dorough on the album, with Gil arranging. We got Wayne Shorter on tenor, a guy named Frank Rehak on trombone, and Willie Bobo on bongos, and in August we did this album. The less said about it, the better, but it did let me play with Wayne Shorter for the first time and I really liked what he was into.

The last thing Gil and I did on *Quiet Nights* in November just wasn't happening. It seemed like we had spent all our energy for nothing and so we just let it go. Columbia brought it out anyway to make some money, but if it had been left up to me and Gil, we would have just let it stay in the tape vaults. That shit made me so mad that I didn't talk to Teo Macero for a long time after that. He just fucked up everything on that record, looking over the musical score, getting in the way of everybody, trying to tell people what they should play and shit. He should have just kept his ass in the recording booth and got us some good sound instead of fucking around with us and fucking up everything. I started to get that motherfucker fired after that record. I called up Goddard Lieberson, who was the president of Columbia at that time. But when Goddard asked me if I wanted Teo fired, I just couldn't do it to him like that.

Before the last session for *Quiet Nights* in November, I finally agreed to do an interview for *Playboy* magazine. Marc Crawford, who had written the story on me for *Ebony,* introduced me to Alex Haley, who wanted to do the interview. I didn't want to do it at first. So Alex said, "Why?"

I told him, "It's a magazine for whites. White people usually ask you questions just to get inside your mind, to see what you're thinking. And then after that, they don't want to give you credit for thinking what you told them, what they asked you about." Then I told him that another reason that I didn't want to do it was because *Playboy* didn't have black or brown or Asian women in there. "All they have," I told him, "are blond women with big tits and flat asses or no asses. So who the fuck wants to see that all the time? Black guys like big asses, you know, and we like to kiss on the mouth and white women don't have no mouths to kiss on." Alex talked to me and went to the gym with me and even got in the ring with me and took a few punches upside his head. *That* impressed me. So I told him, "Listen, man, if I tell you all of this, why don't they make me part of the company for giving you all this information they want me to give you?" He said that he couldn't do that. So I told him if they would give him $2,500 for the interview, then I'd do it. They agreed and that's how they got the interview.

But I didn't like what he did with the interview. Alex made up some things, although it was good reading. In the piece he talked about how the little colored trumpet player—me—always lost out to the white trumpet player when they were picking the best trumpet player in Illinois. This was when I was in high school in a competition for the All State Music Band. And Alex wrote that I always felt bad about that. Fuck that shit! It wasn't true. I might have lost but I didn't feel bad because I *knew* I was a bad motherfucker and so did the white boy. Where's *his* ass at now anyway? I didn't like that Alex dressed shit up. Alex is a good writer but he's very dramatic. I knew later why he was doing it, that's just the way he writes, but I didn't know it before he did that piece on me.

We finished playing Chicago in December 1962—myself, Wynton, Paul, J. J., and Jimmy Cobb; Jimmy Heath came in for one gig taking the place of Sonny Rollins, who left again to form his own group and to go back and woodshed some more. I think it was around this time that he was supposed to be heard practicing on the Brooklyn Bridge high up in the girders; at least that's what everybody was saying. Everybody except me and Jimmy Cobb were talking about leaving the band either to make some more money or to go out on their own to play their own music. The rhythm section wanted to work as a trio led by Wynton, and J. J. wanted to stay around L.A. because he could make a lot of money doing studio gigs and be home with his family. That left just Jimmy Cobb and me, and that wasn't enough to make a band.

At the beginning of 1963 I had to cancel bookings in Philadelphia, Detroit, and St. Louis. Each time I canceled, the promoters sued me for expenses and so I had to pay out over $25,000. Then I was booked to play the Blackhawk in San Francisco and I decided not to take Paul and Wynton. I was having trouble with them because they wanted more money and wanted to play their own music. They said they were tired of playing just my book, and they wanted something fresh to do, and by this time they were in great demand. But more than that, I think, Wynton wanted to be a leader, his own man, and after five years with me he thought he was ready for that responsibility. I think he and Paul just wanted to get out from under me because everyone else had left.

I asked the Blackhawk if I could come a week later after I got myself together, and they agreed. I went on out with a new group, with Jimmy Cobb the only leftover from the previous band. But after a few days he left to join Wynton and Paul. Now I had a whole new band.

I had hired George Coleman on saxophone because I figured I should start from the ground up. Coltrane had recommended him, and he agreed to join the band. I asked him who were some other people he liked to play with and he recommended Frank Strozier on alto and Harold Mabern on piano. Now I needed a bass player. I had met Ron Carter (who was from Detroit) in Rochester, New York, back in 1958 when he had come backstage after a show; he knew Paul Chambers from Detroit. Ron was in the Eastman School of Music at the time, studying bass. I saw him again in Toronto a few years later, and I remember him talking to Paul a lot about what we were playing. At that time we were into the modal thing on *Kind of Blue*. After he graduated, Ron came to New York and was working around, and then I saw him with Art Farmer and Jim Hall's quartet.

Paul had already told me Ron was a motherfucker of a bass player. So when Paul was about to leave and I heard Ron was playing, I went to check him out and loved what he was doing. So I asked him if he would join the band. He was committed to Art, but he told me that if I asked Art and Art said yes, then he would like to join my band. I asked Art after the set was over and although Art didn't really want to let Ron go, he agreed.

Before I left New York, I had had tryouts for the band and that's where I got all those Memphis musicians—Coleman, Strozier, and Mabern. (They had gone to school with the great young trumpet player Booker Little, who soon after this died of leukemia, and the pianist Phineas Newborn. I wonder what they were doing down there when all them guys came through that one school?) I didn't have to try out Ron because I had already heard him, but he did rehearse with us. And I had heard this great little seventeen-year-old drummer who was working with Jackie McLean named Tony Williams, who just blew my fucking mind he was so bad. I wanted him to go to California with me as soon as I heard him, but he had commitments to gigs with Jackie. He told me he had Jackie's blessing to join my band after they finished those gigs. Man, just hearing that little motherfucker made me excited all over again. Like I said earlier, trumpet players love to play with great drummers and I could definitely hear right away that this was going to be one of the baddest motherfuckers who had ever played a set of drums. Tony was my first choice, and Frank Butler from L.A. was only a fill-in until Tony came into the band.

We played the Blackhawk and everything went pretty well for a new group, although I knew right away that Mabern and Strozier weren't the players I was after. They were very good musicians, but they just belonged in another kind of band. Next we played a date down in L.A. at John T's It Club and there I decided I wanted to record some music. I replaced Mabern on piano with a great piano player from England named Victor Feldman, who could play his ass off. He also played vibraphone and drums. On the recording date we used two of his tunes: the title track "Seven Steps to Heaven" and "Joshua." I wanted him to join the band, but he was making a fortune playing studio work in L.A., so he'd be losing money if he came with me. I came back to New York looking for a piano player. I found him in Herbie Hancock.

I had met Herbie Hancock about a year or so earlier when the trumpet player Donald Byrd brought him by my house on West 77th Street. He had just joined Donald's band. I asked him to play something for me on my piano, and I saw right away that he could really play. When I needed a new piano player I thought of Herbie first and called him to come over. I was having Tony Williams and Ron Carter over so I wanted to know how he would sound with them.

They all came over and played every day for the next couple of days, and I would listen to them over the intercom system I had hooked up in my music room and all over the house. Man, they sounded too good together. On around the third or fourth day, I came downstairs and joined them and played a few things. Ron and Tony were already in the band. I told Herbie to meet us at the recording studio the next day. We were finishing up *Seven Steps to Heaven*. Herbie asked me, "So does that mean I'm in the group?"

"You're making the record with me, ain't you?" I said.

I knew right away that this was going to be a motherfucker of a group. For the first time in a while I found myself feeling excited inside, because if they were playing that good in a few days, what would they be playing like in a few months? Man, I could just hear that shit popping all over the place. We finished *Seven Steps to Heaven* and then I called Jack Whittemore and told him to get as many playing gigs as he could for the rest of the summer, and he booked me solid.

We finished the new album in May 1963 and we went out on the road to the Showboat in Philadelphia. I remember Jimmy Heath being in the audience. After I got through playing my solo, I went down and asked him what he thought of the band, because I respected his opinion. "Man, they're great, but I wouldn't want to be getting up there playing with them every night. Miles, them motherfuckers are gonna set everybody on fire!" That's just what I thought, only I found myself loving to play with them. Man, they were so quick to catch on to everything. And he was right; they were great. So we played Newport, Chicago, St. Louis (where VGM made a record, *Miles Davis Quintet: In St. Louis*), and a few other places.

After we played the States for a few weeks, we went over to Antibes in the south of France, close to Nice on the Mediterranean, and played that festival there. Man, we just killed them over there. Tony just blew everyone away because no one had heard of him, and the French pride themselves on keeping up with what's happening in jazz. He just lit a big fire under everyone in the group. He made me play so much that I forgot about all the pain in my joints which had been bothering me a lot. I was beginning to realize that Tony and this group could play anything they wanted to. Tony was always the center that the group's sound revolved around. He was something else, man.

He was the one who started me to playing "Milestones" again in public, because he loved it so. Not long after he had come into the band he said that he thought the album *Milestones* was "the definitive jazz album of all time" and that it had "the spirit in it of everyone who plays jazz." I was so stunned that I could only say, "No shit!?" Then he told me that the first music he "fell in love with" was my music. I just loved him like a son. Tony played to the sound, and he played real hip, slick shit to the sounds he heard. He changed the way he played every night and played different tempos for every sound every night. Man, to play with Tony Williams you had to be real alert and pay attention to everything he did, or he'd lose you in a second, and you'd just be out of tempo and time and sound real bad.

After we played Antibes (CBS-France recorded that performance as *Miles Davis in Europe*) we came back to the States and went out in August to play the Monterey Jazz Festival out in northern California, just south of San Francisco. While we were there Tony sat in with these two old musicians, Elmer Snowden, a guitarist who was in his late sixties then, and Pops Foster, a bassist, who was in his seventies, I think. Their drummer had never shown up. So he played with them two guys he had never heard of, had never heard their music, and was a motherfucker; just turned Pops and Elmer and the whole entire festival out. That's how bad that young little motherfucker was. Then a little later after he got through playing with them, he went on with us and really kicked ass. All this from a seventeen-year-old who nobody had hardly heard of before the beginning of the year. By now, a lot of people were saying that Tony was going to be the greatest drummer who had ever lived. And I'll tell you this: he had the potential, and nobody *ever* played as well with me as Tony did. I mean it was scary. But then Ron Carter and Herbie

Hancock and George Coleman weren't no slouches either, so I knew we had a good thing going.

I stayed in California for a while doing a musical score with Gil Evans. It was for a play called *Time of the Barracuda,* and Laurence Harvey was the star. They were doing the play in L.A. and so Gil and I stayed at the Chateau Marmont in West Hollywood. Laurence would come by to listen to the music we were doing. He had always been a big fan of mine, coming everywhere I played in Los Angeles, so he really wanted me to do this music. I was also an admirer of his acting, and I thought doing the score was a good idea. We finished the musical score but then the play folded because of disagreements between Laurence and some other people; I never did know what went on. They paid us for what we did, and Columbia recorded it but never brought it out. I guess it's somewhere in their tape vault. I liked what we did on that music. We had a full orchestra, and the record was produced by Irving Townsend. I think what probably happened was that the musicians union wanted a live band in the pit during the play instead of some taped music. After that Gil and I didn't do that much together musically. We remained close friends, but I was just going in another direction with this new band.

In August of 1963, my mother's husband, James Robinson, died back in East St. Louis. I didn't go to the funeral because that really ain't my thing. But I talked to my mother on the phone and she didn't sound too well herself. Like I said, she had cancer and it hadn't gotten any better. Things didn't look too good, and her husband dying just made it worse. My father had died the year before, so she was thinking about all that kind of shit when I spoke with her. My mother was a real strong woman, but I found myself for the first time worrying about her. That was hard for me to do because I'm not the worrying type, so I tried to put it out of my mind. And then some shit happened that just fucked up everybody's head.

I won another *Down Beat* poll on trumpet and my new band finished second to Monk's in the group category. I wasn't going into the studios first of all because I was still angry with Teo Macero for fucking up *Quiet Nights* like he did, and also because I was starting to get tired of recording in studios and just wanted to do more live music. I have always thought musicians played better in live situations and so that studio shit had gotten boring to me. Instead I had scheduled a benefit for the civil rights registration drives that were being sponsored by the NAACP and also by the Congress of Racial

Equality (CORE) and the Student Nonviolent Coordinating Commit-
tee (SNCC). This was the height of the civil rights era, with black
consciousness on the rise. The concert was to be held at Philharmonic Hall in February 1964, and Columbia was going to tape the
performance.

We just blew the top off that place that night. It was a motherfucker the way everybody played—and I mean everybody. A lot of
the tunes we played were done up-tempo and the time never did fall,
not even once. George Coleman played better that night than I have
ever heard him play. There was a lot of creative tension happening
that night that the people out front didn't know about. We had been
off for a while as a band, each doing other things. Plus it was a benefit
and some of the guys didn't like the fact that they weren't getting
paid. One guy—and I won't call his name because he has a great
reputation and I don't want to cause him no grief, plus he's a very
nice guy on top of everything else—said to me, "Look, man, give me
my money and I'll contribute what I want to them; I'm not playing
no benefit. Miles, I don't make as much money as you do." The
discussion went back and forth. Everyone decided that they were
going to do it, but only this one time. When we came out to play,
everybody was madder than a motherfucker with each other and so
I think that anger created a fire, a tension that got into everybody's
playing, and maybe that's one of the reasons everybody played with
such intensity.

About two weeks after the concert, on the last day of February,
my brother Vernon called in the middle of the night and told Frances
that my mother had just died in Barnes Hospital in St. Louis. Frances
told me when I got home early in the morning. I knew that they had
put my mother there, and I meant to go over and see her, but I didn't
know it was so serious. Damn, I had done it again. I hadn't read my
father's note when he gave it to me and now I hadn't gone to see my
mother before she died.

The funeral was to take place in a few days, and Frances and I
were going to fly out to East St. Louis to attend. The plane taxied out
to take off and then it came back because the pilot had to check
something out. When they got the plane back to the gate, I just got
off and went home. The pilot was saying they were experiencing
engine problems and I'm superstitious about shit like that. The plane
coming back with engine trouble told me I wasn't supposed to go.

Frances went on out to the funeral, which was held at the St.
Luke's AME Church in East St. Louis. I just went back home and

cried like a motherfucker all night, cried until I was almost sick. I know that a lot of people found it strange that I didn't come to my own mother's funeral, and some of them probably don't understand it to this day, probably thought I didn't care nothing about my mother. But I loved her and learned a lot from her and miss her. I really didn't know just how much I loved my mother until I knew she was dead. Sometimes, when I'm alone in my house, I feel her presence like a warm wind filling up the room, talking to me, coming to see how I am. She had a great spirit, and I believe her spirit is still watching out for me today. She also knows and understands why I didn't come to that funeral. The image I will always carry around of my mother is when she was strong and beautiful. That's the one I always want to have of her.

Things had started to go bad for me and Frances around this time. She wanted us to have a child together, and I didn't want no more children, so we used to argue a lot about that. And that would lead to other shit and we would fight. I was in a lot of pain from the sickle-cell anemia, so I was drinking more than I had in the past and I was snorting a lot of cocaine. That combination can make you real irritable, because with the coke you don't get no sleep, and when you try to take the edge off that with alcohol, well, you just end up with a bad hangover and still real irritable. Like I said, Frances was the only woman that I had ever been jealous of. And being jealous and using drugs and drinking, I even thought she was fucking a homosexual friend of hers, a dancer, and I accused her of it. She just looked at me like I was crazy, which I was at the time. But I didn't know it; I thought I was sane and on top of the world.

I didn't want to go nowhere, even to people we knew like Julie and Harry Belafonte, who lived right around the corner. I didn't want to see Diahann Carroll, so when Frances wanted to go, I'd tell her to go with Roscoe Lee Browne, the great actor, or Harold Melvin, who was an excellent hairdresser. So they would take her places. Because I don't dance I didn't want her to dance with nobody else. Crazy shit like that. I remember one time we were in a nightclub in Paris and a French comedian danced with Frances. I just left her out there on the floor and went back to the hotel where we were staying. See, I'm a Gemini and I can be real nice one minute and into something else the next. I don't know why I'm like that, I just am and I accept that that's the way I am. When it would get real bad, Frances would go down to Harry and Julie Belafonte's house until I cooled off.

And then there were all the women calling me at home. If Frances picked up the phone while I was talking to one, I'd get mad about that and we'd argue and have a fight. I had turned into something like the Phantom of the Opera. I used to sneak around through this tunnel under my building, all paranoid and shit, used to find myself down in there sometimes like a madman. I was a mess and getting worse. Strange people were coming to the house delivering my cocaine and Frances didn't like that.

My children must have seen what was going on. My daughter, Cheryl, was going to Columbia University, and Gregory was trying to box. Gregory was a very good boxer; I had taught him a lot of shit I knew. He idolized me and wanted to be like me, even play the trumpet. But I used to tell him that he had to do his own thing. He wanted to be a professional fighter, but I wouldn't let him because I was thinking that he might get hurt. I loved boxing for myself, but I think I wanted something better for Gregory, although neither of us knew what that was. Later he went to Vietnam. I don't know why that boy did that, but he said he needed some discipline. He felt he didn't have no purpose in his life at the time. Little Miles was too young then to feel the tensions between me and Frances, but the other kids knew and felt bad about how things were going. Although Frances wasn't their real mother, she had been very good to them and they liked her a lot. I felt that Frances and I would eventually work things out.

Then the shit hit the fan in the group when George Coleman quit. Tony Williams never liked the way George played, and the direction the band was moving in revolved around Tony. George *knew* that Tony didn't like the way he played. Sometimes when I would finish my solo and start to go in the back, Tony would say to me, "Take George with you." Tony didn't like George because George played everything almost perfectly, and Tony didn't like saxophone players like that. He liked musicians who made mistakes, like being out of key. But George just played the chords. He was a hell of a musician, but Tony didn't like him. Tony wanted somebody who was reaching for different kinds of things, like Ornette Coleman. Ornette's group was his favorite band. He also loved Coltrane. I think Tony was the one who brought Archie Shepp to the Vanguard one night to sit in, and he was so awful that I just walked off the bandstand. He couldn't play, and I wasn't going to stand up there with this no-playing motherfucker.

Another reason George left was that because my hip was bothering me a lot I sometimes couldn't make gigs, and they would have to play as a quartet. He used to complain how free Herbie, Tony, and Ron played when I wasn't there. They didn't want to play traditionally when I wasn't there, and they felt that George got in the way. George could play free if he wanted to; he just didn't want to. He preferred the more traditional way. One night in San Francisco he had played free, I guess just to prove a point to everyone, and it fucked up Tony's head.

I want to clear up the story about me wanting to get Eric Dolphy in my band when George left. Eric was a beautiful guy as far as his personality went, but I never liked his playing. He could play; I just didn't like the *way* he played. A lot of people *loved* it; I know Trane did, and Herbie, Ron, and Tony did, too. When George quit, Tony did bring up Eric's name, but I didn't even consider him seriously. Sam Rivers was the man Tony was really pushing because he knew him from Boston and Tony's like that; he was always pushing people he knew. Afterwards, around 1964 when Eric Dolphy died, I got a lot of criticism because I was quoted in a Leonard Feather blindfold test in *Down Beat* saying that Eric played "like somebody was standing on his foot." The magazine came out just about the time Eric died, and everyone thought that was so cold-blooded. But I had said that months before.

My first choice to replace George was Wayne Shorter, but Art Blakey had made him musical director of the Jazz Messengers and he couldn't leave then. So we hired Sam Rivers.

We traveled to Tokyo to play some concerts over there. It was my first trip to Japan, and Frances went along and learned all about Japanese food and culture. By this time I had a road manager named Ben Shapiro, so he took a lot of business off my shoulders, like paying the band, getting hotels and flights, and shit like that. That left me free to enjoy myself. We played Tokyo and Osaka. I'll never forget my arrival in Japan. Flying to Japan is a long-ass flight. So I brought coke and sleeping pills with me and I took both. Then I couldn't go to sleep so I was drinking, too. When we landed there were all these people to meet us at the airport. We're getting off the plane and they're saying, "Welcome to Japan, Miles Davis," and I threw up all over everything. But they didn't miss a beat. They got me some medicine and got me straight and treated me like a king. Man, I had a ball, and I have respected and loved the Japanese people ever since. Beautiful people. They have always treated me great. The concerts were a big success.

When I got back to the States I was feeling no pain whatsoever. I was in Los Angeles when I got the great news I had been waiting for: Wayne Shorter had left the Jazz Messengers. I called Jack Whittemore and told him to call Wayne. In the meantime I told everyone in the band to call him, too, because they loved the way he played as much as I did. So he was getting all these calls from everyone begging him to join the band. When he finally called I told him to come on out. To make sure he did, I sent that motherfucker a first-class ticket so he could come out in style; that's how bad I wanted him. And when he got there the music started happening. Our first gig together was to be at the Hollywood Bowl. Getting Wayne made me feel real good, because with him I just knew some great music was going to happen. And it did; it happened real soon.

things were changing in this country and they seemed to be changing real fast. Music was changing a lot in 1964, too.

A lot of people started saying that jazz was dead, and blaming the way-out "free thing" that people like Archie Shepp, Albert Ayler, and Cecil Taylor were playing and the fact that it didn't have no melodic line, wasn't lyrical, and you couldn't hum it. Now, I'm not saying these musicians weren't serious about what they were doing. But people started to turn off to them. Coltrane was still going strong and so was Monk; people still liked them a lot. But the way-out free thing (even Trane went there just before he died) wasn't what a lot of people wanted to hear.

Where just a few years back the music we were playing was the cutting edge, was getting real popular and finding a wide audience, all that started to stop when the critics—white critics—started supporting the free thing, pushing that over what most everybody else was doing. Jazz started to lose its broad appeal around this time.

In place of jazz, a lot of people were listening to rock music—the Beatles, Elvis Presley, Little Richard, Chuck Berry, Jerry Lee Lewis, Bob Dylan; and the Motown sound was the new rage—Stevie Wonder, Smokey Robinson, the Supremes. James Brown was starting to get hot, too. I think some of pushing the free thing among a lot of the white music critics was intentional, because a lot of them thought that people like me were just getting too popular and too powerful in the music industry. They had to find a way to clip my wings. They loved the melodic, lyrical thing we were doing in *Kind of Blue,* but the popularity of it and the influence we got from doing it scared them.

When those critics had pushed the way-out thing and people started to turn off, the critics dropped it like a hot potato. But by then everybody was turning off to what most of us were doing; all of a sudden jazz became passé, something dead that you put under a glass in the museum and study. All of a sudden rock 'n' roll (and hard rock in a few short years) was in the forefront in the media. White rock 'n' roll stolen from black rhythm and blues and people like Little Richard and Chuck Berry and the Motown sound. All of a sudden white pop music was being pushed on television and everywhere else. Before this, so-called white American popular music wasn't into anything. But now that they were stealing, they sounded half-assed new, had a little dip in it, a little bounce, a little half-assed hipness. But it still was square, wasn't happening yet. Because of what people now thought jazz was—non-melodic, not hummable—a lot of serious musicians had a hard time from then on.

A lot of jazz clubs were closing down, so a lot of jazz musicians were leaving this country for Europe. Red Garland went back home to Dallas, Texas, complaining that there was no place to play. Wynton Kelly had died suddenly, and Paul Chambers was just about dead (if he hadn't already died by then).

I still don't believe that Ornette Coleman, Cecil Taylor, John Coltrane, and all of the other way-out guys realize how they had been used by all those white critics back then.

I didn't personally like a lot of the things that were happening, not even the things that Trane was doing; I preferred what he had done in my band, maybe during the first two or three years. Now it seemed he was just playing for himself and not for the group. I have always felt that what the group does together is what makes music happen.

Anyway, the public's attitude toward the music my new group was playing was at best indifferent, even though our concerts were packed and the records sold well. I think that happened because I was a celebrity, so people were coming to see this famous black rebel who might do anything. Some were still coming to hear the music, and a lot that weren't liked what they heard, but I think the majority were just indifferent. We were playing a searching kind of music, but the times had changed. Everybody was dancing.

You got to remember that the people in a band, the quality of the musicians, is what makes a band great. If you have talented, quality musicians who are willing to work hard, play hard, and do it *together*, then you can make a great band. In the last years that Trane was with my group, he started playing for himself, especially during the last year. When that happens the magic is gone out of a band and people who used to love to play together start not caring anymore. And that's when a band falls apart, and all the music gets stale.

I knew that Wayne Shorter, Herbie Hancock, Ron Carter, and Tony Williams were great musicians, and that they would work as a group, as a musical unit. To have a great band requires sacrifice and compromise from everyone; without it, nothing happens. I thought they could do it and they did. You get the right guys to play the right things at the right time and you got a motherfucker; you got everything you need.

If I was the inspiration and wisdom and the link for this band, Tony was the fire, the creative spark; Wayne was the idea person, the conceptualizer of a whole lot of musical ideas we did; and Ron and Herbie were the anchors. I was just the leader who put us all together. Those were all young guys and although they were learning from me, I was learning from them, too, about the new thing, the free thing. Because to be and stay a great musician you've got to always be open to what's new, what's happening at the moment. You have to be able to absorb it if you're going to continue to grow and communicate your music. And creativity and genius in any kind of artistic expression don't know nothing about age; either you got it or you don't, and being old is not going to help you get it. I understood that we had to do something different. I knew that I was playing with some great young musicians that had their fingers on a different pulse.

At first Wayne had been known as free-form player, but playing with Art Blakey for those years and being the band's musical director had brought him back in somewhat. He wanted to play freer than he could in Art's band, but he didn't want to be all the way out, either. Wayne has always been someone who experimented *with* form instead of someone who did it *without* form. That's why I thought he was perfect for where I wanted to see the music I played go.

Wayne was the only person that I knew then who wrote something like the way Bird wrote, the only one. It was the way he notated on the beat. Lucky Thompson used to hear us and say, "Goddamn, that boy can write music!" When he came into the band it started to grow a lot more and a whole lot faster, because Wayne is a real composer. He writes scores, writes the parts for everybody just as he wants them to sound. It worked exactly like that except when I changed some things. He doesn't trust many people's interpretations of his music, so he would bring out the whole score and everyone would just copy their parts from that, rather than go through the melody and changes and pick our way through the music like that.

Wayne also brought in a kind of curiosity about working with musical rules. If they didn't work, then he broke them, but with a musical sense; he understood that freedom in music was the ability to know the rules in order to bend them to your satisfaction and taste. Wayne was always out there on his own plane, orbiting around his own planet. Everybody else in the band was walking down here on earth. He couldn't do in Art Blakey's band what he did in mine; he just seemed to bloom as a composer when he was in my band. That's why I say he was the intellectual musical catalyst for the band in his arrangement of his musical compositions that we recorded.

I was learning something new every night with that group. One reason was that Tony Williams was such a progressive drummer. He would listen to a record and memorize the whole record, all the solos, the whole thing. He was the only guy in my band who ever told me, "Man, why don't you practice!" I was missing notes and shit trying to keep up with his young ass. So he started me to practicing again because I had stopped and didn't even know it. But man, I can tell you this: there ain't but one Tony Williams when it comes to playing the drums. There was nobody like him before or since. He's just a motherfucker. Tony played on top of the beat, just a fraction above, and it gave everything a little edge because it *had* a little edge. Tony played polyrhythms all the time. He was a cross between Art Blakey and Philly Joe Jones, Roy Haynes and Max Roach. Those were his idols, and he had a little bit of all their shit. But his shit was definitely his own. When he first came with me he wasn't using the sock cymbal, so I made him play that. I also told him to use his foot because he had been listening to Max and Roy a lot, and Max doesn't use his foot. But Art Blakey uses his. (The only players around during this time who played like this were Tony, Alphonse Mouzon, and Jack DeJohnette.)

Ron was less musical than Tony in the sense that he played what he heard. He didn't know musical forms like Tony and Herbie Hancock did, but then he had that zip that Wayne and Herbie needed. Tony and Herbie always had eye contact, but they couldn't have made it as a unit without Ron. It would take Ron four or five days to really get into something, but when he got it, man, you'd better watch out. Because that motherfucker would be laying it down, and you'd better get up and play your ass off or you were going to be left behind and look *real* bad. And everybody's ego was too big for that. Tony would lead the tempo, and Herbie was like a sponge. Anything you played was cool with him; he just soaked up everything. One time I told him that his chords were too thick, and he said, "Man, I don't know what to play some of the time."

"Then Herbie, don't play nothing if you don't know what to play. You know, just let it go; you don't have to be playing all the time!" He was like someone who will drink and drink until the whole bottle is gone just because it's there. Herbie was like that at first; he would just play and play and play because he could and because he never did run out of ideas and he loved to play. Man, that motherfucker used to be playing so much piano that I would walk by after I had played and fake like I was going to cut both of his hands off.

When he first came with us, I told Herbie, "You're putting too many notes in the chord. The chord is already established and so is the sound. So you don't have to play all the notes that are in the bottom. Ron's got the bottom." But that was the only thing I had to tell him, except to do it slow sometimes rather than so fast. And not to overplay; don't play nothing sometimes, even if you sit up there all night. Don't just play because you have eighty-eight keys to play. Piano players and guitar players, man, they do that kind of shit; they're always playing too much, so you've always got to bring them back in. The only guitar player I had heard up until this time that I liked was Charlie Christian. He played the electric guitar like a horn and influenced the way I played trumpet. Oscar Pettiford, the bass player, played like Charlie Christian, too, and it was Oscar who introduced that concept into the way the modern bass is played, like a guitar. Oscar and Jimmy Blanton. Charlie Christian influenced my approach to the trumpet and Dizzy Gillespie's and Chet Baker's, and also influenced the phrasing of Frank Sinatra and Nat "King" Cole.

I didn't have to write for the band; all I did was arrange the music in a way we could play it after they wrote it, put the finishing touches on everything. Wayne would just write something and give it to me and walk off. He wouldn't say shit. He'd just say, "Here, Mr. Davis, I wrote some new songs." Mr. Davis! Then I'd look at the shit and it would be a motherfucker. A lot of times on the road, there would be this knock at my hotel door, and there would be one of these bad young motherfuckers standing there, with a whole bunch of new tunes for me to look at. They'd hand them to me and walk away, like they were scared. I used to think to myself, What the fuck these motherfuckers scared of, bad as they are?

Usually, guys who write a tune want to hear somebody play solos on it, so all these different solos are written up in there. But a lot of the things they were writing weren't like that, didn't have a lot of different solos, so I didn't treat them like that. They had more to do with ensemble playing and that kind of voicing, blending, and shit. You play the first thing in 8/8, then you could run chords and stuff. But I would change it around. A lot of times I would let Herbie play no chords at all, just solo in the middle register and let the bass anchor that, and the shit sounded good as a motherfucker, because Herbie knew he could do that. See, Herbie was the step after Bud Powell and Thelonious Monk, and I haven't heard anybody yet who has come after him.

One of the first things you've got to have in a great band is confidence in the other guys, that they can do whatever it is that has to be done, whatever you say you're going to play. I had faith in Tony and Herbie and Ron to play whatever we wanted to play, whatever was decided at that moment. That comes from not playing all the time, so the music is fresh. And they liked each other on and off the bandstand, and that always helps a lot. It was like Ron was putting up with Herbie and Tony until he got his chops together and then he would find out what Herbie and Tony were doing. Like Ron would start playing major sevenths in the bass and he and Herbie would lock that up and Tony would dig it and you know Wayne and I dug it, too. Wayne would be sitting up there looking like an angel, but when he picked up his horn he was a motherfucking monster. After a while they had seeped into each other's heads, and Tony and Herbie and Ron locked it up.

When we went out to the Hollywood Bowl to play it was bad from the beginning and it just got better. There isn't any beginning to when a band really starts sounding great, when you get used to playing with one another. It just happens by osmosis. There will be five people in a band and it might just seep into two at first. And then the others hear that and they say, "What? What was that?" Then they do something off what the first two did. And then it's inside everybody.

I loved that band, man, because if we played a song for a whole year and you heard it at the beginning of the year, you wouldn't recognize it at the end of the year. When I played with Tony, who is a little genius, I had to react in my playing to what he was playing. And this goes for the whole band. So the way we all played together changed what we were playing each and every night during that time.

The way I had been playing before these guys came into the band was kind of getting on my nerves. Like a favorite pair of shoes that you wear all the time, after a while you've got to change them. What *was* good about Ornette Coleman was that his musical ideas and his melodies were independent of styles, and being independent like that would make you appear to be creating spontaneously. I have an almost perfect sense of melodic order. But then I discovered after really paying attention to some of the things Ornette was playing and talking about—especially after Tony came into the band, and listening to what he had to say about what Ornette was doing—that when I played one note from my trumpet I was really playing about four and that I was transposing guitar solos to my trumpet voice. In my music with Tony, I started putting the backbeat in the drums out front and on top of everything, like in African music. In Western music, white people at this time were trying to suppress rhythm because of where it comes from—Africa—and its racial overtones. But rhythm is like breathing. So that's what I began to learn in this group and it just pointed the way forward.

On a personal level, I was probably closest to Ron, because he was the paymaster for the band and he used to ride with me when we drove places, and sometimes he would drive. We'd drive down to St. Louis when we would be playing in the area, and I think he was the only one in the band that had met my mother before she died. He met all my friends from school, some of whom had become big gangsters.

When we were up on the bandstand I always stood next to Ron because I wanted to hear what he was playing. Before, I used to always stand next to the drummer, but now I didn't worry about what Tony was playing because you could hear everything he was playing; same thing with Herbie. But back then they didn't have amplifiers and so it was hard sometimes to hear Ron. Also I stood next to him to give him my support, because everyone was talking about me and Wayne and Herbie and Tony and not talking about Ron too much, and so this used to upset him.

Every night Herbie, Tony, and Ron would sit around back in their hotel rooms, talking about what they had played until the morning came. Every night they would come back and play something different. And every night I would have to react.

The music we did together changed every fucking night; if you heard it yesterday, it was different tonight. Man, it was something how the shit changed from night to night after a while. Even *we* didn't know where it was all going to. But we did know it was going somewhere else and that it was probably going to be hip, and that was enough to keep everyone excited while it lasted.

I made six studio dates with this group in four years: *E.S.P.* (1965), *Miles Smiles* (1966), *Sorcerer* (1967), *Nefertiti* (1967), *Miles in the Sky* (1968), and *Filles de Kilimanjaro* (1968). We recorded much more than what was released (some of it came out later on *Directions* and *Circle in the Round*). And there were some live recordings that I guess Columbia will release when they think they can make the most money—probably after I'm dead.

My playbook, the songs we would play every night, started to wear down the band. People were coming to hear those tunes that they had heard on my albums; that's what was packing them in the door: "Milestones," " 'Round Midnight," "My Funny Valentine," "Kind of Blue." But the band wanted to play the tunes we were recording which we never did live, and I know that was a sore point with them. I understood where they were coming from, though, doing all the work on "Kilimanjaro," "Gingerbread Boy," "Footprints," "Circle in the Round," "Nefertiti," all those great tunes we were recording. You bring in new tunes and write out all the parts and then pass them out and then play them and record them. We'd try out shit and see what parts were needed, what parts needed to be changed, and write changes. We would be writing and making changes in stops and starts in rehearsals because we had never seen the tune before. So it was a physical, technical problem. Is this note in G or A? Or is it on the second or third beat? All that work. Then, when you don't play it live where people can hear it in that kind of situation, it can be a drag after all of that work. What was funny was this: the tunes that we used to record live that we played every night were just getting faster and faster, and after a while the speed really limited what we could do with them because they definitely couldn't get no faster than what they were. Instead of developing the new music live which we were playing on records, we found ways to make the old music sound as new as the new music we were recording.

I was paying the band good, like $100 a night back in 1964, and by the time we broke up it was maybe $150 or $200 a night. I was making more money, and I was paying more than anybody else in the business. And then they were getting paid well for the record dates, and because they were playing with me their reputations were as big as anybody's. I'm not bragging, that was just the way things were. You play with me and then you become a leader, because after that, everybody was saying, that's the only place to go. And that was flattering but it was also something that I didn't ask for. But I didn't have problems accepting that role.

The shit in the group used to get funny sometimes. The only trouble I had with that band when I first got them together was that Tony was too young to play in clubs. Whenever we played in clubs they had to have sections where young people could come and drink soft drinks. To make him look older I made Tony grow a moustache; one time I told him to get a cigar. Still, a lot of clubs wouldn't book us because he was underage.

The band revolved around Tony, and Tony loved it when everybody played a little out. That's why he liked Sam Rivers so much. He liked it when a player reached and didn't mind if they made mistakes as long as they were reaching and not just playing straight. So in that way Tony and I were a lot alike.

Herbie was a freak for electronic shit and when he would go on the road, he'd spend a lot of time buying electronic stuff. Herbie wanted to record everything and he'd always come in with a little tape recorder. A lot of times he was late, not real late—and it wasn't on account of any drugs or anything—and he'd walk in on the first downbeat of the first tune. So I'd look at the motherfucker kind of hard, and the very first thing that he would do was to get up under the goddamn piano and fix his tape recorder up so he could record everything. By the time he got finished, we're three-quarters of the way through the tune and he ain't played nothing. So that's why on a lot of those live recordings at the beginning you don't hear no piano. That was always a joke in the band, whether or not Herbie was going to be late.

I remember once when Tony had bought this new tape recorder and was showing it around to everyone. When Tony showed it to Herbie, Herbie started telling him how to operate it. This made Tony mad because Tony wanted to tell us all about the tape recorder himself. But Herbie had already done it, so Tony was mad as hell now. When Tony got mad at someone he wouldn't play behind them when they soloed. So I would tell Ron, "Watch how tonight Tony ain't gonna play behind Herbie when he's soloing." Sure enough, when Herbie started to play his solo, Tony just kind of fluffed off everything he played, didn't give him no kind of support. Herbie would be looking at Tony and wondering what was going on, Tony with his head up in the air just leaving Herbie's ass hanging. And Tony used to get upset with Wayne because Wayne would be drunk sometimes up on the bandstand and missing shit, and Tony would just stop playing. But that's the way Tony was; if he was mad with you, you couldn't expect nothing out of him when you were playing. But as soon as it was somebody else's turn, he'd just pick it right up where he left it before.

One night we were playing at the Village Vanguard, and the owner Max Gordon wanted me to play behind a singer. So I told him I didn't play behind no girl singer. But I told him to ask Herbie and if Herbie wanted to do it then it was okay with me. So Herbie, Tony, and Ron played behind her and the people loved her. I didn't play and neither did Wayne. I asked Max who she was, you know, what was her name. So Max said, "Her name is Barbra Streisand and she's going to be a real big star." So everytime I see her today somewhere I say, "Goddamn," and just shake my head.

In 1964, Frances and I gave a party for Robert Kennedy at our house; he was running for senator of New York and our friend Buddy Gist asked if we would do it. All kinds of people came to that party —Bob Dylan, Lena Horne, Quincy Jones, Leonard Bernstein—and to this day I don't remember meeting Kennedy. People say he was there, but if he was I don't remember meeting him.

Who I do remember meeting around this time was James Baldwin, the writer. Marc Crawford—who knew him well—brought him by. I remember being in awe of him because he was so goddamn heavy, all those great books he was writing, and so I didn't know what to say to him. Later, I found out that he felt the same way about me. But I really liked him right off the bat and he liked me a lot, too. We had great respect for one another. He was a very shy person and I was, too. I thought we looked like brothers. When I say both of us have a shyness I mean an artistic kind of shyness, where you are wary of people taking up your time. I saw this in him, saw that he was aware of it. But here I was with James Baldwin, in my mother-fucking house. I had read his books and loved and respected what he had to say. As I got to know Jimmy we opened up to each other and became real great friends. Every time I went to southern France to play Antibes, I would always spend a day or two out at Jimmy's house in St. Paul de Vence. We would just sit in that great big beautiful house of his telling all kinds of stories, lying our asses off. Then we would go out to that wine garden he had and do the same thing. I really miss seeing him now when I go to southern France. He was a great man.

By now, things had gone really badly in my marriage to Frances. Part of the reason was because I was hardly there, going on the road for long periods of time, and that long stay out in Los Angeles when I was recording *Seven Steps to Heaven* didn't help the relationship either. The pain in my hip seemed to get worse when it got cold, and so I was trying to be where it was warm, but that was only part of it. It was the drugs and drinking and all the other women I was still seeing that was causing all the problems. And she had started drinking, too, and so the arguments we had had gotten really terrible. I was starting to go now to these after-hours joints where everyone was coked out of their minds, and she really hated all of that. I would be gone for a couple of days and wouldn't even call home. Frances would be worried about me and her nerves just wore down to a frazzle. Then, when I did come home, I'd be so tired and worn out from staying up for two days that I'd fall asleep while I was eating my food. The Belafontes invited us over for a Christmas party at the end of 1964—one of the few times I didn't play Chicago at that time of year—and we went and I just didn't say anything to anybody. I was high, and irritated even to be there. That hurt her a lot, too, because Julie was one of Frances's very best friends.

She started doing her own stuff, going out with her friends and pursuing her own interests, and I didn't blame her. I guess we had just been married long enough. The picture of us on the album *E.S.P.*, with me looking up at her, was taken in our garden just about a week before she left for the last time. Around that time I was hallucinating about someone being there in the house. So I was looking in closets, under beds, and I remember now putting everyone out in the cold—

everyone except Frances—because I was looking for this imaginary person. So here I am crazier than a motherfucker, with a butcher knife, and I take her down in the basement with me looking for this person who wasn't even there. She started playing crazy like me and said, "Yes, Miles, there is somebody in this house; let's call the police." The police searched the house and looked at me like I was crazy. Frances left the house when the police came and stayed at a friend's house.

I talked her into coming back home. The loud arguments started again. The kids just didn't know what to do and so they would just stay in their rooms and cry. I think all this is what hurt my sons, Gregory and Miles IV, because it was just hard for them to cope; Cheryl was the only one out of the three of them who came out of all that bullshit well, and I know even *she* got some scars.

After our last argument, when I threw a beer bottle across the room and told her I wanted my dinner done when I got back, she stayed with some friends and then went out to California and stayed with the singer Nancy Wilson and her husband. I didn't know where she was until the newspapers and the television stations said that she and Marlon Brando were going out together. I found out she was staying at Nancy's and called, and talked to her—I had another woman make the call for me. I told her that I was coming out there to get her and then I hung up. Then I realized how badly I had treated her and that it was over. There wasn't anything else left to say, so I didn't. But I can say this right now. Frances was the best wife that I ever had and whoever gets her is a lucky motherfucker. I know that now, and I wish I had known that then.

My hip was operated on in April 1965, and they replaced the hip ball with some bone from my shin, but it didn't work and so they had to do it again that August. That time they put a plastic joint in. My sidemen now had big reputations so they didn't have any problems working while I stayed home and recuperated, watching the Watts riots on television.

I didn't play again until November 1965, at the Village Vanguard. I had to use Reggie Workman on bass because Ron—who would do this kind of shit periodically—couldn't, or wouldn't, break a commitment to someone else. It was a great comeback and the people received the music real well. After that, I went on the road in December to Philly and Chicago, where we played the Plugged Nickel and made a record there. This was the time when Teo Macero made his return, and he did the recording there. Columbia still has some tapes they haven't released from that taping. But Ron came back for this gig and everybody played like we hadn't been separated at all. Like I said, I have always believed not playing with each other for a while is good for a band if they are good musicians and like playing with each other. It just makes the music fresher, and that's what happened at the Plugged Nickel, even though we were playing the same book we had always played. In 1965 the music that people were listening to was freer than ever; it seemed like everyone was playing out. It had really taken root.

I got sick in January 1966 with a liver infection and was laid up again until March. Then I went out west on tour with a group, and again Ron Carter couldn't make it, so I took Richard Davis. This time I played a lot of college dates and found them less demanding than playing in clubs. I was really getting tired of the club scene—playing the same places, seeing the same people, and drinking all that shit I was drinking. The liver infection made me cut out a lot of shit, though, but not everything, at least not yet. We played the Newport Jazz Festival and then I made *Miles Smiles* in November. And on this album you can really hear us pulling away, stretching out.

In 1966 or 1967—I'm not sure just when—I met Cicely Tyson, out by Riverside Park. I had seen her playing a secretary on a television show called "East Side/West Side," starring George C. Scott. She made an impression on me because she wore her hair in an Afro and she was always intelligent when I saw her. I remember wondering what she was like. She had a different kind of beauty that you didn't usually see in black women on television; she was very proud-looking and had a kind of inner-burning fire that was interesting. When we first met, she would say these certain words and I would say something so she would have to say it again. She'd give me that knowing look because she knew I wanted her to say it again so I could see her mouth pout. People don't ever see that look in movies. She hides it and doesn't do it when she's acting. It was a look that I don't think anyone ever saw but me—at least that's what she told me. She's from Harlem, but her parents are from the West Indies and she thinks like a West Indian, too, being proud of her African heritage.

At first we were just friends; it wasn't nothing real serious. I had been walking in Riverside Park down the street from where I lived on West 77th with an artist friend from Los Angeles named Corky McCoy. I saw Cicely. She was sitting on a park bench and when she saw me, she stood up. I think I might have met her once or twice with either Diahann Carroll or Diana Sands by then, I've forgotten. I introduced her to Corky—I thought she and Corky might like each other. After Frances left I had no feelings at all for any woman, or anybody else for that matter, except for the people in my band and a real small group of friends. But Cicely didn't even look at Corky. She was looking at me because she knew I was not with Frances anymore, and then she said, "You come out here every day?"

I said, "Yeah." I could see the interest in her eyes, but I didn't want to be bothered with no woman, Cicely included. Then I told her I didn't come out to the park every day like I had said, but that I came on Thursdays.

"About what time?" she said. She still ain't looked at Corky yet. I said to myself, Oh shit. But I told her what time I came. So every time after that when I went to the park, she would either be there or soon show up. Then she told me where she lived and we started going out together. Because she was a very nice person and I didn't want to lead her on, I said, "Look Cicely, ain't nothing happening. I don't have nothing. I don't have no feelings. I know you like me and everything and that you want our relationship to be a little more serious, but I just can't do nothing about this emptiness I feel inside right now." But Cicely was patient and persistent, and one thing led to another because Cicely is that type of woman who just gets into you, gets inside your blood and your head. We started going out and having fun at first. We went out for a long time without having sex. Then she helped me to stop drinking hard liquor, and I only drank beer after that for a long time. She used to just watch out for me, just took it upon herself to do that for me. After a while she was all inside me and then she was all inside my business, too (but she won't never tell you none of hers). When I made *Sorcerer* in 1967 I put her face on the cover and everybody who didn't already know it knew then that we were a twosome.

I had been staying in Los Angeles off and on for a few months out of every year for the past few years. Joe Henderson had come into the band early in 1967 because I was experimenting with a sextet with two tenors. And it was around that time that I started not even bothering to have breaks in between tunes but playing everything without breaks, seguing from one tune right into the next. My music was really stretching out from scale to scale, so I just didn't feel like breaking up the mood with stops and breaks. I just moved right into the next tune, whatever tempo it was, and just played it like that. My performances were becoming more like musical suites, and this allowed for more and longer periods of improvisation. A lot of people really dug the new move, but others thought that it was radical as a motherfucker and that I was definitely losing my mind.

In April I did some gigs out in California—again without Ron Carter; Richard Davis was with me again. We did our uninterrupted set in Berkeley in front of about ten thousand people in a gymnasium, after a rainstorm caused everything to be moved indoors. Our set just fucked up everybody. And it shocked me when even *Down Beat* gave us a great review.

After Berkeley, we played Los Angeles, and that's where Buster Williams took Richard Davis's place. Hampton Hawes, my friend from Los Angeles, turned me on to him. When we went up to play the Both And Club in San Francisco, Hampton made Herbie Hancock get up off the piano and he played some tunes with us. Hampton was a crazy, beautiful motherfucker who never got the credit he deserved on piano. He was my friend until he died in 1977. We played the West Coast until we came back to New York to record *Sorcerer* in May 1967. Ron Carter came back into the studio and we recorded *Nefertiti* over three days during that month. This time I put my own picture on the cover. It was with this album that people really began to notice what a great composer Wayne Shorter was. We did another recording session that month that produced one side of an album called *Water Babies;* the rest of the album was filled with other musicians because it wasn't released until 1976.

In July, Coltrane died and fucked up everyone. Coltrane's death shocked everyone, took everyone by surprise. I knew he hadn't looked too good and had gained a lot of weight the last time I saw him, not too long before he died. I also knew he hadn't been playing much in public. But I didn't know he was that sick—or even sick at all. I think only a few people really knew that he was sick, if they really knew. I don't know if Harold Lovett—who was our lawyer at this time—even knew. Trane kept everything close to his vest and I wasn't really seeing too much of him because he had been busy with his own thing, and I had with mine. Plus, I had been sick, too, and I think the last time I saw him I talked about what a drag it was to be sick. But he didn't say nothing about he himself not feeling too well. Trane was real secretive like that and he only went to the hospital I think one day before he died on July 17, 1967. He had cirrhosis of the liver and it was hurting him so bad he couldn't take it no more.

Trane's music and what he was playing during the last two or three years of his life represented, for many blacks, the fire and passion and rage and anger and rebellion and love that they felt, especially among the young black intellectuals and revolutionaries of that time. He was expressing through music what H. Rap Brown and Stokeley Carmichael and the Black Panthers and Huey Newton were saying with their words, what the Last Poets and Amiri Baraka were saying in poetry. He was their torchbearer in jazz, now ahead of me. He played what they felt inside and were expressing through riots—"burn, baby, burn"—that were taking place everywhere in this country during the 1960s. It was all about revolution for a lot of young black people—Afro hairdos, dashikis, black power, fists raised in the air. Coltrane was their symbol, their pride—their beautiful, black, revolutionary pride. I had been it a few years back, now he was it, and that was cool with me.

It was this way for many intellectual and revolutionary whites and Asians as well. Even his change to a more spiritual music in the music on *A Love Supreme*—which was like a prayer—reached out and influenced those people who were into peace, hippies and people like that. I heard he played a lot of love-ins, which was becoming the rage all over California for a lot of whites. So he was reaching different groups of people, too. His music was embraced by a lot of different kinds of people, and that was beautiful and I was proud of him, even if I liked his earlier music more. He once told me that even he liked some of the music he did earlier better than what he was doing now. But Trane was on a search, and his course kept taking him farther and farther out; he couldn't turn back even though I think he wanted to.

His death created chaos in the "free thing" because he was its leader. He was like Bird to all those musicians who considered themselves "out"—you know, "free," out in space: he was like a god to them. When he died it was much like when Bird died for a lot of bebop musicians who looked to him for directions, even though he himself had been directionless for a lot of years. Ornette Coleman was still around, and some turned to him. But for most Trane had been their guiding light, and after he was gone they seemed to me like people in a boat in the ocean without compass or paddles. It seemed a lot of what he stood for musically died with him. Even though some of his disciples carried on his message, they carried it to smaller and smaller audiences.

Like he did with Bird, Harold Lovett told me of Trane's death.

Trane's death made me real sad because not only was he a great and beautiful musician, he was a kind and beautiful and spiritual person that I loved. I miss him, his spirit and his creative imagination and his searching, innovative approach to what he was doing. He was a genius, like Bird, and he was greedy about living and his art—especially about drugs and alcohol and music—and it killed him in the end. But his music is what he left us and we can all learn from that.

Around that time everything was in flux again in this country—everything. Music, politics, race relations, everything. Nobody seemed to know where things were going; everybody seemed confused—even a lot of the artists and musicians who all of a sudden seemed to have more freedom than we ever had to do our own thing. Trane's death seemed to put a lot of confusion in a lot of people, because he had had a great influence on a lot of people. Even Duke Ellington seemed to be going in a spiritual direction, as Trane had done in *A Love Supreme,* when Duke wrote a score called "In the Beginning God" in 1965 and then played it in churches all over the United States and Europe.

After Trane's death, Dizzy Gillespie and I both took our bands into the Village Gate for the whole month of August, and while we were there crowds lined up around the block to see us. Sugar Ray Robinson came by along with Archie Moore, the great old champion from St. Louis. I remember when they came down I asked Dizzy to introduce them from the stage and he told me that *I* was the fight fan, so why didn't I do it. But I couldn't get into that kind of thing, so he ended up doing it. The music that our bands played during our engagement there was the talk of New York.

I think that's where I met Hugh Masekela, the very fine South African trumpet player. He had just come over to the States and was doing real good. He was a friend of Dizzy's, who I think had helped sponsor him while he went to music school here. I remember one night riding uptown with him and him being somewhat in awe that he was in the same car with me. He told me that I had been a hero of his and other blacks in South Africa when I stood up to that policeman outside of Birdland that time, and I remember being surprised that they even knew about that kind of thing over there in Africa. Hugh had his own approach to playing the trumpet even then, had his own sound. I thought that was good, although I didn't think he played black American music too well. Every time I saw him I told him to just keep on doing his own thing rather than trying to play what we were playing over here. After a while I think he started listening to me, because his playing got better.

After I played the Village Gate with Dizzy, I toured the United States and then Europe for most of the rest of 1967. It was a long tour with a package that George Wein put together called the Newport Jazz Festival in Europe. But it had too many groups touring together, and after a while shit got all fucked up. Thelonious Monk, Sarah Vaughan, and Archie Shepp were on the tour along with a whole bunch of other motherfuckers. (I even played with Archie a couple of times because Tony Williams asked me to, but I still couldn't get into what he was playing.) And then in Spain, George Wein and I got into this bad argument over money. I like George, and have known him for a long time, but we've had our share of arguments over the years because I don't like some of the bullshit that he does and I tell him. George is all right, mostly he's cool and has been good for music and a lot of musicians, who he's paid good money to, including me. It's just that I can't take the bullshit he hands out sometimes.

As soon as I got back to New York, I took the group into the studio in December 1967, along with Gil Evans—who arranged some things —and added a young guitarist named Joe Beck. I was already moving toward a guitar sound in my music because I was beginning to listen to a lot of James Brown, and I liked the way he used the guitar in his music. I always liked the blues and always loved to play it, so around this time I was listening to Muddy Waters and B. B. King and trying to find a way to get that kind of voicing into my music. I had learned a lot from Herbie, Tony, Wayne, and Ron and had just about absorbed all the things I had picked up from them in the almost three years we had been together. Now I was starting to think about other ways I could approach the music I wanted to play, because I could feel myself starting to want to change but I didn't really know yet what this change was all about. I knew it had something to do with the guitar voice in my music and I was beginning to get interested in what electrical instrumental voicing could do in my music. See, when I used to listen to Muddy Waters in Chicago down on 33rd and Michigan every Monday when he played there and I would be in town, I knew I had to get some of what he was doing up in my music. You know, the sound of the $1.50 drums and the harmonicas and the two-chord blues. I had to get back to that now because what we had been doing was just getting really abstracted. That was cool while I did it, but I just wanted to get back to that sound from where I had come.

It was on this recording date that Herbie first played the electric piano. I had been listening to Joe Zawinul playing it in Cannonball Adderley's group and loved the way it sounded; for me, it was the future. But moving into electrical instruments would also break up my band a little later and send me into a new kind of music.

Joe Beck was a fine player, but he couldn't give me what I wanted at that time. I added another young guitar player, George Benson, at the other sessions—after recording with my regular quintet first—in a recording we did in January, February, and March 1968. One of the tunes George played on, "Paraphernalia," was released on *Miles in the Sky* later that year. The rest of the tracks were released later on.

I wanted to hear the bass line a little stronger. If you can hear a bass line, then any note in a sound that you play can be heard. So we changed the bass line on the tunes we played; we varied them. If I wrote a bass line, we could vary it so that it would have a sound a little bit larger than a five-piece group. By using an electric piano and having Herbie play the bass line and the chords with what the guitar plays and with Ron playing with him, too, in the same register, I felt the music would have a fresh good sound. And it did. When I did these recordings with this kind of voicing, I was moving toward what the critics later would call "fusion." I was just about trying a fresh, new approach.

Around this time, Columbia wanted Gil and me to do a jazz version of the music from the film *Doctor Dolittle*. See, *Porgy and Bess* had been my best-selling album, and so some real dumb motherfucker over there thought that this *Doctor Dolittle* would be a great seller. After listening to that shit I said, "No way, Jose."

I took the band along with Gil to Berkeley, California, and we did a concert there and added a big band. Columbia recorded the concert live and still has the tapes in their vaults. Just before we left to do these concerts, Martin Luther King, Jr., was killed in Memphis, in early April. The country erupted into violence again. King had won the Nobel prize for peace and was a great leader and a beautiful guy, but I just never could go for his non-violent, turn-the-other-cheek philosophy. Still, for him to get killed like that, so violently—just like Gandhi—was a goddamn shame. He was like America's saint, and white people had killed him anyway because they were afraid when he changed his message from just talking to blacks to talking about the Vietnam War and labor and everything. When he died he was talking to everyone, and the powers that be didn't like that. If he had just kept talking only to blacks he would have been all right, but he did the same thing that Malcolm did after he came back from Mecca and that's why he was killed, too, I'm certain of it.

When we got back to New York, I went back into the studio in May to complete the *Miles in the Sky* album with Herbie, Wayne, Ron, and Tony. In June after we had finished *Miles in the Sky*, we went into the studio and began the *Filles de Kilimanjaro* album. Then we went on tour all summer and finished the album later in September.

Things weren't going too well for me and Cicely, and we broke up because I had met a beautiful young singer and songwriter named Betty Mabry, whose picture is on the cover of *Filles de Kilimanjaro*. We also had a song on there named for her, "Mademoiselle Mabry." Man, I was really in love again and felt real good about Betty Mabry. She was twenty-three when I met her and was from Pittsburgh. She was really into new, avant-garde pop music. My divorce from Frances had come through in February of 1968, and so Betty and I were married that September while the group was playing a gig at the Plugged Nickel. We got married in Gary, Indiana, and my brother and sister stood for me.

Betty was a big influence on my personal life as well as my musical life. She introduced me to the music of Jimi Hendrix—and to Jimi Hendrix himself—and other black rock music and musicians. She knew Sly Stone and all those guys, and she was great herself. If Betty were singing today she'd be something like Madonna; something like Prince, only as a woman. She was the beginning of all that when she was singing as Betty Davis. She was just ahead of her time. She also helped me change the way I was dressing. The marriage only lasted about a year, but that year was full of new things and surprises and helped point the way I was to go, both in my music and, in some ways, my lifestyle.

53

54

PHILLY Joe Jones (53) was the drummer on *Milestones* (54) and the quintet sounded great. I knew we had something special when I heard that record. The other members of the quintet, besides Trane, were bass player Paul Chambers (55) and Red Garland on the piano (56).

56

55

WHEN we went in to do recording sessions for *Kind of Blue*, I brought in musical sketches. I didn't write out the music because I wanted spontaneity.

58

57

AFTER a summer-long stand in 1956 at the Cafe Bohemia, we went back into the studio and recorded "'Round Midnight." The song was put in the can for the album *'Round About Midnight.*

CHARLIE Mingus was one of the finest bassists and a great composer. Like me, he was innovative and always changing —and outspoken.

59

60

Oᴜᴛsɪᴅᴇ Birdland, a white policeman told me to move on. I refused and ended up with blood streaming from my head and a resisting arrest charge.

61

Tʜɪs is me leaving jail. I'm with my wife Frances and my lawyer, Harold Lovett.

62

63

A composition called "Concierto de Aranjuez" by Joaquin Rodrigo was the genesis for the album *Sketches of Spain* that Gil Evans and I did together. Gil was real important to me as a friend and a musician. He was the only one who could pick up on what I was thinking musically.

64

THIS photograph of Frances and me was taken in our garden about a week before she left me for the last time.

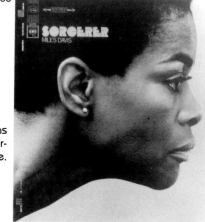

66

65

I met Cicely Tyson in 1966 or '67. She was very proud-looking and had a kind of inner-burning fire.

67

CICELY and I broke up when I met a beautiful singer and songwriter named Betty Mabry. Her photograph is on this album cover and we named a song for her: "Mademoiselle Mabry".

68

69

Art Blakey and I played together and made some records together, too. A lot of musicians in my groups had played with Art before they came to me.

70

Ornette Coleman came on the scene around 1960 and turned the jazz world all the way around. I sat in with Ornette and didn't think he was so hip, especially when he started playing trumpet without any training.

72

71

Clive Davis was the president of Columbia Records. After a rough start, we got along well because he thought like an artist.

Teo Macero, who became my producer at Columbia.

73

75

74

My second great quintet: Herbie Hancock (73) and Ron Carter (74) were the anchors for the band. Wayne Shorter (75) was the idea person, the conceptualizer of many of our musical ideas. Tony Williams was the fire, the creative spark (76).

76

We recorded *Miles Smiles* in 1966.
You really hear us pulling away
musically, stretching out, on this one.

This is the group onstage at Shelly's Manne-Hole in Los Angeles.

THE music I was really listening to in 1968 was Jimi Hendrix (79), James Brown (80), and Sly Stone (81). Jimi Hendrix came from the blues, like me. Around this time I was moving into a guitar-like sound in my music.

CHICK Corea began playing the Fender Rhodes piano when he started playing with me.

82

84

83

KEITH Jarrett and Chick both played electric piano in my working band. Keith hated electrical instruments before he came with me.

WHAT we did on *Bitches Brew* you couldn't write down for an orchestra to play. The session was about improvisation—what makes jazz so fabulous. It sold faster than any other jazz album in history.

I had heard Joe Zawinul play electric piano with Cannonball. I really liked the sound and wanted it in my band.

JACK DeJohnette gave me a certain deep groove that I just loved to play over.

WHEN we went into the studio in 1969, Joe Zawinul and I added a young Englishman named John McLaughlin on guitar.

85

86

87

Betty Mabry was a big influence on my personal life as well as in my musical life. She also helped me change the way I was dressing.

88

Jimi Hendrix's death upset me because he was so young and had so much ahead of him. I decided to go to the funeral with Betty and a friend of hers, though I hated going to them.

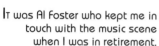

With Sly Stone and James Brown in mind I went into the studio to record *On the Corner*. I really made an effort here to get my music over to young black people.

It was Al Foster who kept me in touch with the music scene when I was in retirement.

I gave my nephew Vincent Wilburn a set of drums when he was about seven, and he fell in love with them.

WHEN I stopped playing I began listening to some avant-garde classical composers like Karlheinz Stockhausen (right) and Paul Buckmaster. I liked the way they used rhythm and space.

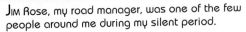

JIM Rose, my road manager, was one of the few people around me during my silent period.

TOWARD the end of this time, Cicely Tyson came back into my love life. She's talking to me and Jim Rose in my yellow Ferrari.

GEORGE Butler kept coming around to see me after I had stopped playing. He gradually talked me back into the studio again. After that, George became my producer at Columbia.

97

98

Cɪᴄᴇʟʏ and the people at Columbia organized
a celebration for me at Radio City Music Hall
in 1983, co-produced by the Black Music
Association (97, 98). Bill Cosby (99) was the
host, and he presented me with an honorary
degree on behalf of the president of Fisk
University. My son Erin (100) came
backstage with me that night.

99

100

101

ALSO at that tribute was Elwood Buchanan, my first great teacher from Lincoln High in East St. Louis. Back then he told me, "You got enough talent to be your own trumpet man."

PRINCE wrote a song for my first Warner album, *Tutu*, but when he heard what was on the tape we sent him, he didn't think his tune fit. A great musician has to have the ability to stretch, and Prince can certainly stretch.

103

MORE and more I've been drawing and painting. I get obsessed with it like I do with music and everything else that I care about.

104

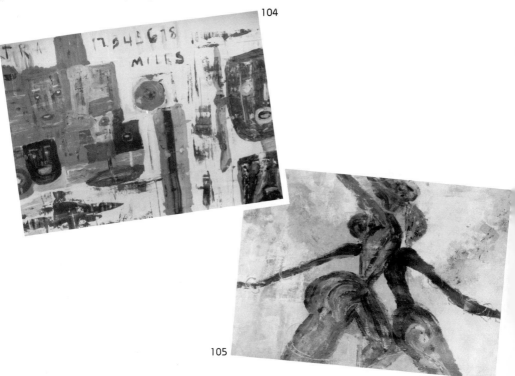

105

Joseph Foley McCreary—"Foley"—has a funk-blues-rock-edged tone to his sound. Marcus Miller recommended him to me.

I like playing with young musicians. I want to keep creating, changing. Music isn't about standing still and becoming safe.

This was my first album for Warner Bros., called *Tutu* after Bishop Desmond Tutu, the Nobel Peace Prize laureate. The song "Full Nelson" is named for Nelson Mandela.

108

Tommy LiPuma produced *Tutu*. He has great focus and concentration in the studio.

110

GREAT musicians are like great fighters. They have a
higher sense of theory going on in their heads. I feel
strong creatively now, and I feel I'm getting even
stronger.

Chapter 14

1968

was full of all kinds of changes, but for me, the changes that were happening in my music were very exciting and the music that was happening everywhere was incredible. These things were leading me into the future and into *In a Silent Way*.

A lot of things were changing in music around 1967 and 1968 and a lot of new shit was happening. One of them was the music of Charles Lloyd, who had become very popular. When his band was really happening he had Jack DeJohnette and a young piano player named Keith Jarrett. He was the leader, but it was those two guys who were making the music really happen. They were playing a cross between jazz and rock, very rhythmic music. Charles never was any kind of player, but he had a certain sound on the saxophone that was kind of light and floating and worked with what Keith and Jack were putting under and around it. His music was very popular for a couple of years and so a lot of people started paying attention. Our two groups shared a bill at the Village Gate at the end of 1967 or early 1968. Man, the place was packed. I knew Jack from when he filled in for Tony, and when Charles's group was in town I would go over and listen. He started accusing me of trying to steal his musicians from him. Charles didn't stay around for too long but made a lot of money during the time he was hot. I hear he's rich and selling real estate today, so more power to him.

The music I was really listening to in 1968 was James Brown, the great guitar player Jimi Hendrix, and a new group who had just come out with the hit record, "Dance to the Music," Sly and the Family Stone, led by Sly Stewart, from San Francisco. The shit he was doing was badder than a motherfucker, had all kinds of funky shit up in it. But it was Jimi Hendrix that I first got into when Betty Mabry turned me on to him.

I first met Jimi when his manager called up and wanted me to introduce him to the way I was playing and putting my music together. Jimi liked what I had done on *Kind of Blue* and some other stuff and wanted to add more jazz elements to what he was doing. He liked the way Coltrane played with all those sheets of sound, and he played the guitar in a similar way. Plus, he said he had heard the guitar voicing that I used in the way I played the trumpet. So we started getting together. Betty really liked this music—and later, I found out, she liked him physically, too—and so he started to come around.

He was a real nice guy, quiet but intense, and was nothing like people thought he was. He was just the opposite of the wild and crazy image he presented on the stage. When we started getting together and talking about music, I found out that he couldn't read music. Betty had a party for him sometime in 1969 at my house on West 77th. I couldn't be there because I had to be in the studio that night recording, so I left some music for him to read and then we'd talk about it later. (Some people wrote some shit that I didn't come to the party for him because I didn't like having a party for a man in my house. That's a lot of bullshit.)

When I called back home from the studio to speak to Jimi about the music I had left him, I found out he didn't read music. There are a lot of great musicians who don't read music—black and white—that I have known and respected and played with. So I didn't think less of Jimi because of that. Jimi was just a great, natural musician—self-taught. He would pick up things from whoever he was around, and he picked up things quick. Once he heard it he really had it down. We would be talking, and I would be telling him technical shit like, "Jimi, you know, when you play the diminished chord . . ." I would see this lost look come into his face and I would say, "Okay, okay, I forgot." I would just play it for him on the piano or on the horn, and he would get it faster than a motherfucker. He had a natural ear for hearing music. So I'd play different shit for him, show him that way. Or I'd play him a record of mine or Trane's and explain to him what we were doing. Then he started incorporating things I told him into his albums. It was great. He influenced me, and I influenced him, and that's the way great music is always made. Everybody showing everybody else something and then moving on from there.

But Jimi was also close to hillbilly, country music played by them mountain white people. That's why he had those two English guys in his band, because a lot of white English musicians liked that American hillbilly music. The best he sounded to me was when he had Buddy Miles on drums and Billy Cox on bass. Jimi was playing that Indian kind of shit, or he'd play those funny little melodies he doubled up on his guitar. I loved it when he doubled up shit like that. He used to play 6/8 all the time when he was with them white English guys and that's what made him sound like a hillbilly to me. Just that concept he was doing with that. But when he started playing with Buddy and Billy in the Band of Gypsies, I think he brought what he was doing all the way out. But the record companies and white people liked him better when he had the white guys in his band. Just like a lot of white people like to talk about me when I was doing the nonet thing—the *Birth of the Cool* thing, or when I did those other albums with Gil Evans or Bill Evans because they always like to see white people up in black shit, so that they can say they had something to do with it. But Jimi Hendrix came from the blues, like me. We understood each other right away because of that. He was a great blues guitarist. Both him and Sly were great natural musicians; they played what they heard.

So, that's the way my head was as far as music was going. First, I had to be comfortable with what I was going to be playing. Then, I had to find the right musicians. It was a process of playing with different people and picking my way forward. I spent time listening to and feeling what certain people could play and give, and what they couldn't, and picking and choosing the ones who would fit, and eliminating the ones who wouldn't. People eliminate themselves when there's nothing happening—or they should.

The group disbanded sometime in late 1968. We continued to play gigs and sometimes made some concerts together—at least Herbie, Wayne, Tony, and I did—but for all intents and purposes the group broke up when Ron decided to leave for good because he didn't want to play electric bass. Herbie had already recorded "Watermelon

Man" and wanted to form a group of his own. Tony felt the same way. So they both left the group at the end of 1968. Wayne stayed with me a couple of years longer.

It had been a great learning experience for everyone. Bands don't stay together for ever and ever, and although it was hard for me when they left me, it was really time for all of us to move on. We left each other in a positive place and that's all you can ask for.

The changes in my band started happening in July 1968 when I replaced Ron Carter on bass with Miroslav Vitous, a young bass player from Czechoslovakia. (Ron still made a couple more studio dates with me, but he quit the working band that made club dates.) Miroslav was only a temporary replacement until I got Dave Holland. I had seen and heard Dave in June 1968, when I played a concert over in England, and he knocked me out. Since I knew Ron was going to be leaving soon I talked with Dave about joining my band. He had other commitments, so when he was through with those at the end of July, I called him in London and asked him to join us. He came over and opened with us when we played Count Basie's club up in Harlem. My interest was in finding an electronic bass player because of the sound it added to my band. I was still on the lookout for someone who would eventually play that instrument all the time in my band, because I didn't know then if Dave would want to switch to playing that instrument. But for the time being he could replace Ron on gigs I had lined up, and we could cross the other bridge when we came to it.

I had also started using both Chick Corea and Joe Zawinul on piano in some of my studio recording dates that year. I would have three piano players on some of those dates—Herbie, Joe, and Chick. On a couple of those dates I used two bass players—Ron and Dave. I also started using Jack DeJohnette on drums sometimes instead of Tony Williams, and started putting "Directions in Music by Miles Davis" on the front of my album covers so that nobody could be mistaken about *who* was the creative control behind the music. After that thing Teo Macero did on *Quiet Nights*, I wanted to control whatever music I put on record. I was moving more and more to using electronic instruments to make up the sound that I wanted, and I felt that saying "Directions in Music by Miles Davis" would indicate that.

I had heard Joe Zawinul playing electric piano on "Mercy, Mercy, Mercy" with Cannonball Adderley, and I really liked the sound of the instrument and wanted it in my band. Chick Corea began playing the electric Fender Rhodes piano when he started playing with me, and so did Herbie Hancock, who liked playing the Rhodes right away after he got into it; Herbie always liked electronic gadgets anyway, so he took to the Rhodes like a fish to water. But Chick wasn't sure about playing it when he first came with me, but I *made* him play it. He didn't like me telling him what instrument to play until he really got into it but then he really liked it, too, and made his reputation playing it.

See, the Fender Rhodes has one sound and that sound is itself. It has no other sound. You always know what it is. I'm crazy about the way Gil Evans voices his music, so I wanted to get me a Gil Evans sound in a small band. That required an instrument like the synthesizer, which can get all those different instrumental sounds. I could hear that you could write a bass line with the voicings that Gil did with his big band. We could get some harmony on top with the synthesizer, and that makes the whole band sound fuller. Then you double the bass when you double that; it works better than if you had a regular piano. After I got this into my head and saw how that affected the music I was doing, I didn't need a piano anymore. It didn't have nothing to do with me just wanting to go electric, like a lot of people have said, just to be having some electrical shit up in my band. I just wanted that kind of voicing a Fender Rhodes could give me that a regular piano couldn't. The same thing for the electric bass; it gave me what I wanted to hear at the time instead of the stand-up bass. Musicians have to play the instruments that best reflect the times we're in, play the technology that will give you what you want to hear. All these purists are walking around talking about how electrical instruments will ruin music. Bad music is what will ruin music, not the instruments musicians choose to play. I don't see nothing wrong with electrical instruments as long as you get great musicians who will play them right.

After Herbie left the working band in August of 1968, Chick Corea took his place. I think Tony Williams hipped me to him because they both were from Boston, and Tony knew him from up there. He had worked with Stan Getz, and when I called him to work with me he was working with Sarah Vaughan. Around the first of the year of 1969, Jack DeJohnette replaced Tony on drums, so we had a new band except for me and Wayne (although Herbie and Tony would keep making record dates with me).

In February 1969 we went into the studio: Wayne, Chick, Herbie, Dave, Tony instead of Jack on drums (because I wanted Tony's sound), Joe Zawinul, and I added a guitarist, another young Englishman, named John McLaughlin, who had come over here to join Tony Williams's new group, Lifetime (it had Larry Young on organ). Dave Holland had introduced Tony and me to John when we were over in England where we first heard him. Then Dave loaned Tony a tape of John playing, and Tony let me hear it. I heard him play with Tony up at Count Basie's and he was a motherfucker, so I asked him to make the date. He told me he had been listening to me for a long time and that he might be nervous going into the studio with one of his idols. So I told him, "Just relax and play like you did up at Count Basie's and everything will be all right." And he did.

This was the *In a Silent Way* recording session. I had called Joe Zawinul and told him to bring some music to the studio because I loved his compositions. He brought a tune called "In a Silent Way," and it became the album's title tune. (The other two tunes on the album are mine.) I had recorded some of Joe's other tunes like "Ascent" and "Directions" in the November 1968 recording sessions we did together. "Ascent" was a tone poem very similar to "In a Silent Way," only it wasn't as compelling. When Joe brought "In a Silent Way," I saw what he was doing, only this time he had put it together better. (With the tunes I wrote for the November 1968 session, like "Splash," you can hear that I'm moving toward a more rhythmic, blues-funk sound.)

We changed what Joe had written on "In a Silent Way," cut down all the chords and took his melody and used that. I wanted to make the sound more like rock. In rehearsals we had played it like Joe had written it, but it wasn't working for me because all the chords were cluttering it up. I could hear that the melody that Joe had written— which was hidden by all the other clutter—was really beautiful. When we recorded I just threw out the chord sheets and told everyone to play just the melody, just to play off that. They were surprised to be working in this way, but I knew from when I had brought in music that nobody had ever heard for *Kind of Blue* that if you've got some great musicians—and we did, both then and now—they will deal with the situation and play beyond what is there and above where they think they can. That's what I did with *In a Silent Way*, and the music on there came out beautiful and fresh.

Joe never did like what I did with his composition, and I don't think he likes it even today. But it worked and that's all that really matters. Today many people consider Joe's tune a classic and the beginning of fusion. If I had left that tune the way Joe had it, I don't think it would have been praised the way it was after the album came out. *In a Silent Way* was a collaborative thing that Joe and I did. Some people don't like the way I work. Some musicians feel sometimes I don't give them enough credit. But I have always tried to credit people who did things for me. People were walking around mad because I took credit for arranging *In a Silent Way*, but I *did* arrange the music by changing it like I did.

After we finished *In a Silent Way*, I took the band out on the road; Wayne, Dave, Chick, and Jack DeJohnette were now my working band. Man, I wish this band had been recorded live because it was really a bad motherfucker. I think Chick Corea and a few other people recorded some of our performances live, but Columbia missed out on the whole fucking thing.

We toured through the spring and up until August, when we went back into the studio again and recorded *Bitches Brew*.

Nineteen sixty-nine was the year rock and funk were selling like hotcakes and all this was put on display at Woodstock. There were over 400,000 people at the concert. That many people at a concert makes everybody go crazy, and especially people who make records. The only thing on their minds is, How can we sell records to that many people all the time? If we haven't been doing that, then how can we do it?

That was the atmosphere all around the record companies. At the same time, people were packing stadiums to hear and see stars in person. And jazz music seemed to be withering on the vine, in record sales and live performances. It was the first time in a long time that I didn't sell out crowds everywhere I played. In Europe I always had sellouts, but in the United States, we played to a lot of half-empty clubs in 1969. That told me something. Compared to what my records used to sell, when you put them beside what Bob Dylan or Sly Stone sold, it was no contest. Their sales had gone through the roof. Clive Davis was the president of Columbia Records and he signed Blood, Sweat and Tears in 1968 and a group called Chicago in 1969. He was trying to take Columbia into the future and pull in all those young record buyers. After a rough start he and I got along well, because he thinks like an artist instead of a straight businessman. He had a good sense for what was happening; I thought he was a great man.

He started talking to me about trying to reach this younger market and about changing. He suggested that the way for me to reach this new audience was to play my music where they went, places like the Fillmore. The first time we had a conversation I got mad with him because I thought he was putting down *me* and all the things I had done for Columbia. I hung up on him after telling him I was going to find another record company to record for. But they wouldn't give me a release. After we went back and forth in these arguments for a while, everything finally cooled down and we got all right again. For a while, I was thinking about going over to Motown Records, because I liked what they were doing and figured that they could understand what I was trying to do better.

What Clive really didn't like was that the agreement I had with Columbia allowed me to get advances against royalties earned, so whenever I needed money, I would call up and get an advance. Clive felt that I wasn't making enough money for the company to be giving me this type of treatment. Maybe he was right, now that I'm looking back on all of it, but right from a strictly business position, not an artistic one. I felt that Columbia should live up to what they had agreed to. They thought that since I sold around 60,000 albums every time I put out a record—which was enough for them before the new thing came around—that that wasn't enough to keep on giving me money.

So this was the climate with Columbia and me just before I went into the studio to record *Bitches Brew*. What they didn't understand was that I wasn't prepared to be a memory yet, wasn't prepared to be listed only on Columbia's so-called classical list. I had seen the way to the future with my music, and I was going for it like I had always done. Not for Columbia and their record sales, and not for trying to get to some young white record buyers. I was going for it for myself, for what I wanted and needed in my own music. *I* wanted to change course, *had* to change course for me to continue to believe in and love what I was playing.

When I went into the studio in August 1969, besides listening to rock music and funk, I had been listening to Joe Zawinul and Cannonball playing shit like "Country Joe and the Preacher." And I had met another English guy, named Paul Buckmaster, in London. I asked him to come over sometime and help me put an album together. I liked what he was doing then. I had been experimenting with writing a few simple chord changes for three pianos. Simple shit, and it was funny because I used to think when I was doing them how Stravinsky went back to simple forms. So I had been writing these things down, like one beat chord and a bass line, and I found out that the more we played it, it was always different. I would write a chord, a rest, maybe another chord, and it turned out that the more it was played, the more it just kept getting different. This started happening in 1968 when I had Chick, Joe, and Herbie for those studio dates. It went on into the sessions we had for *In a Silent Way*. Then I started thinking about something larger, a skeleton of a piece. I would write a chord on two beats and they'd have two beats out. So they would do one, two, three, da-dum, right? Then I put the accent on the fourth beat. Maybe I had three chords on the first bar. Anyway, I told the musicians that they could do anything they wanted, play anything they heard but that I had to have this, what they did, as a chord. Then they knew what they could do, so that's what they did. Played off that chord, and it made it sound like a whole lot of stuff.

I told them that at rehearsals and then I brought in these musical sketches that nobody had seen, just like I did on *Kind of Blue* and *In a Silent Way*. We started early in the day in Columbia's studio on 52nd Street and recorded all day for three days in August. I had told Teo Macero, who was producing the record, to just let the tapes run and get everything we played, told him to get *everything* and not to be coming in interrupting, asking questions. "Just stay in the booth and worry about getting down the sound," is what I told him. And he did, didn't fuck with us once and got down everything, got it down real good.

So I would direct, like a conductor, once we started to play, and I would either write down some music for somebody or I would tell him to play different things I was hearing, as the music was growing, coming together. It was loose and tight at the same time. It was casual but alert, everybody was alert to different possibilities that were coming up in the music. While the music was developing I would hear something that I thought could be extended or cut back. So that recording was a development of the creative process, a living composition. It was like a fugue, or motif, that we all bounced off of. After it had developed to a certain point, I would tell a certain musician to come in and play something else, like Benny Maupin on bass clarinet. I wish I had thought of video taping that whole session because it must have been something and I would have liked to have been able to see just what went down, like a football or basketball instant replay. Sometimes, instead of just letting the tape run, I would tell Teo to back it up so I could hear what we had done. If I wanted something else in a certain spot, I would just bring the musician in, and we would just do it.

That was a great recording session, man, and we didn't have any problems as I can remember. It was just like one of them old-time jam sessions we used to have up at Minton's back in the old bebop days. Everybody was excited when we all left there each day.

Some people have written that doing *Bitches Brew* was Clive Davis's or Teo Macero's idea. That's a lie, because they didn't have nothing to do with none of it. Again, it was white people trying to give some credit to other white people where it wasn't deserved because the record became a breakthrough concept, very innovative. They were going to rewrite history after the fact like they always do.

What we did on *Bitches Brew* you couldn't ever write down for an orchestra to play. That's why I didn't write it all out, not because I didn't know what I wanted; I knew that what I wanted would come out of a process and not some prearranged shit. This session was about improvisation, and that's what makes jazz so fabulous. Any time the weather changes it's going to change your whole attitude about something, and so a musician will play differently, especially if everything is not put in front of him. A musician's attitude *is* the music he plays. Like in California, out by the beach, you have silence and the sound of waves crashing against the shore. In New York you're dealing with the sounds of cars honking their horns and people on the streets running their mouths and shit like that. Hardly ever in California do you hear people talking on the streets. California is mellow, it's about sunshine and exercise and beautiful women on the beaches showing off their bad-ass bodies and fine, long legs. People there have color in their skin because they go out in the sun all the time. People in New York go out but it's a different thing, it's an inside thing. California is an outside thing and the music that comes out of there reflects that open space and freeways, shit you don't hear in music that comes out of New York, which is usually more intense and energetic.

After I finished *Bitches Brew*, Clive Davis put me in touch with Bill Graham, who owned the Fillmore in San Francisco and the Fillmore East in downtown New York. Bill wanted me to play San Francisco first, with the Grateful Dead, and so we did. That was an eye-opening concert for me, because there were about five thousand people there that night, mostly young, white hippies, and they hadn't hardly heard of me if they had heard of me at all. We opened for the Grateful

Dead, but another group came on before us. The place was packed with these real spacy, high white people, and when we first started playing, people were walking around and talking. But after a while they all got quiet and really got into the music. I played a little of something like *Sketches of Spain* and then we went into the *Bitches Brew* shit and that really blew them out. After that concert, every time I would play out there in San Francisco, a lot of young white people showed up at the gigs.

Then Bill brought us back to New York to play the Fillmore East, with Laura Nyro. But before that, we played Tanglewood for Bill with Carlos Santana and a group that was called the Voices of East Harlem. I remember this gig because we got there a little late and I was driving my Lamborghini. So when I arrived—the concert was outdoors—there was a dirt road. I drove down that with all this dust flying everywhere. I pulled up in this cloud of dust and Bill was there waiting for me, worried as hell. When I got out, I had on this full-length animal-skin coat. Bill's looking at me like he wants to get mad, right? So I say to him, "What is it, Bill? You were waiting for somebody else to get out of that car?" And that just cracked him up.

Those gigs I did for Bill during this time were good for expanding my audience. We were playing to all kinds of different people. The crowds that were going to see Laura Nyro and the Grateful Dead were all mixed up with some of the people who were coming to hear me. So it was good for everybody.

Bill and I got along all right, but we had our disagreements because Bill is a tough motherfucking businessman, and I don't take no shit, either. So there were clashes. I remember one time—it might have been a couple of times—at the Fillmore East in 1970, I was opening up for this sorry-ass cat named Steve Miller. I think Crosby, Stills, Nash and Young were on that program, and they were a little better. Anyway, Steve Miller didn't have shit going for him, so I'm pissed because I got to open for this non-playing motherfucker just because he had one or two sorry-ass records out. So I would come late and *he* would have to go on first, and then when we got there, we just smoked the motherfucking place and everybody dug it, including Bill!

This went on for a couple of nights and every time I would come late, Bill would be telling me about "it's being disrespectful to the artist" and shit like that. On this last night, I do the same thing. When I get there I see that Bill is madder than a motherfucker because he's not waiting for me inside like he normally does, but he's standing *outside* the Fillmore. He starts to cut into me with this bullshit about "disrespecting Steve" and everything. So I just look at him, cool as a motherfucker, and say to him, "Hey, baby, just like the other nights and you *know* they worked out just fine, right?" So he couldn't say nothing to that because we had torn the place down.

After this gig, or somewhere around this time, I started realizing that most rock musicians didn't know anything about music. They didn't study it, couldn't play different styles—and don't even talk about reading music. But they were popular and sold a lot of records because they were giving the public a certain sound, what they wanted to hear. So I figured if they could do it—reach all those people and sell all those records without really knowing what they were doing—then I could do it, too, only better. Because I liked playing the bigger halls instead of the nightclubs all the time. Not only could you make more money and play to larger audiences, but you didn't have the hassles you had playing all those smoky night-clubs.

So it was through Bill that I met the Grateful Dead. Jerry Garcia, their guitar player, and I hit if off great, talking about music—what they liked and what I liked—and I think we all learned something, grew some. Jerry Garcia loved jazz, and I found out that he loved my music and had been listening to it for a long time. He loved other jazz musicians, too, like Ornette Coleman and Bill Evans. Laura Nyro was a very quiet person offstage and I think I kind of frightened her. Looking back, I think Bill Graham did some important things for music with those concerts, opened everything up so that a lot of different people heard a lot of different kinds of music that they wouldn't normally have heard. I didn't run into Bill again until we did some concerts for Amnesty International in 1986 or '87.

Around this time I met a young black comedian who was doing an opening act for some of our concerts, Richard Pryor. Man, he was a funny motherfucker. He didn't have a reputation yet, but I knew he was going to be a big star. I could just feel it in my bones. I booked our band into the Village Gate and hired Richard to open up for us. I have forgotten where I first heard him, but I just wanted people to know how great this motherfucker was. I paid him out of my own pocket and produced the whole thing. I think we were there for two weekends and the band and Richard just tore the place up. Richard opened and then we had some Indian music played by this sitar player and then my band played. It was really successful and I even made some money on the whole thing. Richard and I became good friends after that, and we would hang out and get high and just have a great time together. A lot of comedians are a drag once they get off the stage, but Richard—and Redd Foxx—were just as funny offstage as on. Richard used to leave his wife at my house when he would go out on the road, because at the time, he didn't have a permanent place of his own. But Richard was funny, man, even back then and off the stage, too.

I met Bill Cosby coming through the Chicago airport around this time. After I got to know him later and we became close friends, he told me that I had met him back in Philly when he would come around to my shows. He told me I had been a big influence on his life, but I don't remember meeting him back then. He was doing "I Spy" at the time and was a big star. I liked to watch his show. So when we met in the airport, I just told him that I liked his show. I remember him telling me, "Thanks, Miles, but I just hope they give me one woman to have a relationship with before the show is over. They're acting like black people don't go to bed, or have love lives like white people do. I hope they just give me a love scene with one woman one time, just let me have a kissing scene just once." And that was it. He was saying this as he was moving through to catch a plane and I was doing the same thing. I remember thinking, Yeah, he's right. But I don't think they ever did.

Things were going pretty well with my music, but they weren't going too well in my relationship with my wife Betty. She started lying to me and trying to get me to give her my money. She started signing shit when we were out on the road, you know, bringing a friend into the hotel and signing my name to their bills. She started causing me a lot of trouble. Harold Lovett, my lawyer, was drinking too much by this time and so we weren't as close as we'd been. He was fucking up, but I felt loyal to him because he had stood by me when nobody else did. His shit was starting to get on my nerves by this time. He never did like Betty and used to tell me the only reason I was with her was because she looked like Frances. She did, especially if you saw her from across a room. He thought that was the reason I was with her, and he was probably right. He thought she didn't have no class and was just using me and it turned out that he was right—for once.

I remember when we went to Europe to play at the end of the summer of 1969, after we had finished *Bitches Brew*. I ran into Bill

Cosby and his wife, Camille. We were playing in Antibes, I think it was, and Bill was over there on vacation. He came to the show with Camille and afterwards we all went out to a club. Bill and Camille are up on the floor dancing, and Betty's dancing with some French guy and she's real high. Camille has got on this beautiful white lace jumpsuit with holes in it like a basketball net. While they're out there dancing, Betty's dancing wild all over the place and she steps in the holes at the bottom of Camille's jumpsuit with the heels of her shoes and tears Camille's jumpsuit like a motherfucker. She don't even know she did it. After she finds out, she apologizes and everything, and I tell Bill that I will pay for it, but Bill and Camille won't hear that because he just says it was a mistake and they felt bad for Betty. But *I* know that Betty's getting too far out of control and that shit just embarrassed me like a motherfucker.

See, Betty was too young and wild for the things I expected from a woman. I was used to a cool, hip, elegant woman like Frances, or Cicely, who could handle herself in all kinds of situations. But Betty was a free spirit—talented as a motherfucker—who was a rocker and a street woman who was used to another kind of thing. She was raunchy and all that kind of shit, all sex, but I didn't know that when I met her—and if I did, I guess, I just didn't pay much attention. But that was the kind of shit she would do and with the other stuff she was doing I just got tired of it.

After we left Bill and Camille, I went to London to see Sammy Davis, Jr., who was over there opening up in *Golden Boy*. I also saw Paul Robeson; I tried to see him whenever I went to London until he came back to the States. I was hanging out with people who had a lot of class, but Betty wasn't comfortable around those kinds of people. She only liked rockers, and that's cool, but I have always had a lot of good friends who weren't musicians, and Betty couldn't deal with those kinds of people and so we were just moving away from each other.

Later on in New York I ran into this beautiful Spanish girl who wanted to go to bed with me. I go over to her place and she tells me that Betty is going with her boyfriend. When I ask her who he is she tells me, "Jimi Hendrix." She was a blond, fine motherfucker. So she takes off her clothes and she has a body that just wouldn't wait. I tell her, "If Betty wants to fuck Jimi Hendrix, that's their thing, and I ain't got nothing to do with *that*, and it ain't got nothing to do with you and me, either." She tells me that if Betty's going to be fucking her man, then she's going to fuck me.

I tell her, "It don't go like that, because I don't fuck anybody for reasons like that. If you're going to fuck me, then you gotta want to do it because *you* want to do it and not because Betty is fucking Jimi."

She put on her clothes and we just talked. Man, that shit I told her just fucked her up. Because she was so fine that she was used to men just falling down over themselves to get her. But I wasn't like that and have never been like that. Just because a woman is fine don't mean nothing to me and never did; I've always had fine women. For me to really get into them they also have to have a mind and think about something other than how fine they are.

After that, my relationship with Betty just went downhill. After I told her what I knew about her and Jimi, I asked her for a divorce— I *told* her I was getting a divorce. She said, "Naw, you ain't either, fine as I am, you know you don't want to give up this good thing!"

"Oh yeah? Well, bitch, I'm divorcing you, and I already got the papers made out so you'd better sign them if you know what's good for your ass!" She did, and that was the end of that.

Betty and I broke up then in 1969, but because things had been going so bad between us I had already started seeing two beautiful, great women, who both made a big impact on my life, Marguerite Eskridge and Jackie Battle. Both of them were real spiritual women, into health food and things like that. They were both real quiet, but very strong women who had great confidence in themselves. Plus, they were very nice people who weren't into me because I was a star but because they genuinely cared about me. Beautiful as Betty was physically, she didn't have any confidence in herself as a person. She was a high-class groupie, who was very talented but who didn't believe in her own talent. Jackie and Marguerite didn't have that kind of problem, and so I was relaxed with them.

I first saw Marguerite in the audience of one of my concerts and had somebody tell her that I'd like to talk to her, buy her a drink. This was at a nightclub in New York, maybe the Village Gate or the Village Vanguard. This was early in 1969. Marguerite was one of the prettiest women I had ever seen. So I started going out with her. But she wanted me all to herself, wanted an exclusive relationship. I had to keep my relationship with Jackie on the side, so she couldn't know about it. We went together on and off for about four years. For a while she had an apartment in the building I owned on West 77th Street. But she didn't really like the musician's life, all the clubs and alcohol and drugs. It was just too fast for her. She was real quiet and a vegetarian and she was from Pittsburgh too, like Betty. Man, Pittsburgh's got some fine women. And she was twenty-four years old when we met. Real beautiful woman, you know, brown-skinned, tall, beautiful skin, eyes, and hair. Great body. We were together about four years; she's the mother of my youngest son, Erin.

She was with me in Brooklyn in October of 1969. We had just got through playing the Blue Coronet Club over in Brooklyn and I had driven Marguerite back to her house in Brooklyn (she hadn't moved into the apartment in my building yet). We were sitting outside her house, just talking and kissing—you know, the shit that lovers do— in my car when this car pulled up next to mine with these three black dudes inside. At first I didn't think nothing of it, thought that they might be some people who had just caught the show and wanted to say hello. But the next thing I knew I heard these shots and felt this sting in my left side. The guy must have shot about five bullets at me, but I had on a leather suit that was kind of loose-fitting. If it hadn't been for that leather jacket and the fact they shot through the door of a well-built Ferrari, I would have been dead. I was so shocked I didn't have time to be scared. None of the bullets hit Marguerite, and I was glad about that, but it scared the shit out of her.

We went inside and called the police and they came—two white guys—and searched *my* car, even though I was the one who had been shot. Then they said they found a little marijuana in my car and arrested Marguerite and me and took us down to the station. But they let us go without pressing charges because they didn't have no evidence.

Now, in the first place, everyone who knows me *knows* that I have never liked marijuana, never liked to smoke it. So that was a bunch of bullshit they were trying to hang on me. They just didn't like it that a black guy was in this expensive foreign car with a real beautiful woman. They didn't know what to make of that. When they looked up my record I guess they found out that I was a musician and had trouble in the past with drugs, so they were going to try and pin some shit on me just for the hell of it. Maybe they would get a promotion for busting a famous nigger. *I* was the one who called them; if I had drugs on me, I would have gotten rid of them before they arrived. I'm not *that* crazy.

I offered a $5,000 reward for information on whoever it was that shot me. A few weeks later I was sitting in a bar uptown when some guy came up and told me that the guy who had shot me had gotten killed, shot by someone who didn't like it that he had done that. I didn't know the guy's name who told me, and he didn't tell me the name of the gunman who was supposed to be dead now. All I know is what the guy told me, and I never saw him again after that. I later found out that the reason I had been shot was because some black promoters in Brooklyn hadn't liked the fact that white promoters were getting all the bookings. When I played the Blue Coronet that night, they thought I was being an asshole by not letting the black promoters do the booking.

Now I can go along with black guys getting cut in on the action. But nobody had told me shit, and here's some guy trying to kill me over something I didn't know nothing about. Man, life is a bitch sometimes. For a while after this happened, I started carrying brass knuckles everywhere I went until I got busted about a year later in Manhattan on Central Park South for not having a registration sticker on my car, and the brass knuckles fell out of my bag after the police searched me. Now I admit that I didn't have no sticker on my car, and that the car wasn't even registered. But the cops in the patrol car couldn't see that from across the street when they turned around and came back.

Again, the reason that they stopped and came back was because I was sitting in my red Ferrari, dressed in a turban, cobra-skinned pants, and a sheepskin coat, with a real fine woman—I think it was Marguerite, again—outside the Plaza Hotel. The two white cops who saw this probably thought that I was a drug dealer and that's why they came back. Needless to say, if I had been a white person sitting in that Ferrari, they would have gone about their business.

Jackie Battle was also a very special woman. She was from Baltimore and she was about nineteen or twenty when I met her, around the same time I met Marguerite. I met Jackie at the United Nations, where she was the secretary of someone I knew over there. I used to see her at a lot of concerts because she was really into music and was an artist herself, a painter, printmaker, and designer. She was a beautiful woman, tall, light brown–skinned—beautiful skin—with beautiful eyes and a beautiful smile, the works, but with one of the most spiritual karmas I had ever run across. We just started going out. She was very mature for her age, she was already her own person, knew what she wanted out of life and didn't take no bullshit from anyone. She is very soft-spoken, nice and calm, but underneath all of that is a very strong person who knows her own worth. After I got past her beauty, it was her head that made me love and respect her so much. The way she thought about things and the way she looked at the world was something special. And she really cared about me, too, even when I was so crazy into cocaine. Once we were in Phoenix, and I got all this coke from a doctor. Man, it was pure. So I was taking this cocaine around the clock and then I went and played the concert. When I came back from playing, Jackie was all drugged up on sleeping pills, about to go out. Now, Jackie don't get high, ain't even into drugs. After I got her straight, I asked her, "Jackie, why did you take all of my sleeping pills like that? You could have killed yourself!"

So she tells me, tears all in her eyes, "If you're gonna kill yourself taking all that coke and shit like you been doing, then I want to be dead before you. So that's why I took them. Because at the rate you're going you're gonna be dead soon and I don't want to be around without you."

Man, that shit just fucked me up. I was shocked. And then I remembered the coke and went into the bathroom to my stash and it was gone. I came back and asked where the coke was, and she told me that she had flushed it down the toilet. Now *that* fucked me up, too. Man, she was something else.

Her family lived in New York and I got to know them real well, her mother, Dorothea, and her brother, Todd "Mickey" Merchant, who is also a very good artist and used to do some paintings for me. I would call up her mother and ask her to make some gumbo for me —because she's a great cook—and she would do it and bring it down to my house. If she had to go somewhere, she'd leave it with someone I could pick it up from. They're a real close-knit family and they're all special people. When I first started going out with Jackie, her brother asked me, "Nigga, what the fuck do you want with my sister?"

And so I said, "What the fuck do you mean, what do I want with your sister? What does any man want with a fine, nice woman?"

Then he said, "Okay, man, but don't be fucking around and fucking over my sister, you know, because I don't give a fuck how famous you are; you fuck over her and you gonna have to answer to me." So when I broke up with Betty I had two beautiful young spiritual women to be around, Jackie and Marguerite. Looking back it was probably a shame that I knew them at the same time, like I did, because if I could have given one of them my full attention, who

knows what might have happened. But I don't like to deal in specu-
lation.

I had a policy with the group that they couldn't bring their girlfriends on tour because I felt it distracted them. But I brought *my*
girlfriends, and this was beginning to cause some problems with
Wayne, Chick, and Jack, because they all wanted to bring their old
ladies along. I felt that it was *my* band and so I had the right to set
policy. I wouldn't mind their women being there as long as it didn't
stop them from playing, which it usually did.

Before we went out to California, Jack called and told me he was
taking his wife, Lydia, who was about eight months pregnant. First
he tried to get me to cancel the tour because he said that Lydia might
have the baby at any time and he should be around when this happened. But I told him I couldn't do that, so that's when he said he
would have to take Lydia along. The problem with this was that Jack
changed the way he played when Lydia was around. He started styling and shit and not playing like he normally did because he was
trying to look hip. So we had this argument about Lydia, and Jack
threatened to leave the tour. I finally told him he could bring Lydia
and stick her in front of the fucking drums if he wanted, just as long
as he played them fucking drums. This argument continued right
onto the plane out to California. My girlfriend Jackie got into the
argument on Jack and Lydia's side, and I threatened to send *her* ass
home, too. But Jackie just hung in there and argued and shit because
she wasn't scared of nothing. I just finally let it go.

We got to Los Angeles after stops at the Monterey Jazz Festival
and in San Francisco. In Los Angeles, we played Shelly's Manne-
Hole. By this time Anna Maria, Wayne's girlfriend, is there, too,
along with Lydia and Jackie. So then another woman comes, Jane
Mandy, Chick's girlfriend. Jack is all grins and shit, and so I know
he's not going to do nothing but style. I love the way Jack plays, but
when women come around that motherfucker is just up into being
hip and playing for the crowd instead of the band. But you couldn't
tell him that.

The first two nights we're there Lydia comes backstage both
nights. She's an artist, too, and a good one, and a real nice person. I
liked her a lot. But when she came backstage, some other kind of
shit went down with Jack, and I didn't like that—Jack's not playing
nothing. The third night I saw her sitting there by the bandstand. I
went out into the audience and sent a note to Jack through Shelly
that said, "If Lydia doesn't move, we aren't going to play."

Now, there are lines wrapped around the block and Shelly's think-ing about that. But I'm thinking about the music we ain't going to hear because of Lydia being there and making Jack play hip instead of great. Jack is madder than a motherfucker now, thinks I'm really fucking with his family, and so now the shit done *really* got thick. After a while, everybody else in the band is laughing—even Shelly— and then Shelly comes up and actually gets down on his knees and starts to beg me. "Please play. Miles, please play." That's when the shit got real funny to me. I went up and played and that night Jack played his ass off. I guess he was trying to show me that I was wrong about him not being able to play whenever his wife came around. After this incident, I did drop that rule about my players not being able to bring their girlfriends on tour, as long as it didn't affect the way they played. Later Keith Jarrett used to do that same shit when he was in my band. His wife would come along, and he would play some shit that he thought was hip, and him and his old lady would look at each other like it was the greatest thing in the world. But to me it wasn't nothing but real cute shit Keith was playing, and I had to tell him that it wasn't knocking me out. So he stopped doing it.

I was changing my attitude about a lot of things, like the look of my wardrobe. I was working all these clubs where there was a lot of smoke, and it would get in the fabric of my suits. Plus, everyone was starting to dress a little looser at concerts, at least the rock musicians were, and that might have affected me. Everybody was into black-ness, you know, the black consciousness movement, and so a lot of African and Indian fabrics were being worn. I started wearing Afri-can dashikis and robes and looser clothes plus a lot of Indian tops by this guy named Hernando, who was from Argentina and who had a place in Greenwich Village. That's where Jimi Hendrix bought most of his clothes. So I started buying wraparound Indian shirts from him, patch suede pants from a black designer named Steven Bur-rows, and shoes from a place in London called Chelsea Cobblers. (There was a guy there named Andy who in one night could make you the hippest pair of shoes you could imagine.) I had moved away from the cool Brooks Brothers look and into this other thing, which for me was more what was happening with the times. I found I could move around on stage much better. I wanted to move on stage, play in different places, because there are areas on stage where the music and the sound are much better than other places. I was starting to explore for those places.

*i*n a *Silent Way* began a great creative period for me from 1969. That record opened up a lot of music in my head that just kept coming out for the next four years. In that time I think I must have gone into the studio close to fifteen times and finished about ten albums (some coming out sooner than others, but all recorded during this time): *In a Silent Way, Bitches Brew, Miles Davis Sextet: At Fillmore West, Miles Davis: At Fillmore, Miles Davis Septet: At the Isle of Wight, Live-Evil, Miles Davis Septet: At Philharmonic Hall, On the Corner, Big Fun, Get Up With It. (Directions* and *Circle in the Round* came out later, with recordings I made during this period.) But all the music was different and this was causing a lot of critics a lot of problems. Critics always like to pigeonhole everybody, put you in a certain place in their heads so they can get to you. They don't like a lot of changing because that makes them have to work to understand what you're doing. When I started changing so fast like that, a lot of critics started putting me down because they didn't understand what I was doing. But critics never did mean much to me, so I just kept on doing what I had been doing, trying to grow as a musician.

Wayne Shorter left the band in late fall of 1969 and I broke up the band for a while until I could find replacements. I replaced Wayne with a young white saxophonist from Brooklyn named Steve Grossman. Wayne had told me ahead of time he was leaving. So when I went into the studio in November I already had Steve Grossman in mind and wanted to hear how he sounded with the band. I also added a Brazilian percussionist from Brooklyn named Airto Moreira. Airto had been in this country for a couple of years and played in Cannonball Adderley's band with Joe Zawinul. I think it was either Cannonball or Joe who turned me on to him (I forgot how I found out about Steve). Airto was a great percussionist, and I have had percussionists in my band ever since. Airto turned me on to what his kind of talent and voice could do for the sound of my band. When he first came with me he played too loud and didn't listen to what was happening with the music. I would tell him to stop banging and playing so loud and just to listen more. Then for a while he wouldn't play nothing and so I had to go back and tell him to play a little more. I think he was afraid of me, and when I told him not to play so much it just confused him. But then he started listening more and when he did play again he was playing in the right places.

During this time and for the next five years I was using a lot of different musicians on my records (and in my working group, too) because I was always looking to see which combinations played what best. I was using so many different people that I began to lose track of all of them, but I had a group of core musicians: Wayne Shorter (even after he left) and Gary Bartz, Steve Grossman, Airto Moreira, Mtume Heath, Bennie Maupin, John McLaughlin, Sonny Sharrock, Chick Corea, Herbie Hancock, Keith Jarrett, Larry Young, and Joe Zawinul on pianos and electric keyboards; Harvey Brooks, Dave Holland, Ron Carter, and Michael Henderson on basses; Billy Cobham and Jack DeJohnette on drums; and three Indians—Khalil Balakrishna, Bihari Sharma, and Badal Roy. And then others, like Sonny Fortune, Carlos Garnett, Lonnie Liston Smith, Al Foster, Billy Hart, Harold Williams, Cedric Lawson, Reggie Lucas, Pete Cosey, Cornell Dupree, Bernard Purdee, Dave Liebman, John Stobblefield, Azar Lawrence, and Dominique Gaumont. I used all of these musicians in all kinds of combinations, some more than others, some maybe only once. After a while they became known in the musical world as "Miles's Stock Company Players."

The sound of my music was changing as fast as I was changing musicians, but I was still looking for the combination that could give me the sound that I wanted. Jack DeJohnette gave me a certain deep groove that I just loved to play over, but then Billy Cobham gave me a more rock-like sound. Dave Holland played the stand-up bass and I could groove behind that in a way that I couldn't when Harvey

Brooks brought in his electric bass sound. The same thing with Chick, Herbie, Joe, Keith, and Larry, too. I was seeing it all as a process of recording all this music, just getting it all down while it was flowing out of my head.

In 1970 I was asked to play on the televised Grammy Awards show. After I played, Merv Griffin, the host, ran up and grabbed me by my wrist and started talking all this stupid bullshit. Man, it was embarrassing. I started to knock the jive motherfucker out right there on television, live. He ran up talking this nonsense that most television talk hosts say because they ain't got nothing else to say and don't know—or care—about what you're really doing. They just talk to take up space. I don't like that kind of bullshit and so after that I didn't go on too many of them talk shows except for Johnny Carson's, Dick Cavett's, and Steve Allen's. Steve was the only one out of the three who knew a little something about what I was doing. At least Steve Allen tried to play the piano and could ask intelligent questions.

Johnny Carson and Dick Cavett didn't show me anything about understanding what I was trying to do; they were nice guys, but they didn't seem to know anything about music. Most of these TV talk-show hosts were only trying to communicate with some tired, old white people from somewhere nobody ever heard about. My music was too much for them because their ears were used to Lawrence Welk. Those talk shows would take a black man on television back then only if he grinned, became a clown, like Louis Armstrong did. They could dig that. I loved the way Louis played trumpet, man, but I hated the way he had to grin in order to get over with some tired white folks. Man, I just hated when I saw him doing that, because Louis was hip, had a consciousness about black people, was a real nice man. But the only image people have of him is that grinning image off TV.

I figured if I went on those kind of shows, then I would have to tell the motherfuckers that they were just too sad for words, and I *know* they didn't want to hear that. So most of the time I just didn't go on. After a while even Steve Allen's show was too white and silly for me to have to deal with. I only went on his show because Steve is a decent human being. And I had known him for a long time. But he wanted to pay me only union scale for playing. After a while I stopped going on any of those shows altogether, and Columbia got upset because they saw the shows as a way to sell more records.

In 1970 my son Gregory returned from a couple of years in Vietnam. He came back a changed person. From then on he cost me a lot of trouble, headaches, and money while he lived with me. Eventually he moved upstairs into one of my vacant apartments on West 77th Street. He was always getting into trouble after Vietnam. Gregory and his brother, Miles IV, caused me a lot of problems and sadness. I love both of them, but my disappointment is so great, that's about all I can say. Their sister, Cheryl, graduated from Columbia University and went back to St. Louis, made me a grandfather, and teaches in the school system there. I feel good about her. But kids can be a big disappointment for their parents and I guess my two eldest sons are a big disappointment to me. And, maybe I was to them because of the shit I took Frances through that they saw. But whatever happens or happened, they got to pull their own lives together for themselves, because, in the end, they're the only ones who can do it. Gregory was a good boxer and won some championships in the army, but I didn't want him to be a boxer and that was a mistake that I made. All I can do about it now is say I'm sorry, and hope that they both pull their lives together.

By 1970 I was making between $350,000 and $400,000 a year from everything—stocks, albums, royalties, and gigs. I had had my house redone, all in curves and circles, at least the two floors I live on. I brought in a friend named Lance Hay from Los Angeles to put it all together. I wanted everything round, no corners and very little furniture. So he started with the bathroom and did it up all in *faux* black marble, with a step-in pool and a three-tiered curved ceiling covered with plaster that looked like stalactites. Lance put a porthole in for a window. Man, it was something else, so I told him to finish the rest of the house. He made me a cylindrical, wood-paneled kitchen with *faux* marble. He used ottomans and put in Mediterranean-looking arches and tiled floors and blue carpeting. I thought it was beautiful. It reminded me of somewhere on the Mediterranean instead of New York. When somebody asked me why I did it, I told them, "I just got tired of living in a George Washington–kind of house." I wanted a house with round steps rather than square steps with corners. I think the tune I wrote called "Circle in the Round" grew out of the same concept.

That spring I recorded the *Jack Johnson* album, the soundtrack to the movie about the boxer's life. The music was originally meant for Buddy Miles, the drummer, and he didn't show up to pick it up. When I wrote these tunes I was going up to Gleason's Gym to train with Bobby McQuillen, who was now calling himself Robert Allah (he had become a Muslim). Anyway, I had that boxer's movement in mind, that shuffling movement boxers use. They're almost like dance steps, or like the sound of a train. In fact, it did remind me of being on a train doing eighty miles an hour, how you always hear the same rhythm because of the speed of the wheels touching the tracks, the plop-plop, plop-plop, plop-plop sound of the wheels passing over those splits in the track. That train image was in my head when I thought about a great boxer like Joe Louis or Jack Johnson. When you think of a big heavyweight coming at you it's like a train.

Then the question in my mind after I got to this was, well, is the music black enough, does it have a black rhythm, can you make the rhythm of the train a black thing, would Jack Johnson dance to that? Because Jack Johnson liked to party, liked to have a good time and dance. One of the tunes on there, called "Yesternow" was named by James Finney, who was my hairdresser—and Jimi Hendrix's, too. Anyway, the music fit perfectly with that movie. But when the album came out, they buried it. No promotions. I think one of the reasons was because it was music you could dance to. And it had a lot of stuff white rock musicians were playing, so I think they didn't want a black jazz musician doing that kind of music. Plus, the critics didn't know what to do with it. So Columbia didn't promote it. A lot of rock artists heard the record and didn't say nothing in public about it, but came up and told me that they loved the record. Early in 1970 I recorded "Duran" and I thought I had a hit, but Columbia didn't release it until way later, in 1981. "Duran" was named for Roberto Duran, the great Panamanian boxing champion.

The beginning of the summer I had both Chick Corea and Keith Jarrett on electric piano in my working band, and that shit they was playing together was really kicking ass. They were in the band together about three or four months. Keith had his own group while he was playing with me, but it didn't interfere because we kept our scheduling separate so he could play in both. I don't think the two-piano idea set too well with Chick, although he never did say nothing to me personally. I knew what Keith was playing before he came with me and I also knew where he could go. Before he came with me he hated electrical instruments, but he changed his mind while he was with my band. Plus, he learned to stretch out more and play in different styles. He went into the studio with the band in May and out on the road after that.

I was trying to play the music I grew up on now, that roadhouse, honky-tonk, funky thing that people used to dance to on Friday and Saturday nights. But these were musicians who were used to playing a jazz style and so it was new for them. Things take time, you know, you just don't learn something new and do it overnight. It has to get down inside your body, up into your blood before you can do it correctly. But they were getting there, so I wasn't worried.

That summer I joined a birthday celebration for Louis Armstrong's seventieth birthday. Flying Dutchman, the record label, asked me and a bunch of other musicians if we would record a vocal album that would be released on Pops's birthday. I agreed, and we all sang —Ornette Coleman, Eddie Condon, Bobby Hackett, I think Dizzy, and a few more musicians. I didn't usually do those kinds of things but this was for Pops and he was just a beautiful guy. You can't play nothing on trumpet that doesn't come from him, not even modern shit. I can't ever remember a time when he sounded bad playing the trumpet. Never. Not even one time. He had great feeling up in his playing and he always played on the beat. I just loved the way he played and sang. I didn't get to know him well, I only met him a couple of times, once at some big affair and the other time when I was playing somewhere and he heard me and came up and told me afterwards that he like the way I played. Man, I felt so good when he told me that. But I didn't like the way he was portrayed in the media with him grinning all the time, and he said some things about modern music that didn't set too well with me; he put a lot of modern guys down. Back then I said, "Pops was a trailblazer, too, so he shouldn't be knocking it." Then the next year, 1971, Louis Armstrong died and his wife had that bullshit funeral for him where she didn't have no jazz musicians playing. Pops had said he wanted to have a New Orleans–type funeral, but his wife didn't like that so she whitened it all the way up. Man, it was a shame.

In June of 1970, I think it was, we started work in the studio on an album that would be called *Live-Evil*. I saw the album as a kind of extension of *Bitches Brew*, although it would turn into something different. I was learning how to play my trumpet over all of this electrical sound and that was really an eye-opener. For instance, the Fender Rhodes electric piano puts a cushion under a trumpet and a trumpet always needs a cushion because it's so brassy-sounding, so piercing. Now, Dizzy has his drummer put all these staples in his big sock cymbal; he has about twenty-four of them in there so the cymbal vibrates when the drummer hits it, and the space between the notes and the cymbal is filled up with this vibrating sound that Dizzy really likes. But the Fender Rhodes does the same thing, only better, because if you hit a chord on an electric instrument, the chord comes out clean, perfectly clear.

I heard the same kind of musical figures for *Live-Evil* that I had heard for *Bitches Brew*, only a little bit more worked out because I had gone through them when we did that record. On "What I Say," I gave Jack DeJohnette this drum rhythm, this little figure that I wanted him to play throughout the tune. I just wanted him to lock everything in with that figure, but I wanted it to have some fire. For me that piece sets up that album, gives it the mood, the kind of rhythm I wanted. And, you know, it's funny, because on this album I was hearing things up in the upper register. On "What I Say" I played a lot of high notes on trumpet, notes I usually don't play because I don't hear them. But I heard them a lot after I started playing this new music.

I was recording so much at this time that a lot of what went on in the studio I just forgot, and sometimes the images just run into each other and I can't figure out which was which. But I remember in *Live-Evil* we turned my name around on one tune, which became "Sivad" instead of Davis; another was "Selim" instead of Miles. "Evil" is the reverse of "live," and some of the recordings were live, at the Cellar Door in Washington, D.C. But that reversal was the concept of the album: good and bad, light and dark, funky and abstract, birth and death. That's what I was trying to say with those two paintings on the front and back. One gets into love and birth and the other into evil and a feeling of death.

Bitches Brew sold faster than any other album I had ever done, and sold more copies than any other jazz album in history. Everyone was excited because a lot of young rock fans were buying the album and talking about it. So that was good. All that summer, I was touring and playing rock halls with Carlos Santana, the Chicano guitarist who plays Latin rock. Man, that motherfucker can play his ass off. I loved the way he played, and he's a very nice person. We got to know each other real well over that summer and we have kept in touch. We were both recording for Columbia. I was opening up for Carlos, and I felt comfortable with that because I liked what he was doing. Even when we weren't playing together, if I was in the same city where he was playing I would go and catch his concerts. I think he was recording his album *Abraxas* around this time, and I used to go in the studio to hear what they were doing. He told me he learned all about how to use silence in his music from me. We would hang out, me, him, and the music critic Ralph Gleason.

In August 1970 I played the Isle of Wight concert in England. They were trying to do a Woodstock-like thing over there and so they invited all these rock and funk groups like Jimi Hendrix, Sly and the Family Stone, and a whole bunch of white rock groups to play on this big farm off the southern coast of England. People came from all over the world to that concert; they said they had over 350,000 people. I had never seen that many people out in front of me before. By that time my music was really into percussions and rhythms. The people seemed to like what was happening, especially when we got into the real rhythmic things. Some of the critics were talking about how aloof I was, but that didn't bother me; I had been this same way all of my life.

I took Jackie Battle with me over to that concert. I had to talk her into going because she wasn't going to go. Man, it took days to convince her.

Jimi Hendrix was there, too. He and I were supposed to get together in London after the concert to talk about an album we had finally decided to do together. We had come close once to doing one with the producer Alan Douglas, but the money wasn't right or we were too busy to get it together. We had played a lot with each other at my house, just jamming. We thought that maybe the time was right to do something together on a record. Now the roads were so crowded coming back into London after that concert that we couldn't get to the meeting on time, and so by the time we got into London Jimi wasn't there. I was going to France, I think it was, to do a few more gigs and then back to New York. Gil Evans called and told me that he and Jimi were going to get together and that he wanted me to come down and participate. I told him that I would. We were waiting for Jimi to come when we found out that he had died in London, choked to death on his own vomit. Man, that's a hell of a way to go. What I didn't understand is why nobody told him not to mix alcohol and sleeping pills. That shit is deadly and had already killed Dorothy Dandridge, Marilyn Monroe, my good friend Dorothy Kilgallen, and Tommy Dorsey. Jimi's death upset me because he was so young and had so much ahead of him. So I decided I would go to his funeral in Seattle even though I hated going to them. That funeral

was such a drag that I said I would never go to another one after that
—and I haven't.

The white preacher didn't even know Jimi's name and kept on
mispronouncing it, calling him this, calling him that. Man, it was
embarrassing. Plus, the motherfucker didn't even know nothing
about who Jimi was, nothing about his accomplishments. I hated to
see such a great person as Jimi Hendrix given that kind of mistreat-
ment, after all he had done for music.

Right after Jimi's funeral, Chick Corea and Dave Holland left the
band, and I brought in Michael Henderson on bass. Michael had
been playing with Stevie Wonder's band and with Aretha Franklin.
He knew the kind of bass figures I wanted, and I was real happy to
have him in the group. But before he came on permanently, Miroslav
Vitous made a couple of gigs as Dave's replacement. And then Gary
Bartz replaced Steve Grossman and I found myself with a whole new
band.

I was getting away from using a lot of solos in my group sound,
moving more toward an ensemble thing, like the funk and rock
bands. I wanted to have John McLaughlin on guitar, but he liked
what he was doing in Tony Williams's Lifetime band. I did get him
to play with us at the Cellar Door in Washington, D.C., on a gig we
did there later in the year. The tapes we did on this gig were mixed
into the *Live-Evil* album. By now I was using the wah-wah on my
trumpet all the time so I could get closer to that voice Jimi had when
he used a wah-wah on his guitar. I had always played trumpet like a
guitar and the wah-wah just made the sound closer. By this time
there were a lot of fusion groups popping up all over the place:
Wayne Shorter and Joe Zawinul's Weather Report; Chick Corea's
Return to Forever; Herbie Hancock's group, called Mwandishi; and
then a little later, John McLaughlin formed his band, the Mahavishnu
Orchestra. Everyone was chanting now, into peace and love. Even I
had stopped drinking and doing drugs for a while and was into eating
health foods and taking care of myself. I was trying to quit smoking
but that was harder for me to quit than anything else.

In 1971 I was voted Jazzman of the Year by *Down Beat* magazine
and my band was voted the top band of the year. They also voted me
top trumpet player. I don't think too much about those kinds of
things, although I know what they mean to someone's career. Don't
get me wrong; I'm happy to have won them, but it's just something I
can't really get into.

Airto Moreira quit early in 1971 and I got Jimmy Heath's son, Mtume, to replace him on percussion. We didn't record for a while because you have to let a band get used to playing together before you record anything. We went out on the road to try to get things together.

Mtume was a freak for history, and I knew him from his father, so we used to talk a lot. I'd tell him old stories and he'd tell me about things that had happened in African history, because he was really into that. Plus, he was an insomniac like me. So I could call him up at four in the morning because I knew he was going to be awake. I remember one time in 1975, Mtume had a knee operation and was laid up in the hospital. I told him we had to play and that he had to get on out of there. He said he didn't know if he could make it. So I tell him that I'm going to take him to Jamaica and nurse him back to health. I send a limo by to get him and we take a plane to Jamaica and swim and stuff like that for about ten days. I knew this Jamaican healer through a friend who had turned me on to him for my own hip problems, and he had helped me with massages and herbs. It got Mtume back together and he was able to make the gigs. I felt toward him like a son because I had watched him grow up.

We did the same tours we always did during the year and played to great audiences everywhere. We played the Hollywood Bowl with the Band, who were real hot around this time; they used to be Bob Dylan's back-up band when he went out on the road. At this concert our band was getting more and more into a lot of free-form things, so I think we went right past a lot of that audience.

After Jimi died, I realized that no matter how great a musician he was, no matter how much *I* personally loved his music—the way he played the guitar—very few young blacks had heard of him, because for them he was too far over into white rock. Black kids were listening to Sly Stone, James Brown, Aretha Franklin, and all them other great black groups at Motown. After playing a lot of these white rock halls I was starting to wonder why I shouldn't be trying to get to young black kids with my music. They were into funk, music they could dance to. It took me a while to really get into the concept all the way, but with this new band I started to think about it.

Jack DeJohnette left the group late in 1971, around the same time Keith Jarrett left. I wanted the drummer to play certain funk rhythms, a role just like everybody else in the group had. I didn't want the band playing totally free all the time, because I was moving closer to the funk groove in my head. Now, Jack could play drums like a motherfucker in a groove; he could really do that shit, but he also wanted to do other things, play a little freer, be a leader, do things his *own* way, so he left. I tried out Leon Ndugu Chancler (who later played on Michael Jackson's and Stevie Wonder's albums in the eighties). Chancler went to Europe with me during the summer of 1971, but he didn't work out and when I got back Jack DeJohnette came back for a few gigs. So did Billy Hart. But after Gary Bartz, Keith, and Jack left my working band, I got my musicians from funk groups and not jazz bands because that's the way I was going. Those guys were the last pure jazz players I've had in my bands up until today.

As 1971 closed out I found my hip starting to bother me again. I had had a good year but things seemed to be a little out of focus. Plus I had said in an interview that Columbia Records was a racist place to be, and it was. Now they seemed to be interested in pushing only white music. People at the label got mad with me, but I had renewed my contract with them for three years for $300,000; that is, $100,000 per year plus royalties. I wanted them to push black music like they were pushing white rock and that sad-assed hillbilly shit they were doing. In the early sixties they had had Aretha Franklin at Columbia before she went over to Atlantic, and they never did know what to do with her. After she left Columbia, she became a huge star, and she could have been the same over at Columbia. I told the truth about what was happening, and they got mad. Fuck them! All I wanted was for them to do something about it, but they wouldn't.

I was getting interested in seeing the black sound develop and that's where my head was moving toward, more rhythmic stuff, more funk rather than white rock. I had met Sly and he had given me one of his albums; I liked it. He also gave me that album of Rudy Ray Moore's, who was a real funny comedian back then, raunchy, you know, out there. The people at Columbia who own Epic—the label Sly was on—wanted to see if I could get Sly to record quicker. But Sly had his own way of writing music. He got his inspiration from the people in his group. When he wrote something he would write the music to be played live, rather than for a studio. After he got big he always had all these people around his house and at his recording sessions. I went to a couple and there were nothing but girls every-where and coke, bodyguards with guns, looking all evil. I told him I couldn't do nothing with him—told Columbia I couldn't make him record any quicker. We snorted some coke together and that was it.

But when I first heard Sly, I almost wore out those first two or three records, "Dance to the Music," "Stand," and "Everybody Is a Star." I told Ralph Gleason, "Listen to this. Man, if you know a promoter you better get him to get Sly, because he's something else, Ralph." This was before Sly got real big. Then he wrote a couple of other great things, and then he didn't write nothing because the coke had fucked him up and he wasn't a trained musician.

It was with Sly Stone and James Brown in mind that I went into the studio in June 1972 to record *On the Corner*. During that time everyone was dressing kind of "out street," you know, platform shoes that were yellow, and electric yellow at that; handkerchiefs around the neck, headbands, rawhide vests, and so on. Black women were wearing them real tight dresses that had their big butts sticking way out in the back. Everyone was listening to Sly and James Brown and trying at the same time to be cool like me. I was my own model, with a little bit of Sly and James Brown and the Last Poets. I wanted to videotape people coming into a concert who were wearing all those types of clothes, especially black people. I wanted to see all those different kinds of outfits and the women trying to hide them big bad asses, trying to tuck them in.

I had gotten into the musical theories of Karlheinz Stockhausen, a German avant-garde composer, and an English composer who I had met in London in 1969, Paul Buckmaster. I was into both of them before I did *On the Corner* and, as a matter of fact, Paul stayed with me during the time I was recording. He was also in the studio. Paul was into Bach and so I started paying attention to Bach while Paul was around. I had begun to realize that some of the things Ornette Coleman had said about things being played three or four ways, independently of each other, were true because Bach had also composed that way. And it could be real funky and down. What I was playing on *On the Corner* had no label, although people thought it was funk because they didn't know what else to call it. It was actually a combination of some of the concepts of Paul Buckmaster, Sly Stone, James Brown, and Stockhausen, some of the concepts I had absorbed from Ornette's music, as well as my own. The music was about spacing, about free association of musical ideas to a core kind of rhythm and vamps of the bass line. I liked the way Paul Buckmaster used rhythm and space; the same thing with Stockhausen.

So that was the concept, the attitude I tried to get into the music in *On the Corner*. A music where you could tap your feet to get another bass line. I also wanted to get out of playing them little clubs, and playing that kind of music will start to get you out of the clubs. All the electrical equipment and all that sound was too much for small club like the ones jazz was mostly played in. On the other hand, I had also found out it was hard to play acoustical instruments in big halls because nobody heard what you were playing. With acoustical instruments in those large halls, you couldn't hear the musical phrase and the accompaniment that went with it. You couldn't hear all the notes in the piano in a large group. People's ears were getting strained in the audience listening to acoustical instruments because they had gotten used to listening to instruments being amplified. The choral horns had gotten higher up in the treble clef in everything they were playing. Plastic was coming in and plastic has a different sound. Music has changed to reflect what's happening today. It's more electrical because that's what people's ears tune into. The sound's gone up, that's all.

I decided to go electric all the way (Yamaha gave me some equipment in 1973). Before that I had bought a real cheap sound system that was all right for the clubs I was playing in at the time, but it wasn't good for the big halls, because nobody could hear each other. So the sound just kept getting higher because when it's higher you can make people feel things better. (But today, Prince might be bringing that low sound back, because he has that double bass. You don't hear a bass line in Prince's music because he takes keyboard bass and doubles it with regular bass just like Marcus Miller does.)

That's the way electronics came to me. First I got a Fender bass, then a piano, and then I had to play my trumpet against that. So then I got an amplifier hook-up with a microphone on my trumpet. Then I got the wah-wah to make me sound more like a guitar. Then the critics started saying that they couldn't hear my tone anymore. I said, Fuck them. If I don't play what the drummer wants then he won't play for me. If he can't hear me, then he can't play. That's how the groove thing got started with me. I started playing against all of that.

When I started playing against that new rhythm—synthesizers and guitars and all that new stuff—first I had to get used to it. At first there was no feeling because I was used to the old way of playing things like with Bird and Trane. Playing the new shit was a gradual process. You just don't stop playing the way you used to play. You don't hear the sound at first. It takes time. When you do hear the new sound, it's like rush, but a slow rush. In the new music, before you know it, you have played four or five minutes, which is a long time. But you don't have to blast because you've got an amplifier. And the smoother you play a trumpet, the more it sounds like a trumpet when you amplify it. It's like mixing paint: with too many colors you get nothing but mud. An amplified trumpet doesn't sound good when you play real fast. So I learned to play two-bar phrases, and that's where I was going with my new music. It was exciting because I was learning as I was doing it, just like when I had Herbie and Wayne and Ron and Tony in my band. Only this time it was coming from me and that made me feel real good.

I replaced Jack DeJohnette on drums with Al Foster. I had come across him when I went to the Cellar club on 95th Street in Manhattan to visit my old friend Howard Johnson, who used to sell me clothes at Paul Stuart. Now he owned this club and restaurant, and I used to go there to eat because they had some of the best fried chicken in the world (still do). One night when I went in to eat, Howard had this band there led by a bass player named Earl Mays, who used to play in one of Dizzy's bands. They had a great little band. A guy named Larry Willis was on piano, and I forgot who the rest of the musicians were, but Al Foster was on drums. He knocked me out because he had such a groove and he would just lay it right in there. That was the kind of thing I was looking for, and so I asked him to join the band, and he did. Before that happened I asked Columbia to come up to the Cellar to record them and they did. Teo Macero was the producer, and I guess it's in the vault along with a lot of my stuff.

Al Foster didn't record with me on *On the Corner;* he first recorded with me on *Big Fun.* Al could set shit up for everybody else to play off and then he could keep the groove going forever. He was a lot like Buddy Miles and that's who I wanted my drummer to play like then. I liked Billy Hart, too, but for what I wanted in a drummer, Al Foster had all of it.

It was with *On the Corner* and *Big Fun* that I really made an effort to get my music over to young black people. They are the ones who buy records and come to concerts, and I had started thinking about building a new audience for the future. I already had gotten a lot of young white people coming to my concerts after *Bitches Brew* and so I thought it would be good if I could get all these young people together listening to my music and digging the groove.

Gary Bartz left the band around this time, and between 1972 and around mid-1975, I alternately used Carlos Garnett, Sonny Fortune, and Dave Liebman in my working band. I liked the way both Dave and Sonny played. But with all these young guys in the band they were acting toward me like I was God or their father.

I had another run-in with the police that July because of an argument I had had with one of my tenants, a white woman. She had gotten into an argument with Jackie Battle, and I had just told her to mind her own fucking business. Things got loud and the police came and arrested *me* on my own property. If the woman had been black, nothing else would have been said. She was the one who started all the shit by yelling at everybody. The police said that I hit her but they couldn't find no evidence of that so they had to let me go. Later the woman apologized to me for causing me all those problems. But if you're a black man in this country and you get into it with a white woman, ain't no way you can win most of the time and that's a shame. They ought to pick more fair-minded people to be police officers, because the job's too important to have any kind of racist white person walking around with a gun and a license to kill.

That incident reminded me of the time when I first moved into the house on West 77th Street and this white guy, who I had hired to do some work on the house, asked me when I answered the door, "Where is the owner?" Now I'm standing there all clean and shit and he's asking if he can see the owner. He just refused to believe a black person could own a house like that in that particular neighborhood. If you're black you get it in all kinds of ways.

I got into some controversy with the Grammy Awards people in 1971 by saying that most of the awards went to white people copying black people's shit, sorry-assed imitations rather than the real music. I said we ought to give out Mammy Awards to black artists. Give the musicians their awards and then have them tear them up right on television. Live. I hated the way they were treating black musicians by giving all the Grammys to white guys acting like black guys. That shit is tired and sickening, but they get mad if you say something about it. You're just supposed to let them take your shit, grit your teeth, but don't get mad and just bear the pain while they make all the money and all the glory. It's strange the way many white people think. Strange and deadly.

Earlier in the year I had a gallstone operation, and I had broken up with Marguerite Eskridge. She didn't like the pace of my life and that I was also going out with other women. But more than that, I think, she didn't like just sitting around waiting for me. I remember one time when we were in Italy and we were on the plane and she just started crying. I asked why, and she said, "You want me to be like a member of your band and I can't do it. I can't just jump when you snap your fingers. I can't keep up with you."

Man, Marguerite was so beautiful that when we would go places in Europe people would just follow her around. She liked to go to museums and I remember once—it might have been in Holland—when she went into a museum that these people were just gawking at her wherever she went. This was unsettling to her also. She had been a model but she wasn't really into that kind of thing. She was a special person and I will always have a place in my heart for her. When we were just about to break up, she told me that if I needed anything to call her and she would come, but she couldn't regularly take all the other shit and all the people. The last time we had sex she got pregnant with our son, Erin. After she told me she was pregnant, I told her that I would stay with her, but she said I didn't have to. She had Erin and just kind of took herself out of my daily life. I would see her from time to time, but she started living her life on her own terms. I respected that. She was a real spiritual lady who I will always love. Later she moved to Colorado Springs taking our son, Erin, with her. She still lives there today.

After Marguerite left, Jackie Battle and I became a team almost. I still went out with other women sometimes, but I was mostly with her. Jackie and I had a great relationship. She was almost in my blood, we were so close. I had never felt this way about a woman other than Frances. But I took her through a lot of things, because I know I was hard to put up with. She was always trying to keep me off coke, and I would stop for a while and then I would start again. One time when we were on a plane in San Francisco, this stewardess walked up and handed me a matchbox full of coke that I just started snorting right there in the seat. Man, sometimes it got so crazy after I had been snorting coke and dropping seven or eight Tuinals (downers), I would think I would hear voices and begin looking under rugs, in the radiators, under the sofas. I would swear that people were in the house.

I used to drive Jackie crazy with this kind of behavior, especially when I ran out of coke. Then I would be looking for it in the car, going through her bag because she would always be throwing it out every time she found some. Once I had run out of coke and we were getting on a plane to go somewhere. I thought Jackie might have hidden the coke in her purse, so I took her purse and started going through it to see if she had it there. I came across this package of Woolite powdered soap and I remember breaking it open and swearing it was cocaine because it was white powder. After I tasted it I knew it was soap and I felt so embarrassed.

In October 1972 I wrecked my car on the West Side Highway. Jackie wasn't with me; she was at home asleep, where I should have been. I think we had just come off the road that night from playing somewhere and everyone was a little tired. I didn't feel like going to sleep although I had taken a sleeping pill. Jackie was staying at my house, and I wanted to go out somewhere, but she just wanted to sleep. So then I left; I think I was going to some after-hours place in Harlem. Anyway, I fell asleep at the wheel and ran my Lamborghini into a divider and broke both my ankles. When they called Jackie and told her, she had a fit when she got to the hospital.

Jackie and my sister, Dorothy, who had flown in from Chicago to help out, cleaned up my house while I was in the hospital. They found these Polaroid snapshots of women doing all kinds of things. I used to just watch these women freak out on themselves. I didn't make them do it or anything like that; they would just do it because they thought it would please me, and they gave me the pictures to look at. I think these pictures upset Jackie and Dorothy a lot. But *I* was upset that they had come into my house and gone through my private things like that. At that time I liked the house dark all the time; I guess because my mood was dark.

I think that incident had a lot to do with Jackie's getting fed up with me. Women were calling there all the time. And Marguerite lived in the apartment upstairs and would come down to keep the house when Jackie went out on the road with me. I was laid up for almost three months, and when I got home, I had to walk on crutches for a while, which further fucked up my bad hip.

When I came home from the hospital, Jackie made me vow that I would stay off drugs, and I did for a hot minute. Then I got that craving again. I remember one day she had put me out on the patio by the garden in back of my house. It was a nice fall day, not too cold, not too warm. I had this hospital bed I was sleeping in so that I could raise and lower my legs. Jackie had a bed and was sleeping out in the garden next to me when it was nice outside. At night of course we came inside and slept. This particular day we were resting out in the garden, and my sister, Dorothy, was sleeping upstairs in the house. All of a sudden I got a craving for cocaine. I got up on my crutches and called a friend, who came and picked me up to go and score. I did that, and when I got back both Jackie and my sister were hysterical because they figured I had probably gone to buy drugs. They both got really, really angry. But Dorothy, because she is my sister, stayed; Jackie left and went back to her apartment, which she had never given up, and took the phone off the hook so she wouldn't talk to me. When I finally got her on the phone and asked her to come back, she said no. When Jackie said no, she meant no. I knew that it was over and I was sorrier than a motherfucker. I had given her a ring that my mother had given me. I sent Dorothy down to get my mother's ring.

Jackie used to tell me all the right things. Without her, my life for the next two years just went over into the dark zone. It was coke around the clock without any letup and I was in a lot of pain. I started going out with this woman named Sherry "Peaches" Brewer for a while. She was a beautiful woman, too. She had come to New York from Chicago to be in the Broadway musical *Hello Dolly*, with Pearl Bailey and Cab Calloway. We hung out together, and she was a very nice person, a very good actress. Then I was going out with a model named Sheila Anderson, who was another tall, fine-looking woman. But I was keeping more and more to myself.

By this time I was making around a half million dollars a year, but I was also spending a lot of money on all the things I was doing. I was spending a lot on cocaine. Everything had started to blur after I had that car accident.

Columbia released *On the Corner* in 1972, but they didn't push it, so it didn't do as well as we all thought it would. The music was meant to be heard by young black people, but they just treated it like any other jazz album and advertised it that way, pushed it on the jazz radio stations. Young black kids don't listen to those stations; they listen to R & B stations and some rock stations. Columbia marketed it for them old-time jazz people who couldn't get into what I was doing now in the first place. It was just a waste of time playing it for them; they wanted to hear my *old* music that I wasn't playing anymore. So they didn't like *On the Corner,* but I didn't expect that they would; it wasn't made for them. That just became another sore spot in my relationship with Columbia, and the problems were really adding up by this time. A year later, when Herbie Hancock put out his *Headhunters* album and it sold like hotcakes in the young black community, everybody at Columbia said. "Oh. So that's what Miles was talking about!" But that was too late for *On the Corner,* and watching the way *Headhunters* sold just pissed me off even more.

While recovering from my car accident, I studied a lot more of Stockhausen's concepts of music. I got further and further into the idea of performance as a process. I had always written in a circular way and through Stockhausen I could see that I didn't want to ever play again from eight bars to eight bars, because I never end songs; they just keep going on. Some people around this time felt that I was trying to do too much, trying to do too many new things. They felt I should just stay where I was, stop growing, stop trying different kinds of things. But it don't go like that for me. Just because I was forty-seven years old in 1973 didn't mean I was supposed to sit down in some rocking chair and stop thinking about how to keep doing interesting things. I had to do what I was doing if I was going to keep thinking of myself as a *creative* artist.

Through Stockhausen I understood music as a process of elimination and addition. Like "yes" only means something after you have said "no." I was experimenting a lot, for example, telling a band to play rhythm and hold it and not react to what was going on; let me do the reacting. In a way I was becoming the lead singer in my band, and I felt that I had earned that right. The critics were getting on my nerves, saying that I had lost it, that I wanted to be young, that I didn't know what I was doing, that I wanted to be like Jimi Hendrix, or Sly Stone, or James Brown.

But with Mtume Heath and Pete Cosey joining us, most of the European sensibilities were gone from the band. Now the band settled down into a deep African thing, a deep African-American groove, with a lot of emphasis on drums and rhythm, and not on individual solos. From the time that Jimi Hendrix and I had gotten tight, I had wanted that kind of sound because the guitar can take you deep into the blues. But since I couldn't get Jimi or B. B. King, I had to settle for the next best player out there and most of them were white at that time. White guitar players—at least most of them —can't play rhythm guitar like black cats can, but I couldn't find a black guy who could play the way I wanted him to who wasn't leading his own band. (It stayed like this until I got my present guitarist, Foley McCreary.) I tried out Reggie Lucas (who has become a big record producer these days, doing Madonna's records), Pete Cosey (who was close in his playing to Jimi and Muddy Waters), and an African guy named Dominique Gaumont.

I would try exploring one chord with this band, one chord in a tune, trying to get everyone to master these small little simple things like rhythm. We would take a chord and make it work for five minutes with variations, cross rhythms, things like that. Say Al Foster is playing in 4/4, Mtume might be playing in 6/8, or 7/4, and the guitarist might be comping in another time signature, or another rhythm altogether different. That's a lot of intricate shit we were working off this one chord. But music is real mathematical, you know? Counting beats and time: shit like that. And then I was playing over and under and through all of this, and the pianist and bass were playing somewhere else. Everyone had to be alert to what everyone else was doing. At the time, Pete gave me that Jimi Hendrix and Muddy Waters sound that I wanted, and Dominique gave me that African rhythmic thing. I think that could have been a real good band if we had all stayed together, but we didn't. There was too much happening with my health.

I started to think about retiring from music seriously in 1974. I was in São Paulo, Brazil, and had been drinking all this vodka and I smoked some marijuana—which I never did, but I was having such a great time and they had told me it was so good. Plus I took some Percodan and was doing a lot of coke. When I got back to my hotel room, I thought I was having a heart attack. I called the front desk and they sent up a doctor and he put me in the hospital. They had tubes up my nose and IVs attached to me. The band was scared; everyone thought I was going to die. I thought to myself, This is it. But I pulled through that one. Jim Rose, my road manager, told everyone that I was probably just having heart palpitations from all the drugs and that I would be all right the next day, and I was. They had to cancel the show that night and reschedule it the following night. I played and blew everybody's mind I was playing so good.

They just couldn't believe it. One day I looked on the verge of death and then the next day I was playing my ass off. I guess they were looking at me the way I used to look at Bird, in total amazement. But that's the kind of stuff that makes legends. And I had a ball with all those beautiful women down in Brazil. They were all over me and I found them great in bed. They loved to make love.

After we got back from Brazil we started a tour of the United States playing with Herbie Hancock's group. Herbie had a big hit album and he was really well liked among the young black kids. We agreed to be his opening act. Deep down that pissed me off. When we played Hofstra University on Long Island in New York, Herbie—

who is one of the nicest people on earth, and I love him—came back to my dressing room just to say hello. I told him that he wasn't in the band and that the dressing room was off limits to anybody who wasn't in the band. When I thought about it later, I realized that I was just angry about having to open up for one of my ex-sidemen. But Herbie understood and we cleaned it up later.

I was touring all over with Herbie and we were killing everybody. Most of the audiences were young and black and that was good. That's what I wanted, and I was finally getting there. My band was getting real hot and tight by this time. But my hip was a mess, and playing amplified was starting to get to me, too. I was just getting sick of everything, and on top of that, I was sick physically, too.

We played New York and a bunch of other cities. Then I went to St. Louis to play a concert and Irene, my children's mother, showed up at the party afterwards. She started just putting me down in front of my family and friends and musicians. It brought tears to my eyes. I remember the look on everybody's faces, like they were waiting for me just to knock Irene out. But I couldn't do that because I knew where her pain was coming from, from the fact that both our sons were failures and she was blaming me for that. Although it was embarrassing for me to hear it like that, I also knew that some of the things she was saying were true. I was crying because I knew I had to accept a lot of blame. It was a very painful experience.

Right after I saw Irene in St. Louis, I collapsed and they rushed me to Homer G. Phillips Hospital. I had a bad bleeding ulcer and a friend of mine, Dr. Weathers, came over and fixed me up. It was all that drinking and the pills and drugs and shit. I had been spitting up blood a lot but I wasn't really thinking about it until I got to St. Louis. I had been in and out of hospitals so much that it was almost becoming routine. I had just had nodes removed from my larynx. Now here I was in the hospital again. We were supposed to play Chicago the next day and so we had to cancel that.

When I finished all the gigs with Herbie and came back to New York in the summer of 1975, I was thinking seriously about quitting. I played Newport in 1975 and then played the Schaefer Music Festival in Central Park. Then I felt so sick that I canceled a concert I was scheduled to play in Miami. By the time I canceled, all my musicians and their equipment were already there and so the promoters of the concert kept all the sound equipment and tried to sue us. Right after this I decided to quit. By this time the band was Al

Foster on drums, Pete Cosey on guitar, Reggie Lucas on guitar, Michael Henderson on bass, Sam Morrison (who had just replaced Sonny Fortune) on saxophone, and Mtume on percussions. I was doubling up on keyboards.

I quit primarily because of health reasons, but also because I was spiritually tired of all the bullshit I had been going through for all those long years. I felt artistically drained, tired. I didn't have anything else to say musically. I knew that I needed a rest and so I took one, the first one I had had since I had begun playing professionally. I thought that after I was a little better physically I would probably start to feel better spiritually also. I was sick and tired of going in and out of hospitals and hobbling around, on and off stage. I was beginning to see pity in people's eyes when they looked at me, and I hadn't seen that since I was a junkie. I didn't want that. I put down the thing I loved most in life—my music—until I could pull it all back together again.

I thought I might be gone for maybe six months, but the longer I stayed away the more uncertain I was whether I was going to come back at all. And the more I stayed away, the deeper I sank into another dark world, almost as dark as the one I had pulled myself out of when I was a junkie. Once again it was a long, painful road back to sanity and light. In the end it took almost six years and even then I was doubtful whether I could truly come all the way back.

from 1975 until early 1980 I didn't pick up my horn; for over four years, didn't pick it up once. I would walk by and look at it, then think about trying to play. But after a while I didn't even do that. It just went out of my mind because I was involved in doing other things; other things which mostly weren't good for me. But I did them anyway and, looking back, I don't have any guilt about doing them.

I had been involved in music continuously since I was twelve or thirteen years old. It was all I thought about, all I lived for, all I completely loved. I had been obsessed with it for thirty-six or thirty-seven straight years, and at forty-nine years of age, I needed a break from it, needed another perspective on everything I was doing in order to make a clean start and pull my life back together again. I wanted to play music, but I wanted to play it differently than I had in the past and I also wanted to play in big halls *all* the time instead of in little jazz clubs. For the time being, I was through with playing little jazz clubs because my music and its requirements had just outgrown them.

My health was also a factor, and it was getting harder and harder for me to play constantly like I was because my hip wasn't getting any better. I hated limping around the stage like I was, being in all that pain and taking all them drugs. It was a drag. I have a lot of pride in myself and in the way I look, the way I present myself. So I didn't like the way I was physically, and didn't like people looking at me with all that pity in their eyes. I couldn't stand that shit, man.

I couldn't play two weeks in a club without having to go to the hospital. Drinking so much, snorting all the time, and fucking all night. You can't do all of that and create music like you want to. You got to do one or the other. Artie Shaw told me one time, "Miles, you can't play that third concert in bed." What he meant was that if you do two concerts and you're doing all that other stuff, then that third concert you're supposed to play when you're doing one-nighters is going to be played in bed because you're going to be wasted. After a while, all that fucking ain't nothing but tits and asses and pussy. After a while there is no emotion in it because I put so much emotion into my music. The only reason I didn't get staggering drunk was because when I played all that shit came out of my pores. I never did get drunk when I drank a lot, but I would throw up the next day at exactly twelve noon. Tony Williams would come by some time in the morning and at 11:55 he would say, "Okay, Miles, you got exactly five minutes before it's time for you to throw up." And then he'd leave the room and I would go into the bathroom at exactly twelve o'clock and throw up.

Then there was the business side of the music industry, which is very tough and demanding and racist. I didn't like the way I was being treated by Columbia and by people who owned the jazz clubs. They treat you like a slave because they're giving you a little money, especially if you're black. They treated all their white stars like they were kings or queens, and I just hated that shit, especially since they were stealing all their shit from black music and trying to act black. Record companies were still pushing their white shit over all the black music and they *knew* that they had taken it from black people. But they didn't care. All the record companies were interested in at that time was making a lot of money and keeping their so-called black stars on the music plantation so that their white stars could just rip us off. All that just made me sicker than I was physically, made me sick spiritually, and so I just dropped out.

I had invested my money pretty good and Columbia still paid me for a couple of years while I was out of the music industry. We worked out a deal so that they could keep me on the label, and that was cool enough to keep some money coming from royalties. In the seventies, my deal with Columbia was that I got over a million dollars to deliver albums, plus royalties. Plus I had a few rich white ladies who saw to it that I didn't want for money. Mostly during those four or five years that I was out of music, I just took a lot of cocaine (about $500 a day at one point) and fucked all the women I could get into my house. I was also addicted to pills, like Percodan and Seconal, and I was drinking a lot, Heinekens and cognac. Mostly I snorted coke, but sometimes I would inject coke and heroin into my leg; it's called a speedball and it was what killed John Belushi. I didn't go out too often and when I did it was mostly to after-hours places up in Harlem where I just kept on getting high and living from day to day.

I'm not the best person in the world about picking up after myself and keeping a house clean and neat because I didn't never have to do any of that stuff. When I was young, either my mother or my sister, Dorothy, did it, and later my father had a maid. I've always been clean about my personal hygiene, but the other shit I never learned to do and, frankly, I didn't even think about doing it. When I started living by myself after I broke up with Frances, Cicely, Betty, Marguerite, and Jackie, the maids who I had during this time just stopped coming, I guess because of how crazy I was acting. They were probably afraid to be alone with me. I would have a maid from time to time but I couldn't keep anyone steady because cleaning up after me got to be a very big job. The house was a wreck, clothes everywhere, dirty dishes in the sink, newspapers and magazines all over the floor, beer bottles and garbage and trash everywhere. The roaches had a field day. Sometimes I would get someone to come in or one of my girlfriends would do it, but mostly the house was filthy and real dark and gloomy, like a dungeon. I didn't give a fuck because I never thought about it, except during those very few times that I was sober.

I became a hermit, hardly ever going outside. My only connection with the outside world was mostly through watching television—which was on around the clock—and the newspapers and magazines I was reading. Sometimes I got information from a few old friends who would drop by to see me to see if everything was all right, like Max Roach, Jack DeJohnette, Jackie Battle, Al Foster, Gil Evans (I saw Gil and Al more than anybody else), Dizzy Gillespie, Herbie Hancock, Ron Carter, Tony Williams, Philly Joe Jones, Richard Pryor, and Cicely Tyson. I got a lot of information from them but sometimes I wouldn't even let them come in.

I changed managers again through this period. I hired Mark Rothbaum, who had worked for my former manager Neil Reshen for a while, and later became Willie Nelson's manager. My road manager, Jim Rose, was around. But the person who was around the most after a while and who ran errands for me was a young black guy named Eric Engles, who I knew through his mother. Eric stayed with me most of the time during those silent years. If I didn't cook for myself or if one of my girlfriends didn't, Eric would run up to the Cellar, my friend Howard Johnson's place, and get me some fried chicken. It was good that I had Eric because there were times during this period when I didn't leave my house for six months or more.

When my old friends came by to see how I was living they would be shocked. But they didn't say nothing because I think they were afraid if they had, I would just put them out, which I would have. After a while many of my old musician friends stopped coming by, because a lot of time I wouldn't let them in. They got sick and tired of that shit so they just stopped coming. When all those rumors got out about me doing a lot of drugs during that time they were all on the money, because I was. Sex and drugs took the place that music had occupied in my life until then and I did both of them around the clock.

I had so many different women during this period that I lost track of most of them and don't even remember their names. If I met them on the street today I probably wouldn't even recognize most of them. They were there one night and gone the next day and that was that. Most of them are just a blur. Toward the end of my silent period, Cicely Tyson came back into my love life, although she had always been a friend and I would see her from time to time. Jackie Battle came by to check on me, but we were no longer lovers, just real good friends.

I was interested in what some people would call kinky sex, you know, getting it on in bed sometimes with more than one woman. Or sometimes I would watch them just freaking out on themselves. I enjoyed it, I ain't going to lie about that. It gave me a thrill—and during this period I was definitely into thrills.

Now, I know people reading this will probably think I hated women, or that I was crazy, or both. But I didn't hate women; I loved them, probably too much. I loved being with them—and still do—doing what a lot of men secretly wish they could do with a whole lot of beautiful women. For those men it's a dream, just some kind of fantasy, but I made it real in my life. A lot of women also want to do all these kinds of things, like be in bed with several handsome men —or women—doing everything they ever fantasized about in their secret imaginations. All I was doing was what my imagination told me to do, fulfilling my most secret desires and nothing else. I was doing it in private and wasn't hurting nobody else, and the women I was with loved it as much as or more than I did.

I know what I'm talking about here is disapproved of in a country that is as sexually conservative as the United States. I know that most people will consider all of this a sin against God. But I don't look at it that way. I was having a ball, and I don't regret ever having done it. And I don't have a guilty conscience, either. I would admit that taking all the cocaine that I was probably had something to do with it, because when you're snorting good cocaine your sex drive needs satisfaction. After a while, all of this got routine and boring, but only after I had had my fill of it.

A lot of people thought I had lost my mind, or was real close to losing it. Even my family had their doubts. My relationship with my sons—which was never what it should have been—hit rock bottom during this time, especially with Gregory, who was now calling himself Rahman. He would just cause me all kinds of grief, like getting arrested, getting into accidents, and just generally being a pain in the ass. I know he loved me and really wanted to be like me. He used to try to play trumpet, but he played so bad it was just terrible to listen to, and I would scream at him to stop. He and I were having a lot of arguments, and I know the way I was using drugs wasn't good for him to see. I know I wasn't a proper father, but that just wasn't my thing, never was.

In 1978 I went to jail for non-support. This time it was Marguerite who had me put there because I wasn't giving her any money for Erin. It cost me $10,000 to get out of jail and I have tried not to neglect that duty in my life since then. For the last few years, Erin has been staying and traveling with me, so now I have full responsibility for him.

When I didn't have coke my temper was real short and things would just get on my nerves. I couldn't handle that. I didn't listen to any music or read anything during this period. So I would snort coke, get tired of that because I wanted go to sleep, then take a sleeping pill. Even then, I didn't want to go to sleep, so I'd go out at four A.M. and prowl the streets like a werewolf or Dracula. I'd go to an after-hours joint, snort more coke, get tired of all the simple motherfuckers who hang out in those joints. So I'd leave, come home with a bitch, snort some, take a sleeping pill.

All I was doing was bouncing up and down. That was four people, because being a Gemini I'm already two. Two people without the coke and two more with the coke. I was four different people; two of them people had consciences and two didn't. I would look into the mirror and see a whole fucking movie, a horror movie. In the mirror I would see all those four faces. I was hallucinating all the time. Seeing things that weren't there, hearing shit that wasn't there. Four days without sleeping and taking all those drugs will do that to you.

I did some weird shit back in those days, too many weird things to describe. But I'll tell you a couple. I remember one day when I was really paranoid from snorting and staying up all the time. I was driving my Ferrari up West End Avenue and I passed these police-men sitting in a patrol car. They knew me—all of them knew me in my neighborhood—so they spoke to me. When I got about two blocks away from them, I became paranoid and thought that there was a conspiracy to get me, bust me for some drugs. I look down in the compartment on the door and see this white powder. I never took coke out of the house with me. It's winter and snowing and some snow got inside the car. But I didn't realize that; I thought it was some coke that someone had planted in the car just so I could get busted. I panicked, stopped the car in the middle of the street, ran into a building on West End Avenue, looked for the doorman, but he wasn't there. I ran to the elevator and got on and went up to the seventh floor and hid in the trash room. I stayed up there for hours with my Ferrari parked in the middle of West End Avenue with the keys in it. After a while I came to my senses. The car was still sitting where I had left it.

I did that another time just like that and a woman was on the elevator. I thought that I was still in my Ferrari, so I told her, "Bitch, what are you doing in my goddamn car!" And then I slapped her and ran out of the building. That's the kind of weird sick shit that a lot of drugs will make you do. She called the police and they arrested me and put me in the nut ward at Roosevelt Hospital for a few days before letting me out.

Another time, I had a white woman dealer and sometimes—when nobody was at my house—I would run over to her place to pick up some coke. One time I didn't have no money, so I asked her if I could give it to her later. I had always paid her and I was buying a lot of shit from her, but she told me, "No money, no cocaine, Miles." I tried to talk her into it, but she wasn't budging. Then the doorman calls upstairs and tells her her boyfriend is on his way up. So I ask her one more time, but she won't do it. So I just lay down on her bed, and started to take off my clothes. I know her boyfriend knows I got a reputation for being big with the ladies, so what's he going to think when he sees me on her bed like that? So now she's begging me to leave, right? But I'm just laying there with my dick in one hand and my other hand held out for the dope, and I'm grinning, too, because I know she's going to give it to me and she does. She cursed me like a motherfucker on my way out, and when the elevator opened and her boyfriend passed me, he kind of looked at me funny, you know, like, "Has this nigger been with my old lady?" I never went back by there after that.

After a while this shit got boring. I got tired of being fucked up all the time. When you're high like that all the time, people start taking advantage of you. I didn't never think about dying, like I hear some people do who snort a lot of coke. None of my old friends were coming around, except Max and Dizzy, who would come by just to check on me. Then I started to miss them guys, the old guys, the old days, the music we used to play. One day I put up all these pictures all over the house of Bird, Trane, Dizzy, Max, my old friends.

Around 1978, George Butler, who used to be at Blue Note Records but was now at Columbia, started calling me and dropping by. There had been changes at Columbia since I had left. Clive Davis was no longer there. The company was now run by Walter Yetnikoff, and Bruce Lundvall was over the so-called jazz arm of the company. There were still some old people who had been there when I retired, like Teo Macero and some others. When George started telling them that he would like to see if he could convince me to record again, a lot of them told him it was useless. They didn't believe I would ever play again. But George took it upon himself to convince me to come back. It wasn't easy for him. In the beginning I was so indifferent to what he was talking about that he must have thought I would never do it. But he was so goddamn persistent and so pleasant when he would come by, or call and talk on the telephone. Sometimes we would just sit around watching television and not saying nothing.

He wasn't exactly the kind of guy I had been hanging around with all these years. George is conservative and has a Ph.D. in music. He was an academic kind of guy, reserved, laid back. But he was black, and he seemed honest and really loved the music I had done in the past.

Sometimes we'd talk and then we'd get into when I was going to start playing again. At first I didn't want to talk about it, but the more he came, the more I thought about it. And then one day I started messing around on the piano, fingering out a few chords. It felt good! So more and more I started thinking about music again.

Around this same time, Cicely Tyson started coming to see me again. She had been dropping by throughout all of this, but now she started coming by more often. We had this real tight spiritual thing. She kind of knows when I'm not doing too well, when I'm sick and shit. Every time I would get sick, she would just show up because she could feel something was wrong with me. Even when I got shot that time in Brooklyn she said she knew something had happened to me. I used to always say to myself that if I ever married someone again after Betty, it would be Cicely. She just started coming around and I stopped seeing all those other women. She helped run all those people out of my house; she kind of protected me and started seeing that I ate the right things, and didn't drink as much. She helped get me off cocaine. She would feed me health foods, a lot of vegetables, and a whole lot of juices. She turned me on to acupuncture to help get my hip back in shape. All of a sudden I started thinking clearer, and that's when I really started thinking about music again.

Cicely also helped me understand that I had an addictive personality, and that I couldn't ever be just a social user of drugs again. I understood this, but I still took a snort or two now and then. At least I cut it way down with her help. I started drinking rum and Coke instead of cognac, but the Heinekens stayed around for a little while longer. Cicely even got me off cigarettes; she taught me that they were a drug, too. She told me she didn't like kissing me with all that cigarette smell on my breath. She said she would stop kissing me if I didn't stop, so I did.

One of the other important reasons that I came back to music was because of my nephew Vincent Wilburn, my sister's son. I had given Vincent a set of drums when he was about seven, and he fell in love with them. When he was about nine I let him play a song with me and the band one time when we played in Chicago. He sounded pretty good for a kid even then. After he came out of high school, he went to the Chicago Conservatory of Music. So he was serious about music most of his life. Dorothy would complain about him and his friends always being down in the basement playing all the time. I just told her to leave him alone, because I was just like that. From time to time I would call and he would play something for me over the telephone. He could always play. But I would give him advice, tell him what to do and what not to do. Then when I didn't play for those four years or so, Vincent came to New York to stay with me. He would always be asking me to play something for him, show him this, show him that. I wasn't into doing that at the time, so I would just tell him, "Naw, Vincent, I don't feel like it." But he would stay on my case. "Uncle Miles"—he always called me "Uncle Miles," even after he was in my band—"Why don't you play something?" Sometimes he would get on my nerves with that shit. But he always kept music in front of me when he was there, and I used to look forward to his visits.

It was hell trying to get off all those drugs, but I eventually did because I have a very strong will to do whatever I put my mind to. That's what helped me to survive. I got it from my mother and father. I had had my rest and a whole lot of fun—and misery and pain—but I was ready to go back to music, to see what I had left. I knew it was there, at least I felt it was in me and had never left, but I didn't really know for sure. I was confident in my ability and my will to move on. During those years people were even saying that I'd been forgotten. Some people just wrote me off. But I ain't never listened to that kind of shit.

I really believe in myself, in my ability to make things happen in music. I never think about not being able to do something, especially music. I *knew* I could pick up my horn again whenever I wanted to, because my horn is as much a part of me as my eyes and hands. I knew it would take time to get back to where I was when I was *really* playing. I knew I had lost my embouchure because I hadn't played in so long. That would take time to build back up to where it was before I retired. But otherwise, I was ready when I gave George Butler a call in early 1980.

Chapter 17

Whe I decided to come back and play music again, I didn't have a band. But I did have Al Foster to begin with on drums and Pete Cosey on guitar. Al and I had talked a lot about the kind of music I wanted to play. It had been in my head, but now I had to hear it played by a band to know if it was real. I knew I had to go someplace different from where I had been the last time I had played, but I also knew I couldn't go back to the real old music, either. I still didn't know who to get in the band because while I was off I hadn't listened to music and so I didn't know who was around, or who could play. That was all a mystery to me, but I wasn't worried because things like that just work themselves out. One of the first things I told George Butler that I wanted to do was to call some rehearsals and listen to what was out there. George was going to be my producer at Columbia. I was through with Teo Macero. I said I would only work with George and everybody agreed with that. Plus, George convinced me that he wouldn't interfere with what I would be doing in the studio; he trusted my musical judgment and taste. I felt good about going into the studio again. We set a date for early spring, 1980.

I was still under a contract from 1976 but wanted to negotiate a new one; however, they wouldn't do this. But although we agreed upon a date for me to go into the studio, a lot of people were skeptical about me showing up. Other people had tried to get me back into the studio to record one project or another, but after a while I wouldn't even talk to them, so they stopped. To these people, just because my name was on a contract didn't mean that I would honor it and show. They just said they were going to wait until I showed up at the studio and when they saw me there with their own eyes, in the flesh, *then* they would believe it. It had taken George almost a year to convince me to come back.

When I decided to come back, George Butler had Columbia send me a Yamaha grand piano as a present; they just sent it over to the house on West 77th Street. It was a beautiful piano and I used to pick out tunes on it, but the funny thing about getting that piano was that I wasn't using an acoustical piano in my band anymore. I didn't even have a piano player in the band. But I appreciated the present, and the piano was a wonderful instrument.

In April my nephew Vincent Wilburn brought in his Chicago friends to play with me: Randy Hall, Robert Irving, and Felton Crews. He stayed until June and after we had got it together we made *The Man with the Horn*. Vincent played drums on some of the tracks. Dave Liebman turned me on to Bill Evans, a saxophonist who played on the date and was later a member of my working band. Dave had been Bill's teacher, and when he told me Bill could play, I said send him over. I have always relied on musicians I respect, especially if they have played with me, to recommend other musicians. They know what I want and expect.

We got Angela Bofill to sing on that date as backup to Randy Hall, who co-wrote with Robert Irving the title song, "The Man with the Horn" and a couple of other tunes. I wrote three songs for that album for women I knew: "Aida," "Ursula," and "Back Seat Betty," which was for Betty Mabry. The feeling says everything about them. I also wrote the rest of the songs. After things got going, I relented and let Teo Macero come back, and I think it was he who got Barry Finnerty and Sammy Figueroa; Barry played guitar and Sammy played percussion. I didn't know anything about either one of them, but I had heard Sammy playing on an album of Chaka Khan's—who I just love —and I had liked what he did there. So Teo called him up. I remember when Sammy first got to the studio, he came up and spoke to me. I just told him, "play, don't talk." He said he had to tune his drums up. I told him again just to play. He said, "But Miles, my drums sound horrible when they're not tuned properly, so I'm not gonna play them like that." So I told him, "Motherfucker, you'd better play!" So he did and I hired him.

My chops weren't up because I hadn't played for so long, so I started using the wah-wah. One day somebody hid my wah-wah—I think it was Sammy, because he was always trying to get me to play without it. At first, that fucked me up, but after I started playing without it for a while I was all right.

Playing with this group got me back in touch with music. When I was retired, I wasn't hearing any melodies in my head because I wouldn't let myself think about music. But after being in the studio with those guys, I started hearing melodies again, and that made me feel good. Plus, I learned that although I had not played the trumpet for almost five years, I hadn't retired from it. It was still there, all that shit I learned over all them years of playing; the instrument, how to approach it, was still in my blood. The only thing I had to work on was building my technique, my embouchure, back to where it had been.

After I had recorded with Vincent and his friends, I knew I couldn't use nobody but Vincent, Bill Evans, and Bobby Irving in my working band. After I listened to what we had done, I realized that we needed something else, some other kind of music to make a whole album. Despite all that time in the studio, we used only two songs from those sessions on the album. It wasn't that they weren't good musicians; they were. It's just that I needed something else to satisfy what *I* wanted to do. So I called Al Foster to play the drums on these songs, and Bill Evans brought in Marcus Miller. I kept Sammy Figueroa and Barry Finnerty, as well as Bill Evans, and we started rehearsing in my house.

The rehearsals went real good and everybody was playing what I wanted, except for Barry Finnerty when we were rehearsing the last track on the album. One night we were over at my house rehearsing. Barry is playing this shit I don't like on his guitar, so I tell him not to play it, but he keeps playing the way he wants. After he did it several times I told him to go outside and play everything he wanted to play for *himself,* and then come back in and play what *I* wanted. Now, Barry is a very good musician, but he's also a very opinionated guy and doesn't like it when somebody tells him what to play. He comes back in after a while and we start all over again and he played the same thing, so I told him not to play anymore. I went into the kitchen and got a bottle of Heineken and poured the beer on his head. He started telling me how he could be electrocuted because he was playing electric guitar. So I just told him, "Fuck that shit; I told you not to play that chord, motherfucker, and I mean *don't* play it and if you *got* to play it, then play it across the street like I told you." So when I told him that he got real scared. The next day we were going into the studio, and I got Mike Stern to play guitar in the band. I think the sax player Bill Evans brought him in. He was the other guitarist on *The Man with the Horn* and I kept him in my working band.

I liked the way we were playing together, but I felt I needed another kind of percussionist. So I got Mino Cinelu, a percussionist from Martinique, to take Sammy's place. Mino was a prima donna–like guy, light-skinned, curly hair, thought he was a ladies' man. But I liked the way he played, so I put up with the rest of his silly shit. I had first met Mino in a club in New York where I used to hang out called Mikell's. The club is run by Mike and Pat Mikell (Mike's black and Pat is a nice, foxy Italian woman; James Baldwin's brother, David, was the bartender there for many years). The club is on Columbus Avenue and 97th Street and always has great music, especially on weekends. Anything could happen at Mikell's in terms of music. I remember one night when I was there and not playing, Stevie Wonder came in and sat in with Hugh Masekela until early in the morning. Sly Stone used to do the same thing when he was in town and Hugh was playing there. I first heard Mino at Mikell's in May 1981 when he was playing in a group called Civily Jordon and Folk. That's also where I first heard the guitarist Cornell Dupree, who had made a record with me, *Get Up With It,* the one that is dedicated to Duke Ellington. I heard him in Mikell's playing with a group called Stuff, which was a very good group. Anyway, when Mino came into the group, everything was starting to fall into place. I could see where we could have a hell of a group.

Bill Evans, my former piano player, had died in the summer of 1980. His death made me real sad, because he had turned into a junkie, and I think he died from complications of that. The year before Bill died, Charlie Mingus had died, so a lot of my friends were going. Sometimes it seemed like just a few of us were left from the old days. But I was trying not to think about the old days, because in order to stay young I believe a person has to forget the past.

I hadn't stopped using drugs entirely at this time, although I had cut down a lot. My favorite things in the world to get high on were champagne, beer, cognac, and cocaine. I really enjoyed them. But I could see where one day I wouldn't be able to do any of them anymore, because my doctor had told me that on top of everything else that was wrong with me, I also had diabetes. Alcohol is a no-no for diabetics. It was only a matter of time before I had to stop everything. And although I knew it in my mind, I wasn't prepared emotionally to quit.

By the spring of 1981, I felt ready to play again out in public. I felt that I was ready and that my band was, too. So I called my manager, Mark Rothbaum, and told him to call Freddie Taylor, a promoter up in Boston, who then booked us into a small club in the Cambridge area called Kix. I had also agreed to play George Wein's Newport Jazz Festival on the first weekend of July, so the Kix gig, which was booked for four days at the end of June, would be a good warm-up for that. We also had to get a road group together; I had had a good crew with me when I retired, with guys like Jim Rose and Chris Murphy. A good road crew is almost as necessary as a great band when you go on the road because they take care of all the everyday shit that musicians don't think about, like setting up everything and making sure things run smoothly so that all the musicians have to think about is playing. Jim Rose, who had been driving a cab while I was in retirement, heard from a black female passenger that I was going to play Newport, so he called up Mark Rothbaum, who it so happened had been looking for him. I always thought that Jim was the best road manager I ever had. Jim came by a couple of times when I was retired, but eventually I had lost contact with him. When he agreed to come back, man, that was a big relief. Chris Murphy came back, too; he had also been driving a cab. When I saw those guys—both with long hair—I just hugged them, I was so glad they had come back.

I had bought a brand-new, canary-yellow 308 GTSI Ferrari sports coupe, with a targa top. Jim Rose and I drove up to Boston and Chris drove the truck with the equipment. When Jim and I left the house, we got a little coke and after we crossed the George Washington Bridge I drove all the way up like a bat out of hell. I know this scared Jim a little because I was really hitting the speed. But I found that I was finally starting to lose my interest in coke because after we got to Boston I gave it away to someone and then turned some down. So that's how I knew I was winning my battle with it.

The rest of the band had flown up to the gig, but I wanted everyone to see me arriving to work in my new Ferrari. I wanted them to *know* that I was really back, even if I was only staying right across the street from the club and could have just walked across the street every night. A little show biz don't hurt sometimes.

My band had Marcus Miller, Mike Stern, Bill Evans, Al Foster, and Mino Cinelu. Everyone got along real well. The first night we played, there were lines, but a lot of people were just waiting to see if I was really going to show up to play. After I did, the place was jam-packed; there were people everywhere. Man, people were crying when they saw me and crying when I played. It was something. One night, there was this little crippled black guy who had cerebral palsy sitting down front in a wheelchair. He looked about thirty-five years old, but I really don't know how old he was. I was playing this blues, and he was sitting right in front of the stage. I played it to him because I knew that *he* knew what the blues were. Halfway through my solo, I looked into this guy's eyes, and he was crying. He reached up his withered arm, which was trembling, and with his shaking hand he touched my trumpet as though he was blessing it—and me. Man, I almost lost it right then and there, almost broke down myself and cried. I wanted to meet the guy, but when I went outside they had taken him away. Now, I don't ever get sad about not meeting somebody I don't know, and especially a man, but I wanted to tell him how much his gesture had meant to me. What he had done when he reached up his hand like that can only come from a heart that understands. I wanted to thank him for what he had done because it meant a lot to me, coming back to play after all I had gone through. It was almost like he was telling me everything was all right and that my playing was as beautiful and strong as ever. I needed that, needed it right at that moment to go on.

I think we got $15,000 a night for those four days in Boston, which was some nice money for a club that seated around 425 people. We did two shows a night and the club made money, too. Then we played the Newport Jazz Festival at Avery Fisher Hall in New York City. A lot of critics hated what we did there and said I didn't play long enough. On the other hand, a lot of people dug it, so it was even Stephen. We got a lot of money for the Newport thing; I think about $90,000 for two shows. Both shows were sold out, and so that made everyone feel good. In September I went to Japan and they paid me $700,000 for eight shows, plus transportation and food and hotels. That was a great trip we made over there. Everybody played well and the Japanese people loved what we did.

Columbia brought out *The Man with the Horn* in the fall of 1981, and although the record sold well, the critics universally didn't like the music. They said my playing sounded weak and that I was "only a shadow of my former self." But I knew it was going to take a while to get my chops together. I could feel them getting stronger each day that I played, and I was practicing every day. But Columbia thought that I might not stay around for too long, so they sent along a crew to record all my live performances, which was okay with me. I knew that I wasn't going to be retiring unless my health gave out on me. I was feeling a whole lot better than I had been feeling, although that wasn't saying much.

Cicely Tyson had been staying at my house most of the summer, at least while she was in town. She had a place in Malibu, California, right on the water, and another place available to her at a resort called Gurney's out at Montauk, Long Island, right on the ocean. Cicely had become a big star since we were last together. She had made a lot of movies and a lot of money, and she was probably more famous than I was. But I had had some influence on her, too; I mean, she got her accent in the film *The Autobiography of Miss Jane Pittman* in 1974 from copying my voice, the way *I* talk—that's where that voice came from. Anyway, when she was in town, she would be over to my place.

On Thanksgiving Day in 1981, Cicely and I got married at Bill Cosby's house in Massachusetts by Andrew Young. Max Roach was there, along with Dizzy Gillespie, Dick Gregory, and a few other people like my manager, Mark Rothbaum. It was a nice ceremony, but if you look at the pictures of that wedding, you can see I was real sick. I had that gray look of almost-death in my face. Cicely saw it. I told her I felt like I could die at any minute. During the summer I had shot some dope in my leg and it had fucked it up. I was going to see Dr. Phillip Wilson over at New York Hospital a few times a week for therapy when I was in New York and a Dr. Chin that Cicely had turned me onto. I was going to Dr. Wilson for physical therapy and to the other doctor for herbs and acupuncture. I was still smoking three or four packs of cigarettes a day. One day Dr. Wilson just asked me if I wanted to live. I said, "Yeah, I want to live."

So he said, "Well, Miles, if you want to live, you've got to cut all this stuff out, including smoking." He kept telling me this, but I just kept on doing what I was doing.

I even went to bed with a woman I knew five days after Cicely and I were married, because I didn't feel that sex thing for Cicely anymore. I respected her as a woman and felt like she was a good friend to me, but I also needed that sex thing that I couldn't get from her. So I got it in other places. In January Cicely went to Africa to make some kind of film for the State Department. After she left I went a little wild with the drinking once again. I had stopped using cocaine by this time, but I had replaced it with a lot of beer drinking. That was the time when my right hand was paralyzed by a stroke. I called it a stroke, and some other people called it "Honeymoon Syndrome," which is supposed to happen when you sleep embracing someone and that pressure on your hand and arm cuts off the blood circulation to the arm and it damages the nerves. I don't know exactly what happened, except that when I reached for a cigarette one night while Cicely was gone, my fingers and my hand were stiff and I couldn't bend them. I said, "What the fuck is this?!" I could close my hand but I couldn't open it. It scared the shit out of me. Cicely said she felt that too while she was over in Africa, and, sure enough, the phone rang and she was asking me what was wrong. I told her that I couldn't move my hand and my fingers. She told me that that sounded like a stroke and so she came on back.

I should have known something was wrong because I hadn't been feeling good and when I peed my urine was filled with blood. When we had come back from playing Japan, I caught a touch of pneumonia and flew all night and day to get back to New York to do the television show "Saturday Night Live." I remember Marcus Miller asking me, "What hurts?" before we did that show, and I told him: "What *don't* hurt!" I felt so sick that if I had sat down, I didn't believe I could get up again. All through that show I just walked my ass off, while I was playing and even while I wasn't playing; I just walked the whole time. I guess everyone thought that I was crazy, but I was only trying to keep myself together and that was the only way I could think of doing it. I started feeling this numbness in my hand and fingers right after I did that television show. I should have done something about it then, but I didn't. So after that stroke, or whatever it was, and the doctor's warnings, and Cicely telling me she wasn't going to kiss me no more with all the cigarette smell on my breath, I just stopped everything cold turkey, just like I had done with my heroin problem. Stopped everything just like that.

This was 1982, and my doctor told me that if I had sex anytime in the next six months that I could have another stroke. That was tough, because a hard-on comes spontaneously; sex is that way for me, too. And if you don't go and do it right then, then you lose it. I couldn't do nothing, and Cicely said, "If you don't want to do anything, I'll just wait." So she waited six months.

I was still weak through all of this and couldn't play. I didn't even have enough strength to pee straight. The urine would go all down my leg. Dr. Chin gave me herbs that he said would clean me all the way up in about six months. I started taking these herbs and I had all kinds of shit coming out; mucus, everything. Dr. Chin also said that after I took the herbs for six months, I would want to have sex. I said, "Bullshit," but to myself. But he was right, because right after the six months were over I had the urge again. Somehow through all of this I lost most of my hair, and this just really fucked me up because I have always been vain about my appearance.

For the next two or three months after I had that stroke and couldn't use my fingers, I went to physical therapy at New York Hospital three or four times a week. Jim Rose drove me. Man, this was the scariest shit that had ever happened to me, because with my hand and fingers bunched up and stiff like they were, I thought I would never play again. At least that thought sometimes crept into my mind. That was more frightening than death to me; to live when my mind was working and not be able to play what I was thinking about. After a time of doing the herbs and the physical therapy, not drinking or smoking, eating good solid food, getting a lot of rest, and drinking Perrier water instead of beer or liquor, my fingers all of a sudden started getting some life back in them. I started swimming every day again like I used to, which helped increase my breathing capacity and stamina. I could feel my health coming back after a while, could feel myself growing stronger.

In April 1982, I got the band back together again to tour Europe in early May. I knew that I looked like death waiting to eat a soda cracker. I was so thin and had lost most of my hair; just a few strands of it were sticking up. I slicked them back and eventually I got myself a hair weave. I was so weak a lot of the time that I had to play while sitting down. Some days I'd feel good and others I'd feel like getting back on the airplane and going home. But the band was playing better and better together. I was trying to get Al Foster to play more funk licks on drums, but he didn't seem to be listening to me. Other than that, everything was going fine with the band and my chops were getting stronger all the time. When I felt good I would walk all over the stage, playing into the wireless mike attached to the bell of my trumpet. But I always played keyboard sitting on a stool. Although I was looking very sick, I was, in fact, feeling stronger than I had felt in a long, long time. I had lost a lot of weight because of the diet I was on, fish and vegetables, food that keeps the weight off. That's why I looked so frail.

My health wasn't good, but we were able to keep stories of my stroke out of the newspapers and away from the media. No one knew of the problem until a few months later when Leonard Feather published an interview I had given when I said I couldn't use my hand. By the time the interview was published, we had already completed our European tour.

As it turned out, the biggest problem I had on this tour was with Cicely and a friend of hers who went with us all over Europe. Man, they were a pain in the ass on that trip with their prima donna bullshit of "Get me this," "Get me that," like Perrier water, to the band roadies. They were buying clothes like there wasn't going to be no tomorrow. Me and the rest of the band—five people—and the road crew didn't have but two bags each, while Cicely and her friend soon had over eighteen bags for the two of them. It got to be ridiculous. Chris and Jim, my two main road people, along with Mark Allison and Ron Lorman (the two other roadies), had to carry all their shit *and* Cicely's and her friend's. Jim and Chris got really mad about having to do it. I was making $25,000 dollars a night by this time and we were paying both Jim and Chris real well for what they were doing. But there just wasn't enough money to pay them for the way that Cicely and her friend were treating them. Jim and Chris thought that if they complained to me about Cicely, I would have probably blown up at them since she was my wife. And maybe I would have; I don't know.

Since Cicely had become a star actress, her personality had changed. She demanded everything, gave a lot of people a hard time, treated a lot of people like they were nothing. Now, I know I got a bad reputation for treating people bad, too. But I don't just fuck with people just because I'm famous and I think I can. That's the shit that Cicely started doing after she became a star; she just gave everyone grief. She just treated the roadies like they were her servants.

Cicely was starting to get on my nerves real bad, so when we got to Rome I told Jim that I wanted a separate room from her. I stayed in another room for the three days we were in Rome, and Cicely didn't know where I was. After I had been there for three days and we had played the concert, I rejoined her in our room. I had told her I needed a rest and that I would see her after the concert.

I had had another little break from Cicely in Paris when I had Jim Rose take me over to see my old girlfriend, Juliette Greco. We are still good friends and I always like to see her when I'm in Paris. She is still doing her thing, is still a big star all over France. We just talked about what I did when I wasn't playing, the old days, and what she was doing. It was good seeing her, always was.

I started to draw a lot on this trip to Europe. It started with just a little doodling. Cicely had bought me some sketch pads the summer before, but I didn't use them much. But now, on this trip, when I wasn't thinking about music and playing, I found myself thinking about drawing and painting. I think it was therapeutic at first, something to do with my spare time now that I wasn't smoking or drinking or snorting. I had to keep myself occupied so that I wouldn't start thinking about doing those kinds of things again.

When I came back to music I started to hear something I had thought might happen. More and more musicians were going over to the guitar as their main instrument because of the influence of pop music and because most of the kids nowadays really get off on that instrument. Plus, it allows you to sing. The new musicians were mainly playing electric guitar or bass, or electric piano. Or, they were becoming just pure singers or writers of popular songs. That's where the black kids who where gifted in music were going, and there was nothing anyone could do about it.

Fewer and fewer black musicians were playing jazz and I could see why, because jazz was becoming the music of the museum. A lot of musicians and critics are at fault for letting it happen. No one wants to be dead before their time, you know, when they're twenty-one, and that's what was going to happen to someone who went into jazz. At least that's the way it looked to me. The only way that wasn't going to happen was if somehow they got the ear of the young people again, and I didn't see that happening. I didn't even go to listen to most jazz groups anymore, because they were only playing the same musical licks that we played way back with Bird, over and over again; that, along with some of the things that Coltrane introduced, and maybe Ornette. It was boring to hear that shit. These musicians had become victims of the critics, most of whom are lazy and don't want to work too hard to understand contemporary musical expression and language. That's too much like work for them, so they just put it down every time. Dumb, insensitive critics have destroyed a lot of great music and musicians who just weren't as strong as I was in having the ability to say, "Fuck y'all."

Even though the jazz scene seemed to be stagnant, there were some good young musicians coming up, like Lester Bowie, and the Marsalis brothers, Wynton and Branford. Wynton played trumpet and everybody was saying that he was one of the best trumpet players to come along in a long time. I think he was playing with Art Blakey's band at the time. Branford was the older, a saxophone player, also playing with Art Blakey. I think it was around 1981 that I first started hearing about them from some of the musicians I knew. I don't know what was happening to Freddie Hubbard, who I thought was going to be a great trumpet player. A lot of good trumpet players were off the scene now: Lee Morgan had gotten killed, and Booker Little had died young like Clifford Brown, and then Woody Shaw had gone off the deep end from drugs before he could get all the recognition I thought he would get. But there were guys like Jon Faddis and a player from Mississippi named Olu Dara, who I heard was great, but who I had never heard play. Dizzy was still playing great and so was Hugh Masekela, Art Farmer, and a few other guys.

Some of the new developments in music were kind of interesting, but I found the most interesting stuff happening in white rock music. Some of the fusion music was okay, especially some of the stuff that Weather Report, Stanley Clarke, and a few other guys were doing. But I saw room for a new kind of music to express itself. I felt that some of the things being done in rap music might get to be real interesting, but that was a little ways off. Then there was the music of Prince, who I was hearing for the first time. His shit was the most exciting music I was hearing in 1982 around the time of my European tour. Here was someone who was doing something different, so I decided to keep an eye on him.

We got back to the States in the spring of 1982, and then toured the United States and Canada during the summer. With all the playing I could really hear my technique and sound and tone coming back. Things were going better than I expected. I even took a little time off and went down to Lima, Peru, with Cicely, who was a judge at the Miss Universe contest. All I did for three or four days was swim and lie around the hotel pool and rest and eat good seafood. I was even starting to look like myself again, only my motherfucking hair wouldn't grow back and that was pissing me off.

We were mostly playing the tunes on the album *We Want Miles,* which were recorded live when we went on tour that first time in 1981. They were tunes like "Jean-Pierre" (named after Frances's son), "My Man's Gone Now" (from *Porgy and Bess*), "Back Seat Betty," and "Fast Track." We were playing a tune called "Kix," too, which was named after the club in Boston.

We Want Miles was released in late summer 1982, and in the fall of 1982 I took the group into the studio to record *Star People* (I think these two albums were the last ones I worked on with Teo Macero). That was the session when we recorded "Come and Get It," which was now the opening number at our live performances. I also put a song on that album called "Star on Cicely," which Gil Evans arranged. The title track "Star People" is a long blues and I really think I got into the solos I play on it.

On the last tunes we did on *Star People* around the end of 1982 and the beginning of 1983, we brought in John Scofield to play some guitar tracks, and I just kept him in the band. Barry Finnerty was gone by now. John made his first gig with us at New Haven, Connecticut, close to the end of the year, and stayed on when we played the Felt Forum at Madison Square Garden on the last day of 1982. We shared that gig with Roberta Flack. I liked the subtleties of John Scofield's playing. My sax player Bill Evans had recommended John, just like he had Mike Stern. I felt that two guitarists with different styles would create a tension that would be good for the music. I also felt that if Mike listened to John, then he might learn something about understatement. On "It Gets Better" on *Star People,* John is featured as the lead soloist with Mike playing in the background. This was a blues, too. Now with John Scofield in the band I started playing more blues because Mike had been more rock-oriented. The blues was John's thing, along with a good jazz touch, so I felt comfortable playing the blues with him.

As John came into the band Marcus Miller was leaving, and this hurt me a lot, because Marcus was the best bass player I had had in a long, long time. Plus, he was a funny motherfucker who kept everyone in the band loose. He was just a nice guy to be around, mature and really into the music. That motherfucker could play four or five instruments—guitar, bass, saxophone, and some other things. Marcus was really in demand as one of the best studio musicians in the United States; everybody wanted him to play on their albums. He was also getting into a lot of producing and writing, so playing with me was cutting into the money he could make. (But he'd be back later.)

Marcus recommended a guy named Tom Barney, who stayed around for about a month or two and got in on one of the recordings that went on *Star People.* Then I got Darryl Jones from Chicago on the recommendation of my nephew, Vincent. Darryl was nineteen years old at the time. Darryl came to New York in May 1983 and met me in my house. I told him that we were going to play a little bit, but if I don't like what he plays, that don't mean he can't play. I put on a tape of one of our records and tell him to play along with it. Then I put on a blues and ask him to play with that. After that I ask him if he can play a B-flat blues and he plays a little and then he don't play it. So I ask him again, "Can you play a B-flat blues?" He starts playing it slower than he had before. I ask him if he can play it slower, and so he plays it even slower. I go into my bedroom with Vincent and tell him that this motherfucker can really play, so tell him he got the gig. Vincent goes out and tells Darryl, but he wants to hear it from me. So I go out and punch him on the shoulder and tell him he's got the gig.

It was around this time that I changed managers. I fired Mark Rothbaum after a dispute we had and on Cicely's advice I hired some Jewish guys from Philadelphia, the Blank brothers, Lester and Jerry and Lester's son Bob, who was working with them. But I had enjoyed hanging out with Mark Rothbaum. In 1982 he had brought me and Cicely out to Las Vegas and introduced me to Willie Nelson and his wife, Connie. Mark manages Willie and also Emmylou Harris, Kris Kristofferson, and some other stars. We had a nice time in Las Vegas. I got to know Willie Nelson real well. He was down-to-earth and cool with me. I have always liked the way he sang. After this, Willie came to a place called Red Rocks, in Denver, Colorado, where I was playing. He came to see me play a few times after that.

In the spring of 1983 the band went back to Europe. Chris Murphy quit in Torino, Italy, because he said he couldn't take Cicely any longer. Now that the Blanks were running things, they were trying to penny-pinch their way through the tour, nickel-and-diming everyone to death. But a tour takes cash money to make it run smooth, and they were holding back on the money. That's when I began to see that having them might be a big mistake. The Blanks turned out to be a horror show because they could hardly get us dates. I think they got us a few dates in Europe during all of 1983, including a tour of Japan in May, but that was all. That's how incompetent they were.

Throughout this period Cicely and I were living at 315 West 70th Street while my house on West 77th was being gutted; we lived there until we moved out to California, to Malibu, where she had her place on the beach. I spent a lot of money fixing up my place on 77th Street so that it could be like Cicely wanted. But ironically I wound up having to sell the place under pressure from the Blank brothers, because I owed them money. But really, I think that Cicely was behind having the house gutted so that she could make a fresh start there, without having to think about all the other women who had been in there before her. Having my house gutted like that really fucked me up for a while.

At least the music we were playing really turned me on. The guys in the band played so well and they were great to be around. The only problems I had with them was that they were reading the critics, who were saying the music we were playing wasn't happening. They were young musicians, trying to make their reputations and they thought they were playing with someone that everyone would love. They expected the critics to say everything we played was great. But the critics didn't, and that disturbed them. I had to hip them to how critics felt about me—at least some of them.

I told them that so-called critics had done the same thing to Bird when he first started playing that great music he was playing, and that they had also criticized Trane and Philly Joe when they were in my band. I hadn't listened to them then and I wasn't about to listen to them now. After this, me and the guys in my band got closer than ever, and they stopped paying attention to critics.

I could communicate with the band just by giving them a certain look. That look told them to play something different from what they had been playing, and after a while the music really started coming together. I listened to what everybody was playing in my band. I listen constantly and if anything is just a little off, I hear it right away and try to correct it on the spot while the music is happening. That's what I'm doing when I have my back turned to the audience—I can't be concerned with talking and bullshitting with the audience while I'm playing because the music is talking to them when everything's right. If the audience is hip and alert, they know when the music is right and happening. When that's the case, you just let things groove and enjoy what's going on.

Al Foster was the person closest to me in my new band because he had been with me the longest. He was a real spiritual person, nice to be around. It was Al that kept me in touch with the music scene when I was out for those years. I used to talk to him almost every day when I was retired. I really trusted him during that time. It's hard for me to relax with people I don't know well, hard for me to trust them even after I've known them for a while. Maybe it comes from where I was raised. People out there in the East St. Louis area just don't get into people right away. If they are laughing and talking with you, that's just a mask so they can check you out. I think it has something to do with a country mentality. Country people are skeptical of other people, and I'm like that no matter how sophisticated I've gotten. Most of the time my best friends are the musicians in my current band, and it was the same thing with the guys in the new band. I liked Bill Evans and Darryl Jones in my new band (and Marcus Miller before he left). I liked John Scofield, too, and Mike Stern, even though I had to let him go. So we were all close; all up against the critical world.

We Want Miles won a Grammy for 1982 (given out in 1983) and I was named Jazz Musician of the Year in *Jazz Forum*. We played Japan, and some festivals in this country and in Canada, and in the late summer and early fall of 1983, we started laying down tracks for *Decoy,* some of which were live recordings. When we went into the studio I added Branford Marsalis on soprano saxophone and Robert Irving (who had first recorded with me on *The Man with the Horn*) on synthesizer, an instrument that I wanted to bring into the band. Gil Evans did some arranging. I wanted to add Branford to my band, but he couldn't do it because he was committed to playing with his brother Wynton. I had heard Branford when we played a gig together in St. Louis. I think he was playing with Herbie Hancock, Wynton, Tony Williams, and Ron Carter in a group that was calling themselves the Reunion band. I had liked what he had done and asked him if he could make some recordings with me.

I took the band to Europe for a few dates in the fall of 1983. This tour was something special because the people were so happy to see me, and they really got into the music. I remember one date in particular in Warsaw, Poland. We didn't even have to go through customs; they just waved us on through. Everybody was wearing "We Want Miles" buttons. The leader of the Soviet Union, Yuri Andropov, sent his personal limousine (or one just like it) to take me everywhere I wanted to go while I was in Warsaw. They told me that he loved my music and thought that I was one of the greatest musicians of all time. They also told me that he had wanted to come to my concert, but that he was too sick. He sent his personal regards, wishing that I have a great concert and saying that he was sorry that he couldn't be there. They put me up at the very best hotel in Warsaw and treated me like a king. When I got through playing my concert, people stood and cheered, and chanted that they hoped that I live a hundred years. Man, that was something!

Chapter 18

When I got back to the States, Cicely and the people at Columbia had organized a celebration for me at Radio City Music Hall in November 1983 called "Miles Ahead: A Tribute to an American Music Legend," co-produced by the Black Music Association. Bill Cosby was the host and they had all kinds of musicians there that night: Herbie Hancock, J. J. Johnson, Ron Carter, George Benson, Jackie McLean, Tony Williams, Philly Joe Jones, and a whole bunch of others. They even had an all-star band conducted by Quincy Jones that played a few arrangements by Slide Hampton of some of Gil Evans's arrangements from *Porgy and Bess* and *Sketches of Spain*. The president of Fisk University gave me an honorary degree in music.

It was cool up until this point and I had really enjoyed myself. Then, they wanted me to give a speech and the only thing I could think of to say was "Thank you," which I did. I think this pissed some people off because they thought I was ungrateful, which I wasn't. But I can't be giving no long speeches because that isn't me. I said what I thought was real and I meant it from the bottom of my heart. Before they wanted me to talk, I had played a half-hour set with my band. They wanted me to play with some of the old guys, but I couldn't do that because I don't believe in going back. It was a beautiful night, and I was happy that they honored me the way that they did. But right after this, I got sick and had to go into the hospital to have another operation on my hip. Then I caught pneumonia. As a result, I was out of action for about six months.

When I came back, we played the usual concerts, and *Decoy* won a Grammy for Best Album. Al Foster left the band for a while because he wouldn't play the kind of drums I wanted him to play. He never did like the rock thing. I used to ask him over and over again to play that funky backbeat, but he just wouldn't play it and so I brought in my nephew, Vincent Wilburn, on drums because that was his thing. I hated to see Al go because we were close, but the music comes before everything. Al and Vincent played alternately with me on my next album, *You're Under Arrest,* in 1985. Vincent joined my working band in 1985 (I think it was March), right after Al left for good, and stayed with me for about two years.

In November 1984, I won the Sonning Music Award for lifetime achievement in music. The award is given in Denmark, and I was the first jazz musician and the first black ever to win it. The award is usually given to classical musicians; Leonard Bernstein, Aaron Copland, and Isaac Stern had won it in the past. I was happy and honored that they gave me that award. They wanted me to make a record with Denmark's best musicians, so in February 1985 I went back over to record and they got together a big band. All of the music was written by the Danish composer Palle Mikkelborg. It is a mixture of orchestra and electronic music, synthesizers. I took Vincent over with me to get a certain sound on the drums. He recorded with us on this album. John McLaughlin is on guitar and Marilyn Mazur is on percussion. Columbia was supposed to release the album, but they reneged on me and so I had to get a grant from the National Endowment for the Arts to finish the album, which was to be called *Aura.*

That was the beginning of the end of my relationship with Columbia. That and the way that George Butler was treating me and Wynton Marsalis. I really liked Wynton when I first met him. He's still a nice young man, only confused. I knew he could play the hell out of classical music and had great technical skills on the trumpet, technique and all of that. But you need more than that to play great jazz music, you need feelings and an understanding of life that you can only get from living, from experience. I always thought he needed that. But I was never jealous of him or anything like that. Shit, man, he was young enough to be my son, and I wanted the best for him.

But the more famous he became the more he started saying things —nasty, disrespectful things—about me, things I've never said about musicians who influenced me and who I had great respect for. I've disagreed with and spoken out about many musicians I didn't like, but never against someone who had influenced me in the way I had influenced Wynton's playing. When he started hitting on me in the press, at first it surprised me and then it made me mad.

George Butler was the producer for both of us, and I felt that he was more concerned about Wynton's music than he was about mine. George likes that classical shit, and he was pushing Wynton to record more of that. Wynton was getting a lot of play because he was playing classical music and by this time he was winning *all* the awards, both in classical and in jazz music. A lot of people thought I was getting jealous of Wynton because of this. I wasn't jealous; I just didn't think he was playing as good as people said he was playing.

The press was trying to play Wynton off me. They compared me with Wynton, but never with some white trumpet player, like Chuck Mangione. Just the way they compare Richard Pryor, Eddie Murphy, and Bill Cosby to each other. They don't compare them to people like Robin Williams, or somebody else who is white. When Bill Cosby first won all those awards for his television show, you could hear a pin drop at the awards ceremony, because all those other television networks had turned him down. I know, because Cicely and me were there. White people want to see blacks crawling around and Uncle Tomming. Or, they like to see blacks angry with each other, like Wynton and me.

So all these white people are praising Wynton for his classical playing and that's all right. But then they turn around and rank him *over* Dizzy and me in jazz, and he knows he can't hold a candle to all the shit we have done and are going to do in the future. What makes it so bad is that Wynton is listening to all their shit and believing them. If he keeps on, they're going to fuck him up. They even got him putting down his own brother for playing the kind of music he wants to play. Now you know that's some bullshit right there, good as Branford can play.

They got Wynton playing some old dead European music. Why doesn't he play some of the American black composers, give them some play? If the recording companies really want to do classical stuff with black guys, why don't they do some black classical composers or even young white classical composers instead of all that old shit? I'm not saying that music isn't good, but it's been done over and over and over again. Wynton's playing their dead shit, the kind of stuff anybody can do. All you've got to do is practice, practice, practice. I told him I wouldn't bow down to play that music, that they should be glad someone as talented as he is is playing that tired-ass shit.

Wynton ought to learn from the way they did me and all the rest of the guys who came before him, how they try to set you up so they can put you down if you miss one motherfucking note. Wynton's taking off from playing his own shit to play their shit and he ain't got time to do that, because he's still got a lot to learn about improvisational music. I don't see why our music can't be given the respect of European classical music. Beethoven's been dead all these years and they're still talking about him, teaching him, and playing his music. Why ain't they talking about Bird, or Trane, or Monk, or Duke, or Count, or Fletcher Henderson, or Louis Armstrong like they're talking about Beethoven? Shit, *their* music is classical. We're all Americans now, and sooner or later whites are going to have to deal with that and with all the great things that black people have done here.

They've also got to accept that we do things differently. Our music isn't the same on Friday and Saturday night. Our food isn't the same. Most black people don't sit up there and listen to Billy Graham and those other sorry preachers, who sound just like Ronald Reagan. We aren't into that kind of shit and Wynton isn't either, not really. But they had him believing that this was the thing to do, that it was hip and everything. But it wasn't, at least it wasn't hip to me.

I had just recorded *You're Under Arrest* in the late part of 1984 and the early part of 1985. This was the last record that I officially recorded with Columbia. But this time, Bob Berg had replaced Bill Evans on saxophone in the band, Steve Thornton had taken Mino Cinelu's place, and my nephew Vincent Wilburn had recorded on the drums, in place of Al Foster. The singer Sting was on that album, too, because Darryl Jones was recording with him and asked if he could bring him over, so I said he could. Sting plays the French policeman's voice on the album. He is a nice guy, although I didn't know at the time that he was trying to hire Darryl as a bass player for his band.

The concept for *You're Under Arrest* came out of the problems that black people have with policemen everywhere. The police are always fucking with me when I drive around out in California. They didn't like me driving around in a $60,000 yellow Ferrari, which I was doing at the time I made this record. Plus, they didn't like me, a black person, living in a beachfront house in Malibu. That's where the concept for *You're Under Arrest* came from: being locked up for being part of a street scene, being locked up politically. Being subjected to the looming horror of a nuclear holocaust—plus being locked up in a spiritual way. It's the nuclear threat that is really a motherfucker in our daily lives, that and the pollution that is everywhere. Polluted lakes, oceans, rivers; polluted ground, trees, fish, everything.

I mean, they're just fucking up everything because they're so fucking greedy. I'm talking about whites who are doing this, and they're doing it all over the world. Fucking up the ozone layer, threatening to drop bombs on everybody, trying to always take other people's shit, and sending in armies when people don't want to give it up. It's shameful, pitiful, and dangerous what they're doing, what they have been doing all these years, because it's fucking with everyone. That's why on "Then There Were None" I have the synthesizer creating sounds like flaming, howling winds which were supposed to be a nuclear explosion. Then you hear my lonely trumpet, which is supposed to be a baby's wailing cry, or the sad cry of a person who has survived the bomb's explosion. That's why those bells are there in that tolling, mourning kind of sound. They're supposed to be ringing for the dead. I put that countdown in there, "5, 4, 3, 2 . . ." and then, at the end of the record, you hear my voice saying, "Ron, I meant for you to push the *other* button."

You're Under Arrest did real good; it sold over 100,000 albums in a few weeks. But I didn't like what was happening at Columbia. When the opportunity came to move over to Warner Bros. Records, I told my new manager, David Franklin, to do it. David was Cicely's manager, and she had recommended him to me. I had already decided that I wanted a black person to manage my business. But David fucked up on the negotiations by giving up too much to Warners, like the rights to all my publishing. They gave us a lot of money to come over to Warner Bros., in the seven figures, just to sign. But I didn't like the idea of giving up my publishing rights to them. That's why you don't see my own songs on my new albums; Warner Bros. would get the rights to use those tunes, not me. So until we renegotiate that point you're going to always see someone else's tunes on my albums.

I was doing my usual touring all over the world between 1984 and 1986. Nothing new there, just lots of music being played in places I had seen now many, many times, so visiting those places wasn't new to me anymore. The thrill was gone. It just becomes a routine, so it's the music that keeps you going. If the music is cool, then everything else gets better and easier to deal with. If it isn't, well, then that can make things a little bit rough, because a long tour can get tiring and boring. But I'm used to it. As a matter of fact, since I've gotten so deeply into painting, I spend a lot of my time on the road going to museums and visiting painters' and sculptors' studios and buying a lot of art. This is new for me and I just love doing it, having the money to buy art from all over the world. I'm building up a good international collection that I'm dividing between my house in Malibu and my apartment in New York.

More and more I've been drawing and painting; I do it several hours a day now when I'm at home. When I'm on the road, too. It's soothing for me to paint, and I just love seeing what comes out of my imagination. It's like therapy for me, and keeps my mind occupied with something positive when I'm not playing music. I get obsessed with painting just like I get obsessed with music and everything else that I care about. Like, I love good movies and so I try to watch a lot of them.

I don't read a lot of books, never have, never found the time for it. But I read all the magazines I can get my hands on and newspapers. That's where I get a lot of my information. Plus, I like to watch the CNN all-day news program on television. But I take my reading with a grain of salt; I just never have trusted many writers, because so many of them are so dishonest, especially journalists. Man, they will make up anything to get a good story. I think my distrust of writers started with my not liking most of the journalists I ran into, and especially those who used to write all those lies about me. Most of them are white. I like poets and some novelists. I used to love poetry, especially the black poets—The Last Poets, LeRoi Jones, Amiri Baraka—in the 1960s, because the shit the poets were saying and writing about was true, although I know a lot of people—black and white —didn't want to admit that it was true, then or now. But it was, and everybody who knows anything about this country and who is aware of truth knows that what they were writing was the truth.

I remember on one of the trips I was taking to Japan to play—I think it was in 1985—I got sick on the way in Anchorage, Alaska, because I had eaten all these sweets that I wasn't supposed to eat while we were in France. I'm a fiend when it comes to good pastry, and the French make the best as far as I'm concerned. We had just finished a concert in France and were flying to Japan, and I had brought all these goodies on the plane with me. I'm a diabetic and I know I shouldn't be doing this, but sometimes I can't help myself; I'm an obsessive-type person. We stopped off in Anchorage, and I was going into a sugar or insulin shock about the time we got there. The symptoms are low energy and nodding and falling asleep like a junkie. Jim Rose stuck me in a hospital there, because he's hip to my medical condition and he was watching me like a hawk. The Japan Airlines people wouldn't let me get back on board the plane until they had me together.

It was a scare, and so after this I started taking insulin shots every day. I've had a lot of problems since then with some of the immigration officials in certain countries thinking my insulin syringes are going to be used for shooting heroin or some other drug. Once I had to throw a fit at the airport in Rome, Italy, when the immigration people were giving me a hard time about my syringes and the medication I take for my various ailments. I started cussing everyone out. Diabetes is a very serious disease and it can kill you, so I have to be careful of what I eat. The older you get, the more serious the disease gets; your pancreas starts fucking up and you can get cancer. It cuts off circulation in your arms and legs and toes, and I've got poor circulation anyway, especially in my legs, which are skinnier than anything anybody can imagine anyway. I can remember going to hospitals, and the doctors would be trying to draw blood from my arms and legs. They couldn't find any veins, first, because I used to be a junkie and had collapsed some of them, and second, because my legs and arms are so skinny. They would be just sticking me everywhere trying to find a vein. One day, Jim Rose said, "Try his feet, see if you can get the blood out of there." And so they tried that and that's where they've been getting it mostly ever since.

Man, I've got scars all over my body, except on my face. My face is in good shape. Shit, I look in the mirror and say, "Miles, you're a handsome motherfucker!" Seriously, my face is in good shape, and I haven't had a face lift either. But I have scars everywhere else and all my friends who have known me for a while say that I like to show my scars off to them. Maybe I do. They are like medals to me, badges of honor, the history of my survival, the story of how I kept on getting up from bad shit, terrible adversity and just kept on getting up, doing the best that I could. I can see where I would be proud of my scars, because they show me that I didn't let this shit get me down, that you can win if you got the heart and tenacity and soul to keep on trying.

By 1985 Cicely and I were spending a lot of time out in Malibu, first at a cottage she had, and then in a house that I bought. The house was right on the ocean and we had our own private beach. The warm weather was better for my hip, plus, I got more rest while I was in California; it just wasn't as hectic as New York City. I got rid of the Blank brothers as my managers and stopped them from over-seeing my money. In New York, we now stayed at Cicely's four-teenth-floor apartment on Fifth Avenue off 79th Street, overlooking Central Park. Her apartment was nice, but I missed the house over on West 77th Street. Besides David Franklin, who was now my man-ager as well as Cicely's (he also handled Roberta Flack, Peabo Bry-son, and Richard Pryor, until they fell out), I kept Peter Shukat as my lawyer (he had been with me since 1975) and Steve Ratner as my personal accountant and business manager. Jim Rose also stayed on as my road manager.

But 1985 was the year that my relationship with Cicely started to go bad. It didn't happen suddenly, but was building up over a lot of little different things. There were even signs that our shit wasn't doing too well spiritually.

Cicely and I should never have gotten married in the first place, because I never felt that way about her you know, sexually attracted; I think we would have done much better if we had just stayed friends. But she was insistent on us getting married and Cicely's a very persistent and stubborn woman, who, most of the time, gets whatever she wants. What really bothered me about Cicely was how she wanted to control everything in my life, like who I saw, who my friends were, who would come over and all that. Another thing that bothered me a lot was the way she treated things I bought her. I used to buy her presents, bracelets and watches and rings, you know, nice jewelry and clothes and things. But I found out later that when I would buy her some expensive gift, a lot of the time she would take it back and just get the money and keep that. Then I found out a lot of other people were fed up with her shit also.

One day in 1985 a package came to our house in Malibu. The package was for Cicely and when she opened it up there was a bloody dagger in it. It made me and her gasp. It kind of scared me and I asked her what it meant. She didn't say nothing, just that she would take care of it. The package had a note in it, but she never let me read it or told me what it said. Even today it's a mystery to me. But whatever it was it didn't have a good meaning. After that happened, and because she never told me what the reason behind it was, I started to feel real funny around her.

Cicely was especially jealous of a woman taking her place in my life, but after a while she didn't have no place in my life, even though she turned down a lot of movie offers just to stay around me. Cicely's like two different women, one nice, the other one totally fucked up. For example, she used to bring her friends around anytime she wanted, but she didn't want my friends coming around. And she had some friends who I couldn't stand. One time we argued about one friend in particular, and I just slapped the shit out of her. She called the cops and went down into the basement and was hiding there. When the police came, they asked me were she was. I said, "She's around here somewhere. Look down in the basement." The cop looked in the basement and came back and said, "Miles, nobody's down there but a woman, and she won't talk to me. She won't say nothing."

So I said, "That's her, and she's doing the greatest acting job ever." Then the cop said he understood—she didn't look like she was hurt or nothing. I said, "Well, she ain't hurt bad; I just slapped her once."

The cop said, "Well, Miles, you know when we get these calls we have to investigate."

"Well, if she's beating my ass you gonna come with your guns ready, too?" I asked him.

They just laughed and left. Then I went down and told Cicely, "I told you to tell your friend not to call over here no more. Now if you don't tell him, I'm gonna tell him." She ran to the phone and called him up and told him, "Miles don't want me talking to you anymore." Before I knew it I had slapped her again. So she never did pull that kind of shit on me again. Things started to get *really* bad with Cicely over an incident with a woman, a white woman, who was just a friend of mine. I had met her one day in the elevator of the building where Cicely and I lived on Fifth Avenue and 79th Street. It was in 1984, and I was on crutches from my hip operation. We just started talking and became friends. That was it. I would say hello and stop to talk with her whenever I saw her. Gradually Cicely got jealous of her. Finally one day she jumped the woman in broad daylight and beat her up. The woman had her seven-year-old son with her. Cicely thought I was going with the woman; she had convinced herself I was. But I wasn't.

Sometime later, in 1986, right before a concert I was playing with B. B. King at the Beacon Theatre in New York, Cicely and I had an argument and she jumped on my back and pulled my hair weave right out of my head. That was the last straw. We continued to stay together and even go out after that, but now when I look back on everything, I knew that was the beginning of the end. The shit got so crazy that someone, and I believe it was Cicely, called the *National Enquirer* and told them that I was having an affair with this woman that Cicely had beat up. The *Enquirer* called up my friend, but she wouldn't talk to them. Cicely herself even tried to call up my friend, acting like a reporter from the *Enquirer.* Man, that shit got sick. After a while, Cicely had to go to Africa, first to make a film, and then because she was Chairperson of the United Nations Children's Fund for 1985–86 and she had to tour the drought-stricken areas over there. I bought her a Rolls-Royce automobile as a present when she returned. When they delivered it, she couldn't believe it. She thought someone was playing a joke on her.

Cicely has done movie and TV roles where she played an activist or something like that, a person who cared a lot about black people. Well, she ain't nothing like that. She loves to sit up with white people, loves to listen to their advice about everything and believes almost everything they tell her.

After all these things happened I just told her to leave me alone and do her own thing. We got together a couple of times after that, once with Sammy Davis, Jr., and his wife, Altovise, at one of Sammy's Las Vegas performances. As a matter of fact, I saw my first wife, Frances, at that performance. She was looking good as usual and when she came over to the table to say hello, it just put Cicely into one of her real deep funks. There was a lot of tension. Frances can pick up on that kind of stuff immediately so she just stayed a little while and left. I saw her the next night also, at a concert of Harry Belafonte's. Afterward me and Cicely went to the reception, and Frances was there because she's tight with the Belafontes. I told her that I had been calling Cicely "Frances" every time I spoke to her for the last month, kind of a Freudian slip. And it was true. I guess because I still cared a lot for Frances. But everybody there felt weird when I said that.

Me and Cicely were on our way out, so I guess I didn't really care what I said to her by this time because of all the grief she had caused me. Plus, when I look back over my life, Frances was the best wife I ever had and I made a mistake when I broke up with her. I know that now. I think her and Jackie Battle were the best women I had back in those crazy old days. But I didn't feel that way about Cicely, despite the fact that I admit that she helped save my life. But because she saved my life don't mean she has the right to control my life and that's where she went wrong.

One time in 1984 or '85 (I've forgotten exactly when it was), Cicely and I went to a party. Leontyne Price was there and she came up to me and Cicely and started talking to us. I hadn't seen Leontyne for quite a while, but I have always been one of her fans because in my opinion she is the greatest female singer ever, the greatest opera singer ever. She could hit anything with her voice. Leontyne's so good it's scary. Plus, she can play piano and sing and speak in all those languages. Man, I love her as an artist. I love the way she sings *Tosca*. I wore out her recording of that, wore out two sets. Now, *I* might not do *Tosca*, but I loved the way Leontyne did it. I used to wonder how she would have sounded if she had sung jazz. She should be an inspiration for every musician, black or white. I know she is to me.

Anyway, after we had been talking for a while at this party, she turned to Cicely and told her, "Girl, you got the prize, you got the prize, child. I've been after this motherfucker for years!" See, Leontyne's direct like that. Comes right out and says what's on her mind. I love that about her, because that's the way I am. So when Leontyne said that, Cicely just smiled, didn't know what to say. I don't think Cicely even got it, that Leontyne was talking about me being "the prize."

Darryl Jones left my band in 1985 after he had recorded that *Dream of the Blue Turtles* album with Sting. After that he made the movie *Bring on the Night* with Sting over in Paris and then he started making gigs with him and me. One day when we were touring Europe during the summer of '85, I asked Darryl what he was going to do when he had a gig with me and one with Sting on the same date. He said he didn't know. So I told him he'd better think about it because it was bound to happen. I could understand why Darryl was considering leaving, because Sting was going to be paying him a lot of money, much more than I could afford to pay him. I started thinking that this was like déjà vu, you know, the same type of things that I had done when *I* wanted a musician. Now it was being done to me. By the time we got to Tokyo in August 1985, John Scofield had already told me that this was to be his last tour with me, and now I'm thinking about Darryl leaving, too. I was walking to my hotel room in downtown Tokyo, dragging my headphones to my Walkman on the ground. Darryl saw me and said, "Yo, Chief [a lot of my musicians call me "Chief"], your headphones are dragging on the ground!"

I snatched up the headphones and turned around and told Darryl, "So fucking what? You're not with us anymore, so what does it mean to you? Go tell that shit to your new leader, Sting!" I was mad with Darryl for thinking about leaving me because I really loved the way he played, and I knew he was going to go with Sting; I could just feel it in my bones. I could see that what I said had hurt him, could see the pain in his face. I mean, Darryl had grown to be almost like a son to me, you know, because him and my nephew Vincent were tight. I was just hurt that he was going to be leaving me to go and play with Sting. I could understand that shit on a money level and I could understand it intellectually. But at that moment I couldn't get to it emotionally and so I just reacted out of pain. Later he came up to my room and we had a long talk and I understood where he was coming from. When he was about to leave, I got up and said, "Hey, Darryl, I understand, man. God bless you in everything that you do, man, because I love you and I love the way you play."

Before my relationship with Cicely fell completely apart, she gave me a big birthday party for my sixtieth birthday in May 1986. She had it on a yacht in Marina del Rey, California, and it was a surprise. I didn't know nothing about it until I got to the yacht and saw all of those people there: Quincy Jones; Eddie Murphy; Camille Cosby; Whoopi Goldberg; Herbie Hancock; Herb Alpert; Billy Dee Williams and his wife; Roscoe Lee Browne; Leonard Feather; Monte Kay; Roxie Roker; Lola Falana; Sammy Davis's wife, Altovise; the mayor of Los Angeles, Tom Bradley (who gave me a citation from the city); and Maxine Waters, a California politician who is originally from St. Louis. My manager, David Franklin, was there, too, and a whole lot of other people, including the Warner Bros. Records chairman, Mo Ostin. My brother and sister were there, and my daughter, Cheryl.

The nicest thing about that party was that Cicely gave me a painting of my mother, father, and grandfather done by this painter named Artis Lane. That really touched me and brought me closer to her for a while. That was a nice thing Cicely did by having that painting done, because I didn't have any pictures of my parents. I will always cherish and treasure what she did with that painting.

And, the party was all a surprise. *Jet* magazine even covered the whole thing in a four- or five-page spread with all kinds of pictures. It was a great party, and I really felt good being there and seeing everybody else there having fun. I think that surprise birthday party kept Cicely and me together for longer than we would have if she hadn't given the party.

I recorded my first album for Warner Bros. in 1986, called *Tutu*, after Bishop Desmond Tutu, the Nobel Peace Prize laureate. The song "Full Nelson" is named for Nelson Mandela. At first we were going to call the album *Perfect Way*, but Tommy LiPuma, my new producer at Warner's, didn't like that title, so they came up with *Tutu*, and I really liked that. At first I didn't care what they called it, but after I heard the name *Tutu* I said, yeah, that would work. That was the first album where I worked with Marcus Miller as much as I did. The album started with some music that George Duke, the piano player, sent to me. As it turned out, we didn't use George's music on the album, but Marcus heard it and wrote something off it. Then I told Marcus to write something else. He did, but I didn't like that, so it went back and forth like that for a while until we came up with something that we both liked.

When we recorded *Tutu* we didn't decide on any music in advance. The only thing we decided was what key a song was going to be in. Marcus wrote most of the music on *Tutu*, but I told him what I wanted, like an ensemble here and four bars there. With Marcus I don't have to do much because he knows what I like. He would just put down some tracks and I would come in and record over them. He and Tommy LiPuma would stay up all night getting the music on tape, and then I could come and put my trumpet voice over what they did. First, they programmed the drums on tape, the bass drum and then two or three other rhythms and then the keyboards.

Then Marcus brought in this guy named Jason Miles, who is a synthesizer programming genius. He started working with the music, and it kept happening like that. It just kept growing; it was a group effort. George Duke arranged a lot of music on *Tutu*. Then we brought in all the other musicians, like Adam Holzman on synthesizer, Steve Reid on percussion, Omar Hakim on drums and percussion, Bernard Wright on synthesizers, Paulinho da Costa on some percussion, Michael Urbaniak on electric violin, me on trumpet, and Marcus Miller on bass guitar and everything else.

I have found that taking my working band into the studio is too much trouble these days. The band might not feel good that day at the recording session, or at least some people in the band might not. So you've got to deal with that. And if one or two musicians don't feel good that day, then they throw everybody else off. Or, they might not feel like playing the style you want or need for the record you're doing and that might cause problems. Music to me is all about styles, and if somebody can't do what you ask for and need, then they look at you all funny and feel bad and insecure. You've got to teach them what you want them to do, show them right there in the studio in front of everybody else, and a lot of musicians can't take that kind of shit, so they get mad. That holds things up. Doing it the old way, recording like we used to, is just too much trouble and takes too much time. Some people say they miss that spontaneity and spark that comes out of recording with a band right there in the studio. Maybe that's true; I don't know. All I know is that the new recording technology makes it easier to do it the way we have been doing it. If a musician is really professional he will give you what you want in terms of performance in the studio by playing off and against the band that's already down on tape. I mean, the motherfucker *can* hear what is being played, can't he? And that's all that is important in music ensemble playing; hearing what everyone else is doing and playing off or against that.

It's a matter of style, and what you and your producers want to hear on record. Tommy LiPuma's a great producer for the kinds of things *he* wants to hear on a record. But I like raw shit, live, raunchy, get down, get back in the alley shit, and that isn't really what he likes or understands. Rather than get myself, the working band, and Tommy into all kinds of hassles by trying to bring my working band into the studio to record music that I might like, but Tommy doesn't, we do it this way, laying down tracks on tape, with me and Marcus and whoever we decide we need to do an album. I use mostly Marcus on all the instruments, because that motherfucker can play almost anything: guitar, bass, saxophone, piano, and then he does some of the synthesizer programming with Jason Miles. Marcus has such concentration in the studio, man, it's scary. That motherfucker's really one of the most focused people I have ever known. He don't miss nothing and he can work all day and night without losing focus. Makes everybody else work their asses off, too. And he's having a good time while he's working, laughing at your stories and jokes, keeping everybody loose. But he's getting the record done.

Tommy LiPuma's the same way. He's an Italian guy, loves to collect paintings. But give him some pasta and a great bottle of wine and he will work your ass off, too. He has great focus and concentration in a studio and he's a lot like Marcus in that he will be smiling and laughing and making you do the solo over a thousand fucking times. But you do it because you know it's best for the record and because they got such great personalities. You don't know how tired you are until the next day when you can't get your ass out of bed and then you be cussing them motherfuckers out.

I also like Marcus because he's just an unbelievably sweet guy. When Marcus was getting married, he called me up and asked what he should do because he said he was so nervous. I told him to drink some orange juice and do some push-ups and if that didn't calm him down, to do it all over again. Man, he laughed about that so hard he dropped the fucking phone. But he did it and he said it calmed him down. He's a funny guy, likes to laugh, so I'm always telling him funny stories when we're together because I like to hear and see him laugh. Marcus always brings out the funny guy in me. In the studio we make a great team, you know. Marcus is so hip and into the music that he even *walks* in tempo, ain't never out of tempo in whatever he does. So now I don't mind going into the studio so much because I know I'm going to be in there with people who know how to take care of business.

Prince wanted to put a song on *Tutu,* even wrote a song for it, but when we sent him the tape and he heard what was on there, he didn't think his tune fit. Prince has high musical standards, like me. So, he just pulled his song meant for the album until we can do something else at a later date. Prince also records for Warner Bros. and it was through people over there that I first found out that he loved my music and considered me one of his musical heroes. I was happy and honored that he looked at me in that way.

After my bass player Darryl Jones went on tour with Sting, I first got Angus Thomas and then Felton Crews to take his place. Mike Stern and then Robben Ford came in on guitar in place of John Scofield. Darryl would call me up from time to time whenever he was in town and finally, one day in October 1986, around the time I was doing the "Dick Cavett Show," he called me up in New York and told me that he wasn't playing with nobody. I asked him why he didn't come back and play with me, and so he did. Robben Ford didn't stay in the working band for too long. Marcus Miller sent me a tape of a guitarist named Joseph Foley McCreary, who calls himself Foley. He was from Cincinnati. I could hear right away that he was a motherfucker, just the kind of player I was looking for, and he was black. He was a little raw, but I figured we could work that out. We had also brought Marilyn Mazur into the band on percussion in August 1985. I had first run into her over in Denmark when I won the Sonning Award, and I did that recording with Palle Mikkelborg for that still-unreleased album, *Aura*. When she called me I added her, and I kept Steven Thornton in the band on percussion because he gave me that African sound that I liked. Going into the fall of 1986 the band consisted of Bob Berg on tenor saxophone, Darryl Jones back on bass, Robben Ford on guitar, Adam Holzman and Robert Irving on keyboards, Marilyn Mazur and Steve Thornton on percussion, Vince Wilburn on drums, and myself on trumpet.

With this band I did the Amnesty International concert in the summer of 1986 out at Giants Stadium, the Meadowlands in New Jersey. The day before, we had played the Playboy Jazz Festival out in Los Angeles and we had gone on stage at about eleven at night. We came into Newark early in the morning and no one was there to meet us. So we got in a limo and a van to take everyone to hotels. Then when it was time for us to play, we got over there to the Meadowlands and it had been raining all morning. Everything was wet. Man, that place was packed. Bill Graham was coordinating all the stage setups and shit. They had one of those revolving stages where one group is playing out front to the people, while another group is setting up on the other stage. This works in theory if everything is cool and it hasn't been raining. Every time they tried to set us up, the wind blew water from the roof of the stage down on our equipment. So Jim Rose and his crew really couldn't set up. I heard that Bill Graham was screaming at Jim to get set up until somebody showed him all the water coming off the roof. Then he understood.

This whole thing was like a madhouse, because everything was being broadcast live on television all over the world. And we didn't have no sound check or nothing. Somehow, everything went all right. I think Santana played with us and then we played about twenty minutes. People seemed to really like what we did.

After we played, all these real famous white rock stars were coming up to me to say hello. All the guys from U2, Bono, Sting, all the guys from the Police, Peter Gabriel, Ruben Blades. All kinds of people. Some of them really looked afraid to come up to me, and somebody told me that some of them were afraid because of my reputation for bluntness and liking to be left alone. I was feeling good and so I was happy to meet some of the musicians I had never met. It was a real nice time after all that rain and shit that had almost messed up everything.

Some other things happened that year. I did a "Great Performances" program for PBS, a ninety-minute show they televised across the country. They had TV crews follow me around and they filmed an entire concert at the New Orleans Jazz and Heritage Festival. They also did a lot of interviews. We were supposed to do a dance number that George Faison and I had worked on, but that didn't work out. I also wrote the musical score for a film called *Street Smart* that starred Christopher Reeve, the actor who played Superman, and the great black actor Morgan Freeman. I got the music together for that film in the last part of 1986 and the early part of 1987.

Another thing that happened in 1986 that I think is worth mentioning is the incident between me and Wynton Marsalis. It was in Vancouver, Canada, at a festival we were both playing. We were playing at this outdoor amphitheater that was jam-packed. Wynton was scheduled to play the next night. So here I was playing and getting off on what I was doing. All of a sudden I feel this presence coming up on me, this body movement, and I see that the crowd is kind of wanting to cheer or gasp or something. Then Wynton whispers in my ear—and I'm still trying to play—"They told me to come up here."

I was so mad at him for doing that shit like that, I just said, "Man, get the fuck off the stage." He looked a little shocked when I said it to him like that. After I said that, I said, "Man, what the fuck are you doing up here on stage? Get the fuck off the stage!" And then I stopped the band. Because we were playing some set pieces and when he came up like that I was trying to give the band some cues. He wouldn't have fit in. Wynton can't play the kind of shit we were playing. He's not into that kind of style and so we would have had to make adjustments to the way he was going to be playing.

When Wynton did that to me, that showed me he didn't have no respect for his elders. First of all, I'm old enough to be his father and he had already talked real bad about me in the papers and on television and in magazines and shit. He never apologized for the shit he had said about me. We ain't tight friends, like me and Dizzy and Max and some other guys. As close as me and Dizzy are, I wouldn't ever do that to him or him to me. We would ask each other in front. Wynton thinks that music is about blowing people away up on stage. But music isn't about competition, but about cooperation, doing shit together and fitting in. It's definitely not about competition, at least not to me. That kind of attitude has no place in music as far as I'm concerned.

Selfishness and no respect is why I didn't like Ornette Coleman trying to play the trumpet and violin like he did when he first came on the scene. I mean, he couldn't play either one of those instruments. That was an insult to people like me and Diz. I certainly wouldn't walk up on stage and try to play saxophone if I couldn't play.

Before, in the old days, all the great trumpet players like Fat Girl and Dizzy and all of us used to jam together all the time. Well, them days are gone, those times have changed. It ain't like it was with all of us back in the old days. Yeah, we used to try to cut one another, but we knew each other, too, and there was a lot of love going on between us. Even that time when Kenny Dorham came into the Cafe Bohemia and blew me away the first night and I got him the next. There was a lot of respect and love in that kind of competition.

But it's not like that with Wynton (at least I haven't seen that kind of respect out of him toward me) or with hardly any of the other younger musicians today. They all want to be stars right away. They all want to have what they call their own styles. But all these young guys are doing is playing somebody else's shit, copying all the runs and licks that other guys already laid down. There are a few young guys out there who are developing their own style. My alto player, Kenny Garrett, is one of them.

Another interesting experience I had in 1986 was that I did an episode of "Miami Vice," playing a pimp and a dope dealer. When I did that role, someone asked me how I felt acting and I told them, "You're acting all the time when you're black." And it's true. Black people are acting out roles every day in this country just to keep on getting by. If white people really knew what was on most black people's minds it would scare them to death. Blacks don't have the power to say these things, so they put on masks and do great acting jobs just to get through the fucking day.

Acting wasn't that hard. I knew how to play a pimp because I knew a little bit about that from the old days. Don Johnson and Phillip

Michael Thomas, the actors on the show, just told me, "Man, it's nothing, nothing but lies, Miles. Nothing but lies. So just think of it that way," and I did. Playing a pimp was easy because there's a little of that in every man.

I didn't like so much that I had to play a pimp, although I did it. I didn't like the idea of reinforcing some stereotypical view that a lot of people have of black men. I was mostly playing a businessman in that part, a male sort of madame. So in my mind I wasn't playing a pimp, but a kind of businessman and so that's the way I played the role. Cicely even told me that she liked what I did, that she thought I was good in it and that made me feel real good, because I respect her judgment as an actress and as an artist.

I also did a Honda commercial, and that one commercial got me more recognition than anything else I have ever done. After I did "Miami Vice" and that Honda commercial, people who hadn't ever heard of me started speaking to me on the streets, black and white and Puerto Rican and Asian kids, people who didn't even know what I did, started speaking to me after I did those things. Man, now ain't that a bitch. After you make all this music, please all these people with your playing, and are known all over the world, you find out that all it takes is one commercial to put you over the top in people's minds. All you've got to do in this country today is just be on television and you're more known and respected than anyone who paints a great painting or creates great music or writes a great book or is a great dancer. People were already calling me "Mr. Tyson," or saying, "I know who you are. You're that guy who's married to Cicely Tyson!" And they would be sincere when they said that. It taught me that a bad, untalented person who is on television or in the movies can be more recognized and respected than a genius who doesn't appear on the screen.

I made the usual round of festivals all over the United States and Europe throughout the rest of 1986. *Tutu* sold well and I was pleased about that. And a lot of people liked the album, even some of the critics and old fans who had been getting on my case for years. I went into 1987 feeling good, although I had to find a replacement for Garth Webber on guitar (Robben Ford had quit earlier because he was getting married and wanted to make his own record; he had recommended Garth Webber because he was such a nice guy and would play his ass off). Mino Cinelu, who had left the band, wanted to come back on percussion and I decided to bring him back again in place of Steve Thornton. Bob Berg left the band also, because he didn't like the fact that I had brought in a saxophonist named Gary Thomas to share duties with him. But it was good that he left because I got Kenny Garrett to come in on alto saxophone, soprano sax, and flute. Kenny had been playing with Art Blakey before he joined me and I could hear right away that he was a great young player.

All I needed now, in 1987, was a guitar player who could play what I wanted; I was sure that I was going to find him or her somewhere. And I still wasn't pleased with the way my nephew Vincent was playing on the drums, because he was always dropping the time, and if there's anything I can't stand in a drummer it's to drop the time. I was trying to let him know how I felt about it by telling him every night when he did it. I know he was trying hard and doing the best that he could, but I didn't want to hear no excuses; all I wanted from him was not do it. His being my nephew made the situation particularly hard for me, because I felt so close to him, felt toward him like he was my own son. I had known him all of his life and had given him his first set of drums, and I really loved him. So it was a difficult situation, one that I was hoping would just work itself out for the good of everybody.

t he year 1987 started off with Cicely taking me down to Washington to a party she was invited to attend by President Reagan and his wife, Nancy. They were giving a Lifetime Achievement Award to Ray Charles and some other prominent people, with an awards show at the Kennedy Center. Cicely and I went down to help Ray celebrate. Ray's been a friend for a long time, and I just love his music. That's the only reason I went; I have never liked that kind of political shit.

First we had dinner at the White House with the President and the Secretary of State, George Shultz. When I met the President I wished him good luck in trying to do what he was doing, and he said, "Thanks, Miles, because I'm going to need it." He's a nice enough guy when you meet him in person. I guess he was doing the best he could. He's a politician, man, who happens to lean to the right. Others lean to the left. Most of them politicians are stealing the country blind. It don't matter whether they are Republicans or Democrats; they are all in it for what they can take. The politicians don't care anymore about the American people. All they think about is how they're going to get rich just like everybody else who is greedy.

Reagan was nice to us, respectful and everything. But Nancy is the one who has the charm between those two. She seemed like a warm person. She greeted me warmly and I kissed her hand. She liked that. Then we met Vice President Bush and his wife and I didn't kiss her hand. When Cicely asked me why I didn't kiss Barbara Bush's hand, I told her that I thought she was George's mother. Cicely looked at me like she thought I was crazy. But I don't know those people, don't keep up with them, and they don't know me either. Cicely keeps up with that kind of shit and it's important to her, but not me. Hell, here these people are giving a lifetime award to Ray Charles, and most of them didn't even know who he was.

On the way to the dinner at the White House I rode in a limousine with Willie Mays. Me and Willie and Cicely and Fred Astaire's widow and Fred MacMurray and his wife, I think. When we got into the car, one of them white women said, "Miles, the limo driver says he likes the way you sing and he's got all your records." Right away I was mad, so I looked at Cicely and say under my breath, "Cicely, why you bring me down here to get insulted like this?" She didn't say nothing and just looked straight ahead with that plastic grin on her face.

Billy Dee Williams was also in the car with us, so Billy, Willie, and me started having some fun by talking that black shit that black men talk, you know. But this was embarrassing Cicely. Fred MacMurray's sitting in the front of the limo and he's real sick, almost can't walk. The two white women are in the back with us, right? So one of them turns to me and says, "Miles, I know your mammy's proud of you coming down to meet the President."

Everything in the car got quiet, real quiet. I know everybody was thinking to themselves, of all the motherfuckers to say this to, why did she say this to Miles? They were just waiting for me to go off on this old-ass broad.

I turned to her and said, "Listen, my mother ain't no motherfucking mammy, you hear what I'm telling you! That word is out of style and people don't use it anymore. My mother was more elegant and proper than you could ever be, and my father was a doctor. So don't you ever say anything like that to a black person anymore, you hear what I'm saying to you?" When I was telling her this, I never did raise my voice one time. But she knew what I was saying because I was looking her in her fucking eyes and if looks could have killed she would have been dead. She got the message and apologized. After that I was silent.

We got to the dinner given by the Secretary of State, and I'm at the table with former Vice President Mondale's wife, Joan, Jerry Lewis, some antique dealer, and I think it was David Brinkley's wife, who was a real nice, hip, sweet woman who knew what was happening. I'm dressed in the Japanese designer Kohshin Satoh's hip, long black waistcoat with tails. It had this red snake on the back trimmed in white sequins. I also had on two vests made by Kohshin, one red and the other white broadcloth, and I had silver chains crossing this, and some shiny black leather pants. When I went to the toilet to pee, everybody else is lined up with all the same old shit on, so they couldn't stand me. But one guy told me that he loved my outfit and asked "Who did it for you?" I told him, and he walked away pleased, but the rest of them uptight white men were madder than hell.

There were only about ten black people in the whole place, including the ones I mentioned before and Quincy Jones. I think Clarence Avon and his wife were there. And Lena Horne was there, too. Maybe there were twenty black people there.

At the table where I was sitting, a politician's wife said some silly shit about jazz, like "Are we supporting this art form just because it's from here in this country, and is it art in its truest form, or are we just being blasé and ignoring jazz because it comes from here and not from Europe, and it comes from black people?"

This came from out of the blue. I don't like questions like that because they're just questions from someone who's trying to sound intelligent, when in fact they don't give a damn about it. I looked at her and said, "What is it? Jazz time or something? Why you ask me some shit like that?"

So she said, "Well, you're a jazz musician, aren't you?"

So I said, "I'm a musician, that's all."

"Well, then, you're a musician, you play music . . ."

"Do you *really* want to know why jazz music isn't given the credit in this country?"

She said, "Yes, I do."

"Jazz is ignored here because the white man likes to win everything. White people like to see other white people win just like you do and they can't win when it comes to jazz and the blues because black people created this. And so when we play in Europe, white people over there appreciate us because they know who did what and they will admit it. But most white Americans won't."

She looked at me and turned all red and shit, then she said, "Well, what have you done that's so important in your life? Why are you here?"

Now, I just hate shit like this coming from someone who is ignorant, but who wants to be hip and has forced you into a situation where you're talking to them in this manner. She brought this on herself. So then I said, "Well, I've changed music five or six times, so I guess that's what I've done and I guess I don't believe in playing just white compositions." I looked at her real cold and said, "Now, tell me what have you done of any importance other than be white, and that ain't important to me, so tell me what your claim to fame is?"

She started to twitch and everything around her mouth. She couldn't even talk she was so mad. There was a silence so thick you could cut it with a knife. Here this woman was supposedly from the hippest echelons of society talking like a fool. Man, it was depressing.

Ray Charles was up there sitting with the President, and the President was looking around to see how to act. I felt sorry for him. Reagan just looked embarrassed.

That was some of the sorriest shit I've ever been around. That was a hell of a feeling I had down there in Washington, feeling embarrassed because those white people down there who are running the country don't understand nothing about black people and don't want to know! It was sickening to be put in a position where you've got to teach dumbass white people who really don't want to know in the first place, but feel obligated to ask them silly questions. Why should some motherfucker make me feel bad because of their ignorance? They can go to a store and buy a record of people they're honoring and inviting down. They could read a book and learn something. But that's too much like giving us the respect we deserve. They stay stupid and make me and a lot of other black people feel bad because of their ignorance. And the President sitting up there and don't know what to say. Man, they should have written down something hip for him to say, but they ain't got nobody hip nowhere around him. Just a bunch of sorry motherfuckers with plastic smiles, acting all proper and shit.

When we left, I told Cicely, "Don't you ever as long as you fucking live bring me to no more of this shit, make me feel sad for white folks. I'd rather have my heart fail doing some other shit than I would have it fail doing some sorry shit like this. Let me run my Ferrari into a bus or something." She didn't say nothing. But, man, I'll never forget that image of her crying when Ray was listening to all them blind and deaf kids from the Ray Charles School in Florida singing, and the white people looking at Cicely trying to make up their minds if they should cry or fake it or something. After I saw that, I whis-pered to Cicely, "Let's get out of here as soon as this shit is over. You can handle this kind of shit, I can't." After this, I knew it was over between us and didn't want to have anything to do with her. So from that time on we basically lived apart.

Later in 1987 I broke off with my manager David Franklin because of the way he was handling things. Jim Rose and I had already fallen out when I punched him out because of a dispute over money that started with David. So he left and I had to get a new road manager in 1987, Gordon Meltzer.

What happened with Jim Rose was this. After our gigs Jim always collects the money, so on this one particular gig (in late 1986 or early 1987, in Washington), I asked him for it. He told me that he had given it to David Franklin's assistant down in Atlanta. I told Jim, "Fuck them, it's my money, so give it to me." I said this because some funny things were happening with my money lately and I wanted to see it myself. He was resisting giving me the money so I hit him upside the head and just took it. He quit working for me after that. I hated that it had come to that between me and Jim, because Jim had been with me through thick and thin. Anyway, I had bought an apartment in New York on Central Park South, and a lot of other things, and I was really starting to pay attention to how my money was being handled.

So eventually I fired David and made Peter Shukat my manager as well as my lawyer. I got into the problem that a lot of people who make a lot of money get into sometimes: you find yourself depending on other people to handle your money. And all this was happening at the time that I was making the final break with Cicely.

When I got Cicely and David Franklin out of my life, I felt a whole lot better. Marcus Miller and I had already started working on the music for the film *Siesta,* a film that was set in Spain and starred Ellen Barkin and Jodie Foster. The music was to be a little like what Gil Evans and I had done on *Sketches of Spain.* So I asked Marcus to try to work up some music with some of that feeling. In the mean-time, *Tutu* won a Grammy Award in 1987, and that made me feel good. We did our usual gigs at festivals and concerts all over the United States, Europe, South America, and the Far East—Japan and now China. We were also playing concerts now in Australia and New Zealand.

I think one of the most memorable things that happened to me during that year at a concert (besides when my band played well) was when I went to Oslo, Norway, in July. We flew into Oslo, and when we got off the plane, there was a swarm of reporters waiting for me. We were walking across the tarmac toward the airport when all of a sudden this guy came up and said, "Excuse me, Mr. Davis, but we have a car waiting for you over here. You don't have to go through customs." I looked over to where he was pointing and there was this long-ass white limo sitting there, one of the longest I have ever seen. I got in the car and we drove right off the tarmac and went into town. I didn't even have to bother going through customs. This kind of treatment in Norway is done only for visiting heads of state, presidents, prime ministers, kings and queens, and so forth. The producer of the festival told me this. Then he added, "And it's done for Miles Davis." Man, that made my day. I mean, how could I help but play my ass off that night?

All over Europe I'm treated that way—like royalty. You can't help playing better when people treat you that way. Same thing in Brazil, Japan, China, Australia, New Zealand. The only place where I'm not given the respect I get everywhere else is in the United States. And the reason why this is is because I'm black and I don't compromise, and white people—especially white men—don't like this in a black person, especially a black man.

One of the most painful things I had to do in 1987 was let my nephew Vincent go. I had known for a long time that I was going to have to let Vincent go because he kept dropping the time. I would show him shit but he just wouldn't do it. I'd give him a tape to listen to but he wouldn't even do that. It hurt me to tell him that because I really love him, but I had to do it for the music. So after I told him, I waited a few days and then I called his mother, my sister, Dorothy, and told her. I told her that Vincent wasn't in the band anymore and asked if he had told her. She said, "Naw, he didn't tell me." Then I told Dorothy I was coming to play in Chicago. She said, "Well, Miles, you could at least let him play here because of all his friends; it's going to be embarrassing for him."

"Dorothy, music don't have friends like that. I've been telling Vincent what to do for years and he won't do it, so I got to let him go. I'm sorry."

Then Dorothy's husband, Vincent's father and my good friend for years, Vincent Sr., got on the phone and asked me to give him another chance. I said, "No, I can't." After Vincent got off the phone I asked Dorothy if she was coming to my concert and she said she didn't think so, because she would probably stay home with Vincent. So I said, "Well, fuck you, Dorothy!"

She said, "Well, hang up the phone; I didn't call you, you called me!"

So I did. That's the kind of shit that goes on between a brother and sister who love each other. It's emotional. Plus it involved her only son. I knew where she was coming from. So I didn't mind when none of them showed up at the concert, although it did hurt me a little.

I let him go in early March and picked up a great drummer from Washington, D.C., named Ricky Wellman. I had heard a record that he did with a group called Chuck Brown and the Soul Searchers, so I had Mike Warren, my personal secretary (who is also from D.C.), call him and tell him I was interested in hiring him. He said he was interested, so I sent him a tape and told him to learn it, and we got together. Ricky had been playing what they call go-go music for a long time. But he had that thing that I wanted in my band.

The band I had in 1987 was a motherfucker, man. I loved the way they were playing. People all over loved this band. See, all this interweaving stuff was up in what they played, you know, Ricky playing off Mino Cinelu, and Darryl Jones was up under that shit and giving foundation, and Adam Holzman and Robert Irving doing their thing on the synthesizer, and me and Kenny Garrett (sometimes Gary Thomas on tenor sax) weaving our voices through all of that, and Foley, who was my new guitar player, playing that funky blues-rock-funk, almost Jimi Hendrix–like music he plays. They were great and I truly had finally found the guitar player that I had been looking for. Everybody in that band could dialogue with each other from the beginning and that was good. My band was right and my health was good and so was everything else in my life.

In 1987 I was really getting into the music of Prince and the music of Cameo and Larry Blackmon, and the Caribbean group called Kassav. I love the things they're doing. But I really love Prince, and after I heard him, I wanted to play with him sometime. Prince is from the school of James Brown, and I love James Brown because of all the great rhythms he plays. Prince reminds me of him and Cameo reminds me of Sly Stone. But Prince got some Marvin Gaye and Jimi Hendrix and Sly in him, also, even Little Richard. He's a mixture of all those guys and Duke Ellington. He reminds me, in a way, of Charlie Chaplin, he and Michael Jackson, who I also love as a performer. Prince does so many things, it's almost like he can do it all;

write and sing and produce and play music, act in films, produce and direct them, and both him and Michael can really dance.

They both are motherfuckers, but I like Prince a little better as an all-around musical force. Plus he plays his ass off as well as sings and writes. He's got that church thing up in what he does. He plays guitar and piano and plays them very well. But it's the church thing that I hear in his music that makes him special, and that organ thing. It's a black thing and not a white thing. Prince *is* like the church to gay guys. He's the music of the people who go out after ten or eleven at night. He comes in on the beat and plays on top of the beat. I think when Prince makes love he hears drums instead of Ravel. So he's not a white guy. His music is new, is rooted, reflects and comes out of 1988 and '89 and '90. For me, he can be the new Duke Ellington of our time if he just keeps at it.

When Prince asked me to come to Minneapolis to bring in the new year of 1988 and maybe we could play a song or two together, I went. In order to become a great musician the musician has to have the ability to stretch and Prince can certainly stretch. Me and Foley went out to Minneapolis. Man, Prince has got a hell of a complex out there. Record and movie equipment, plus he had an apartment for me to stay in. The whole thing seems like it's about half a block. He's got sound stages and everything. Prince put on a concert to aid the homeless of Minneapolis and charged people $200 per person to get in. The concert was held in his new Paisley Park Studios. The place was packed. At midnight, Prince sang "Auld Lang Syne" and asked me to come up and play something with the band and I did, and they taped it.

Prince is very nice, a shy kind of person, a little genius, too. He knows what he can and cannot do in music and in everything else. He gets over with everyone because he fulfills everyone's illusions. He's got that raunchy thing, almost like a pimp and a bitch all wrapped up in one image, that transvestite thing. But when he's singing that funky X-rated shit that he does about sex and women, he's doing it in a high-pitched voice, in almost a girl's voice. If I said "Fuck you" to somebody they would be ready to call the police. But if Prince says it in that girl-like voice that he uses, then everyone says it's cute. And he isn't out in the public eye all the time; he's a mystery to a lot of people. Me and Michael Jackson are the same way. But he's really like his name, man, a prince of a person when you get to know him.

But he shocked me when he said he wanted to do an entire album with me. He also wants our two groups to tour together. That would be very interesting. I don't know when or if it will happen, but it certainly is an interesting idea for a tour.

Prince came to my sixty-second birthday party held at a restaurant in New York. All the people from Cameo came, Hugh Masekela, George Wein, Nick Ashford and Valerie Simpson, Marcus Miller, Jasmine Guy, and the guys in my band who were in town; Peter, my lawyer and manger; Gordon, my road manager; and Michael, my valet. There were about thirty people there for a sit-down dinner. We all had a very nice time.

Nineteen eighty-eight was a very good year for me, with the exception that Gil Evans, who was probably my best and oldest friend, died of peritonitis in March. I knew Gil was sick, because at the end he could hardly see or hear. I also knew he had gone down to Mexico to see if he could find someoné to help cure his illness. But Gil knew he was going to die and so did I. We just never talked about it. As a matter of fact, I called his wife, Anita, the day before he died and asked her, "Where the fuck is Gil?" She told me he was in Mexico, then the next day she called and said that her son, who was down there with him, had called and said that Gil was doing this and that. The day after this she called and said that Gil was dead. Man, that just left a hole in me.

But a week after he died, I was talking to him and we had a conversation that went something like this. I was in my apartment in New York, sitting on my bed looking at the picture I have of him on the table across from my bed, by the window. The lights were dancing in through my window. All of a sudden a question came into my head for Gil and I asked him, "Gil, why did you die like you did, you know, down in Mexico?" And then he said, "That's the only way I could do it, Miles. I had to go down to Mexico to do it." I knew it was him because I could tell his voice anywhere. It was his spirit coming to talk to me.

Gil was real important to me as a friend and as a musician, because our approach to music was the same. He liked all styles, like I do, from ethnic music to tribal vamps. But we used to talk about doing things for years and only just about two months before he died, he called me up and said he was ready to do a project that we had talked about doing some twenty years ago. I think it was something he wanted to do from *Tosca*. I didn't want to do nothing like that now, but that's the way he was. Gil was my best friend, but he never was together in terms of being organized, and he would take so long to do things. He should have lived someplace other than this country. If he had, he would have been recognized as the national treasure that he was and been subsidized by the government, or something like the National Endowment for the Arts. He should have lived in a place like Copenhagen where he would have been appreciated. He still had—somewhere—about five or six songs I wrote that he was going to write arrangements to. To me Gil is not dead.

While he was here he never had the money he needed to do what he wanted to do. Plus, he had to support his house and his son, who was named after me.

I will miss Gil, but not in the same way other people miss people. So many people have died that I was close to that I guess I just don't have those kinds of feelings anymore. Hell, right before Gil died, James Baldwin died and so every time I'm in southern France I'm always thinking about going by to see Jimmy. But then I realize that he's dead. No, I won't be thinking about Gil being dead, like I won't be thinking about Jimmy being dead, because my head doesn't work that way. I'll miss them, but Gil is still in my head, like Jimmy is, like Trane and Bud and Monk and Bird and Mingus and Red and Paul and Wynton, and all them other great motherfuckers, like Philly Joe, who are no longer here. All my best friends are dead. But I can hear them, I can put myself into their heads, into Gil's head.

Man, Gil was something. One time when Cicely was accusing me of this and that, of going out with all kinds of women, I told Gil. He wrote something down on a piece of paper and gave it to me and said, "Give her this." I did and she stopped fucking with me like she had been. You know what he wrote on the paper? "You might love me, but you don't own me. And I might love you, but I don't own you." That's the kind of friend Gil was, someone I could go to who really understood and loved me for what I am.

Siesta came out in 1988. The movie came and went in the bat of an eye; it was gone from the theaters before it even got there. Almost the same thing happened with the other film that I wrote the music for, *Street Smart,* only it stayed around a little longer than *Siesta* and got very good reviews; the critics even liked my music. But they trashed *Siesta,* although everyone liked the music that Marcus and I did.

Another wonderful thing that happened to me in 1988 was that on November 13 at the Alhambra Palace in Granada, Spain, I was knighted and inducted into The Knights of Malta—or to use their formal name, The Knights of the Grand Cross in and for the Sovereign Military Hospitaler Order of St. John of Jerusalem of Rhodes and of Malta. I was inducted along with three Africans and a doctor from Portugal. I have to admit that I don't know what all those words in the order's name actually mean, but I'm told that as a member I can get into thirty or forty countries without a visa. I was also told that I was chosen for this honor because I have class, because I'm a genius. The only thing they asked of me is not to be prejudiced against any person and to continue to do what I do, which is contributing to the only worldwide cultural contribution to come out of America—jazz, or as I prefer to call it, black music.

I was honored by the award, but on the day of the ceremony, I was so sick I could hardly make it there. I had what used to be called "walking pneumonia," or bronchial pneumonia. Man, that shit floored me for a couple of months, forced me to cancel my entire winter tour in early 1989, and that alone cost me over a million dollars. I was in the hospital in Santa Monica, California, for three weeks. I had tubes up my nose and in my arms, needles everywhere. Anyone who came into my room had to wear a mask because there was a danger I could be infected by germs brought in by visitors or even by doctors or nurses. I was pretty sick all right, but I didn't have AIDS like that bullshit gossip rag *The Star* said I did. Man, that was a terrible thing that paper did to me. It could have ruined my career and fucked up my life. That story made me madder than a motherfucker when I found out about it. It wasn't true, of course, but a lot of people didn't know that, and they believed the story.

After I got out of the hospital in March my sister, Dorothy, my brother, Vernon, and my nephew, Vince, who used to play drums in my band, all came to my house in Malibu and took care of me. Dorothy cooked for me and helped me get back on my feet. My girlfriend was there, too, and we rode horses and took long walks. Pretty soon the walking pneumonia walked on out of me and I was well enough to go back on tour, good as new.

Not too long after, on June 8 in a ceremony at The Metropolitan Museum of Art in New York City, I received the 1989 New York State Governor's Arts Award, presented by Governor Mario Cuomo. I think eleven other people and organizations received awards, too, in that ceremony. I was very proud to be honored again.

Around the same time my third Warners album, *Amandla,* came out. The reviews were good and so were the sales. And Columbia announced that it was releasing *Aura* in September 1989. I made that album back in 1985 and since then I've moved on elsewhere musically. Something new happens in music almost every day, it seems. But *Aura* is a good album, and I'm looking forward to seeing what kind of response it gets, especially after four years.

Today my mind is concentrating and my body's like an antenna. It helps me with my painting, too, which I'm doing more and more of these days. I paint about five or six hours a day, practice a couple of hours, and write music a lot, too. I've really gotten into painting and I'm starting to have a lot of one-man shows. I had a couple in New York in 1987, and I had several all over the world in 1988: I had a few in Germany, one in Madrid, Spain, and a couple in Japan. And people are buying paintings of mine that are selling for as much as $15,000. The show in Madrid sold out and the ones in Japan and Germany almost sold out.

Painting helps me with my music, too. I'm waiting for Columbia to put out that record I made in Denmark of Palle Mikkelborg's music, *Aura*. I think it's a masterpiece, I really do. And I'm writing stuff for the band that we don't record. I have a guy out in California by the name of John Bigham who is just a great musical writer. He's a young black guy, around twenty-three, and he writes beautiful, funky music. He's a guitarist. He writes off a computer, and when he starts trying to explain his shit to me, he loses me talking all them technical computer terms. But he don't know how to finish nothing. So I told him, "John, don't worry about it; send it to me and I'll finish it." So he does. He don't know about orchestration. He just hears sounds that are unbelievable. He keeps telling me that he wants to learn all that kind of stuff, all about orchestration and so on, but I tell him not to worry about that because *I* know about that. I'm afraid that if he does learn it, it will fuck with his natural gift. Because that's what happens sometimes, you know. A guy like Jimi Hendrix or Sly or Prince might not do what they have done if they had known all the rest of that technical stuff because it might have gotten in their way, and they might have done something else had they known all that other stuff.

As far as where my music is going, I'm always trying to hear something new. One day I asked Prince, "Where's the bass line in that composition?"

He said, "Miles, I don't write one, and if you ever hear one I'm gonna fire the bass player because a bass line gets in my way." He told me he wouldn't tell that to nobody else, but he knew that I understood that because he had heard that same kind of concept in some of my music. Now when I get musical ideas, I take them right away to the synthesizer. I write down musical figures on anything I can get my hands on when I hear them. I see myself still growing as an artist and that's the way I always want it; I always want to grow.

I had to drop Darryl Jones from my band on bass in 1988. He started getting dramatic, too show biz for my band. He always had to be fixing something, breaking the strings on his bass so he could stand up there and pose, looking like something's going to happen. He was a dramatic motherfucker, especially after he came out of Sting's band, that rock and roll big arena thing, which is all show business. I really loved Darryl; he's a very nice, hip cat. But he wasn't playing what I wanted. I got a guy named Benjamin Rietveld from Hawaii to take Darryl's place. Mino Cinelu also left the band to go with Sting's new band. At first I replaced him with a percussionist named Rudy Bird, and then Marilyn Mazur came back and I let Rudy go. Now my regular percussionist is Munyungo Jackson. The other new face in the band is Kei Akagi on keyboards. Kenny Garrett is still on saxophones, Ricky Wellman on drums, Adam Holzman on keyboards, and Foley on lead bass.

I'm trying to keep my artistic juices flowing. I would like to write a play someday, maybe a musical. I have even been experimenting with some rap songs, because I think there's some heavy rhythms up in that music. I heard that Max Roach said that he thought that the next Charlie Parker might come from out of rap melodies and rhythms. Sometimes you can't get those rhythms out of your head. I was listening a lot to the music of Kassav, that West Indian group that plays a music called "Zouk." They're a great group and I think they have influenced some of the music on *Amandla*, which means "freedom" in Zulu, the South African language.

About the only downer for me in 1988 besides that hospitalization for pneumonia that I mentioned earlier was the divorce from Cicely. We said when we got married that if we broke up we wouldn't do this kind of thing to each other, that we each had our own money going in and that we would keep our own separate careers. But she broke her word about that. She didn't have to sic those lawyers on me like she did, trying to serve me divorce papers everywhere I went. It was a drag trying to duck them until I got myself together. The whole thing could have been settled more amicably. But all of that is over now because the property settlement was signed in 1988 and the divorce came through in 1989, and I'm very happy about that. Now I can get on with other women in my life.

I have met another woman whom I really feel comfortable with. She's a lot younger than me, over twenty years younger. We don't go out that often because I don't want her subjected to all the bullshit that comes to women who have gone out with me. I don't want to mention her name because I want our relationship to stay out of the public eye. But she's a very nice, loving woman who loves me for myself. We have a good time together now, although she knows she doesn't own me and I can see other women if I want to. I also met a nice woman in Israel a couple of years ago when I played there. She's a sculptor and is very talented. We see each other sometimes in the United States. She's also a very nice person, although I don't know her as well as the woman I know in New York who is my main interest.

When I hear jazz musicians today playing all those same licks we used to play so long ago, I feel sad for them. I mean, it's like going to bed with a real old person who even smells real old. Now, I'm not putting down old people because I'm getting older myself. But I got to be honest, and that's what it reminds me of. Most people my age like old, stuffy furniture. I like the new Memphis style of sleek high-tech stuff, a lot of it coming from Italy. Bold colors and long, sleek, spare lines. I don't like a lot of clutter or a lot of furniture either. I like contemporary stuff. I have to always be on the cutting edge of things because that's just the way I am and have always been.

I love challenges and new things; they reenergize me. But music has always been healing for me, and spiritual. When I'm playing well and my band is too, then I'm most of the time in a good mood, if my health is good also. I'm still learning every day. I learn things from Prince and Cameo. For example, I like the way Cameo does their live shows. The live performances start slow, but you have to watch the middle of their concerts because that's where their shit starts picking up unbelievable speed and just flies on out from there. I learned when I was fifteen that a show, a live show, has to have an opening, a middle, and an ending. If you know that, your shows will sound like the highlights of an average show all the way through. You will have a 10 for the beginning, a 10 for the middle, and a 10 for the ending, with different mood swings, of course, and you can't beat that with a stick.

Seeing the way Cameo featured the other musicians first helped me to do the same thing in my shows. We open up and then I play, and then the band plays, and then I play again. Then Benny plays on bass and then Foley plays on guitar, which takes the feeling to another place because of his funk-blues-rock-edged tone. Then after we run through the first couple of tunes, we play "Human Nature," which is a change of pace. It's an ending, sort of, to the first set's movement. But we make the song into something else. And then from there on it's up and out, but with a groove. It don't start until Benny and the rest of the band—especially Foley—play, because I really play after that. When Darryl Jones was in the band and playing real hip stuff, he and I used to play off each other, and sometimes me and Benny. But mostly Benny handles the anchor stuff, and he's really a motherfucker at that. (He's going to be a great bass player. He almost already is.) Then everyone might take turns playing solos after that.

Billy Eckstine told me and a singer a long time ago to walk into the applause when people like what you're doing. He was saying this to the singer: "Don't wait until it dies down." I do that now when they're applauding, just walk into the applause. I start another number while the people are still applauding. Even if you get a bad start on that number, they can't hear it because they're applauding. So you go right into it. That's the way we play live concerts, and it works the way we set it up. People all over the world like it and that's the barometer of what you're doing, not the critics; the people. They don't have no hidden agenda or hidden motives. They paid their money to see you, and if they don't like what you are doing, they're going to let you know, and quick.

a lot of people ask me where music is going today. I think it's going in short phrases. If you listen, anybody with an ear can hear that. Music is always changing. It changes because of the times and the technology that's available, the material that things are made of, like plastic cars instead of steel. So when you hear an accident today it sounds different, not all the metal colliding like it was in the forties and fifties. Musicians pick up sounds and incorporate that into their playing, so the music that they make will be different. New instruments like synthesizers and all them other things people play make everything different. Instruments used to be wood, then it was metal, and now it's hard plastic. I don't know what it's going to be in the future but I know it's going to be something else. The worst musicians don't *hear* the music today, so they can't play it. Only when I started *hearing* the upper register did I play there. I could only play in the middle to lower registers before because that's all I heard. It's the same thing with old musicians trying to play the music today. I was like them before Tony and Herbie and Ron and Wayne came into my band. They made me hear differently and I'm grateful to them for that.

I think Prince's music is pointing toward the future, that and a lot of what they're doing in Africa and the Caribbean. People like Fela from Nigeria and Kassav from the West Indies. A lot of the white musicians and bands are taking a lot from them, like Talking Heads,

Sting, Madonna, and Paul Simon. A lot of good music is also coming out of Brazil, too. But a lot of that music is happening around Paris, because that's where a lot of African and West Indian musicians are going to play, especially the ones that speak French. The English-speaking ones go to London. Someone told me recently that Prince was thinking about moving some of his operations to a place outside of Paris so he could soak up a lot of what's happening there. That's why I say he's one of the main musicians today who are pointing the way to the future. He understands that the sound has to go international; it's already there.

One of the reasons I like playing with a lot of young musicians today is because I find that a lot of old jazz musicians are lazy motherfuckers, resisting change and holding on to the old ways because they are too lazy to try something different. They listen to the critics, who tell them to stay where they are because that's what *they* like. The critics are lazy, too. They don't want to try to understand music that's different. The old musicians stay where they are and become like museum pieces under glass, safe, easy to understand, playing that tired old shit over and over again. Then they run around talking about electronic instruments and electronic musical voicing fucking up the music and the tradition. Well, I'm not like that and neither was Bird or Trane or Sonny Rollins or Duke or anybody who wanted to keep on creating. Bebop was about change, about evolution. It wasn't about standing still and becoming safe. If anybody wants to keep creating they have to be about change. Living is an adventure and a challenge. When people come up to me and ask me to play something like "My Funny Valentine," some old thing that I might have done when they were fucking this special girl and the music might have made them both feel good, I can understand that. But I tell them to go buy the record. *I'm* not there in that place any longer and I have to live for what is best for me and not what's best for them.

People my age who used to listen to me "way back when" don't even buy records anymore. If I had to depend on them buying my records—even if I did play what they wanted—I would starve to death and miss out on communicating to people who *do* buy records: young people. And even if I wanted to play those old tunes I couldn't find people who could play the way we used to play. The ones who are alive are leaders of their own bands, playing what *they* want to. I know they wouldn't want to give that up to come into a band led by me.

George Wein once wanted me to get Herbie and Ron and Wayne back together to make a tour. But I told him that wouldn't work because there would be too many problems for them playing as sidemen. The tour could have made a lot of money, but so what? Music ain't just about making money. It's about feeling, especially the music we play.

Take someone like Max Roach, who is like my brother. If today Max wrote something and asked me to play on it with, say, Sonny Rollins or somebody like that, I don't know if I could make it because I don't play that way no more. It's not that I don't love Max, because I do. But in order for me to make a date like that he'd have to write something that both he and I liked. Here's another example. I had a chance to work with Frank Sinatra a long time ago. He sent somebody for me at Birdland, where I was working. But I couldn't make it because I wasn't into what he was into. Now, it ain't that I don't love Frank Sinatra, but I'd rather listen to him than maybe get in his way by playing something that *I* want to play. I learned how to phrase from listening to Frank, his concept of phrasing, and also to Orson Welles.

But take someone like Palle Mikkelborg over in Denmark, who I did that *Aura* album with. When you hang around him over there you might hear almost anything. Same thing with Gil Evans. What Gil did for Sting's new album is a motherfucker, for Sting that is. Did you see what happened in the *Playboy* Jazz Poll after Sting made that record with Gil? The people who read the magazine—mostly white people—voted Sting's group the Best Jazz Group of the year. Now ain't that something! A black group couldn't get that kind of recognition if they were, say, crossing over from fusion-jazz to rock. No white people would vote them the best dogcatchers of the year. But they will vote for Sting like that. Sting's last album was a motherfucker, but you don't hear nobody's personality but his and he ain't no jazz musician. A song that Sting writes with lyrics tells you what to think. But with an instrumental composition you can think whatever you want to. It's like you don't have to read *Playboy* in order to know what position to put a girl in in order to make love. That's for lazy people. Most popular music is about "Baby, I love you. Come here and give it to me." There are millions of records with lyrics like that. So it becomes a cliché and then you have all these people copying that and they don't do nothing but copy clichés off each other. That's why it's hard to be original in the recording studio because of all those records out there for everyone to listen to.

I don't like the music Trane was playing at the end of his life. I never did listen to his records after he left my group. He was playing the same thing over and over again that he had started playing when he was with me. At first the group he had with Elvin Jones, McCoy Tyner, and Jimmy Garrison was all right. Then they became a cliché of themselves and wasn't nobody playing nothing for me but Elvin and Trane. I didn't like what McCoy was doing after a while because all he was doing was banging the hell out of the baby grand piano and that wasn't hip for me. I mean guys like Bill Evans, Herbie Hancock, and George Duke know how to play that instrument. But all Trane and them were doing was playing in the mode and I had already done that. McCoy didn't have no touch after a while. He got monotonous and the way that Trane played after a while got monotonous, too, if you sat and listened to him for too long. After a while I couldn't see or hear nothing there, and I didn't like what Jimmy Garrison was doing either. But a lot of people liked it and that's cool. When Elvin and Trane would play duets together, I thought what they were doing *then* was cool. This is only my opinion, though; I could be wrong.

The musical sound is very different today than it was when I first started playing. You got all these echo chambers and shit. Like in the movie *Lethal Weapon* with Danny Glover and Mel Gibson, they had scenes in a place that was made out of steel. So the public is getting used to hearing steel clanging together, and guys in the West Indies, like in Trinidad, write music like that with steel drums and all that kind of stuff. And the synthesizer has changed everything whether purist musicians like it or not. It's here to stay and you can either be in it or out of it. I choose to be in it because the world has always been about change. People who don't change will find themselves like folk musicians, playing in museums and local as a motherfucker. Because the music and the sound has gone international and there ain't no sense in trying to go back into some womb where you once were. A man can't go back into his mother's womb.

Music is about timing and getting everything in rhythm. It can sound good if it's Chinese as long as the right things are in place. But as complex as people try to make my music out to be, I like it simple. That's the way I hear it even if it's complex to them.

I love drummers. I learned so much about drums from Max Roach when we were playing together with Bird and living together on the road. He would always be showing me shit. He taught me that the drummer is always supposed to protect the rhythm, have a beat inside, protect the groove. The way you protect the groove is to have a beat in between a beat. Like "bang, bang, sha-bang, sha-bang." The "sha" in between the "bang" is the beat in between the beat, and that little thing is the extra groove. When a drummer can't do that, then the groove is off and there ain't nothing worse in the world than to have a drummer in that no groove bag. Man, that shit is like death.

Now, a musician and artist like Marcus Miller is the type who represents today. He can play everything and is open to all things that are musical. He understands things like not having to have a live drummer in the studio. You can program a drum machine and then have a drummer play along with it if you want to. The drum machine is good because you can always take what it plays in one place and put it in another place because it always keeps the same tempo. Most drummers have a habit of dropping tempo or rushing it, and that can fuck up what you're doing. Drum machines don't do that, so they're good for recording. But I've got to have a live, great drummer like Ricky Wellman to keep everything goosed up. In the music we play live the sections are always changing, and that perks up a drummer who can change with the flow. When you play live, you've got to keep the interest there and in that situation a great drummer is better than a drum machine.

Like I said earlier, a lot of jazz musicians are lazy. White people give them an attitude by saying, "You don't have to study, you're natural. You just pick up the horn and blow." But that's not true. And all black people don't have rhythm, either. There are a lot of white dudes who can play their asses off, especially in those rock groups. And the drummers in those groups don't drop no tempos and can play with the drum machine also. But a lot of black jazz drummers don't want to and can't do that kind of thing. They want to stay "natural," because that's what white critics tell them they are.

It's always been a gift with me hearing music the way I do. I don't know where it comes from, it's just there and I don't question it. Like I can hear when the time drops one beat, or I can hear when it's Prince playing the drums instead of a drum track. It's just something I've always had. I mean, I can start my tempo off and go to sleep and come back and be at the same tempo I was in before I went to sleep. I've never questioned whether I was right or wrong about things like that. Because I stop if the tempo is off, if it is wrong. I mean, it just stops me from doing anything. And when an engineer makes a bad splice on a tape it stops me cold because I hear it right away.

For me, music and life are all about style. Like if you want to look and feel rich, you wear a certain thing, a certain pair of shoes, or shirt, or coat. Styles in music produce certain kinds of feeling in people. If you want someone to feel a certain way, you play a certain style. That's all. That's why it's good for me to play for different kinds of people because I pick up things from them that I can use. There are places that I haven't played in yet that I would like to, like Africa and Mexico. I'd love to play in those places and I will someday.

When I'm out of this country I play different because of the way the people treat me, with a lot of respect. I appreciate that and show it in my playing. I want to make them feel good like the way they make me feel good. My favorite places to play, I think, are Paris, Rio, Oslo, Japan, Italy, and Poland. In the United States I like to play in New York, Chicago, the San Francisco area, and Los Angeles. People aren't too bad in these places, but sometimes they still fuck with me, rub me the wrong way.

When I stopped playing, I heard that a lot of people were saying, "Miles stopped, what we gonna do now?" The reason a lot of people felt that way, I suppose, has something to do with what Dizzy once said. He said, "If you look at Miles, look at the musicians who have been with him; Miles raises leaders, a lot of them." And I suppose that's true. So a lot of musicians have looked at me for direction. But I didn't feel a burden because of this, because of being considered a forerunner by a lot of people, the point man, so to speak. I never felt it was just me by myself. I wasn't carrying a whole load. There were others, like Trane and Ornette. Even in my own bands it wasn't just me, never was. Like with Philly Joe and Trane. Philly Joe set the time up and he made Paul Chambers play, and Red Garland used to tell *me* what ballads he wanted to play, and not the other way around. And Trane would sit there and say nothing, but play his ass off. He never did say much. He was like Bird when it came to talking about music. They both just talked with their horns. In the band I had with Herbie, Tony, Ron, and Wayne, Tony set the shit up and we followed him. They all wrote things for the band, and we wrote some things together. But with Tony back there the tempo never dropped; if anything, it got faster and the rhythm shit was on. In the band with Keith Jarrett and Jack DeJohnette, Keith and Jack dictated where the sounds went and what they played, the rhythms they laid down. They altered the music and then the music just pushed itself out into something else. Can't nobody else play music like that because they didn't have Keith and Jack. Same thing with every other band I put together.

But that was my gift, you know, having the ability to put certain guys together that would create a chemistry and then letting them go; letting them play what they knew, and above it. I didn't know exactly what they would sound like together when I first hooked up guys. But I think it's important to pick intelligent musicians because if they're intelligent and creative then the music can really fly.

Just like Trane's style was his own, and Bird's and Diz's their own, I don't want to sound like nobody but myself. I want to be myself, whatever that is. But in music, I have such feeling for different phrases, and when I'm really enjoying something, it's like I'm one with it. The phrase is me. I play things my way and then I try to go above it. The hardest tune I ever had to play in my life was "I Loves You, Porgy," because I had to make the trumpet sound and phrase just like a human voice. I see colors and things when I'm playing. If I hear a song of someone's, I'm always wondering why he put a certain note where he did and why he did other things the way he did. My sound comes from my high school teacher, Elwood Buchanan. I even loved the way he held his horn. People tell me my sound is like a human voice and that's what I want it to be.

My best musical ideas for compositions come to me at night. Duke Ellington was the same way. He wrote all night and slept all day. I guess at night everything is quiet and so you can block what little noise there is out and concentrate. I also think I write better out in California because it's so quiet out there; I live by the ocean. At least it's that way for now. I'll take Malibu over New York when I write.

I play some chords that some of the guys in my band call "Milesian Chords." It's the way you can play any chord, any sound and it won't sound wrong unless someone plays the wrong thing behind it. See, the thing that is played behind a chord governs where it should or shouldn't fit. You just don't play a cluster of unrelated chords and leave it like that. You have to bring it back to something to resolve it. Like if we play in a minor key, I usually show them all kinds of possibilities with playing that, from flamenco music to a passacaglia, at least some people call it that. A passacaglia is when you have the same bass line and I play triads in order for a soloist to play against a minor chord. You have to have a feel for this. It's the same thing I did with Trane. If you listen to Khachaturian, the Russian composer, and Hernspach, a brilliant British composer, both of them play and write things in a minor chord. There's a whole lot of shit you can play if you study it.

To me, great musicians are like great fighters who know self-defense. They have a higher sense of theory going on in their heads, like African musicians. But we ain't in Africa, and we don't play just chants. There's some theory under what we do. If you put diminished chords underneath, those chords make a chant sound and you get it down much fuller, and you can understand because it's got these different sounds under it. And you can do it better now because people have been hearing such great music for the last twenty years. Coltrane, myself, Herbie Hancock, James Brown, Sly, Jimi Hendrix, Prince, Stravinsky, Bernstein. Then you got people like Harry Parch and John Cage. Cage's music sounds like glass and things falling. A lot of people are into that. So people are ready for a whole lot of different kinds of music. And if they can stomach Martha Graham and what she does and what she did with Cage back in 1948 at Juilliard when I saw them both there, then people are ready for all kinds of shit.

But it's still the black thing that is leading the way, like break dancing, hip-hop, and rap. Even the music they are doing on commercials is hip these days, man. They got Baptist gospel music up in some of them. What's funny is that they got white people singing that shit and wearing it out. They're trying to look like us and sing like us and play like us. So now black artists have to do something else. People in Europe and Japan and Brazil ain't fooled by that. It's only the stupid people here who are.

I like traveling, although not as much as I used to because I do it so much, but I still get off on it, because you get to meet all kinds of different people and experience many different cultures. One of the things that I've seen is that black people are a lot like Japanese people. Both of them like to laugh. Both Japanese people and black people aren't as uptight as white people are. A black person is thought to be an Uncle Tom when he laughs around white people, but Japanese people aren't thought of like that because they have money and power. Asian people also don't have a lot of expression around their eyes, especially Chinese people. They look at you funny. But I've picked up on how Japanese women hit on men from the side of their eyes, and now I can do it.

The finest women in the world for me are Brazilian, Ethiopian, and Japanese women. And here I mean a combination of beauty, femininity, intelligence, the way they carry themselves, their body carriage, and the respect they have for a man. Japanese, Ethiopian, and Brazilian women respect men and don't ever try acting like a man—at least the ones I've known. Most American women don't know how to treat a man, it seems to me, especially a whole lot of black women, mostly the older ones. Most of them are in competition with you, no matter what you do for them. I think it's because of their hair and the brainwashing this country has put on them about not having long, blond, straight hair, so they believe they're not beautiful—but they are. But I think this applies mostly to older black women who bought all that white woman beauty bullshit. A lot of the younger black women I have met are real hip and don't have the problems that a lot of the older ones do. But many of them also have serious problems about how they look. A lot of black women think that all black men want and desire white women, even though they may be treating their black women like queens. This fucks them up. Most white women tend to treat a man better than a black woman does, because most white women don't have those hangups that black women have. I know this is going to make a lot of black women mad but that's just the way I see it.

See, a lot of black women see themselves as teachers or mothers when it comes to a man. They've got to be in control. The only black woman in my life who didn't act like that was Frances. She never did nothing like that in seven years we were together. She was cool and wasn't in competition with anything because she had a lot of confidence in herself. And when you're confident in yourself—know that you're fine and feminine and that men just drool when they see you, —you can handle that man. Frances had a lot of confidence in her body because she was a dancer and knew when she walked down the street she was going to stop traffic. She was an artist and most women who are artistic have a broader and deeper thing.

But a lot of them black women who are executives and don't have confidence are a pain in the fucking ass. They're always in competition and always got something fucked up to say. If a man gets into some shit that makes you mad, you can fight him, physically speaking. But with a woman it's different. If they make you mad you can't be beating on them. So you have to let it slide. But if you let it slide too many times with know-it-all, competitive broads, they're going to keep getting up in your face with their lips all stuck out, pushing and pushing you. Then, you get mad and might hit them. I used to get in those situations a lot with pushy women and I used to hit a few. But I don't like that kind of feeling or doing that to a woman. When I see it coming I just avoid it these days.

A lot of black women don't know how to deal with an artist— especially them old-timey ones, or those ones who are deep into their careers. An artist might have something on his mind at any time. So you just can't be fucking with him and taking him away from what he's thinking or doing. That shit is horrible if an artist has a woman who don't respect when he has to be creative. A lot of the older women didn't understand that, because being an artist wasn't respected when I was growing up. But white women have been around artists a long time and understand the importance of what art does in society. So black women got a lot of catching up to do in this area. But they'll get there. In the meantime, people like me have got to do what makes us happy. I got to go with whoever understands and respects me.

Most of the African women I've met aren't like American black women. They're different and know better how to treat their men. But I love them real black African women from Ethiopia and, I think, the Sudan. They got those high cheekbones and straight noses and those are the faces I draw mostly in my paintings and sketches. Iman, the African model, looks like that. She's so beautiful and elegant and graceful. Then you got the other kind of black beauty in women, those with full lips, big eyes, and heads slanted like Cicely's head. Cicely had a look in private that you'll never see in the movies, especially when she got mad or when I got mad at her. It was sensuous. I used to pretend that I was mad just so she would get that look on her face. I used to love it.

I like flirting with women. You can get a lot from them with just a wink. It's a nice way to flirt without opening up your mouth and saying something. I can always tell by a woman's eyes whether she's interested in me or not, especially when you see and feel something that is a little more than just a stare. Women in the West do with their eyes what Japanese women do with their bodies. If you see that little something in the eyes of Western women and if you agree with it, then you react. If you don't, then you just turn your head. But if you feel something spiritual there, a certain connection, then you go for it.

The type of woman I like for myself has to have a certain kind of carriage, and be lean and confident in her body, like a dancer. It's in the way she walks or does things or dresses. I can see it in one glance. There are a lot of fine women out there who don't have that thing that I like. They have to have that sex thing, that electricity that tells me something special is there. Sometimes it's in their mouths, like Jacqueline Bisset's mouth. She's got that sex thing written all over her face, and Cicely had it for me at one time. When I see it I get a feeling in my stomach. It's like I get a rush, like from a snort of cocaine—a big one. It's the anticipation of being with someone like that that makes me feel so good. That feeling is so great that it is almost better than any orgasm. Nothing can match that.

I like that way that Japanese women flirt with a man. They will stand not in your direct eyesight, but almost where you can't see them when you're looking out of the corner of your eye. They'll be there where you almost can't see them, but they'll be there. They won't be looking at you directly, either. It's interesting. Say there are four Asian women in a room and you talk to all of them, and you talk to one of them, say, five minutes longer than you did with the rest, the other three just move on out. They just leave and start circulating elsewhere.

I love women. I never needed any help or ever had any trouble finding women. I just like to be with them, talking and shit like that. But I never have messed with a musician's girlfriend. Never. Even if she hadn't been with him for very long. You never know when you might have to hire a musician to play with you. You don't want no shit like that getting in the way of what you will be playing together. But all other women—except good friends—are fair game.

Women are funny though, and many times aren't what they seem to be. Women mess with other women in a way that people don't even notice. I used to see it a lot when I was working in the clubs. I used to think that all them fine girls were coming down to the clubs to look at and pick up musicians. Then I found out that a lot of them were coming down to see each other. And here I was thinking they were coming down to hit on me and listen to the music and shit. But musicians are vain motherfuckers when it comes to their public, *especially* women. Musicians are the most self-centered of all the artists because they think that they're the hippest and that the shit they do is the most important. They think that they're irresistible to women because they've got some instrument in their mouths or hands. They feel they are God's gift to women. And a lot of this is true, from the way a lot of people hang around us giving us everything we want and shit. At least we musicians think it's true because of the way people treat us. But see, a lot of women who like women know this, too. They know a lot of other ladies are going to be hanging around us so they get on that scene, too, so they can cop.

In the past I have gone with all races of women, probably as many white ones as black ones. I'm not into a race thing when it comes to the race of a woman I'm with. Like the old saying goes, "A hard dick ain't got no conscience," and it don't have no race consciousness, either. I have always married black women, though, but it's not a conscious thing. If you ask me what color woman I prefer, I'd have to say I like a woman my mother's color, or lighter. I don't know why that is, but that's the way I am. I think I've had one girlfriend who was darker than me and you know that was dark, because I'm midnight black myself.

American women are bolder than all the women in the world when it comes to men. They will come right up to you if they really dig you and start hitting on you. Especially if you're someone as famous as I am. They don't care and they don't have no shame about it. But that kind of shit just turns me off. All they're trying to do is go to bed and fuck my press clippings and try to get into my bank account so I can buy them gifts and things. But I can see that kind of shit coming a mile away now. It used to get past me sometimes, but not now. I don't mess with a woman who approaches me. That turns me off. I want them to at least let me *think* that's it's me picking them.

White people in America get all up in your face because they think they're God's gift to the whole fucking world. It's sickening and pitiful the way they think, how backwards, stupid, and disrespectful many of them are. They think they can come right up to you and get right into your business because they're white and you're not. When I'm on airplanes they do that a lot; get right up in your face. I ride first class, so I know they wonder what I'm doing there if they don't recognize me. So they look at me strangely. One time when I was sitting on a plane and some white woman did this to me, I asked her if I was sitting on something that belonged to her. She just smiled this tight smile and left me alone. But you got some white people who are cool and don't do that kind of shit. You got hip people in all races and stupid ones, too. Some of the most stupid motherfuckers I have ever met have been black people. Especially the ones who believe all them lies white people spread about them. They can be some sick motherfuckers when you find them like that.

America is such a racist place, so racist it's pitiful. It's just like South Africa only more sanitized today; it's not as out in front in its racism. Other than that, it's the same thing. But I always have had a built-in thing for racism. I can smell it. I can feel it behind me, anywhere it is. And the way I am, a lot of whites really get mad with me, especially white men. They get even madder when I tell them off when they get out of line. They just think they can do any kind of shit to a black person here.

Look at what's happening to our kids, how they have gone so far into drugs, especially black kids. One reason for this, at least among black kids, is that they don't know about their heritage. It's a shame the way our country has treated black people and our contributions to this society. I think the schools should teach kids about jazz or black music. Kids should know that America's only original cultural contribution is the music that our black forefathers brought from Africa which was changed and developed here. African music should be studied as much as European ("classical") music.

When kids don't learn about their own heritage in school, they just don't care about school. They turn to dope, to crack, because nobody cares about them. Plus they see some easy money to be made selling crack, so they get into that underground connection and attitude. I know about this because I was into it when I was on drugs. I understand these kids and what they are thinking. I know that a lot of them drop into the underground culture because they know they ain't gonna get no fairness from white people. So they play sports or music, they become entertainers and athletes, because it's a chance for them to make a lot of money and get out of where they are at. It's either sports, entertainment, or the underground. That's why I respect Bill Cosby so much, because he's doing the right thing, setting the right example, by buying black art and contributing to black colleges. I wish more black people with money would follow his example. Start a publishing house or a record company, some business that will employ black people and clean up the bullshit image white people have of black Americans. Black people need that.

In Europe and Japan they respect black people's culture, what we have contributed to the world. They know what it is. But white Americans would rather push a white person like Elvis Presley, who is just a copy of a black person, than to push the real thing. They give all this money to white rock groups, to promote and publicize them, give them a lot of awards for trying to be like black artists. But that's all right because everyone knows that Chuck Berry started the shit, not Elvis. They know Duke Ellington was the "King of Jazz" and not Paul Whiteman. Everybody knows that. But you won't see it in the history books unless we get the power to write our own history and tell our story ourselves. Nobody else is going to do it for us and do it like it is supposed to be done.

For example, when he was alive Bird never got his due. Only a few white critics like Barry Ulanov and Leonard Feather recognized Bird and bebop. But for most white critics, Jimmy Dorsey was their man, like Bruce Springsteen or George Michael is today. Outside of a few places, hardly anybody had heard of Charlie Parker. But a lot of black people—the hip ones—knew. Then when white people finally found out about Bird and Diz it was too late. Duke Ellington and Count Basie and Fletcher Henderson never got their due. Louis Armstrong had to start grinning like a motherfucker to finally get his. White people used to talk about how John Hammond discovered Bessie Smith. Shit, how did he discover her when she was there already? And if he had really "discovered" her and did what he was supposed to, what he did for other white singers, she wouldn't have died the way she did on that Mississippi back road. She had an accident and bled to death because no white hospital would take her in. It's like, how did Columbus discover America when the Indians were already here? What kind of shit is that, but white people's shit?

The police fuck with me by stopping me all the time. This kind of shit happens to black people every day in this country. It's like what Richard Pryor said, "When you're black and you hear a white man go 'Yah hoo,' you better know it's time to get on up and get outta there, because you know something stupid is next."

I remember one time when Milton Berle, the comedian, came down to see me when I was playing at the Three Deuces. I was in Bird's band at the time. I think this was in 1948. Anyway, Berle was sitting at a table listening to us and somebody asked him what he thought of the band and the music. He laughed and turned to this group of white people he was with and said that we were "headhunters," meaning we were fucking savages. He thought it was funny, and I remember all those white people laughing at us. Well, I never forgot that. Then I saw him on an airplane about twenty-five years after that and we were both riding in first class. I went up and introduced myself to him. I said, "Milton, my name is Miles Davis and I'm a musician."

He started smiling and said, "Oh, yeah, I know who you are. I really love your music." He seemed happy that I had come up to him.

Then I said, "Milton, you did something to me and some people in the band I was playing with some years ago that I've always remembered, and I always told myself that if I ever got close enough to breathe on you that I was gonna tell you the way I felt when you said what you said that night." He was looking at me kind of funny now because he didn't know what he had said. And I could feel some of the anger of that night coming back so it must have been showing in my face. I told him what he said and I told him how they had all laughed at us. Now his face was turning red because he was embarrassed, and he had probably forgotten all about it. So then I told him, "I don't like what you called us that night, Milton, and none of the band liked it either after I told them what you said. Some of them also heard what you said."

He looked all pitiful and everything and then he said, "I'm very, very sorry."

And I said, "I know you are. But you're only sorry now, sorry after I told you, because you weren't sorry then." And then I turned around and went back to my seat and sat down and didn't say another word to him.

That's the kind of thing I'm talking about. Some white people—and black people, too—will laugh at you one minute and then turn around and say that they love you the next. They do it all the time; try to divide and conquer people with shit like that. But I've got a long memory of what has happened to us in this country. The Jewish people keep reminding the world of what happened to them in Germany. So black people have to keep reminding the world of what happened in the United States, or as James Baldwin once told me, "these yet to be United States." We've got to watch out for those divide-and-conquer techniques that whites have used on us all these years, keeping us apart from out real inner selves and our real inner strength. I know people get tired of hearing it but black people have got to keep saying it, throwing our conditions up into these people's faces until something is done about the way they have treated us. We've just got to keep it in front of their eyes and their ears like the Jews have done. We've got to make them know and understand just how evil the things are that they did to us over all these years and are still doing to us today. We've just got to let *them* know that *we know what they are doing* and that we're not going to lighten up until they stop.

The older I get the more I learn about playing this trumpet and the more I learn about a lot of other things. I used to like to drink and I really liked cocaine, but I don't even think about them things anymore. Cigarettes either. I just stopped doing those kinds of things. Cocaine was a little harder for me to stop, but I stopped that, too. It's just willpower, believing you can do what you want to do. When I don't want to do something I just say to myself, "Fuck it." Because you have to do it yourself. Nobody else can do it for you. Other people might be trying to help, but you've got to do it alone most of the time.

Nothing is out of the question the way I think and live my life. I'm always thinking about creating. My future starts when I wake up every morning. That's when it starts—when I wake up and see the first light. Then, I'm grateful, and I can't wait to wake up, because there's something new to do and try every day. Every day I find something creative to do with my life. Music is a blessing and a curse. But I love it, wouldn't have it no other way.

In my life I have few regrets and little guilt. Those regrets I do have I don't want to talk about. I'm more relaxed with myself and with everybody else now. I think my personality is nicer. I'm still suspicious of people, but less than I was in the past, and I'm less hostile, too. I'm still a very private person, though, and don't like being around a lot of people I don't know. But I don't jump all over people like I used to or cuss people out. Hell, I even introduce the members of my band now at concerts and even talk a little bit to the audience.

I've got this reputation for being a hard person to get along with. But people who really know me know that isn't true, because we get along fine. I don't like being the center of attention all the time. I just do what I have to do and that's it. But I got some good friends, like Max Roach, Richard Pryor, Quincy Jones, Bill Cosby, Prince, my nephew Vincent, and a few other people. I think Gil Evans was my best friend. The people in my band are good friends and so are my horses out in Malibu. I love horses and other animals. But a lot of the people who really know me best are some of the guys I grew up with back in East St. Louis, even though I hardly see them anymore. I think about them and when we do see each other it's like we never left. They talk to me as though I just left their house.

They can tell me some shit about what I'm playing and I will listen to them before I listen to a critic. Because I know they know what I'm trying to do and what I'm supposed to sound like. If Clark Terry, who I consider one of my best friends, came up to me and told me I was playing shit, man, I'd take that seriously. I'd take it to heart. Same thing with Dizzy, who is my mentor and one of my closest friends in the whole world. If he told me something about my playing, I would listen. But I've always been the way I am, been like this all my life. Nobody can say nothing bad about me to my good friends because they won't even listen. It's the same way with me; I ain't gonna listen to no bad shit about somebody I know.

Music has always been like a curse with me because I have always felt driven to play it. It has always been the first thing in my life and it still is. It comes before everything. But I've made a kind of peace with my musical demons that allows me to live a more relaxed life. I think painting has helped me a lot. The demons are still there, but now I know that they're there and when they want to be fed. So I think I've gotten most things under control.

I'm a very private person, and it costs a lot of money to maintain privacy when you're as famous a person as I am. It's real, real hard and that's one of the reasons I have to make money; so that I can keep my life private. You have to pay for fame—mentally, spiritually, and in *real* money.

I don't go out much, hardly ever these days. I've had enough of that kind of thing. People come up trying to get a photograph with me. Fuck that shit. That's why people in the limelight can't live normal lives, because of the way some people mess with them. It's not natural. That's one of the main reasons I don't like to go out. But when I'm with my horses or my good friends, I can relax and not worry about that. I've got a horse named Kara, one named Kind of Blue, and another one called Gemini. Gemini's got a lot of spirit because he's got some Arabian in him. I like to ride him the best. But he does me a favor by letting me ride him because I can't ride that good. I'm still learning, and he knows that. So when I do things wrong he just kind of looks at me like, "What the fuck is *this* motherfucker doing on my back again? Don't he know I'm a pro?" But I like animals, understand them and them me. But people? People are weird.

I have always been able to predict things before they happened. Always. I believe that some of us can predict the future. For example, I was swimming one day at the United Nations Plaza Hotel in New York and this white guy was swimming with me. All of a sudden he said to me, "Guess where I'm going?" And I said, "You're going to New Orleans." And he was! Man, that shit fucked him up. He just broke up and looked at me real funny and asked how I knew. But I couldn't tell him that. I just knew. I don't know why and I don't ask questions about it. I just know that the ability has always been there.

I'm an instinctive kind of person who sees things in people that other people don't see. I hear things that other people don't hear and don't think are important until many years later, when they finally hear them or see them themselves. By then, I'm someplace else and I've forgotten what they're seeing. I stay current and on top of things by having the ability to forget things that are unimportant. It doesn't matter to me that other people think something's important if I don't. That's only their opinion. I have mine and usually I trust what I feel and hear above everybody else when it comes to some shit about me and what I'm doing.

For me, music has been my life, and musicians I have known and loved and grown from have become my family. My blood family is my family because of parents, relatives, and blood. But for me, my family are the people I associate with in my profession—other artists, musicians, poets, painters, dancers, and writers—but not critics. Most people leave whatever money they have when they die to their other relatives, their cousins, aunts, sisters, or brothers. But I don't believe in that. I feel if you're going to leave something, leave it to the people who helped you do what you did. If that's blood relatives, fine, but if it isn't, I don't believe in giving it to relatives. See, I would think of leaving money to Dizzy or Max, or somebody like that, or a couple of girlfriends who helped me a lot. I wouldn't want people to find some cousin in Louisiana or someplace who I ain't never seen and give them my money when I'm dead just because we got the same blood. Fuck that!

I want to share with people who helped me through all of this shit I've come through, who helped me be more creative—and I've had several real fertile creative periods in my life. The first one was from 1945 to 1949, which was the beginning. Then, after I got off drugs, 1954 to 1960 was a hell of a fertile time for me musically. And 1964 to 1968 wasn't so bad, but I would say that I was feeding a lot of

Tony's and Wayne's and Herbie's musical ideas. Same thing when I did *Bitches Brew* and *Live-Evil,* because that's a combination of people and things—Joe Zawinul, Paul Buckmaster, and others—all I did was get everyone together and write a few things. But I think right now is the best creative period I have ever gone through, because I'm painting and writing music and playing on top of what I know.

I don't like throwing God up into anybody's face and I don't like it thrown in mine. But if I have a religious preference, I think it would be Islam, and that I would be a Muslim. But I don't know about that, or any organized religion. I've never been into that, using religion as a crutch. Because I personally don't like a lot of things that are happening in organized religion. It don't seem too spiritual to me, but more about money and power, and I can't go for that.

But I do believe in being spiritual and do believe in spirits. I always have. I believe my mother and father come to visit me. I believe all the musicians that I have known who are now dead do, too. When you work with great musicians, they are always a part of you—people like Max Roach, Sonny Rollins, John Coltrane, Bird, Diz, Jack DeJohnette, Philly Joe. The ones that are dead I miss a lot, especially as I grow older: Monk, Mingus, Freddie Webster, and Fat Girl. When I think about the ones who are dead it makes me mad, so I try not to think about it. But their spirits are walking around in me, so they're still here and passing it on to others. It's some spiritual shit and part of what I am today is them. It's all in me, the things I learned to do from them. Music is about the spirit and the spiritual, and about feeling. I believe their music is still around somewhere, you know. The shit that we played together has to be somewhere around in the air because we blew it there and that shit was magical, was spiritual.

I used to have these dreams where I thought I could see things, see some other stuff, like smoke or clouds, and my mind would make pictures of them. I do that now when I wake up in the morning and want to see my mother or father or Trane or Gil or Philly, or whoever. I just say to myself, "I want to see them," and they're there and I'm talking to them. Sometimes now when I look in the mirror I see my father there. This has been happening since he died and wrote that letter. I definitely believe in the spirit, but I don't think about death; there's too much for me to do to worry about that.

For me, the urgency to play and create music today is worse than when I started. It's more intense. It's like a curse. Man, the music I forget now drives me nuts trying to remember it. I'm driven to it—

go to bed thinking about it and wake up thinking about it. It's always there. And I love that it hasn't abandoned me; I feel really blessed.

I feel strong creatively now and I feel I'm getting stronger. I exercise every day, eat proper food most of the time. Sometimes I get weak for black food, like barbecue, fried chicken, and chitterlings; you know, things I'm not supposed to eat—sweet potato pie, greens, pig feet, stuff like that. But I don't drink or smoke or use drugs anymore, except the ones my doctor prescribes for my diabetes. I feel good, because I have never felt this creative. I feel the best is yet to come. Like Prince says when he's talking about hitting the beat and getting to the music and the rhythm, I'm going to keep "getting up on the one," brother, I'm just going to try to keep my music getting up on the one, getting up on the one every day I play. Getting up on the one. Later.

Acknowledgments

There are many, many people who gave of their time and information to help make this book possible, and the authors would like to acknowledge their invaluable assistance. Hugh Masekela; Max Roach; Peter Shukat; Gordon Meltzer; Herbie Hancock; Wayne Shorter; Ron Carter; Tony Williams; Gil Evans; Dr. Bill Cosby; Jimmy Heath; Sonny Rollins; Ricky Wellman; Kenny Garrett; Jim Rose; Darryl Jones; Vince Wilburn, Jr.; Vince Wilburn, Sr.; Dorothy Davis Wilburn; Frances Taylor Davis; Eugene Redmond; Millard Curtis; Frank Gully; Mr. and Mrs. Red Bonner; Edna Gardner; Bernard Hassell; Bob Holman; Gary Giddins; Jon Stevens; Risasi; Yvonne Smith; Jason Miles; Milt Jackson; Pat Mikell; Howard Johnson; Dizzy Gillespie; Anthony Barboza; *Spin* magazine; Bob Guccione, Jr.; Bart Bull; Rudy Langlais; Art Farmer; Marcus Miller; Branford Marsalis; Dr. George Butler; Sandra Trim-DaCosta; Verta Mae Grosvenor; David Franklin; Michael Warren; Michael Elam; Judith Mallen; Eric Engles; Raleigh McDonald; Olu Dara; Hamiett Bluiet; Lester Bowie; Dr. Leo Maitland; Eddie Randle, Sr.; Roscoe Lee Browne; Freddie Birth; Elwood Buchanan; Jackie Battle; Charles Duckworth; Adam Holzman; George Hudson; James Baldwin; David Baldwin; Gloria Baldwin; Oliver Jackson; Joe Rudolph; Ferris Jackson; Deborah Kirk; Kwaku Lynn; Mtume; Monique Clesca; Odette Chikel; Jo Jo; Walter and Teresa Gordon; Charles Quincy Troupe; Evelyn Rice; Gille Larrain; Ishmael Reed; Lena Sherrod; George

Tisch; Pat Cruz; The Studio Museum of Harlem; Mammie Anderson; Craig Harris; Amiri Baraka; Donald Harrison; Terence Blanchard; Benjamin Rietveld; Kei Akagi; Joseph Foley McCreary; Mickey Bass; Steve Cannon; Peter Bradley; George Coleman; Jack DeJohnette; Sammy Figueroa; Marc Crawford; John Stubblefield; Greg Edwards; Alfred "Junie" McNair; Thomas Medina; George Faison; James Finney; Robben Ford; Nelson George; Bill Graham; Mark Rothbaum; Lionel Hampton; Beaver Harris; Mr. and Mrs. Lee Konitz; Tommy LiPuma; Harold Lovett; Ron Milner; Herb Boyd; Jackie McLean; Steve Rowland; Steve Ratner; Arthur and Cynthia Richardson; Billie Allen; Chip Stern; Dr. Donald Suggs; Milan Simich; Clark Terry; Arthur Taylor; Alvin "Laffy" Ward; Terrie Williams; Sim Copans; Joe Overstreet; Ornette Coleman; Rev. Calvin Butts; C. Vernon Mason; James Brown; Adger Cowans; Susan DeSandes; Clayton Riley; Leonard Fraser; Paula Giddings; John Hicks; Keith Jarrett; Ted Joans; Patti LaBelle; Stewart Levine; Sterling Plumpp; Lynell Hemphill; Fred Hudson; Leon Thomas; Dr. Clyde Taylor; Chinua Achebe; Derek Walcott; August Wilson; Rita Dove; Danny Glover; Terry McMillen; Nikki Giovanni; Asaki Bomani; Judge Bruce Wright; Ed Williams; Abbey Lincoln (Aminata Moseka); K. Curtis Lyle; David Kuhn; Jack Chambers; Eric Nisenson; Ian Carr; and many others who are too numerous to mention, but who contributed information that helped bring this book together.

Special thanks goes to Quincy's agent, Marie Dutton Brown, for her invaluable assistance and close reading of the manuscript, and to her assistant, B. J. Ashanti, for helping to coordinate this very difficult project. The authors also extend special thanks to Mabusha Masekela, nephew of Hugh, who sat down one evening and read the entire manuscript and contributed pertinent information and helpful criticism. The authors would also like to thank the people at Simon and Schuster, specifically Julia Knickerbocker, Karen Weitzman, Virginia Clark, and our great and always supportive editors, Bob Bender and Malaika Adero, who brought the idea for the book to Simon and Schuster. We would also like to thank Fay Bellamy, Pamela Williams, and Cynthia Simmons, who took on the extremely difficult task of transcribing all of the taped interviews and did an outstanding job. And lastly, the authors would like to thank and acknowledge the contributions of Quincy's wife, Margaret Porter Troupe, who read the manuscript several times and provided great criticism and invaluable moral support.

Index

Photo credits

1 —Northwestern University Dental School
2–4 —Edna Gardner
5–8 —Lester Glassner Collection (LGC)
9 —UPI/Bettmann Newsphotos
10–11 —LGC
12–14 —Frank Driggs Collection (FDC)
15 —UPI/Bettmann Newsphotos
16 —LGC
17 —LGC
18 —William P. Gottlieb/Retna
19 —W. P. Gottlieb/Retna
20 —W. P. Gottlieb/Retna
21 —FDC/Magnum
22 —W. P. Gottlieb/Retna
23 —FDC
24 —W. P. Gottlieb/Retna
25 —Carole Reiff © 1985, 1987 by Hal & Florence Reiff
26–33 —FDC
34 —LGC
35 —FDC
36 —UPI/Bettmann Newsphotos
37–40 —FDC
41 —LGC
42 —Carole Reiff © etc.
43 —LGC
44 —Michael Putland/Retna
45 —Carole Reiff © etc.
46 —FDC
47 —LGC
48 —Teppei Inokuchi
49 —Carole Reiff © etc.
50 —FDC
51 —David Redfern/Retna
52 —FDC
53 —FDC
54 —CBS Records
55–56 —FDC
57 —CBS Records
58 —CBS Records
59 —Carol Reiff © etc.
60 —UPI/Bettmann Newsphotos
61 —New York *Daily News*
62–67 —CBS Records
68 —(none)
69 —FDC
70 —Teppei Inokuchi
71–73 —CBS Records
74 —Frans Schellekens/Redken
75 —David Redfern/Retna
76 —FDC
77 —CBS Records
78 —UPI/Bettmann Newsphotos
79 —Joel Axelrad/Retna
80 —David Ellis/Retna
81 —CBS Records
82–83 —FDC
84 —CBS Records
85–86 —FDC
87 —Spencer Richards
88 —Anthony Barboza
89 —Bob Peterson/*Life Magazine* © Time Inc.
90 —CBS Records
91 —Teppei Inokuchi
92 —Spencer Richards
93 —Noel Rutdu/Gamma-Liaison
94–95 —Teppei Inokuchi
96 —David Gahr
97 —Radio City Music Hall
98–100 —Risasi-Zachariah Dais
101 —UPI/Bettmann Newsphotos
102 —UPI/Bettmann Newsphotos
103 —Jon Stevens
104–105 —(none)
106–107 —Teppei Inokuchi
108 —Warner Bros. Records. Photograph by Irving Penn.
109 —Warner Bros. Records
110 —Teppei Inokuchi
111 —Spencer Richards